BETH HENLEY
Collected Plays Volume I

1980–1989

SMITH AND KRAUS PUBLISHERS
Contemporary Playwrights / Anthologies

Lynne Alvarez: Collected Plays
Christopher Durang: 27 Short Plays
Christopher Durang Vol.II: Full-Lengths
Horton Foote: 4 New Plays
Horton Foote Vol.II: Collected Plays
Horton Foote Vol.III: Collected Plays
John Guare Vol.I: War Against the Kitchen Sink
A.R. Gurney Vol.I: Nine Early Plays
A.R. Gurney Vol.II: Collected Plays 1977–1985
A.R. Gurney Vol.III: Collected Plays 1984–1991
A.R. Gurney Vol.IV: Collected Plays 1992–1999
Beth Henley Vol.II: Collected Plays
Israel Horovitz Vol.I: Collected Works
Israel Horovitz Vol.II: New England Blue
Israel Horovitz Vol.III: P.E.C. and 6 New Plays
Israel Horovitz Vol.IV: Two Trilogies
Romulus Linney: 17 Short Plays
Romulus Linney: Adaptations for the American Stage
Jane Martin: Collected Plays
William Mastrosimone: Collected Plays
Terrence McNally Vol.I: 15 Short Plays
Terrence McNally Vol.II: Collected Plays
Marsha Norman: Collected Plays
Eric Overmyer: Collected Plays
Theresa Rebeck Vol.I: Collected Plays 1989–1998
Lanford Wilson: 21 Short Plays
Lanford Wilson Vol.I: Collected Plays 1965–1970
Lanford Wilson Vol.II: Collected Plays 1970–1983
Lanford Wilson Vol.III: The Talley Trilogy
Lanford Wilson Vol.IV: Collected Plays 1987–1997

If you require pre-publication information about upcoming Smith and Kraus books, you may receive our semi-annual catalogue, free of charge, by sending your name and address to *Smith and Kraus Catalogue,4 Lower Mill Road, North Stratford, NH 03590. Or call us at (800) 895-4331, fax (603) 922-3348. WWW.SmithKraus.com.*

BETH HENLEY

Collected Plays Volume I
1980–1989

CONTEMPORARY PLAYWRIGHTS
SERIES

SK
A Smith and Kraus Book

A Smith and Kraus Book
Published by Smith and Kraus, Inc.
PO Box 127, Lyme, NH 03768

First Edition: February 2000
10 9 8 7 6 5 4 3 2 1

The Library of Congress Cataloging-In-Publication Data

Henley, Beth.
[Plays]
Beth Henley : collected plays / Beth Henley. —1st ed.
p. cm. — (Contemporary playwrights series)
Contents: v.1. Crimes of the heart. Am I blue. The wake of Jamey Foster. The Miss Firecracker contest.
The lucky spot. The debutante ball.
ISBN 1-57525-199-X (cloth) — ISBN 1-57525-258-9 (pbk.)
I. Series.

PS3558.E4962 A6 1999
812'.54—dc21   99-052209

CONTENTS

૪૭

Holly Hunter
in *Miss Firecracker Contest.*

photo by Gerry Goodstein

INTRODUCTION

When presented with the task of writing an introduction to two volumes of plays I'd written over a period of twenty-five years, I balked. Going over the galleys proved to be an emotional chore I had not envisioned. Against my will I was revisiting my whole existence: people I loved, people I lost; performances I loathed; skin allergies I endured; tears in alleyways, rides in limousines with open windows and my head out a moon roof screaming. So many years; so many collaborators, critics, and creative soulmates. I have never liked looking back. "Let the dead bury the dead" has been my feeling. Paradoxically I do believe Eugene O'Neill's observation that "The past is the present and the future too." Thus the notion of combing over past plays felt foolishly redundant, in that the past never leaves but lies viruslike in the blood waiting to erupt: inevitably, unexpectedly.

Having experienced such visceral memories going over the galleys and production photographs, I dreaded writing an introduction. It began to seem as though I was drafting my up-and-coming obituary. In an attempt to mitigate my terror, I decided to lie down and without much thought write an impression or memory of each one of the plays. A nonliteral, associative look at the past.

In the process of writing these impressions it occurred to me there were many people who may have more potent observations than I. So, in a deliberate attempt to shield myself from being entirely responsible for an entire introduction to all of these plays, I sent a letter out to some friends and colleagues asking for their input. When I began to receive responses, I was touched and inspired. It became easier for me to get some bits down. I've included my friends' generous memories, along with my own, in accordance with the play that they have chosen to recall. I deeply thank them all.

The plays in this volume are not presented in the order in which they were written, but rather in the order in which they were produced in New York. The actual order they were written in is as follows: *Am I Blue, Crimes of the Heart, The Miss Firecracker Contest, The Wake of Jamey Foster, The Debutante Ball,* and *The Lucky Spot.*

AM I BLUE

Am I Blue was written for a playwriting class at Southern Methodist University in 1972. Originally it was titled *No, I Don't Have a Cat.* That summer I went to the New Orleans French Quarter and heard the song "Am I Blue?" for the first time. I loved it immediately and helplessly. Whenever the bandleader asked for requests I shouted out "Am I Blue?! Am I Blue?!" I stayed all night until the little club was empty and the small, not-really-even-all-that-good band would play the song for me one more time and then just once more again.

When *Am I Blue?* was produced as a major production at SMU in 1974, my recently divorced parents came to Dallas to see it. This was the only play of mine my father ever saw. He died in the summer of 1978. He seemed indifferent to the play but gave me an excellent suggestion concerning the title. "There shouldn't be a question mark in the title. Am I blue. It's a statement, it's a fact."

My mother, on the other hand, loved the play and even cried. Her concern was that I had chosen to present the play under the pseudonym "Amy Peach." There was the practical dilemma of taking the program back to friends and relatives in Mississippi and explaining that her daughter, Beth Henley, was now known as Amy Peach. She also feared I had done this in reaction to the divorce and was ashamed to be their child. Although I could not tell her at the time, the pen name was in fact an early nod to nihilism. At fourteen I went unchaperoned with some girlfriends on a trip to Mississippi State College for Women to see the Miss Mississippi Contest. I was delirious with the first smell of freedom and in a fit of pubescent euphoria ran up to a strange college man and said, "One day I am going to be a writer and I will call myself Amy Peach! Remember that name!" He responded with bitter disdain, "Little girl, if you were just half as cute as you think you are, you'd still be ugly." That was my last fearless attempt at flamboyance.

JIM MCLURE, ACTOR, WRITER, DIRECTOR
One of my first impressions of Beth came during general acting auditions at Southern Methodist University. I was a sophomore, Beth was an incoming freshman, and like all freshmen, had to do an acting audition. It was on the big stage. This beautiful young girl walked to the center of the proscenium and announced in charming Southern accent that she would like to do a speech from *Macbeth*...then she added in a slightly sinister voice..."by William Shakespeare." There ensued a nervous silence in the audience. What was coming?

viii

Maybe the worst Lady Macbeth of all times? Certainly not a traditional one. Beth did her inner preparation then turned to the audience with a fierce intensity… "Is this a dagger which I see before me, the handle towards my hand? Come, let me clutch thee." For the one and only time in my experience I saw the dagger in the air. There was almost a gasp in the audience, an eerie sense of the surreal. It was an electric moment. "My God, who is this person?" I thought. Beth has always been that moment to me—original, courageous, beautiful, and slightly sinister.

CRIMES OF THE HEART

Crimes of the Heart was written in a breakfast nook in a rented house in West Hollywood in 1978. I was inspired by my playwright friend Frederick Bailey who was producing his play *Gringo Planet* at La Mama Hollywood on a budget of five hundred dollars. When writing the play (originally titled *Crimes of Passion*), I thought a lot about how to cut corners: one set, modern dress, nothing that breaks. In the original manuscript I had the lights fade out as the sisters cut into the cake, foreseeing we could never afford a new cake every performance. Later when the play was professionally produced, I was delighted when a prop master divined we could have a fake cake with a smaller real section allowing the sisters to cut, eat, and smear cake every night. I remain impressed by this ingenuously logical solution. How I love theatre magic.

RAY BAKER, ACTOR
One day when we were rehearsing *Crimes of the Heart* for Broadway, Sharon Ullrick (who played Chick) fluffed a line. She said, "I've been on the phone all day, and you better get busy phonin' on the phone yourself!" (She was supposed to say "*callin'* on the phone yourself…") During our next break for notes, Beth, who was at all the rehearsals, said, "Sharon, I like the way you said that line. Leave it that way. I think it sounds kinda funny hearin' 'phone, phonin', phone' all in the same sentence." The moment struck me because I realized that Beth is always writing and rewriting, always creating…and always aware of the details that affect the way any story is heard and understood.

I started writing *The Miss Firecracker Contest* in 1979 in a fourth floor room of a mansion of a wealthy theatre patron in Louisville, Kentucky. The first production of *Crimes of the Heart* was in rehearsal at the Actors Theatre of Louisville and I felt it was important to have a second play going. I still adhere to this early, innate wisdom. A sort of don't-put-all-your-eggs-in-a-basket-that's-headed-for-a-free-fall theory.

Firecracker was originally produced at the Victory Theatre in Burbank, California, in a ninety-nine-seat house. The theatre had only recently opened. Perhaps this was the very first production, as I remember a beauty queen coming up onto the tiny stage, cutting a ribbon and having her photograph taken. Probably a theatre can only do that once.

The notices, as I recall, were "mixed-good," well, maybe just mixed. At any rate, not a lot of people were coming out to Burbank for the play. It was a very good production and I felt dejected by the lukewarm response.

After opening I went to work on a regional production of *Crimes of the Heart* in Baltimore and started eating Italian food every night. I made a phone call to L.A. and got the most glorious news. Oliver Hailey (the playwright) had come to see the production and said, "This play just makes me goofy!" I'll never forget the rapture I felt receiving this confirmation from a playwright I had known and admired only from afar. Oliver Hailey returned with his wife Betsy to see the play a second time and invited the cast to have chili and beer at their beautiful home. That vote of confidence is something I still sail on. "This play just makes me goofy!" will always be one of my most treasured reviews.

FREDERICK BAILEY, ACTOR, WRITER, DIRECTOR
One of my fondest memories in this life goes like this: When I first moved to L.A., Beth Henley was one of four people I knew in town. I was in her back-yard on Hayworth Avenue in Hollywood reading the freshly typed manuscript of *The Miss Firecracker Contest,* in something like 1978. I still have a strong sense-memory sitting in the grass in the cool of the afternoon, turning the pages with another close friend, and savoring the sheer, unpolluted joy of knowing I was only the second person on earth to read this delightful, exciting new stage play by the author of *Crimes of the Heart.*

BELITA MORENO, ACTRESS, DIRECTOR

In 1979, a mutual friend, Stephen Tobolowsky, brought me Beth's new play, *The Miss Firecracker Contest*. He and I had grown up in a section of Dallas where an authentic Miss Firecracker Contest was an annual event. Steve told me that Beth wanted me to read the role of "Popeye," a role I later played on stage. As I read, laughing and sighing my way through, the "Popeye" character told a familiar story I once told Beth, about a midget and a dwarf who married and the tragedy of their life together. It was an odd story but my mother and I had actually attended their wedding years before when I was in college. This is an example of how Beth brings to her plays real events that might seem impossible but are based in truth. In my opinion, it is what makes her plays so strong and at the same time so fragile. The simple, painful truth in Beth's plays is the key to entering her world. And, of course, it makes me think twice about what I tell that gal.

PATRICIA RICHARDSON, ACTRESS

Doing *The Miss Firecracker Contest* and *The Wake of Jamey Foster* gave me two of the luckiest, scariest, happiest experiences I have ever had as an actress and got me pregnant with my first child, too. Okay, my first husband had something to do with that, but I had been unable to get pregnant for three years and then—a few months into *Firecracker* and the summer in an un-air-conditioned theatre and Bingo! I became huge and cranky with child very rapidly and had to leave the show, to the immense relief of everyone else who had been dealing with me, putting thermometers all over the set in order to force the Manhattan Theatre Club into air-conditioning us. There was some Actor's Equity rule about theatres not getting over 99 degrees and we were there. My friend Mac says it was the only time he's ever seen an entire audience strip to the waist for a play. Elaine was very sweaty. And fanned herself incessantly. I was sure if I didn't leave, Mark Linn-Baker would strangle me to death. Justifiable homicide. Sweat and swelling hormones notwithstanding, it was sheer fun, onstage and off.

THE WAKE OF JAMEY FOSTER

The Wake was originally produced at the Hartford Stage Company in the winter of 1981. The company stayed in a run-down apartment complex called

Asylum Apartments. I recall Susan Kingsley (Marshael) reading *Sophie's Choice* by William Styron. She had two children, a boy and a girl, back in Louisville whom she missed a lot. One night after an early preview, we were riding up in the creaky water-stained elevator, Susan reading the book. Her face went ashen and she ripped the book apart, kicking and slamming the walls of the elevator. Not having read the book, I assumed the rage was play induced. All the same I was silent. Susan had a way of letting you know when that would be a good idea.

To get to rehearsal we had to walk under a train station, past freezing hookers, through a mall, and over snowy streets to reach the theatre. Brad Sullivan (Brocker Slade) had a little pug-type dog called Buster. Buster was made to wear four tiny yellow rain boots so his feet wouldn't stick to the icy pavement. He would go with Brad to all of the performances and wait mutely and dutifully in the dressing room.

Later when the play was in previews on Broadway, Buster appeared as The Junkyard Dog in one preview performance at the end of Act Two, Scene Two. It was quickly ascertained that Buster's desperate eagerness to catapult into Brad's arms as soon as Brad whistled was grossly out of character in the part of the tough world-weary Junkyard Dog. Buster was promptly removed from the cast roster.

PATRICIA RICHARDSON, ACTRESS
The Wake was the best and worst experience of doing theatre in and around New York. We were blessed with the genius of Ulu Grosbard and a truly great play. We were sublime to all the critics when we opened in Hartford and raked over the coals by Frank Rich when we moved it to New York. The opening night party was a downhill slide to oblivion for all of us, who ended up on the street in the gutter drunk and depressed beyond reason. We had to perform the show for a few weeks after that debacle, and though there had been many laughs before, there were now none. Beth said that the whole audience was holding the Frank Rich review and reading it while watching the play. When we finally closed the play, it took months to get over the disappointment of not getting to perform it longer. What a joy it had been for me to work again with Belita Moreno (later to be a brilliant "Popeye" in *Firecracker Contest*) and Steve Tobolowsky (who, happily, directed *Firecracker Contest*) and Beth. We had all gone to college together at SMU and had a shared history that was really grounding for me. It was a lesson in acting to be with the brilliant and truthful Susan Kingsley and the amazing Holly Hunter, who replaced mesmerizing Amanda Plummer when we got to New York. I'm so thankful for these experiences

now and save every note that Beth has ever written me somewhere in my house, and every character that I have ever played for her somewhere in my heart.

JONATHAN DEMME, DIRECTOR

I RECALL this amazing Beth Henleyesque moment that I was simultaneously appalled, curiously exhilarated, and most certainly privileged to witness. It was the ultimate image/moment of an unforgettable Beth Henley night.

I FLASHBACK to the beginning of the evening, the night of the Broadway premiere of *The Wake of Jamey Foster,* Beth's follow-up to *Crimes of the Heart.* Lucky to be seated amongst the First Night audience, it was just so galvanizing both as an admirer and friend of Beth to experience this electrifying ground-floor taste of this bold and hilarious and deeply moving play that was unquestionably challenging and thrilling every single person in the house. It was a complete Grand-Slam Home Run all the way up to and including the ecstatic, extended ovation that greeted the curtain calls.

I REMEMBER how giddy and puffed-up all the lucky people were who got to go over to Sardi's with Beth after the show to uncork champagne, await the rave reviews, feast on cannelloni, and generally groove on being there for what was clearly the unforgettable first night of a triumphant follow-up hit to a great new playwright's first gigantic success.

I RECALL (interestingly, in slow motion) the moment when towering stacks of mint next-day's *New York Times* were raced into Sardi's directly from the *Times'* printing press two blocks away and were grabbed by producers, cast members, and friends like prized items at a high-end clearance sale.

I RECALL how bizarre it was to find myself and the waiters suddenly completely alone, minutes later in Sardi's at 11:15 PM, me clutching the *New York Times'* unjustly and absurdly dismissive pan of *The Wake of Jamey Foster.*

And finally, I RECALL the singularly Beth Henleyesque real-life Beth Henley image, as I staggered out of Sardi's to witness Beth Henley dressed in her beautiful premiere outfit, seated on the curb of 45th Street in front of the restaurant, a half-empty bottle of champagne to her left, the crumpled *Times* review on the pavement to her right, bawling her gorgeous eyes out and sobbing to the heavens. I felt sorry for Beth and felt she was wasting her emotions. When a play plays as great as *Jamey Foster* had that night, it was obviously going to have a huge run that no newspaper pan could ever staunch. I pointed that out to Beth, but she was not persuaded.

I REALIZED about a week or so later how little I knew about New York theatre… *The Wake of Jamey Foster*, an extraordinary work by a great new writer, closed very shortly thereafter.

Beth Henley, however, went on and on and continues to create uniquely exceptional plays—often hilarious, always deeply moving, relentlessly humanistic, utterly and magically the work of this one-of-a-kind American author.

And I GOT TO SEE HER weep for her art in the gutters of New York that night long ago, and have been loving her work ever since…

THE DEBUTANTE BALL

In writing *The Debutante Ball* I was struggling with the ending. I had an image of the play closing with Jen, the mother, soothing her daughter, Teddy, as she bathed. I learned, however, that after a miscarriage one isn't to bathe for a matter of days. At first I thought, it's fiction. I'll just cheat this. Then I began to ponder the reality that Teddy would be wearing a sanitary pad. A problem difficult to surmount when nudity is required. As soon as I let go of the idea of having Teddy in the bath, a simple revelation occurred: The mother, not the daughter, would be in the bath. Now the roles were reversed and the daughter was taking care of her mother who was—for the first time in the play—naked and vulnerable, without artifice, with all of her wounds exposed. Resolutions like this intrigue me. It is as though the play is somehow aware of the factual as well as the dramatic truth and I must faithfully follow the clues.

CAMILLA CARR, ACTRESS, WRITER
Every time Beth finishes a new play, she has a reading in her living room. When she revised *The Debutante Ball* and wanted to hear it, Gena Rowlands was reading "Jen," Carol Kane was reading "Bliss," Jennifer Jason Leigh was reading "Teddy." I will certainly never forget that Liza Minelli was there in the audience because when Gena Rowlands' character told Carol Kane's character: "Good then. You just keep on taking those pills, but they're going to kill you just like they killed Judy Garland, only you won't have any fame or money to show for it!"… Beth just slid to the floor. But Gena Rowlands didn't bat an eye. And neither did Liza Minelli.

Ever since I heard Ruth Etting sing "Ten Cents a Dance" I have been fascinated by the idea of Taxi Dancers. There seems to be something heartbreaking and wondrous about a human being paying another human being for the short pleasure and romance of a dance.

A great challenge in choosing to write a play about a taxi dance hall was what to do about music. It is not financially feasible to have a band onstage when you are not writing a musical. Finally I came round to the idea of a jukebox. They would simply have this modern contraption with songs by actual artists. I spent months searching for and listening to old recordings from the 20s and 30s, dedicated to finding the perfect music to go under the dance scene in Act Two. When I started listening to Earl Hines, Bessie Smith, Jimmie Noone, and Valaida Snow, I realized it was the dazzling, wrenching black music that most enthralled me. This music would never be on a 1930s jukebox, which, at the time, would have only ten tunes. All of them white "marshmallow music." The solution was to have Sue Jack shoot the jukebox to smithereens at the end of Act One, and let *The Lucky Spot* be reduced to using Davenport's old race records, from the attic. That Sue Jack would be capable of such violence and destruction informed me tremendously about the despair and rage that lived inside her—unrepentant and unresolved.

There was also the problem of casting a roomful of dancers and patrons. After some thought I devised the idea that Hooker was opening up his dance hall in an isolated rural area. Who would start a business so obviously doomed to fail? A man seeking to rebuild a life from the fractured images of the past. A man that would become the blustering, passionate, much flawed dreamer, Reed Hooker. Again by overcoming a practical dilemma, I was able to make creative headway.

CAROL KANE, ACTRESS

When I have the honor to be one of Beth's characters, I eventually feel a rare and exquisite kind of freedom. This could be thought odd because all of Beth's characters, while gifted with extraordinary dialogue, are shackled with emotional weights the likes of which no human being should ever have to carry. So do I feel so often.

Norman Renee, who directed the magnificent production of *The Lucky Spot* in which I participated, gave me what feels like the key to Beth's magic; he told us in rehearsal one day never never to forget that Beth's characters are filled with hope. Insane, unstoppable hope against all reason. With this hope you are released to fly free in the face of doom.

Amy Madigan, actress
I remember *Lucky Spot* vividly. I read the play and Sue Jack is one of the most beautiful heroines of all time—a liar, a loudmouth, haunted by a past and consumed with trying to make it all right. Her failings make her so real—her love and forgiveness is boundless.

CRIMES OF THE HEART

FOR LEN, C.C., AND KAYO

Lee Anne Fahey, Kathy Bates, and Susan Kingsley
in the Actor's Theatre of Louisville's production of
Crimes of the Heart.

photo by David S. Talbott

ORIGINAL PRODUCTION

Crimes of the Heart was presented on Broadway by Warner Theatre Productions, Inc./Claire Nichtern, Mary Lea Johnson, Martin Richards, and Francine Lefrak, at the Golden Theatre, in New York City, on November 4, 1981. It was directed by Melvin Bernhardt; the set was by John Lee Beatty; costumes were by Patricia McGourty; and the lighting was by Dennis Parichy. The associate producer was Ethel Watt. The cast, in order of appearance, was as follows:

Lenny Magrath . . . . Lizbeth Mackay
Chick Boyle . . . . Sharon Ullrick
Doc Porter . . . . Raymond Baker
Meg Magrath . . . . Mary Beth Hurt
Babe Botrelle . . . . Mia Dillon
Barnette Lloyd . . . . Peter MacNicol

Crimes of the Heart received its New York premiere at the Manhattan Theatre Club, in 1980.

Crimes of the Heart had it's world premiere at Actors Theatre of Louisville, Louisville, Kentucky, February, 1979.

THE CAST

LENNY MAGRATH: 30, the oldest sister
CHICK BOYLE: 29, the sisters' first cousin
MEG MAGRATH: 27, the middle sister
DOC PORTER: 30, Meg's old boyfriend
BABE BOTRELLE: 24, the youngest sister
BARNETTE LLOYD: 26, Babe's lawyer

THE SETTING

The setting of the entire play is the kitchen in the Magrath sisters' house in Hazlehurst, Mississippi, a small southern town. The old-fashioned kitchen is unusually spacious, but there is a lived-in cluttered look about it. There are four different entrances and exits to the kitchen: the back door; the door leading to the dining room, and the front of the house; a door leading to the downstairs bedroom; and a staircase leading to the upstairs room. There is a table near the center of the room, and a cot has been set up in one of the corners.

THE TIME

In the fall, five years after Hurricane Camille

ACT I

The lights go up on the empty kitchen. It is late afternoon. Lenny Magrath, a thirty-year-old woman with a round figure and face, enters from the back door carrying a white suitcase, a saxophone case, and a brown paper sack. She sets the suitcase and the sax case down and takes the brown sack to the kitchen table. After glancing quickly at the door, she gets the cookie jar from the kitchen counter, a box of matches from the stove, and then brings both objects back down to the kitchen table. Excitedly, she reaches into the brown sack and pulls out a package of birthday candles. She quickly opens the package and removes a candle. She tries to stick the candle into a cookie—it falls off. She sticks the candle in again but the cookie is too hard and it crumbles. Frantically, she gets a second cookie from the jar. She strikes a match, lights the candle and begins dripping wax onto the cookie. Just as she is beginning to smile we hear Chick's voice from offstage.

CHICK'S VOICE: Lenny! Oh, Lenny!
  (Lenny quickly blows out the candle and stuffs the cookie and candle into her dress pocket. Chick, twenty-nine, enters from the back door. She is a brightly dressed matron with yellow hair and shiny, red lips.)
CHICK: Hi! I saw your car pull up.
LENNY: Hi.
CHICK: Well, did you see today's paper?
  (Lenny nods.)
CHICK: It's just too awful! It's just way too awful! How I'm gonna continue holding my head up high in this community, I do not know. Did you remember to pick up those panty hose for me?
LENNY: They're in the sack.
CHICK: Well, thank goodness, at least I'm not gonna have to go into town wearing holes in my stockings. *(Chick gets the package, tears it open, and proceeds to take off one pair of stockings and put on another, throughout the following scene. There should be something slightly grotesque about this woman changing her stockings in the kitchen.)*
LENNY: Did Uncle Watson call?
CHICK: Yes, Daddy has called me twice already. He said Babe's ready to come home. We've got to get right over and pick her up before they change their simple minds.
LENNY: *(Hesitantly.)* Oh, I know, of course, it's just—

CHICK: What?

LENNY: Well, I was hoping Meg would call.

CHICK: Meg?

LENNY: Yes, I sent her a telegram: about Babe, and—

CHICK: A telegram?! Couldn't you just phone her up?

LENNY: Well, no, 'cause her phone's…out of order.

CHICK: Out of order?

LENNY: Disconnected. I don't know what.

CHICK: Well, that sounds like Meg. My, these are snug. Are you sure you bought my right size?

LENNY: *(Looking at the box.)* Size extra petite.

CHICK: Well, they're skimping on the nylon material. *(Struggling to pull up the stockings.)* That's all there is to it. Skimping on the nylon. *(She finishes on one leg and starts on the other.)* Now, just what all did you say in this "telegram" to Meg?

LENNY: I don't recall exactly. I, well, I just told her to come on home.

CHICK: To come on home! Why, Lenora Josephine, have you lost your only brain, or what?

LENNY: *(Nervously, as she begins to pick up the mess of dirty stockings and plastic wrappings.)* But Babe wants Meg home. She asked me to call her.

CHICK: I'm not talking about what Babe wants.

LENNY: Well, what then?

CHICK: Listen, Lenora, I think it's pretty accurate to assume that after this morning's paper, Babe's gonna be incurring some mighty negative publicity around this town. And Meg's appearance isn't gonna help out a bit.

LENNY: What's wrong with Meg?

CHICK: She had a loose reputation in high school.

LENNY: *(Weakly.)* She was popular.

CHICK: She was known all over Copiah County as cheap Christmas trash, and that was the least of it. There was that whole sordid affair with Doc Porter, leaving him a cripple.

LENNY: A cripple—he's got a limp. Just, kind of, barely a limp.

CHICK: Well, his mother was going to keep *me* out of the Ladies' Social League because of it.

LENNY: What?

CHICK: That's right. I never told you, but I had to go plead with that mean, old woman and convince her that I was just as appalled and upset with what Meg had done as she was, and that I was only a first cousin anyway and I could hardly be blamed for all the skeletons in the Magraths' closet. It was humiliating. I tell you, she even brought up your mother's death. And that poor cat.

LENNY: Oh! Oh! Oh, please, Chick! I'm sorry. But you're in the Ladies' League now.

CHICK: Yes. That's true, I am. But frankly, if Mrs. Porter hadn't developed that tumor in her bladder, I wouldn't be in the club today, much less a committee head. *(As she brushes her hair.)* Anyway, you be a sweet potato and wait right here for Meg to call, so's you can convince her not to come back home. It would make things a whole lot easier on everybody. Don't you think it really would?

LENNY: Probably.

CHICK: Good, then suit yourself. How's my hair?

LENNY: Fine.

CHICK: Not pooching out in the back, is it?

LENNY: No.

CHICK: *(Cleaning the hair from her brush.)* Alright then, I'm on my way. I've got Annie May over there keeping an eye on Peekay and Buck Jr., but I don't trust her with them for long periods of time. *(Dropping the ball of hair onto the floor.)* Her mind is like a loose sieve. Honestly it is. *(She puts the brush back into her purse.)* Oh! Oh! Oh! I almost forgot. Here's a present for you. Happy Birthday to Lenny, from the Buck Boyles! *(Chick takes a wrapped package from her bag and hands it to Lenny.)*

LENNY: Why, thank you, Chick. It's so nice to have you remember my birthday every year like you do.

CHICK: *(Modestly.)* Oh well, now, that's just the way I am, I suppose. That's just the way I was brought up to be. Well, why don't you go on and open up the present?

LENNY: Alright. *(She starts to unwrap the gift.)*

CHICK: It's a box of candy—assorted cremes.

LENNY: Candy—that's always a nice gift.

CHICK: And you have a sweet tooth, don't you?

LENNY: I guess.

CHICK: Well, I'm glad you like it.

LENNY: I do.

CHICK: Oh, speaking of which, remember that little polka dot dress you got Peekay for her fifth birthday last month?

LENNY: The red and white one?

CHICK: Yes; well, the first time I put it in the washing machine, I mean the very first time, it fell all to pieces. Those little polka dots just dropped right off in the water.

LENNY: *(Crushed.)* Oh, no. Well, I'll get something else for her then—a little toy.

CHICK: Oh, no, no, no, no, no, no! We wouldn't hear of it! I just wanted to let you know so you wouldn't go and waste any more of your hard-earned money on that make of dress. Those inexpensive brands just don't hold up. I'm sorry but not in these modern washing machines.

DOC PORTER'S VOICE: Hello! Hello, Lenny!

CHICK: *(Taking over.)* Oh, look, it's Doc Porter! Come on in, Doc! Please come right on in!

(Doc Porter enters through the back door. He is carrying a large sack of pecans. Doc is an attractively worn man with a slight limp that adds rather than detracts from his quiet seductive quality. He is thirty years old, but appears slightly older.)

CHICK: Well, how are you doing? How in the world are you doing?

DOC: Just fine, Chick.

CHICK: And how are you liking it now that you're back in Hazlehurst?

DOC: Oh, I'm finding it somewhat enjoyable.

CHICK: Somewhat! Only somewhat! Will you listen to him! What a silly, silly, silly man! Well, I'm on my way. I've got some people waiting on me. *(Whispering to Doc.)* It's Babe. I'm on my way to pick her up.

DOC: Oh.

CHICK: Well, good-bye! Farewell and good-bye!

LENNY: 'Bye.

(Chick exits.)

DOC: Hello.

LENNY: Hi. I guess you heard about the thing with Babe.

DOC: Yeah.

LENNY: It was in the newspaper.

DOC: Uh huh.

LENNY: What a mess.

DOC: Yeah.

LENNY: Well, come on and sit down. I'll heat us up some coffee.

DOC: That's okay. I can only stay a minute. I have to pick up Scott; he's at the dentist's.

LENNY: Oh; well, I'll heat some up for myself. I'm kinda thirsty for a cup of hot coffee. *(Lenny puts the coffeepot on the burner.)*

DOC: Lenny—

LENNY: What?

DOC: *(Not able to go on.)* Ah…

LENNY: Yes?

DOC: Here, some pecans for you. *(He hands her the sack.)*

LENNY: Why, thank you, Doc. I love pecans.

DOC: My wife and Scott picked them up around the yard.

LENNY: Well, I can use them to make a pie. A pecan pie.

DOC: Yeah. Look, Lenny, I've got some bad news for you.

LENNY: What?

DOC: Well, you know, you've been keeping Billy Boy out on our farm; he's been grazing out there.

LENNY: Yes—

DOC: Well, last night, Billy Boy died.

LENNY: He died?

DOC: Yeah. I'm sorry to tell you when you've got all this on you, but I thought you'd want to know.

LENNY: Well, yeah. I do. He died?

DOC: Uh huh. He was struck by lightning.

LENNY: Struck by lightning? In that storm yesterday?

DOC: That's what we think.

LENNY: Gosh, struck by lightning. I've had Billy Boy so long. You know. Ever since I was ten years old.

DOC: Yeah. He was a mighty old horse.

LENNY: *(Stung.)* Mighty old.

DOC: Almost twenty years old.

LENNY: That's right, twenty years. 'Cause; ah; I'm thirty years old today. Did you know that?

DOC: No, Lenny, I didn't know. Happy Birthday.

LENNY: Thanks. *(She begins to cry.)*

DOC: Oh, come on now, Lenny. Come on. Hey, hey, now. You know I can't stand it when you Magrath women start to cry. You know it just gets me.

LENNY: Oh-ho! Sure! You mean when Meg cries! Meg's the one you could never stand to watch cry! Not me! I could fill up a pig's trough!

DOC: Now, Lenny…stop it. Come on. Jesus!

LENNY: Okay! Okay! I don't know what's wrong with me. I don't mean to make a scene. I've been on this crying jag. *(She blows her nose.)* All this stuff with Babe and old Granddaddy's gotten worse in the hospital and I can't get in touch with Meg.

DOC: You tried calling Meggy?

LENNY: Yes.

DOC: Is she coming home?

LENNY: Who knows. She hasn't called me. That's what I'm waiting here for—
hoping she'll call.

DOC: She still living in California?

LENNY: Yes; in Hollywood.

DOC: Well, give me a call if she gets in. I'd like to see her.

LENNY: Oh, you would, huh?

DOC: Yeah, Lenny, sad to say, but I would.

LENNY: It is sad. It's very sad indeed.

(They stare at each other, then look away. There is a moment of tense silence.)

DOC: Hey, Jello Face, your coffee's boiling.

LENNY: *(Going to check.)* Oh, it is? Thanks. *(After she checks the pot.)* Look,
you'd better go on and pick Scott up. You don't want him to have to wait
for you.

DOC: Yeah, you're right. Poor kid. It's his first time at the dentist.

LENNY: Poor thing.

DOC: Well, 'bye. I'm sorry to have to tell you about your horse.

LENNY: Oh, I know. Tell Joan thanks for picking up the pecans.

DOC: I will. *(He starts to leave.)*

LENNY: Oh, how's the baby?

DOC: She's fine. Real pretty. She, ah, holds your finger in her hand; like this.

LENNY: Oh, that's cute.

DOC: Yeah. 'Bye, Lenny.

LENNY: 'Bye.

*(Doc exits. Lenny stares after him for a moment, then goes and sits back
down at the kitchen table. She reaches into her pocket and pulls out a somewhat crumbled cookie and a wax candle. She lights the candle again, lets the
wax drip onto the cookie, then sticks the candle on top of the cookie. She
begins to sing the "Happy Birthday Song" to herself. At the end of the song
she pauses, silently makes a wish, and blows out the candle. She waits a
moment, then relights the candle, and repeats her actions, only this time
making a different wish at the end of the song. She starts to repeat the pro-
cedure for the third time, as the phone begins to ring. She goes to answer it.)*

LENNY: Hello…oh, hello, Lucille, how's Zackery?…Oh, no!…Oh, I'm so
sorry. Of course, it must be grueling for you…Yes, I understand. Your
only brother…no, she's not here yet. Chick just went to pick her up…
oh, now, Lucille, she's still his wife, I'm sure she'll be interested…Well,
you can just tell me the information and I'll relate it all to her…Uh-hum,

his liver's saved. Oh, that's good news!…Well, of course, when you look at it like that…Breathing stabilized…Damage to the spinal column, not yet determined…Okay…Yes, Lucille, I've got it all down…Uh-huh, I'll give her that message. 'Bye, 'bye.

(Lenny drops the pencil and paper down. She sighs deeply, wipes her cheeks with the back of her hand, and goes to the stove to pour herself a cup of coffee. After a few moments, the front door is heard slamming. Lenny starts. A whistle is heard, then Meg's voice.)

MEG'S VOICE: I'm home! *(She whistles the family whistle.)* Anybody home?!!

LENNY: Meg? Meg!

(Meg, twenty-seven, enters from the dining room. She has sad, magic eyes and wears a hat. She carries a worn-out suitcase.)

MEG: *(Dropping her suitcase, running to hug Lenny.)* Lenny—

LENNY: Well, Meg! Why, Meg! Oh, Meggy! Why didn't you call? Did you fly in? You didn't take a cab, did you? Why didn't you give us a call?

MEG: *(Overlapping.)* Oh, Lenny! Why, Lenny! Dear, Lenny! *(Then she looks at Lenny's face.)* My God, we're getting so old! Oh, I called for heaven's sake. Of course, I called!

LENNY: Well, I never talked to you—

MEG: Well, I know! I let the phone ring right off the hook!

LENNY: Well, as a matter of fact, I was out most of the morning seeing to Babe—!

MEG: Now just what's all this business about Babe? How could you send me such a telegram about Babe? And Zackery! You say somebody's shot Zackery? !

LENNY: Yes; they have.

MEG: Well, good Lord! Is he dead?

LENNY: No. But he's in the hospital. He was shot in his stomach.

MEG: In his stomach! How awful! Do they know who shot him?

(Lenny nods.)

MEG: Well, who? Who was it? Who? Who?

LENNY: Babe! They're all saying Babe shot him! They took her to jail! And they're saying she shot him! They're all saying it! It's horrible! It's awful!

MEG: *(Overlapping.)* Jail! Good Lord, jail! Well, who? Who's saying it? Who?!!

LENNY: Everyone!! The policemen, the sheriff, Zackery, even Babe's saying it! Even Babe herself!!

MEG: Well, for God's sake. For God's sake.

LENNY: *(Overlapping as she falls apart.)* It's horrible! It's horrible! It's just horrible!!!

MEG: Now calm down, Lenny. Just calm down. Would you like a Coke? Here, I'll get you some Coke. *(Meg gets a Coke from the refrigerator. She opens it and downs a large swig.)* Why? Why would she shoot him? Why? *(Meg hands the Coke bottle to Lenny.)*

LENNY: I talked to her this morning and I asked her that very question. I said, "Babe, why would you shoot Zackery? He was your own husband. Why would you shoot him?" And do you know what she said? *(Meg shakes her head.)*

LENNY: She said, "Cause I didn't like his looks. I just didn't like his looks."

MEG: *(After a pause.)* Well, I don't like his looks.

LENNY: But you didn't shoot him! You wouldn't shoot a person 'cause you didn't like their looks! You wouldn't do that! Oh, I hate to say this—I do hate to say this—but I believe Babe is ill. I mean in-her-head-ill.

MEG: Oh, now, Lenny, don't you say that! There're plenty of good sane reasons to shoot another person and I'm sure that Babe had one. Now what we've got to do is get her the best lawyer in town. Do you have any ideas on who's the best lawyer in town?

LENNY: Well, Zackery is, of course; but he's been shot!

MEG: Well, count him out! Just count him and his whole firm out!

LENNY: Anyway, you don't have to worry, she's already got her lawyer.

MEG: She does? Who?

LENNY: Barnette Lloyd. Annie Lloyd's boy. He just opened his office here in town. And Uncle Watson said we'd be doing Annie a favor by hiring him up.

MEG: Doing Annie a favor? Doing Annie a favor?! Well, what about Babe? Have you thought about Babe? Do we want to do her a favor of thirty or forty years in jail?! Have you thought about that?

LENNY: Now, don't snap at me! Just don't snap at me! I try to do what's right! All this responsibility keeps falling on my shoulders, and I try to do what's right!

MEG: Well, boo hoo, hoo, hoo! And how in the hell could you send me such a telegram about Babe!

LENNY: Well, if you had a phone, or if you didn't live way out there in Hollywood and not even come home for Christmas maybe I wouldn't have to pay all that money to send you a telegram!!!

MEG: *(Overlapping.)* 'Babe's in terrible trouble—Stop! Zackery's been shot—Stop! Come home immediately—Stop! Stop! Stop!'

LENNY: And what was that you said about how old we're getting? When you looked at my face, you said, "My God, we're getting so old!" But you didn't mean we—you meant me! Didn't you? I'm thirty years old today and my face is getting all pinched up and my hair is falling out in the comb.

MEG: Why, Lenny! It's your birthday, October 23rd. How could I forget. Happy Birthday!

LENNY: Well, it's not. I'm thirty years old and Billy Boy died last night. He was struck by lightning. He was struck dead.

MEG: *(Reaching for a cigarette.)* Struck dead. Oh, what a mess. What a mess. Are you really thirty? Then I must be twenty-seven and Babe is twenty-four. My God, we're getting so old.

(They are silent for several moments as Meg drags off her cigarette and Lenny drinks her Coke.)

MEG: What's the cot doing in the kitchen?

LENNY: Well, I rolled it out when Old Granddaddy got sick. So I could be close and hear him at night if he needed something.

MEG: *(Glancing toward the door leading to the downstairs bedroom.)* Is Old Granddaddy here?

LENNY: Why, no. Old Granddaddy's at the hospital.

MEG: Again?

LENNY: Meg!

MEG: What?

LENNY: I wrote you all about it. He's been in the hospital over three months straight.

MEG: He has?

LENNY: Don't you remember? I wrote you about all those blood vessels popping in his brain?

MEG: Popping—

LENNY: And how he was so anxious to hear from you and to find out about your singing career. I wrote it all to you. How they have to feed him through those tubes now. Didn't you get my letters?

MEG: Oh, I don't know, Lenny. I guess I did. To tell you the truth, sometimes I kinda don't read your letters.

LENNY: What?

MEG: I'm sorry. I used to read them. It's just since Christmas reading them gives me these slicing pains right here in my chest.

LENNY: I see. I see. Is that why you didn't use that money Old Granddaddy sent you to come home Christmas, because you hate us so much? We never did all that much to make you hate us. We didn't!

MEG: Oh, Lenny! Do you think I'd be getting slicing pains in my chest if I didn't care about you?! If I hated you? Honestly, now, do you think I would?

LENNY: No.

MEG: Okay, then. Let's drop it. I'm sorry I didn't read your letters. Okay?

LENNY: Okay.

MEG: Anyway, we've got this whole thing with Babe to deal with. The first thing is to get her a good lawyer and get her out of jail.

LENNY: Well, she's out of jail.

MEG: She is?

LENNY: That young lawyer, he's gotten her out.

MEG: Oh, he has?

LENNY: Yes, on bail. Uncle Watson's put it up. Chick's bringing her back right now—she's driving her home.

MEG: Oh; well, that's a relief.

LENNY: Yes, and they're due home any minute now; so we can just wait right here for 'em.

MEG: Well, good. That's good. *(As she leans against the counter.)* So, Babe shot Zackery Botrelle, the richest and most powerful man in all of Hazlehurst, slap in the gut. It's hard to believe.

LENNY: It certainly is. Little Babe—shooting off a gun.

MEG: Little Babe.

LENNY: She was always the prettiest and most perfect of the three of us. Old Granddaddy used to call her his Dancing Sugar Plum. Why, remember how proud and happy he was the day she married Zackery?

MEG: Yes, I remember. It was his finest hour.

LENNY: He remarked how Babe was gonna skyrocket right to the heights of Hazlehurst society. And how Zackery was just the right man for her whether she knew it now or not.

MEG: Oh, Lordy, Lordy. And what does Old Granddaddy say now?

LENNY: Well, I haven't had the courage to tell him all about this as yet. I thought maybe tonight we could go to visit him at the hospital and you could talk to him and…

MEG: Yeah, well, we'll see. We'll see. Do we have anything to drink around here—to the tune of straight bourbon?

LENNY: No. There's no liquor.

MEG: Hell. *(Meg gets a Coke from the refrigerator and opens it.)*

LENNY: Then you will go with me to see Old Granddaddy at the hospital tonight?

MEG: Of course. *(Meg goes to her purse and gets out a bottle of Empirin*

Compound. She takes out a tablet and puts it on her tongue.) Brother, I know he's gonna go on about my singing career. Just like he always does.

LENNY: Well, how is your career going?

MEG: It's not.

LENNY: Why, aren't you still singing at that club down on Malibu Beach?

MEG: No. Not since Christmas.

LENNY: Well, then, are you singing some place new?

MEG: No, I'm not singing. I'm not singing at all.

LENNY: Oh. Well, what do you do then?

MEG: What I do is I pay cold storage bills for a dog food company. That's what I do.

LENNY: *(Trying to be helpful.)* Gosh, don't you think it'd be a good idea to stay in the show business field?

MEG: Oh, maybe.

LENNY: Like Old Granddaddy says, "With your talent all you need is exposure. Then you can make your own breaks!" Did you hear his suggestion about getting your foot put in one of those blocks of cement they've got out there? He thinks that's real important.

MEG: Yeh. I think I've heard that. And I'll probably hear it again when I go to visit him at the hospital tonight, so let's just drop it. Okay? *(She notices the sack of pecans.)* What's this? Pecans? Great, I love pecans! *(Meg takes out two pecans and tries to open them by cracking them together.)* Come on… Crack, you demons! Crack!

LENNY: We have a nutcracker!

MEG: *(Trying with her teeth.)* Ah, where's the sport in a nutcracker? Where's the challenge?

LENNY: *(Getting up to get the nutcracker.)* It's over here in the utensil drawer. *(As Lenny gets the nutcracker, Meg opens the pecan by stepping on it with her shoe.)*

MEG: There! Open! *(Meg picks up the crumbled pecan and eats it.)* Mmmm, delicious. Delicious. Where'd you get the fresh pecans?

LENNY: Oh…I don't know.

MEG: They sure are tasty.

LENNY: Doc Porter brought them over.

MEG: Doc. What's Doc doing here in town?

LENNY: Well, his father died a couple of months ago. Now he's back home seeing to his property.

MEG: Gosh, the last I heard of Doc, he was up in the East painting the walls of houses to earn a living. *(Amused.)* Heard he was living with some Yankee woman who made clay pots.

LENNY: Joan.

MEG: What?

LENNY: Her name's Joan. She came down here with him. That's one of her pots. Doc's married to her.

MEG: Married—

LENNY: Uh huh.

MEG: Doc married a Yankee?

LENNY: That's right; and they've got two kids.

MEG: Kids—

LENNY: A boy and a girl.

MEG: God. Then his kids must be half-Yankee.

LENNY: I suppose.

MEG: God. That really gets me. I don't know why, but somehow that really gets me.

LENNY: I don't know why it should.

MEG: And what a stupid-looking pot! Who'd buy it anyway?

LENNY: Wait—I think that's them. Yeah, that's Chick's car! Oh, there's Babe! Hello, Babe! They're home, Meg! They're home.

(Meg hides.)

BABE'S VOICE: Lenny! I'm home! I'm free! *(Babe, twenty-four, enters exuberantly. She has an angelic face and fierce, volatile eyes. She carries a pink pocketbook.)* I'm home!

(Meg jumps out of hiding.)

BABE: Oh, Meg—Look, it's Meg! *(Running to hug her.)* Meg! When did you get home?

MEG: Just now!

BABE: Well, it's so good to see you! I'm so glad you're home! I'm so relieved.

(Chick enters.)

MEG: Why, Chick; hello.

CHICK: Hello, Cousin Margaret. What brings you back to Hazlehurst?

MEG: Oh, I came on home… *(Turning to Babe.)* I came on home to see about Babe.

BABE: *(Running to hug Meg.)* Oh, Meg—

MEG: How are things with you, Babe?

CHICK: Well, they are dismal, if you want my opinion. She is refusing to cooperate with her lawyer, that nice-looking young Lloyd boy. She won't tell any of us why she committed this heinous crime, except to say that she didn't like Zackery's looks—

BABE: Oh, look, Lenny brought my suitcase from home! And my saxophone! Thank you! *(Babe runs over to the cot and gets out her saxophone.)*

CHICK: Now that young lawyer is coming over here this afternoon, and when he gets here he expects to get some concrete answers! That's what he expects! No more of this nonsense and stubbornness from you, Rebecca Magrath, or they'll put you in jail and throw away the key!

BABE: Meg, come look at my new saxophone. I went to Jackson and bought it used. Feel it. It's so heavy.

MEG: It's beautiful. *(The room goes silent.)*

CHICK: Isn't that right, won't they throw away the key?

LENNY: Well, honestly, I don't know about that—

CHICK: They will! And leave you there to rot. So, Rebecca, what are you going to tell Mr. Lloyd about shooting Zackery when he gets here? What are your reasons going to be?

BABE: *(Glaring.)* That I didn't like his looks! I just didn't like his stinking looks! And I don't like yours much either, Chick-the-Stick! So, just leave me alone! I mean it! Leave me alone! Oooh!

(Babe exits up the stairs. There is a long moment of silence.)

CHICK: Well, I was only trying to warn her that she's going to have to help herself. It's just that she doesn't understand how serious the situation is. Does she? She doesn't have the vaguest idea. Does she now?

LENNY: Well, it's true, she does seem a little confused.

CHICK: And that's putting it mildly, Lenny honey. That's putting it mighty mild. So, Margaret, how's your singing career going? We keep looking for your picture in the movie magazines.

(Meg moves to light a cigarette.)

CHICK: You know, you shouldn't smoke. It causes cancer. Cancer of the lungs. They say each cigarette is just a little stick of cancer. A little death stick.

MEG: That's what I like about it, Chick—taking a drag off of death. *(Meg takes a long, deep drag.)* Mmm! Gives me a sense of controlling my own destiny. What power! What exhilaration! Want a drag?

LENNY: *(Trying to break the tension.)* Ah, Zackery's liver's been saved! His sister called up and said his liver was saved. Isn't that good news?

MEG: Well, yes, that's fine news. Mighty fine news. Why, I've been told that the liver's a powerful important bodily organ. I believe it's used to absorb all of our excess bile.

LENNY: Yes—well—it's been saved.

(The phone rings. Lenny gets it.)

MEG: So! Did you hear all that good news about the liver, Little Chicken?

CHICK: I heard it. And don't you call me Chicken!

(Meg clucks like a chicken.)

CHICK: I've told you a hundred times if I've told you once not to call me Chicken. You cannot call me Chicken.

LENNY: …Oh, no!…Of course, we'll be right over! 'Bye! *(She hangs up the phone.)* That was Annie May—Peekay and Buck Jr. have eaten paints!

CHICK: Oh, no! Are they alright? They're not sick? They're not sick, are they?!

LENNY: I don't know. I don't know. Come on. We've got to run on next door.

CHICK: *(Overlapping.)* Oh, God! Oh, please!! Please let them be alright! Don't let them die!! Please, don't let them die!!

(Chick runs off howling with Lenny following after. Meg sits alone, finishing her cigarette. After a moment, Babe's voice is heard.)

BABE'S VOICE: Pst—Psst!

(Meg looks around. Babe comes tiptoeing down the stairs.)

BABE: Has she gone?

MEG: She's gone. Peekay and Buck Jr. just ate their paints.

BABE: What idiots.

MEG: Yeah.

BABE: You know, Chick's hated us ever since we had to move here from Vicksburg to live with Old Grandmama and Old Granddaddy.

MEG: She's an idiot.

BABE: Yeah. Do you know what she told me this morning while I was still behind bars and couldn't get away?

MEG: What?

BABE: She told me how embarrassing it was for her all those years ago, you know, when mama—

MEG: Yeah, down in the cellar.

BABE: She said our mama had shamed the entire family, and we were known notoriously all through Hazlehurst. *(About to cry.)* Then she went on to say how I would now be getting just as much bad publicity and humiliating her and the family all over again.

MEG: Ah, forget it, Babe. Just forget it.

BABE: I told her, "Mama got national coverage! National!" And if Zackery wasn't a senator from Copiah County, I probably wouldn't even be getting statewide.

MEG: Of course you wouldn't.

BABE: *(After a pause.)* Gosh, sometimes I wonder...

MEG: What?

BABE: Why she did it. Why mama hung herself.

MEG: I don't know. She had a bad day. A real bad day. You know how it feels on a real bad day.

BABE: And that old yellow cat. It was sad about that old cat.

MEG: Yeah.

BABE: I bet if Daddy hadn't of left us, they'd still be alive.

MEG: Oh, I don't know.

BABE: 'Cause it was after he left that she started spending whole days just sitting there and smoking on the back porch steps. She'd sling her ashes down onto the different bugs and ants that'd be passing by.

MEG: Yeah. Well, I'm glad he left.

BABE: That old yellow cat'd stay back there with her.

MEG: God, he was a bastard.

BABE: I thought if she felt something for anyone it woulda been that old cat. Guess I musta been mistaken.

MEG: Really, with his white teeth, Daddy was such a bastard.

BABE: Was he? I don't remember.

(Meg blows out a mouthful of smoke. After a moment, uneasily.)

BABE: I think I'm gonna make some lemonade. You want some?

MEG: Sure.

(Babe cuts lemons, dumps sugar, stirs ice cubes, etc. throughout the following exchange.)

MEG: Babe. Why won't you talk? Why won't you tell anyone about shooting Zackery?

BABE: Oooh—

MEG: Why not? You must have had a good reason. Didn't you?

BABE: I guess I did.

MEG: Well, what was it?

BABE: I...I can't say.

MEG: Why not? *(Pause.)* Babe, why not? You can tell me.

BABE: 'Cause...I'm sort of...protecting someone.

MEG: Protecting someone? Oh, Babe, then you really didn't shoot him?! I knew you couldn't have done it!! I knew it!!!

BABE: No, I shot him. I shot him alright. I meant to kill him. I was aiming for his heart, but I guess my hands were shaking and I—just got him in the stomach.

MEG: *(Collapsing.)* I see.

BABE: *(Stirring the lemonade.)* So I'm guilty. And I'm just gonna have to take my punishment and go on to jail.

MEG: Oh, Babe—

BABE: Don't worry, Meg, jail's gonna be a relief to me. I can learn to play my new saxophone. I won't have to live with Zackery anymore. And I won't have his snoopy old sister, Lucille, coming over and pushing me around. Jail will be a relief. Here's your lemonade.

MEG: Thanks.

BABE: It taste okay?

MEG: Perfect.

BABE: I like a lot of sugar in mine. I'm gonna add some more sugar.

(Babe goes to add more sugar to her lemonade, as Lenny bursts through the back door in a state of excitement and confusion.)

LENNY: Well, it looks like the paint is primarily on their arms and faces; but Chick wants me to drive them all over to Doctor Winn's just to make sure. *(Lenny grabs her car keys off of the counter and as she does so, she notices the mess of lemon and sugar.)* Oh, now, Babe, try not to make a mess here; and be careful with this sharp knife. Honestly, all that sugar's gonna get you sick. Well, 'bye, 'bye. I'll be back as soon as I can.

MEG: 'Bye, Lenny.

BABE: 'Bye.

(Lenny exits.)

BABE: Boy, I don't know what's happening to Lenny.

MEG: What do you mean?

BABE: "Don't make a mess; don't make yourself sick; don't cut yourself with that sharp knife." She's turning into Old Grandmama.

MEG: You think so?

BABE: More and more. Do you know she's taken to wearing Old Grandmama's torn sun hat and her green garden gloves?

MEG: Those old lime green ones?

BABE: Yeah; she works out in the garden wearing the lime green gloves of a dead woman. Imagine wearing those gloves on your hands.

MEG: Poor Lenny. She needs some love in her life. All she does is work out at that brick yard and take care of Old Granddaddy.

BABE: Yeah. But she's so shy with men.

MEG: *(Biting into an apple.)* Probably because of that *shrunken* ovary she has.

BABE: *(Slinging ice cubes.)* Yeah, that *deformed* ovary.

MEG: Old Granddaddy's the one who's made her feel self-conscious about it. It's his fault. The old fool.

BABE: It's so sad.

MEG: God—you know what?

BABE: What?

MEG: I bet Lenny's never even slept with a man. Just think. Thirty years old and never even had it once.

BABE: *(Slyly.)* Oh; I don't know. Maybe she's...had it once?

MEG: She has?

BABE: Maybe. I think so.

MEG: When? When?

BABE: Well...maybe I shouldn't say—

MEG: Babe!

BABE: *(Rapidly telling the story.) Alright* then; it was after Old Granddaddy went back to the hospital this second time Lenny was really in a state of deep depression, I could tell that she was. Then one day she calls me up and asks me to come over and to bring along my Polaroid camera. Well, when I arrive she's waiting for me out there in the sun parlour wearing her powder blue Sunday dress and this old curled up wig. She confided that she was gonna try sending in her picture to one of those lonely hearts clubs.

MEG: Oh, my God.

BABE: Lonely Hearts of the South. She'd seen their ad in a magazine.

MEG: Jesus.

BABE: Anyway, I take some snapshots and she sends them on in to the club, and about two weeks later she receives in the mail this whole load of pictures of available men, most of 'em fairly odd looking. But of course she doesn't call any of 'em up 'cause she's real shy. But one of 'em, this Charlie Hill from Memphis, Tennessee, he calls her.

MEG: He does?

BABE: Yeah. And time goes on and she says he's real funny on the phone; so they decide to get together to meet.

MEG: Yeah?!

BABE: Well, he drives down here to Hazlehurst 'bout three or four different times and has supper with her, then one weekend she goes up to Memphis to visit him; and I think that is where it happened.

MEG: What makes you think so?

BABE: Well, when I went to pick her up from the bus depot, she ran off the bus and threw her arms around me and started crying and sobbing as though she'd like to never stop. I asked her, I said, "Lenny, what's the matter?" And she said, "I've done it, Babe! Honey, I have done it!"

MEG: *(Whispering.)* And you think she meant that she'd done *it?*

BABE: *(Whispering back, slyly.)* I think so.

MEG: Well, goddamn!

(They laugh with glee.)

BABE: But she didn't say anything else about it. She just went on to tell me about the boot factory where Charlie worked and what a nice city Memphis was.

MEG: So, what happened to this Charlie?

BABE: Well, he came to Hazlehurst just one more time. Lenny took him over to meet Old Granddaddy at the hospital and after that they broke it off.

MEG: 'Cause of Old Granddaddy?

BABE: Well, she said it was on account of her missing ovary. That Charlie didn't want to marry her on account of it.

MEG: Ah, how mean. How hateful.

BABE: Oh, it was. He seemed like such a nice man, too—kinda chubby with red hair and freckles, always telling these funny jokes.

MEG: Hmmm, that just doesn't seem right. Something about that doesn't seem exactly right. *(Meg paces about the kitchen and comes across the box of candy Lenny got for her birthday.)* Oh, God. "Happy Birthday to Lenny from the Buck Boyles."

BABE: Oh, no! Today's Lenny's birthday!

MEG: That's right.

BABE: I forgot all about it!

MEG: I know. I did too.

BABE: Gosh, we'll have to order up a big cake for her. She always loves to make those wishes on her birthday cake.

MEG: Yeah, let's get her a big cake! A huge one! *(Suddenly noticing the plastic wrapper on the candy box.)* Oh, God, that Chick's so cheap!

BABE: What do you mean?

MEG: This plastic has poinsettias on it!

BABE: *(Running to see.)* Oh, let me see— *(She looks at the package with disgust.)* Boy, oh, boy! I'm calling that bakery and ordering the very largest size cake they have! That Jumbo Deluxe!

MEG: Good!

BABE: Why, I imagine they can make one up to be about—*this* big. *(She demonstrates.)*

MEG: Oh, at least; at least that big. Why, maybe, it'll even be *this* big. *(She makes a very, very, very, large size cake.)*

BABE: You think it could be *that* big?

MEG: Sure!

BABE: *(After a moment, getting the idea.)* Or, or what if it were *this* big? *(She maps out a cake that covers the room.)* What if we get the cake and it's *this* big?!! *(She gulps down a fistful of cake.)* Gulp! Gulp! Gulp! Tasty treat!

MEG: Hmmm—I'll have me some more! Give me some more of that birth-day cake!

(Suddenly there is a loud knock at the door.)

BARNETTE'S VOICE: Hello...hello! May I come in?

BABE: *(To Meg, in a whisper, as she takes cover.)* Who's that?

MEG: I don't know.

BARNETTE'S VOICE: *(Still knocking.)* Hello! Hello, Mrs. Botrelle!

BABE: Oh, shoot! It's that lawyer. I don't want to see him.

MEG: Oh, Babe, come on. You've got to see him sometime.

BABE: No, I don't! *(She starts up the stairs.)* Just tell him I died—I'm going upstairs.

MEG: Oh, Babe! Will you come back here!

BABE: *(As she exits.)* You talk to him, please, Meg. Please! I just don't want to see him—

MEG: Babe—Babe! Oh, shit...ah, come on in! Door's open!

(Barnette Lloyd, twenty-six, enters carrying a briefcase. He is a slender, intelligent young man with an almost fanatical intensity that he subdues by sheer will.)

BARNETTE: How do you do? I'm Barnette Lloyd.

MEG: Pleased to meet you. I'm Meg Magrath, Babe's older sister.

BARNETTE: Yes, I know. You're the singer.

MEG: Well, yes...

BARNETTE: I came to hear you five different times when you were singing at that club in Biloxi. Greeny's I believe was the name of it.

MEG: Yes, Greeny's.

BARNETTE: You were very good. There was something sad and moving about how you sang those songs. It was like you had some sort of vision. Some special sort of vision.

MEG: Well, thank you. You're very kind. Now...about Babe's case—

BARNETTE: Yes?

MEG: We've just got to win it.

BARNETTE: I intend to.

MEG: Of course. But, ah… *(She looks at him.)* Ah, you know, you're very young.

BARNETTE: Yes. I am. I'm young.

MEG: It's just, I'm concerned, Mr. Lloyd—

BARNETTE: Barnette. Please.

MEG: Barnette; that, ah, just maybe we need someone with, well, with more experience. Someone totally familiar with all the ins and outs and the this and thats of the legal dealings and such. As that.

BARNETTE: Ah, you have reservations.

MEG: *(Relieved.)* Reservations. Yes, I have…reservations.

BARNETTE: Well, possibly it would help you to know that I graduated first in my class from Ole Miss Law School. I also spent three different summers taking advanced courses in criminal law at Harvard Law School. I made A's in all the given courses. I was fascinated!

MEG: I'm sure.

BARNETTE: And even now, I've just completed one year working with Jackson's top criminal law firm, Manchester and Wayne. I was invaluable to them. Indispensable. They offered to double my percentage, if I'd stay on; but I refused. I wanted to return to Hazlehurst and open my own office. The reason being, and this is a key point, that I have a personal vendetta to settle with one Zackery F. Botrelle.

MEG: A personal vendetta?

BARNETTE: Yes, ma'am. You are correct. Indeed, I do.

MEG: Hmmm. A personal vendetta…I think I like that. So you have some sort of a personal vendetta to settle with Zackery?

BARNETTE: Precisely. Just between the two of us, I not only intend to keep that sorry S.O.B. from ever being re-elected to the state senate by exposing his shady, criminal dealings; but I also intend to decimate his personal credibility by exposing him as a bully, a brute, and a redneck thug!

MEG: Well; I can see that you're—fanatical about this.

BARNETTE: Yes; I am. I'm sorry if I seem outspoken. But, for some reason, I feel I can talk to you…those songs you sang. Excuse me; I feel like a jackass.

MEG: It's alright. Relax. Relax, Barnette. Let me think this out a minute. *(She takes out a cigarette. He lights it for her.)*

MEG: Now just exactly how do you intend to get Babe off? You know, keep her out of jail.

BARNETTE: It seems to me that we can get her off with a plea of self-defense, or possibly we could go with innocent by reason of temporary insanity.

But basically, I intend to prove that Zackery Botrelle brutalized and tormented this poor woman to such an extent that she had no recourse but to defend herself in the only way she knew how!

MEG: I like that!

BARNETTE: Then, of course, I'm hoping this will break the ice and we'll be able to go on to prove that the man's a total criminal, as well as an abusive bully and contemptible slob!

MEG: That sounds good! To me that sounds very good!

BARNETTE: It's just our basic game plan.

MEG: But, now, how are you going to prove all this about Babe being brutalized? We don't want anyone perjured. I mean to commit perjury.

BARNETTE: Perjury? According to my sources, there'll be no need for perjury.

MEG: You mean it's the truth?

BARNETTE: This is a small town, Miss Magrath. The word gets out.

MEG: It's really the truth?

BARNETTE: *(Opening his briefcase.)* Just look at this. It's a photostatic copy of Mrs. Botrelle's medical chart over the past four years. Take a good look at it, if you want your blood to boil!

MEG: *(Looking over the chart.)* What! What! This is maddening. This is madness! Did he do this to her? I'll kill him; I will—I'll fry his blood!! Did he do this?

BARNETTE: *(Alarmed.)* To tell you the truth, I can't say for certain what was accidental and what was not. That's why I need to talk with Mrs. Botrelle. That's why it's very important that I see her!

MEG: *(Her eyes are wild, as she shoves him toward the door.)* Well, look, I've got to see her first. I've got to talk to her first. What I'll do is I'll give you a call. Maybe you can come back over later on—

BARNETTE: Well, then, here's my card—

MEG: Okay. Good-bye.

BARNETTE: 'Bye!

MEG: Oh, wait! Wait! There's one problem with you.

BARNETTE: What?

MEG: What if you get so fanatically obsessed with this vendetta thing that you forget about Babe? You forget about her and sell her down the river just to get at Zackery. What about that?

BARNETTE: I—wouldn't do that.

MEG: You wouldn't?

BARNETTE: No.

MEG: Why not?

BARNETTE: Because, I'm—I'm fond of her.

MEG: What do you mean you're fond of her?

BARNETTE: Well, she…she sold me a pound cake at a bazaar once. And I'm fond of her.

MEG: Alright; I believe you. Good-bye.

BARNETTE: Good-bye. *(Barnette exits.)*

MEG: Babe! Babe, come down here! Babe!

(Babe comes hurrying down the stairs.)

BABE: What? What is it? I called about the cake—

MEG: What did Zackery do to you?

BABE: They can't have it for today.

MEG: Did he hurt you? Did he? Did he do that?

BABE: Oh, Meg, please—

MEG: Did he? Goddamnit, Babe—

BABE: Yes, he did.

MEG: Why? Why?

BABE: I don't know! He started hating me, 'cause I couldn't laugh at his jokes. I just started finding it impossible to laugh at his jokes the way I used to. And then the sound of his voice got to where it tired me out awful bad to hear it. I'd fall asleep just listening to him at the dinner table. He'd say, "Hand me some of that gravy!" Or, "This roast beef is too damn bloody." And suddenly I'd be out cold like a light.

MEG: Oh, Babe. Babe, this is very important. I want you to sit down here and tell me what all happened right before you shot Zackery. That's right, just sit down and tell me.

BABE: *(After a pause.)* I told you I can't tell you on account of I'm protecting someone.

MEG: But Babe, you've just got to talk to someone about all this. You just do.

BABE: Why?

MEG: Because it's a human need. To talk about our lives. It's an important human need.

BABE: Oh. Well, I do feel like I want to talk to someone. I do.

MEG: Then talk to me; please.

BABE: *(A decision.)* Alright. *(After thinking a minute.)* I don't know where to start.

MEG: Just start at the beginning. Just there at the beginning.

BABE: *(After a moment.)* Well, do you remember Willie Jay?

(Meg shakes her head.)

BABE: Cora's youngest boy?

MEG: Oh, yeah, that little kid we used to pay a nickel to, to run down to the drugstore and bring us back a cherry Coke.

BABE: Right. Well, Cora irons at my place on Wednesdays now, and she just happened to mention that Willie Jay'd picked up this old stray dog and that he'd gotten real fond of him. But now they couldn't afford to feed him anymore, so she was gonna have to tell Willie Jay to set him loose in the woods.

MEG: *(Trying to be patient.)* Uh huh.

BABE: Well, I said I liked dogs and if he wanted to bring the dog over here, I'd take care of him. You see, I was alone by myself most of the time 'cause the senate was in session, and Zackery was up in Jackson.

MEG: Uh huh. *(Meg reaches for Lenny's box of birthday candy. She takes little nibbles out of each piece, throughout the rest of the scene.)*

BABE: So the next day, Willie Jay brings over this skinny, old dog with these little crossed eyes. Well, I asked Willie Jay what his name was, and he said they called him Dog. Well, I liked the name; so I thought I'd keep it.

MEG: *(Getting up.)* Uh huh. I'm listening. I'm just gonna get me a glass of cold water; do you want one?

BABE: Okay.

MEG: So you kept the name—Dog.

BABE: Yeah. Anyway, when Willie Jay was leaving he gave Dog a hug and said, "Good-bye, Dog. You're a fine ole dog." Well, I felt something for him, so I told Willie Jay he could come back and visit with Dog any time he wanted, and his face just kinda lit right up.

MEG: *(Offering the candy.)* Candy—

BABE: No thanks. Anyhow, time goes on and Willie Jay keeps coming over and over. And we talk about Dog and how fat he's getting and then, well, you know, things start up.

MEG: No, I don't know. What things start up?

BABE: Well, things start up. Like sex. Like that.

MEG: Babe, wait a minute—Willie Jay's a boy. A small boy, about this tall. He's about this tall!

BABE: No! Oh, no! He's taller now! He's fifteen now. When you knew him he was only about seven or eight.

MEG: But, even so—fifteen. And he's a black boy, a colored boy, a Negro.

BABE: *(Flustered.)* Well, I realize that, Meg. Why do you think I'm so worried about his getting public exposure? I don't want to ruin his reputation!

MEG: I'm amazed, Babe. I'm really, completely amazed. I didn't even know you were a liberal.

BABE: Well, I'm not! I'm not a liberal! I'm a democratic! I was just lonely! I was so lonely. And he was good. Oh, he was so, so good. I'd never had it that good. We'd always go out into the garage and—

MEG: It's okay. I've got the picture; I've got the picture! Now. Let's just get back to the story. To yesterday, when you shot Zackery.

BABE: Alright, then. Let's see…Willie Jay was over. And it was after we'd—

MEG: Yeah! Yeah.

BABE: And we were just standing around on the back porch playing with Dog. Well, suddenly, Zackery comes from around the side of the house. And he startled me 'cause he's supposed to be away at the office, and there he is coming from 'round the side of the house. Anyway, he says to Willie Jay, "Hey, boy, what are you doing back here?" And I said, "He's not doing anything. You just go on home, Willie Jay! You just run right on home." Well, before he can move, Zackery comes up and knocks him once right across the face and then shoves him down the porch steps, causing him to skin up his elbow real bad on that hard concrete. Then he says, "Don't you ever come around here again, or I'll have them cut out your gizzard!" Well, Willie Jay starts crying, these tears come streaming down his face, then he gets up real quick and runs away with Dog following off after him. After that, I don't remember much too clearly; let's see…I went on into the living room, and I went right up to the davenport and opened the drawer where we keep the burglar gun…I took it out. Then I—I brought it up to my ear. That's right. I put it right inside my ear. Why, I was gonna shoot off my own head! That's what I was gonna do. Then I heard the back door slamming and suddenly, for some reason, I thought about mama…how she'd hung herself. And here I was about ready to shoot myself. Then I realized—that's right I realized how I didn't want to kill myself! And she—she probably didn't want to kill herself. She wanted to kill him, and I wanted to kill him, too. I wanted to kill Zackery, not myself. 'Cause I—I wanted to live! So I waited for him to come on into the living room. Then I held out the gun, and I pulled the trigger, aiming for his heart, but getting him in the stomach. *(After a pause.)* It's funny that I really did that.

MEG: It's a good thing that you did. It's a damn good thing that you did.

BABE: It was.

MEG: Please, Babe, talk to Barnette Lloyd. Just talk to him and see if he can help.

BABE: But how about Willie Jay?

MEG: *(Starting toward the phone.)* Oh, he'll be alright. You just talk to that lawyer like you did to me. *(Looking at the number on the card, she begins dialing.)* See, 'cause he's gonna be on your side.

BABE: No! Stop, Meg, stop! Don't call him up! Please don't call him up! You can't! It's too awful.

(She runs over and jerks the bottom half of the phone away from Meg. Meg stands, holding the receiver.)

MEG: Babe!

(Babe slams her half of the phone into the refrigerator.)

BABE: I just can't tell some stranger all about my personal life. I just can't.

MEG: Well, hell, Babe; you're the one who said you wanted to live.

BABE: That's right. I did. *(She takes the phone out of the refrigerator and hands it to Meg.)* Here's the other part of the phone.

(Babe moves to sit at the kitchen table. Meg takes the phone back to the counter.)

BABE: *(As she fishes a lemon out of her glass and begins sucking on it.)* Meg.

MEG: What?

BABE: I called the bakery. They're gonna have Lenny's cake ready first thing tomorrow morning. That's the earliest they can get it.

MEG: Alright.

BABE: I told them to write on it, "Happy Birthday Lenny—A Day Late." That sound okay?

MEG: *(At the phone.)* It sounds nice.

BABE: I ordered up the very largest size cake they have. I told them chocolate cake with white icing and red trim. Think she'll like that?

MEG: *(Dialing on the phone.)* Yeah, I'm sure she will. She'll like it.

BABE: I'm hoping.

(Blackout)

END OF ACT I

ACT II

The lights go up on the kitchen. It is later that evening on the same day. Meg's suitcase has been moved upstairs. Babe's saxophone has been taken out of the case and put together. Babe and Barnette are sitting at the kitchen table. Barnette is writing and rechecking notes with explosive intensity. Babe, who has changed into a casual shift, sits eating a bowl of oatmeal, slowly.

BARNETTE: *(To himself.)* Mmm-huh! Yes! I see, I see! Well. We can work on that! And of course, this is mere conjecture! Difficult, if not impossible, to prove. Ha! Yes. Yes, indeed. Indeed—

BABE: Sure you don't want any oatmeal?

BARNETTE: What? Oh, no. No, thank you. Let's see, ah, where were we?

BABE: I just shot Zackery.

BARNETTE: *(Looking at his notes.)* Right. Correct. You've just pulled the trigger.

BABE: Tell me, do you think Willie Jay can stay out of all this?

BARNETTE: Believe me, it is in our interest to keep him as far out of this as possible.

BABE: Good.

BARNETTE: *(Throughout the following, Barnette stays glued to Babe's every word.)* Alright, you've just shot one Zackery Botrelle, as a result of his continual physical and mental abuse—what happens now?

BABE: Well, after I shot him, I put the gun down on the piano bench and then I went out into the kitchen and made up a pitcher of lemonade.

BARNETTE: Lemonade?

BABE: Yes, I was dying of thirst. My mouth was just as dry as a bone.

BARNETTE: So in order to quench this raging thirst that was choking you dry and preventing any possibility of you uttering intelligible sounds or phrases, you went out to the kitchen and made up a pitcher of lemonade?

BABE: Right. I made it just the way I like it with lots of sugar and lots of lemon—about ten lemons in all. Then I added two trays of ice and stirred it up with my wooden stirring spoon.

BARNETTE: Then what?

BABE: Then I drank three glasses, one right after the other. They were large glasses, about this tall. Then suddenly, my stomach kind of swoll all up. I guess what caused it was all that sour lemon.

BARNETTE: Could be.

BABE: Then what I did was...I wiped my mouth off with the back of my hand, like this... *(She demonstrates.)*

f water that had settled there.

:kery, I've made some lemon-

;wer?

)ut to him.

He was looking up at me try-
onade?...You don't want it?
t the idea, he was telling me
got on the phone and called
ss and I told them my hus-
ιg and there was plenty of

tically on his notes.)

e hospital.

: lemonade, I mean besides
hat I was afraid to call the
was afraid they would see
t I had shot him, and they
d me away to jail.

appen. That's what is hap-
y to go right off to the
practically on the brink of

on for you to get yourself

d information as you can

about those incidents on the medical reports. That's all you need to think about. Don't you worry, Mrs. Botrelle, we're going to have a solid defense.

BABE: Please, don't call me Mrs. Botrelle.

BARNETTE: Alright.

BABE: My name's Becky. People in the family call me Babe, but my real name's Becky.

BARNETTE: Alright, Becky.

(Barnette and Babe stare at each other for a long moment.)

BABE: Are you sure you didn't go to Hazlehurst High?

BARNETTE: No, I went away to a boarding school.

BABE: Gosh, you sure do look familiar. You sure do.

BARNETTE: Well, I—I doubt you'll remember, but I did meet you once.

BABE: You did? When?

BARNETTE: At the Christmas bazaar, year before last. You were selling cakes and cookies and…candy.

BABE: Oh, yes! You bought the orange pound cake!

BARNETTE: Right.

BABE: Of course, and then we talked for a while. We talked about the Christmas angel.

BARNETTE: You do remember.

BABE: I remember it very well. You were even thinner then than you are now.

BARNETTE: Well, I'm surprised. I'm certainly…surprised.

(The phone begins to ring.)

BABE: *(As she goes to answer the phone.)* This is quite a coincidence! Don't you think it is? Why, it's almost a fluke. *(She answers the phone.)* Hello…Oh, hello, Lucille…Oh, he is?…Oh, he does?…Okay. Oh, Lucille, wait! Has Dog come back to the house?…Oh, I see…Okay. Okay. *(After a brief pause.)* Hello, Zackery? How are you doing?…Uh huh…uh huh…oh, I'm sorry…Please, don't scream…uh huh…uh huh…You want what?… No, I can't come up there now…Well, for one thing, I don't even have the car. Lenny and Meg are up at the hospital right now, visiting with Old Granddaddy…What?…Oh, really?…Oh, really?…Well, I've got me a lawyer that's over here right now, and he's building me up a solid defense!…Wait just a minute, I'll see. *(To Barnette.)* He wants to talk to you. He says he's got some blackening evidence that's gonna convict me of attempting to murder him on the first degree!

BARNETTE: *(Disgustedly.)* Oh, bluff! He's bluffing! Here, hand me the phone. *(He takes the phone and becomes suddenly cool and suave.)* Hello, this is

Mr. Barnette Lloyd speaking. I'm Mrs....ah, Becky's attorney...Why, certainly, Mr. Botrelle, I'd be more than glad to check out any pertinent information that you may have...Fine, then I'll be right on over. Good-bye. *(He hangs up the phone.)*

BABE: What did he say?

BARNETTE: He wants me to come see him at the hospital this evening. Says he's got some sort of evidence. Sounds highly suspect to me.

BABE: Oooh! Didn't you just hate his voice? Doesn't he have the most awful voice! I just hate! I can't bear to hear it!

BARNETTE: Well, now—now, wait. Wait just a minute.

BABE: What?

BARNETTE: I have a solution. From now on I'll handle all communications between you two. You can simply refuse to speak with him.

BABE: Alright—I will. I'll do that.

BARNETTE: *(Starting to pack his briefcase.)* Well, I'd better get over there and see just what he's got up his sleeve.

BABE: *(After a pause.)* Barnette.

BARNETTE: Yes?

BABE: What's the personal vendetta about? You know, the one you have to settle with Zackery.

BARNETTE: Oh, it's—it's complicated. It's a very complicated matter.

BABE: I see.

BARNETTE: The major thing he did was to ruin my father's life. He took away his job, his home, his health, his respectability. I don't like to talk about it.

BABE: I'm sorry. I just wanted to say—I hope you win it. I hope you win your vendetta.

BARNETTE: Thank you.

BABE: I think it's an important thing that a person could win a lifelong vendetta.

BARNETTE: Yes. Well, I'd better be going.

BABE: Alright. Let me know what happens.

BARNETTE: I will. I'll get back to you right away.

BABE: Thanks.

BARNETTE: Good-bye, Becky.

BABE: Good-bye, Barnette.

(Barnette exits. Babe looks around the room for a moment, then goes over to her white suitcase and opens it up. She takes out her pink hair curlers and a brush. She begins brushing her hair.)

BABE: Good-bye, Becky. Good-bye, Barnette. Good-bye, Becky. Oooh.

(Lenny enters. She is fuming. Babe is rolling her hair throughout most of the following scene.)

BABE: Lenny, hi!

LENNY: Hi

BABE: Where's Meg?

LENNY: Oh, she had to go by the store and pick some things up. I don't know what.

BABE: Well, how's Old Granddaddy?

LENNY: *(As she picks up Babe's bowl of oatmeal.)* He's fine! Wonderful! Never been better!

BABE: Lenny, what's wrong? What's the matter?

LENNY: It's Meg! I could just wring her neck! I could just wring it!

BABE: Why? Wha'd she do?

LENNY: She lied! She sat in that hospital room and shamelessly lied to Old Granddaddy. She went on and on telling such untrue stories and lies.

BABE: Well, what? What did she say?

LENNY: Well, for one thing she said she was gonna have a RCA record coming out with her picture on the cover, eating pineapples under a palm tree.

BABE: Well, gosh, Lenny, maybe she is! Don't you think she really is?

LENNY: Babe, she sat here this very afternoon and told me how all that she's done this whole year is work as a clerk for a dog food company.

BABE: Oh, shoot. I'm disappointed.

LENNY: And then she goes on to say that she'll be appearing on the *Johnny Carson Show* in two weeks' time. Two weeks' time! Why, Old Granddaddy's got a TV set right in his room. Imagine what a letdown it's gonna be.

BABE: Why, mercy me.

LENNY: *(Slamming the coffeepot on.)* Oh, and she told him the reason she didn't use the money he sent her to come home Christmas was that she was right in the middle of making a huge multi-million-dollar motion picture and was just under too much pressure.

BABE: My word!

LENNY: The movie's coming out this spring. It's called, *Singing in a Shoe Factory.* But she only has a small leading role—not a large leading role.

BABE: *(Laughing.)* For heaven's sake—

LENNY: I'm sizzling. Oh, I just can't help it! I'm sizzling!

BABE: Sometimes Meg does such strange things.

LENNY: *(Slowly, as she picks up the opened box of birthday candy.)* Who ate this candy?

BABE: *(Hesitantly.)* Meg.

LENNY: My one birthday present, and look what she does! Why, she's taken one little bite out of each piece and then just put it back in! Ooh! That's just like her! That is just like her!

BABE: Lenny, please—

LENNY: I can't help it! It gets me mad! It gets me upset! Why, Meg's always run wild—she started smoking and drinking when she was fourteen years old, she never made good grades—never made her own bed! But somehow she always seemed to get what she wanted. She's the one who got singing and dancing lessons; and a store-bought dress to wear to her senior prom. Why, do you remember how Meg always got to wear twelve jingle bells on her petticoats, while we were only allowed to wear three apiece? Why?! Why should Old Grandmama let her sew twelve golden jingle bells on her petticoats and us only three!!!

BABE: *(Who has heard all this before.)* I don't know!! Maybe she didn't jingle them as much!

LENNY: I can't help it! It gets me mad! I resent it. I do.

BABE: Oh, don't resent Meg. Things have been hard for Meg. After all, she was the one who found Mama.

LENNY: Oh, I know; she's the one who found Mama. But that's always been the excuse.

BABE: But, I tell you, Lenny, after it happened, Meg started doing all sorts of these strange things.

LENNY: She did? Like what?

BABE: Like things I never wanted to tell you about.

LENNY: What sort of things?

BABE: Well, for instance, back when we used to go over to the library, Meg would spend all her time reading and looking through this old, black book called *Diseases of the Skin.* It was full of the most sickening pictures you'd ever seen. Things like rotting-away noses and eyeballs drooping off down the sides of people's faces and scabs and sores and eaten-away places all over *all* parts of people's bodies.

LENNY: *(Trying to pour her coffee.)* Babe, please! That's enough.

BABE: Anyway, she'd spend hours and hours just forcing herself to look through this book. Why, it was the same way she'd force herself to look at the poster of crippled children stuck up in the window at Dixieland Drugs. You know, that one where they want you to give a dime. Meg would stand there and stare at their eyes and look at the braces on their little crippled-up legs—then she'd purposely go and spend her dime on a double scoop ice cream cone and eat it all down. She'd say to me, "See, I can stand it. I can stand it. Just look how I'm gonna be able to stand it."

LENNY: That's awful.

BABE: She said she was afraid of being a weak person. I guess 'cause she cried in bed every night for such a long time.

LENNY: Goodness mercy. *(After a pause.)* Well, I suppose you'd have to be a pretty hard person to be able to do what she did to Doc Porter.

BABE: *(Exasperated.)* Oh, shoot! It wasn't Meg's fault that hurricane wiped Biloxi away. I never understood why people were blaming all that on Meg—just because that roof fell in and crunched Doc's leg. It wasn't her fault.

LENNY: Well, it was Meg who refused to evacuate. Jim Craig and some of Doc's other friends were all down there and they kept trying to get everyone to evacuate. But Meg refused. She wanted to stay on because she thought a hurricane would be—oh, I don't know—a lot of fun. Then everyone says she baited Doc into staying with her. She said she'd marry him if he'd stay.

BABE: *(Taken aback by this new information.)* Well, he has a mind of his own. He could have gone.

LENNY: But he didn't. 'Cause…'cause he loved her. And then after the roof caved, and they got Doc to the high school gym, Meg just left. She just left him there to leave for California—'cause of her career, she says. I think it was a shameful thing to do. It took almost a year for his leg to heal and after that he gave up his medical career altogether. He said he was tired of hospitals. It's such a sad thing. Everyone always knew he was gonna be a doctor. We've called him Doc for years.

BABE: I don't know. I guess, I don't have any room to talk; 'cause I just don't know. *(Pause.)* Gosh, you look so tired.

LENNY: I feel tired.

BABE: They say women need a lot of iron…so they won't feel tired.

LENNY: What's got iron in it? Liver?

BABE: Yeah, liver's got it. And vitamin pills.

(After a moment, Meg enters. She carries a bottle of bourbon that is already minus a few slugs and a newspaper. She is wearing black boots, a dark dress, and a hat. The room goes silent.)

MEG: Hello.

BABE: *(Fooling with her hair.)* Hi Meg.

(Lenny quietly sips her coffee.)

MEG: *(Handing the newspaper to Babe.)* Here's your paper.

BABE: Thanks. *(She opens it.)* Oh, here it is, right on the front page.

(Meg lights a cigarette.)

BABE: Where's the scissors, Lenny?

LENNY: Look in there in the ribbon drawer.

BABE: Okay. *(Babe gets the scissors and glue out of the drawer and slowly begins cutting out the newspaper article.)*

MEG: *(After a few moments, filled only with the snipping of scissors.)* Alright—I lied! I lied! I couldn't help it…these stories just came pouring out of my mouth! When I saw how tired and sick Old Granddaddy'd gotten—they just flew out! All I wanted was to see him smiling and happy. I just wasn't going to sit there and look at him all miserable and sick and sad! I just wasn't!

BABE: Oh, Meg, he is sick, isn't he—

MEG: Why, he's gotten all white and milky—he's almost evaporated!

LENNY: *(Gasping and turning to Meg.)* But still you shouldn't have lied! It just was wrong for you to tell such lies—

MEG: Well, I know that! Don't you think I know that? I hate myself when I lie for that old man. I do. I feel so weak. And then I have to go and do at least three or four things that I know he'd despise just to get even with that miserable, old, bossy man!

LENNY: Oh, Meg, please, don't talk so about Old Granddaddy! It sounds so ungrateful. Why, he went out of his way to make a home for us; to treat us like we were his very own children. All he ever wanted was the best for us. That's all he ever wanted.

MEG: Well, I guess it was; but sometimes I wonder what we wanted.

BABE: *(Taking the newspaper article and glue over to her suitcase.)* Well, one thing I wanted was a team of white horses to ride Mama's coffin to her grave. That's one thing I wanted.

(Lenny and Meg exchange looks.)

BABE: Lenny, did you remember to pack my photo album?

LENNY: It's down there at the bottom, under all that night stuff.

BABE: Oh, I found it.

LENNY: Really, Babe, I don't understand why you have to put in the articles that are about the unhappy things in your life. Why would you want to remember them?

BABE: *(Pasting the article in.)* I don't know. I just like to keep an accurate record, I suppose. There. *(She begins flipping through the book.)* Look, here's a picture of me when I got married.

MEG: Let's see.

(Babe brings the photo album over to the table. They all look at it.)

LENNY: My word, you look about twelve years old.

BABE: I was just eighteen.

MEG: You're smiling, Babe. Were you happy then?

BABE: *(Laughing.)* Well, I was drunk on champagne punch. I remember that!
(They turn the page.)

LENNY: Oh, there's Meg singing at Greeny's!

BABE: Oooh, I wish you were still singing at Greeny's! I wish you were!

LENNY: You're so beautiful!

BABE: Yes, you are. You're beautiful.

MEG: Oh, stop! I'm not—

LENNY: Look, Meg's starting to cry.

BABE: Oh, Meg—

MEG: I'm not—

BABE: Quick, better turn the page; we don't want Meg crying— *(She flips the pages.)*

LENNY: Why, it's Daddy.

MEG: Where'd you get that picture, Babe? I thought she burned them all.

BABE: Ah, I just found it around.

LENNY: What does it say here? What's that inscription?

BABE: It says "Jimmy—clowning at the beach—1952."

LENNY: Well, will you look at that smile.

MEG: Jesus, those white teeth—turn the page, will you; we can't do any worse than this!
(They turn the page. The room goes silent.)

BABE: It's Mama and the cat.

LENNY: Oh, turn the page—

BABE: That old yellow cat. You know, I bet if she hadn't of hung that old cat along with her, she wouldn't have gotten all that national coverage.

MEG: *(After a moment, hopelessly.)* Why are we talking about this?

LENNY: Meg's right. It was so sad. It was awfully sad. I remember how we all three just sat up on that bed the day of the service all dressed up in our black velveteen suits crying the whole morning long.

BABE: We used up one whole big box of Kleenexes.

MEG: And then Old Granddaddy came in and said he was gonna take us out to breakfast. Remember, he told us not to cry anymore 'cause he was gonna take us out to get banana splits for breakfast.

BABE: That's right—banana splits for breakfast!

MEG: Why, Lenny was fourteen years old and he thought that would make it all better—

BABE: Oh, I remember he said for us to eat all we wanted. I think I ate about five! He kept shoving them down us!

MEG: God, we were so sick!

LENNY: Oh, we were!

MEG: *(Laughing.)* Lenny's face turned green—

LENNY: I was just as sick as a dog!

BABE: Old Grandmama was furious!

LENNY: Oh, she was!

MEG: The thing about Old Granddaddy is he keeps trying to make us happy and we end up getting stomachaches and turning green and throwing up in the flower arrangements.

BABE: Oh, that was me! I threw up in the flowers! Oh, no. How embarrassing!

LENNY: *(Laughing.)* Oh, Babe—

BABE: *(Hugging her sisters.)* Oh, Lenny! Oh, Meg!

MEG: Oh, Babe! Oh, Lenny! It's so good to be home!

LENNY: Hey, I have an idea—

BABE: What?

LENNY: Let's play cards!!

BABE: Oh, let's do!

MEG: Alright!

LENNY: Oh, good! It'll be just like when we used to sit around the table playing Hearts all night long.

BABE: I know! *(Getting up.)* I'll fix us up some popcorn and hot chocolate—

MEG: *(Getting up.)* Here, let me get out that old black popcorn pot.

LENNY: *(Getting up.)* Oh, yes! Now, let's see, I think I have a deck of cards around here somewhere.

BABE: Gosh, I hope I remember all the rules—Are hearts good or bad?

MEG: Bad, I think. Aren't they, Lenny?

LENNY: That's right. Hearts are bad, but the Black Sister is the worst of all—

MEG: Oh, that's right! And the Black Sister is the Queen of Spades.

BABE: *(Figuring it out.)* And spades are the black cards that aren't the puppy dog feet?

MEG: *(Thinking a moment.)* Right. And she counts a lot of points.

BABE: And points are bad?

MEG: Right. Here, I'll get some paper so we can keep score.

(The phone begins to ring.)

LENNY: Oh, here they are!

MEG: I'll get it—

LENNY: Why, look at these cards! They're years old!

BABE: Oh, let me see!

MEG: Hello…No, this is Meg Magrath…Doc. How are you?…Well, good… You're where?…Well, sure. Come on over…Sure, I'm sure. Yeah, come right on over…All right. 'Bye. *(She hangs up.)* That was Doc Porter. He's down the street at Al's Grill. He's gonna come on over.

LENNY: He is?

MEG: He said he wanted to come see me.

LENNY: Oh. *(After a pause.)* Well, do you still want to play?

MEG: No, I don't think so.

LENNY: Alright.

(Lenny starts to shuffle the cards, as Meg brushes her hair.)

LENNY: You know, it's really not much fun playing Hearts with only two people.

MEG: I'm sorry; maybe after Doc leaves, I'll join you.

LENNY: I know; maybe Doc'll want to play, then we can have a game of Bridge.

MEG: I don't think so. Doc never liked cards. Maybe we'll just go out somewhere.

LENNY: *(Putting down the cards. Babe picks them up.)* Meg—

MEG: What?

LENNY: Well, Doc's married now.

MEG: I know. You told me.

LENNY: Oh. Well, as long as you know that. *(Pause.)* As long as you know that.

MEG: *(Still primping.)* Yes, I know. She made the pot.

BABE: How many cards do I deal out?

LENNY: *(Leaving the table.)* Excuse me.

BABE: All of 'em, or what?

LENNY: Ah, Meg? Could I—could I ask you something?

(Babe proceeds to deal out all the cards.)

MEG: What?

LENNY: I just wanted to ask you—

MEG: What?

(Unable to go on with what she really wants to say, Lenny runs up and picks up the box of candy.)

LENNY: Well, just why did you take one little bite out of each piece of candy in this box and then just put it back in?

MEG: Oh. Well, I was looking for the ones with nuts.

LENNY: The ones with nuts.

MEG: Yeah.

LENNY: But there are none with nuts. It's a box of assorted cremes—all it has in it are cremes!

MEG: Oh.

LENNY: Why couldn't you just read on the box? It says right here, "Assorted Cremes," not nuts! Besides this was a birthday present to me! My one and only birthday present; my only one!

MEG: I'm sorry. I'll get you another box.

LENNY: I don't want another box. That's not the point!

MEG: What is the point?

LENNY: I don't know; it's—it's—You have no respect for other people's property! You just take whatever you want. You just take it! Why, remember how you had layers and layers of jingle bells sewed onto your petticoats while Babe and I only had three apiece?!

MEG: Oh, God! She's starting up about those stupid jingle bells!

LENNY: Well, it's an example! A specific example of how you always got what you wanted!

MEG: Oh, come on, Lenny, you're just upset because Doc called.

LENNY: Who said anything about Doc? Do you think I'm upset about Doc? Why, I've long since given up worrying about you and all your men.

MEG: *(Turning in anger.)* Look, I know I've had too many men. Believe me, I've had way too many men. But it's not my fault you haven't had any— or maybe just that one from Memphis.

LENNY: *(Stopping.)* What one from Memphis?

MEG: *(Slowly.)* The one Babe told me about. From the—club.

LENNY: Babe!!!

BABE: Meg!!!

LENNY: How could you?!! I asked you not to tell anyone! I'm so ashamed! How could you? Who else have you told? Did you tell anyone else?

BABE: *(Overlapping, to Meg.)* Why'd you have to open your big mouth?!

MEG: *(Overlapping.)* How am I supposed to know? You never said not to tell!

BABE: Can't you use your head just for once?!! *(Then to Lenny.)* No, I never told anyone else. Somehow it just slipped out to Meg. Really, it just flew out of my mouth—

LENNY: What do you two have—wings on your tongues?

BABE: I'm sorry, Lenny. Really sorry.

LENNY: I'll just never, never, never be able to trust you again—

MEG: *(Furiously, coming to Babe's defense.)* Oh, for heaven's sake, Lenny, we were just worried about you! We wanted to find a way to make you happy!

LENNY: Happy! Happy! I'll never be happy!

MEG: Well, not if you keep living your life as Old Granddaddy's nursemaid—

BABE: Meg, shut up!

MEG: I can't help it! I just know that the reason you stopped seeing this man from Memphis was because of Old Granddaddy.

LENNY: What—Babe didn't tell you the rest of the story—

MEG: Oh, she said it was something about your shrunken ovary.

BABE: Meg!!

LENNY: Babe!!

BABE: I just mentioned it!

MEG: But I don't believe a word of that story!

LENNY: Oh, I don't care what you believe! It's so easy for you—you always have men falling in love with you! But I have this underdeveloped ovary and I can't have children and my hair is falling out in the comb—so what man can love me?! What man's gonna love me?

MEG: A lot of men!

BABE: Yeah, a lot! A whole lot!

MEG: Old Granddaddy's the only one who seems to think otherwise.

LENNY: 'Cause he doesn't want to see me hurt! He doesn't want to see me rejected and humiliated.

MEG: Oh, come on now, Lenny, don't be so pathetic! God, you make me angry when you just stand there looking so pathetic! Just tell me, did you really ask the man from Memphis? Did you actually ask that man from Memphis all about it?

LENNY: (Breaking apart.) No; I didn't. I didn't. Because I just didn't want him not to want me—

MEG: Lenny—

LENNY: (Furious.) Don't talk to me anymore! Don't talk to me! I think I'm gonna vomit—I just hope all this doesn't cause me to vomit! (Lenny exits up the stairs sobbing.)

MEG: See! See! She didn't even ask him about her stupid ovary! She just broke it all off 'cause of Old Granddaddy! What a jackass fool!

BABE: Oh, Meg, shut up! Why do you have to make Lenny cry? I just hate it when you make Lenny cry! (Babe runs up the stairs.) Lenny! Oh, Lenny—

(Meg takes a long sigh and goes to get a cigarette and a drink.)

MEG: I feel like hell.

(Meg sits in despair—smoking and drinking bourbon. There is a knock at the back door. Meg starts. She brushes her hair out of her face and goes to answer the door. It is Doc.)

DOC: Hello, Meggy.

MEG: Well, Doc. Well, it's Doc.

DOC: *(After a pause.)* You're home, Meggy.

MEG: Yeah; I've come home. I've come on home to see about Babe.

DOC: And how's Babe?

MEG: Oh, fine. Well, fair. She's fair.

(Doc nods.)

MEG: Hey, do you want a drink?

DOC: Whatcha got?

MEG: Bourbon.

DOC: Oh, don't tell me Lenny's stocking bourbon.

MEG: Well, no. I've been to the store.

(Meg gets him a glass and pours them each a drink. They clink glasses.)

MEG: So, how's your wife?

DOC: She's fine.

MEG: I hear ya got two kids.

DOC: Yeah. Yeah, I got two kids.

MEG: A boy and a girl.

DOC: That's right, Meggy, a boy and a girl.

MEG: That's what you always said you wanted, wasn't it? A boy and a girl.

DOC: Is that what I said?

MEG: I don't know. I thought it's what you said.

(They finish their drinks in silence.)

DOC: Whose cot?

MEG: Lenny's. She's taken to sleeping in the kitchen.

DOC: Ah. Where is Lenny?

MEG: She's in the upstairs room. I made her cry. Babe's up there seeing to her.

DOC: How'd you make her cry?

MEG: I don't know. Eating her birthday candy; talking on about her boyfriend from Memphis. I don't know. I'm upset about it. She's got a lot on her. Why can't I keep my mouth shut?

DOC: I don't know, Meggy. Maybe it's because you don't want to.

MEG: Maybe.

(They smile at each other. Meg pours each of them another drink.)

DOC: Well, it's been a long time.

MEG: It has been a long time.

DOC: Let's see—when was the last time we saw each other?

MEG: I can't quite recall.

DOC: Wasn't it in Biloxi?

MEG: Ah, Biloxi. I believe so.

DOC: And wasn't there a—a hurricane going on at the time?

MEG: Was there?

DOC: Yes, there was, one hell of a hurricane. Camille, I believe they called it. Hurricane Camille.

MEG: Yes, now I remember. It was a beautiful hurricane.

DOC: We had a time down there. We had quite a time. Drinking vodka, eating oysters on the half shell, dancing all night long. And the wind was blowing.

MEG: Oh, God, was it blowing.

DOC: Goddamn, was it blowing.

MEG: There never has been such a wind blowing.

DOC: Oh, God, Meggy. Oh, God.

MEG: I know, Doc. It was my fault to leave you. I was crazy. I thought I was choking. I felt choked!

DOC: I felt like a fool.

MEG: No.

DOC: I just kept on wondering why.

MEG: I don't know why…'Cause I didn't want to care. I don't know. I did care though. I did.

DOC: *(After a pause.)* Ah, hell— *(He pours them both another drink.)* Are you still singing those sad songs?

MEG: No.

DOC: Why not?

MEG: I don't know, Doc. Things got worse for me. After a while, I just couldn't sing anymore. I tell you, I had one hell of a time over Christmas.

DOC: What do you mean?

MEG: I went nuts. I went insane. Ended up in L.A. County Hospital. Psychiatric ward.

DOC: Hell. Ah, hell, Meggy. What happened?

MEG: I don't really know. I couldn't sing anymore; so I lost my job. And I had a bad toothache. I had this incredibly painful toothache. For days I had it, but I wouldn't do anything about it. I just stayed inside my apartment. All I could do was sit around in chairs, chewing on my fingers. Then one afternoon I ran screaming out of the apartment with all my money and jewelry and valuables and tried to stuff it all into one of those

March of Dimes collection boxes. That was when they nabbed me. Sad story. Meg goes mad.

(Doc stares at her for a long moment. He pours them both another drink.)

DOC: *(After quite a pause.)* There's a moon out.

MEG: Is there?

DOC: Wanna go take a ride in my truck and look out at the moon?

MEG: I don't know, Doc. I don't wanna start up. It'll be too hard, if we start up.

DOC: Who says we're gonna start up? We're just gonna look at the moon. For one night just you and me are gonna go for a ride in the country and look out at the moon.

MEG: One night?

DOC: Right.

MEG: Look out at the moon?

DOC: You got it.

MEG: Well...alright. *(She gets up.)*

DOC: Better take your coat. *(He helps her into her coat.)* And the bottle—

(He takes the bottle. Meg picks up the glasses.)

DOC: Forget the glasses—

MEG: *(Laughing.)* Yeah—forget the glasses. Forget the goddamn glasses.

(Meg shuts off the kitchen lights, leaving the kitchen lit by only a dim light over the kitchen sink. Meg and Doc leave. After a moment, Babe comes down the stairs in her slip.)

BABE: Meg—Meg?

(She stands for a moment in the moonlight wearing only a slip. She sees her saxophone then moves to pick it up. She plays a few shrieking notes. There is a loud knock on the back door.)

BARNETTE'S VOICE: Becky! Becky, is that you?

(Babe puts down the saxophone.)

BABE: Just a minute. I'm coming. *(She puts a raincoat on over her slip and goes to answer the door. It is Barnette.)* Hello, Barnette. Come on in.

(Barnette comes in. He is troubled but is making a great effort to hide the fact.)

BARNETTE: Thank you.

BABE: What is it?

BARNETTE: I've, ah, I've just come from seeing Zackery at the hospital.

BABE: Oh?

BARNETTE: It seems...Well, it seems his sister, Lucille, was somewhat suspicious.

BABE: Suspicious?

BARNETTE: About you?

BABE: Me?

BARNETTE: She hired a private detective, he took these pictures.

(*He hands Babe a small envelope containing several photographs. Babe opens the envelope and begins looking at the pictures in stunned silence.*)

BARNETTE: They were taken about two weeks ago. It seems, she wasn't going to show them to Botrelle straight away. She, ah, wanted to wait till the time was right.

(*The phone rings one and a half times. Barnette glances uneasily toward the phone.*)

BARNETTE: Becky?

(*The phone stops ringing.*)

BABE: (*Looking up at Barnette, slowly.*) These are pictures of Willie Jay and me...out in the garage.

BARNETTE: (*Looking away.*) I know.

BABE: You looked at these pictures?

BARNETTE: Yes—I—well...professionally, I looked at them.

BABE: Oh, mercy. Oh, mercy! We can burn them, can't we? Quick, we can burn them—

BARNETTE: It won't do any good. They have the negatives.

BABE: (*Holding the pictures, as she bangs herself hopelessly into the stove, table, cabinets, etc.*) Oh, no; oh, no; oh, no! Oh, no—

BARNETTE: There—there, now—there—

LENNY'S VOICE: Babe? Are you alright? Babe—

BABE: (*Hiding the pictures*) What? I'm alright. Go on back to bed.

(*Lenny comes down the stairs. She is wearing a coat and wiping white night cream off of her face with a wash rag.*)

LENNY: What's the matter? What's going on down here?

BABE: Nothin! (*Then as she begins dancing ballet style around the room.*) We're—we're just dancing. We were just dancing around down here. (*Signaling to Barnette to dance.*)

LENNY: Well, you'd better get your shoes on, 'cause we've got—

BABE: Alright, I will! That's a good idea! (*As she goes to get her shoes, she hides the pictures.*) Now, you go on back to bed. It's pretty late and—

LENNY: Babe, will you listen a minute—

BABE: (*Holding up her shoes.*) I'm putting 'em on—

LENNY: That was the hospital that just called. We've got to get over there. Old Granddaddy's had himself another stroke.

BABE: Oh. Alright. My shoes are on.
   (She stands. They all look at each other as the lights blackout.)

END OF ACT II

ACT III

The lights go up on the empty kitchen. It is the following morning. After a few moments, Babe enters from the back door. She is carrying her hair curlers in her hands. She goes and lies down on the cot. A few moments later, Lenny enters. She is tired and weary. Chick's voice is heard.

CHICK'S VOICE: Lenny! Oh, Lenny!
    (Lenny turns to the door. Chick enters energetically.)
CHICK: Well…how is he?
LENNY: He's stabilized; they say for now his functions are all stabilized.
CHICK: Well, is he still in the coma?
LENNY: Uh huh.
CHICK: Hmmm. So do they think he's gonna be…passing on?
LENNY: He may be. He doesn't look so good. They said they'd phone us if there were any sudden changes.
CHICK: Well, it seems to me we'd better get busy phoning on the phone ourselves. *(Removing a list from her pocket.)* Now I've made out this list of all the people we need to notify about Old Granddaddy's predicament. I'll phone half if you'll phone half.
LENNY: But—what would we say?
CHICK: Just tell them the facts; that Old Granddaddy's got himself in a coma, and it could be, he doesn't have long for this world.
LENNY: I—I don't know. I don't feel like phoning.
CHICK: Why, Lenora, I'm surprised, how can you be this way? I went to all the trouble of making up the list. And I offered to phone half of the people on it, even though I'm only one-fourth of the granddaughters. I mean, I just get tired of doing more than my fair share, when people like Meg can suddenly just disappear to where they can't even be reached in case of emergency!
LFNNY: Alright; give me the list. I'll phone half.
CHICK: Well, don't do it just to suit me.
LENNY: *(She wearily tears the list into two halves.)* I'll phone these here.
CHICK: *(Taking her half of the list.)* Fine then. Suit yourself. Oh, wait—let me call Sally Bell. I need to talk to her anyway.
LENNY: Alright.
CHICK: So you add Great Uncle Spark Dude to your list.
LENNY: Okay.

CHICK: Fine. Well, I've got to get on back home and see to the kids. It is gonna be an uphill struggle till I can find someone to replace that good-for-nothing Annie May Jenkins. Well, you let me know if you hear anymore.

LENNY: Alright.

CHICK: Good-bye, Rebecca. I said good-bye.

(Babe blows her sax. Chick starts to exit in a flurry then pauses to add.)

CHICK: And you really ought to try to get that phoning done before twelve noon. *(Chick exits.)*

LENNY: *(After a long pause.)* Babe; I feel bad. I feel real bad.

BABE: Why, Lenny?

LENNY: Because yesterday I—I wished it.

BABE: You wished what?

LENNY: I wished that Old Granddaddy would be put out of his pain. I wished on one of my birthday candles. I did. And now he's in this coma, and they say he's feeling no pain.

BABE: Well, when did you have a cake yesterday? I don't remember you having any cake.

LENNY: Well, I didn't…have a cake. But I just blew out the candles anyway.

BABE: Oh. Well, those birthday wishes don't count unless you have a cake.

LENNY: They don't?

BABE: No. A lot of times they don't even count when you do have a cake. It just depends.

LENNY: Depends on what?

BABE: On how deep your wish is, I suppose.

LENNY: Still, I just wish I hadn't of wished it. Gosh, I wonder when Meg's coming home.

BABE: Should be soon.

LENNY: I just wish we wouldn't fight all the time. I don't like it when we do.

BABE: Me, neither.

LENNY: I guess it hurts my feelings, a little, the way Old Granddaddy's always put so much stock in Meg and all her singing talent. I think I've been, well, envious of her 'cause I can't seem to do too much.

BABE: Why, sure you can.

LENNY: I can?

BABE: Sure. You just have to put your mind to it; that's all. It's like how I went out and bought that saxophone, just hoping I'd be able to attend music school and start up my own career. I just went out and did it. Just on hope. Of course, now it looks like…Well, it just doesn't look like things are gonna work out for me. But I know they would for you.

LENNY: Well, they'll work out for you, too.

BABE: I doubt it.

LENNY: Listen, I heard up at the hospital that Zackery's already in fair condition. They say soon he'll probably be able to walk and everything.

BABE: Yeah. And life sure can be miserable.

LENNY: Well, I know, 'cause—day before yesterday, Billy Boy was struck down by lightning.

BABE: He was?

LENNY: *(Nearing sobs.)* Yeah. He was struck dead.

BABE: *(Crushed.)* Life sure can be miserable.

(They sit together for several moments in morbid silence. Meg is heard singing a loud happy song. She suddenly enters through the dining room door. She is exuberant! Her hair is a mess and the heel of one shoe has broken off. She is laughing radiantly and limping as she sings into the broken heel.)

MEG: *(Spotting her sisters.)* Good morning! Good morning! Oh, it's a wonderful morning! I tell you, I am surprised I feel this good. I should feel like hell. By all accounts, I should feel like utter hell! *(She is looking for the glue.)* Where's that glue? This damn heel has broken off my shoe. La, la, la, la, la! Ah, here it is! Now let me just get these shoes off. Zip, zip, zip, zip, zip! Well, what's wrong with you two? My God, you look like doom!

(Babe and Lenny stare helplessly at Meg.)

MEG: Oh, I know, you're mad at me 'cause I stayed out all night long. Well; I did.

LENNY: No, we're—we're not mad at you. We're just…depressed. *(She starts to sob.)*

MEG: Oh, Lenny, listen to me, now, everything's alright with Doc. I mean nothing happened. Well, actually a lot did happen, but it didn't come to anything. Not because of me, I'm afraid. *(Smearing glue on her heel.)* I mean, I was out there thinking, "What will I say when he begs me to run away with him? Will I have pity on his wife and those two half-Yankee children? I mean, can I sacrifice their happiness for mine? Yes! Oh, yes! Yes, I can!" But…he didn't ask me. He didn't even want to ask me. I could tell by this certain look in his eyes that he didn't even want to ask me. Why aren't I miserable! Why aren't I morbid! I should be humiliated! Devastated! Maybe these feelings are coming—I don't know. But for now it was…just such fun. I'm happy. I realized I could care about someone. I could want someone. And I sang! I sang all night long!

I sang right up into the trees! But not for Old Granddaddy. None of it was to please Old Granddaddy!

(Lenny and Babe look at each other.)

BABE: Ah, Meg—

MEG: What—

BABE: Well, it's just—It's…

LENNY: It's about Old Granddaddy—

MEG: Oh, I know; I know. I told him all those stupid lies. Well, I'm gonna go right over there this morning and tell him the truth. I mean every horrible thing. I don't care if he wants to hear it or not. He's just gonna have to take me like I am. And if he can't take it, if it sends him into a coma, that's just too damn bad!

(Babe and Lenny look at each other. Babe cracks a smile. Lenny cracks a smile.)

BABE: You're too late—Ha, ha, ha!

(They both break up laughing.)

LENNY: Oh, stop! Please! Ha, ha, ha!

MEG: What is it? What's so funny?

BABE: *(Still laughing.)* It's not—It's not funny!

LENNY: *(Still laughing.)* No, it's not! It's not a bit funny!

MEG: Well, what is it then? What?

BABE: *(Trying to calm down.)* Well, it's just—it's just—

MEG: What?

BABE: Well, Old Granddaddy—he—he's in a coma!

(Babe and Lenny break up laughing.)

MEG: He's what?

BABE: *(Shrieking.)* In a coma!

MEG: My God! That's not funny!

BABE: *(Calming down.)* I know. I know. For some reason it just struck us as funny.

LENNY: I'm sorry. It's—it's not funny. It's sad. It's very sad. We've been up all night long.

BABE: We're really tired.

MEG: Well, my God. How is he? Is he gonna live?

(Babe and Lenny look at each other.)

BABE: They don't think so!

(They both break up again.)

LENNY: Oh, I don't know why we're laughing like this. We're just sick! We're just awful!

BABE: We are—we're awful!

LENNY: *(As she collects herself.)* Oh, good; now I feel bad. Now, I feel like crying. I do; I feel like crying.

BABE: Me, too. Me, too.

MEG: Well, you've gotten me depressed!

LENNY: I'm sorry. I'm sorry. It, ah, happened last night. He had another stroke.

(They laugh again.)

MEG: I see.

LENNY: But he's stabilized now. *(She chokes up once more.)*

MEG: That's good. You two okay?

(Babe and Lenny nod.)

MEG: You look like you need some rest.

(Babe and Lenny nod again. Meg goes on, about her heel.)

MEG: I hope that'll stay. *(Meg puts the top on the glue. A realization.)* Oh, of course, now I won't be able to tell him the truth about all those lies I told. I mean, finally, I get my wits about me, and he conks out. It's just like him. Babe, can I wear your slippers till this glue dries?

BABE: Sure.

LENNY: *(After a pause.)* Things sure are gonna be different around here… when Old Granddaddy dies. Well, not for you two really, but for me.

MEG: It'll work out.

BABE: *(Depressed.)* Yeah. It'll work out.

LENNY: I hope so. I'm afraid of being here all by myself. All alone.

MEG: Well, you don't have to be alone. Maybe Babe'll move back in here.

(Lenny looks at Babe hopefully.)

BABE: No; I don't think I'll be living here.

MEG: *(Realizing her mistake.)* Well, anyway, you're your own woman. Invite some people over. Have some parties. Go out with strange men.

LENNY: I don't know any strange men.

MEG: Well, you know that Charlie.

LENNY: *(Shaking her head.)* Not anymore.

MEG: Why not?

LENNY: *(Breaking down.)* I told him we should never see each other again.

MEG: Well; if you told him, you can just untell him.

LENNY: Oh, no I couldn't. I'd feel like a fool.

MEG: Oh, that's not a good enough reason! All people in love feel like fools. Don't they, Babe?

BABE: Sure.

MEG: Look, why don't you give him a call right now? See how things stand?

LENNY: Oh, no! I'd be too scared—

MEG: But what harm could it possibly do? I mean, it's not gonna make things any worse than this never seeing him again, at all, forever.

LENNY: I suppose that's true—

MEG: Of course it is; so call him up! Take a chance, will you? Just take some sort of chance!

LENNY: You think I should?

MEG: Of course! You've got to try—You do!

(Lenny looks over at Babe.)

BABE: You do, Lenny—I think you do.

LENNY: Really? Really, really?

MEG: Yes! Yes!

BABE: You should!

LENNY: Alright. I will! I will!

MEG: Oh, good!

BABE: Good!

LENNY: I'll call him right now, while I've got my confidence up!

MEG: Have you got the number?

LENNY: Uh huh. But, ah, I think I wanna call him upstairs. It'll be more private.

MEG: Ah, good idea.

LENNY: I'm just gonna go on; and call him up; and see what happens— *(She has started up the stairs.)* Wish me good luck!

MEG: Good luck!

BABE: Good luck, Lenny!

LENNY: Thanks.

(Lenny gets almost out of sight, when the phone begins to ring. She stops, Meg picks up the phone.)

MEG: Hello? *(Then in a whisper.)* Oh, thank you very much…Yes, I will. 'Bye-'bye.

LENNY: Who was it?

MEG: Wrong number. They wanted Weed's Body Shop.

LENNY: Oh. Well, I'll be right back down in a minute. *(Lenny exits.)*

MEG: *(After a moment, whispering to Babe.)* That was the bakery; Lenny's cake is ready!

BABE: *(Who has become increasingly depressed.)* Oh.

MEG: I think I'll sneak on down to the corner and pick it up. *(She starts to leave.)*

BABE: Meg—

MEG: What?

BABE: Nothing.

MEG: You okay?

(Babe shakes her head.)

MEG: What is it?

BABE: It's—just—

MEG: What?

(Babe gets up and goes to her suitcase. She opens it and removes the envelope containing the photographs.)

BABE: Here. Take a look.

MEG: *(Taking the envelope.)* What is it?

BABE: It's some evidence Zackery's collected against me. Looks like my goose is cooked.

(Meg opens the envelope and looks at the photographs.)

MEG: My God, it's—it's you and…is *that* Willie Jay?

BABE: Yeh.

MEG: Well, he certainly *has* grown. You were right about that. My, oh, my.

BABE: Please don't tell Lenny. She'd hate me.

MEG: I won't. I won't tell Lenny. *(Putting the pictures back into the envelope.)* What are you gonna do?

BABE: What can I do?

(There is a knock on the door. Babe grabs the envelope and hides it.)

MEG: Who is it?

BARNETTE'S VOICE: It's Barnette Lloyd.

MEG: Oh. Come on in, Barnette.

(Barnette enters. His eyes are ablaze with excitement.)

BARNETTE: *(As he paces around the room.)* Well; good morning! *(Shaking Meg's hand.)* Good morning, Miss Magrath. *(Touching Babe on the shoulder.)* Becky. *(Moving away.)* What I meant to say is…how are you doing this morning?

MEG: Ah—fine. Fine.

BARNETTE: Good. Good. I—I just had time to drop by for a minute.

MEG: Oh.

BARNETTE: So, ah, how's your Granddad doing?

MEG: Well, not very, ah—ah, he's in this coma. *(She breaks up laughing.)*

BARNETTE: I see…I see. *(To Babe.)* Actually, the primary reason I came by was to pick up that—envelope. I left it here last night in all the confusion. *(Pause.)* You, ah, still do have it?

(Babe hands him the envelope.)

BARNETTE: Yes. *(Taking the envelope.)* That's the one. I'm sure it'll be much better off in my office safe. *(He puts the envelope into his coat pocket.)*

MEG: I'm sure it will.

BARNETTE: Beg your pardon?

BABE: It's alright. I showed her the pictures.

BARNETTE: Ah; I see.

MEG: So what's going to happen now, Barnette? What are those pictures gonna mean?

BARNETTE: *(After pacing a moment.)* Hmmm. May I speak frankly and openly?

BABE: Uh huh.

MEG: Please do—

BARNETTE: Well, I tell you now, at first glance, I admit those pictures had me considerably perturbed and upset. Perturbed to the point that I spent most of last night going over certain suspect papers and reports that had fallen into my hands—rather recklessly.

BABE: What papers do you mean?

BARNETTE: Papers that pending word from three varied and unbiased experts, could prove graft, fraud, forgery, as well as a history of unethical behavior.

MEG: You mean about Zackery?

BARNETTE: Exactly. You see, I now intend to make this matter just as sticky and gritty for one Z. Botrelle as it is for us. Why, with the amount of scandal I'll dig up, Botrelle will be forced to settle this affair on our own terms!

MEG: Oh, Babe! Did you hear that?!

BABE: Yes! Oh, yes! So you've won it! You've won your lifelong vendetta!

BARNETTE: Well…well, now of course it's problematic in that, well, in that we won't be able to expose him openly in the courts. That was the original game plan.

BABE: But why not? Why?

BARNETTE: Well, it's only that if, well, if a jury were to—to get, say, a glance at these, ah, photographs, well…well, possibly…

BABE: We could be sunk.

BARNETTE: In a sense. But! On the other hand, if a newspaper were to get a hold of our little item, Mr. Zackery Botrelle could find himself boiling in some awfully hot water. So what I'm looking for very simply, is—a deal.

BABE: A deal?

MEG: Thank you, Barnette. It's a sunny day, Babe. *(Realizing she is in the way.)* Ooh, where's that broken shoe? *(She grabs her boots and runs upstairs.)*

BABE: So, you're having to give up your vendetta?

BARNETTE: Well, in a way. For the time. It, ah, seems to me you shouldn't always let your life be ruled by such things as, ah, personal vendettas. *(Looking at Babe with meaning.)* Other things can be important.

BABE: I don't know, I don't exactly know. How 'bout Willie Jay? Will he be alright?

BARNETTE: Yes, it's all been taken care of. He'll be leaving incognito on the midnight bus—heading north.

BABE: North.

BARNETTE: I'm sorry, it seemed the only…way.

(Barnette moves to her—she moves away.)

BABE: Look, you'd better be getting on back to your work.

BARNETTE: *(Awkwardly.)* Right—'cause I—I've got those important calls out. *(Full of hope for her.)* They'll be pouring in directly. *(He starts to leave, then says to her with love.)* We'll talk.

MEG: *(Reappearing in her boots.)* Oh, Barnette—

BARNETTE: Yes?

MEG: Could you give me a ride just down to the corner? I need to stop at Helen's Bakery.

BARNETTE: Be glad to.

MEG: Thanks. Listen, Babe, I'll be right back with the cake. We're gonna have the best celebration! Now, ah, if Lenny asks where I've gone, just say I'm…just say, I've gone out back to, ah, pick up some paw paws! Okay?

BABE: Okay.

MEG: Fine; I'll be back in a bit. Good-bye.

BABE: 'Bye.

BARNETTE: Good-bye, Becky.

BABE: Good-bye, Barnette. Take care.

(Meg and Barnette exit. Babe sits staring ahead, in a state of deep despair.)

BABE: Good-bye, Becky. Good-bye, Barnette. Good-bye, Becky.

(She stops when Lenny comes down the stairs in a fluster.)

LENNY: Oh! Oh! Oh! I'm so ashamed! I'm such a coward! I'm such a yellow-bellied chicken! I'm so ashamed! Where's Meg?

BABE: *(Suddenly bright.)* She's, ah—gone out back—to pick up some paw paws.

LENNY: Oh. Well, at least I don't have to face her! I just couldn't do it! I couldn't make the call!! My heart was pounding like a hammer. Pound! Pound!

Pound! Why, I looked down and I could actually see my blouse moving back and forth! Oh, Babe, you look so disappointed. Are you?

BABE: *(Despondently.)* Uh huh.

LENNY: Oh, no! I've disappointed Babe! I can't stand it! I've gone and disappointed my little sister, Babe! Oh, no! I feel like howling like a dog!

CHICK'S VOICE: Oooh, Lenny! *(Chick enters dramatically, dripping with sympathy.)* Well, I just don't know what to say! I'm so sorry! I am so sorry for you! And for Little Babe, here, too. I mean to have such a sister as that!

LENNY: What do you mean?

CHICK: Oh, you don't need to pretend with me. I saw it all from over there in my own backyard; I saw Meg stumbling out of Doc Porter's pickup truck, not fifteen minutes ago. And her looking such a disgusting mess. You must be so ashamed! You must just want to die! Why, I always said that girl was nothing but cheap Christmas trash!

LENNY: Don't talk that way about Meg.

CHICK: Oh, come on now. Lenny, honey, I know exactly how you feel about Meg. Why, Meg's a low-class tramp and you need not have one more blessed thing to do with her and her disgusting behavior.

LENNY: I said don't you ever talk that way about my sister Meg again.

CHICK: Well, my goodness gracious, Lenora, don't be such a noodle—it's the truth!

LENNY: I don't care if it's the Ten Commandments. I don't want to hear it in my home. Not ever again.

CHICK: In your home?! Why, I never in all my life—this is my Grandfather's home! And you're just living here on his charity; so don't you get highfalutin' with me, Miss Lenora Josephine Magrath!

LENNY: Get out of here—

CHICK: Don't you tell me to get out! What makes you think you can order me around? Why, I've had just about my fill of you trashy Magraths and your trashy ways; hanging yourselves in cellars; carrying on with married men; shooting your own husbands!

LENNY: Get out!

CHICK: *(To Babe.)* And don't think she's not gonna end up at the state prison farm or in some—mental institution. Why, it's a clear-cut case of manslaughter with intent to kill!

LENNY: Out! Get out!

CHICK: *(Running on.)* That's what everyone's saying, deliberate intent to kill! And you'll pay for that! Do you hear me? You'll pay!

LENNY: *(She picks up a broom and threatens Chick with it.)* And I'm telling you to get out!

CHICK: You—you put that down this minute—are you a raving lunatic?

LENNY: *(Beating Chick with the broom.)* I said for you to get out! That means out! And never, never, never come back!

CHICK: *(Overlapping, as she runs around the room.)* Oh! Oh! Oh! You're crazy! You're crazy!

LENNY: *(Chasing Chick out the door.)* Do you hear me, Chick the Stick! This is my home! This is my house! Get out! Out!

CHICK: *(Overlapping.)* Oh! Oh! Police! Police! You're crazy! Help! Help!

(Lenny chases Chick out of the house. They are both screaming. The phone rings. Babe goes and picks it up.)

BABE: Hello?...Oh, hello, Zackery!...Yes, he showed them to me!...You're what!...What do you mean?...What!...You can't put me out to Whitfield...'Cause I'm not crazy... I'm not! I'm not!...She wasn't crazy either...Don't you call my mother crazy!...No, you're not! You're not gonna. You're not! *(She slams the phone down and stares wildly ahead.)* He's not. He's not. *(As she walks over to the ribbon drawer.)* I'll do it. I will. And he won't...

(She opens the drawer; pulls out the rope; becomes terrified; throws the rope back in the drawer and slams it shut. Lenny enters from the back door swinging the broom and laughing.)

LENNY: Oh, my! Oh, my! You should have seen us! Why, I chased Chick the Stick right up the mimosa tree. I did! I left her right up there screaming in the tree!

BABE: *(Laughing; she is insanely delighted.)* Oh, you did!

LENNY: Yes, I did! And I feel so good! I do! I feel good! I feel good!

BABE: *(Overlapping.)* Good! Good, Lenny! Good for you!

(They dance around the kitchen.)

LENNY: *(Stopping.)* You know what—

BABE: What?

LENNY: I'm gonna call Charlie!!! I'm gonna call him right now!

BABE: You are?

LENNY: Yeah, I feel like I can really do it!

BABE: You do?

LENNY: My courage is up; my heart's in it; the time is right! No more beating around the bush! Let's strike while the iron is hot!

BABE: Right! Right! No more beating around the bush! Strike while the iron is hot!

(Lenny goes to the phone. Babe rushes over to the ribbon drawer. She begins tearing through it.)

LENNY: *(With the receiver in her hand.)* I'm calling him up, Babe—I'm really gonna do it!

BABE: *(Still tearing through the drawer.)* Good! Do it! Good!

LENNY: *(As she dials.)* Look. My hands aren't even shaking.

BABE: *(Pulling out a red cord of rope.)* Don't we have any stronger rope than this?

LENNY: I guess not. All the rope we've got's in that drawer. *(About her hands.)* Now they're shaking a little.

(Babe takes the rope and goes up the stairs. Lenny finishes dialing the number. She waits for an answer.)

LENNY: Hello?...Hello, Charlie. This is Lenny Magrath...Well, I'm fine. I'm just fine. *(An awkward pause.)* I was, ah, just calling to see—how you're getting on...Well, good. Good...Yes, I know I said that. Now I wish I didn't say it...Well, the reason I said that before, about not seeing each other again, was 'cause of me, not you...Well, it's just I—can't have any children. I—have this ovary problem...Why, Charlie, what a thing to say!...Well, they're not all little snot-nosed pigs!...You think they are!...Oh, Charlie, stop, stop! You're making me laugh...Yes, I guess I was. I can see now that I was...You are?...Well, I'm dying to see you, too...Well, I don't know when, Charlie...soon. How about, well, how about tonight?...You will?...Oh, you will!...All right, I'll be here. I'll be right here...Good-bye, then, Charlie. Good-bye for now. *(She hangs up the phone in a daze.)* Babe. Oh, Babe! He's coming. He's coming! Babe! Oh, Babe, where are you? Meg! Oh...out back—picking up paw paws.*(As she exits through the back door.)* And those paw paws are just ripe for picking up!

(There is a moment of silence, then a loud, horrible thud is heard coming from upstairs. The telephone begins ringing immediately. It rings five times before Babe comes hurrying down the stairs with a broken piece of rope hanging around her neck. The phone continues to ring.)

BABE: *(To the phone.)* Will you shut up! *(She is jerking the rope from around her neck. She grabs a knife to cut it off.)* Cheap! Miserable! I hate you! I hate you!

(She throws the rope violently around the room. The phone stops ringing.)

BABE: Thank God. *(She looks at the stove, goes over to it, and turns the gas on. The sound of gas escaping is heard. Babe sniffs at it.)* Come on. Come on...Hurry up...I beg of you—hurry up! *(Finally, Babe feels the oven is ready; she takes a deep breath and opens the oven door to stick her head into it. She spots the rack and furiously jerks it out. Taking another breath, she sticks her head into the oven. She stands for several moments tapping her fingers furiously on top of the stove. She speaks from inside the oven…)* Oh, please. Please. *(After a few moments, she reaches for the box of matches with her head still in the oven. She tries to strike a match. It doesn't catch.)* Oh, Mama, please! *(She throws the match away and is getting a second one.)* Mama… Mama…So that's why you done it!

(In her excitement she starts to get up, bangs her head and falls back in the stove. Meg enters from the back door, carrying a birthday cake in a pink box.)

MEG: Babe! *(Meg throws the box down and runs to pull Babe's head out of the oven.)* Oh, my God! What are you doing? What the hell are you doing?

BABE: *(Dizzily.)* Nothing. I don't know. Nothing.

(Meg turns off the gas and moves Babe to a chair near the open door.)

MEG: Sit down. Sit down! Will you sit down!

BABE: I'm okay. I'm okay.

MEG: Put your head between your knees and breathe deep!

BABE: Meg—

MEG: Just do it! I'll get you some water. *(Meg gets some water for Babe.)* Here.

BABE: Thanks.

MEG: Are you okay?

BABE: Uh-huh.

MEG: Are you sure?

BABE: Yeah, I'm sure. I'm okay.

MEG: *(Getting a damp rag and putting it over her own face.)* Well good. That's good.

BABE: Meg—

MEG: Yes?

BABE: I know why she did it.

MEG: What? Why who did what?

BABE: *(With joy.)* Mama. I know why she hung that cat along with her.

MEG: You do?

BABE: *(With enlightenment.)* It's 'cause she was afraid of dying all alone.

MEG: Was she?

BABE: She felt so unsure, you know, as to what was coming. It seems the best thing coming up would be a lot of angels and all of them singing. But I imagine they have high, scary voices and little gold pointed fingers that are as sharp as blades and you don't want to meet 'em all alone. You'd be afraid to meet 'em all alone. So it wasn't like what people were saying about her hating that cat. Fact is, she loved that cat. She needed him with her 'cause she felt so all alone.

MEG: Oh, Babe...Babe. Why, Babe? Why?

BABE: Why what?

MEG: Why did you stick your head into the oven?!

BABE: I don't know, Meg. I'm having a bad day. It's been a real bad day; those pictures; and Barnette giving up his vendetta; then Willie Jay, heading north; and—Zackery called me up. *(Trembling with terror.)* He says he's gonna have me classified insane and send me on out to the Whitfield asylum.

MEG: What! Why, he could never do that!

BABE: Why not?

MEG: 'Cause you're not insane.

BABE: I'm not? ʹ

MEG: No! He's trying to bluff you. Don't you see it? Barnette's got him running scared.

BABE: Really?

MEG: Sure. He's scared to death—calling you insane. Ha! Why, you're just as perfectly sane as anyone walking the streets of Hazlehurst, Mississippi.

BABE: I am?

MEG: More so! A lot more so!

BABE: Good!

MEG: But, Babe, we've just got to learn how to get through these real bad days here. I mean, it's getting to be a thing in our family. *(Slight pause as she looks at Babe.)* Come on now. Look, we've got Lenny's cake right here. I mean don't you wanna be around to give her her cake; watch her blow out the candles?

BABE: *(Realizing how much she wants to be here.)* Yeah, I do, I do. 'Cause she always loves to make her birthday wishes on those candles.

MEG: Well, then we'll give her her cake and maybe you won't be so miserable.

BABE: Okay.

MEG: Good. Go on and take it out of the box.

BABE: Okay. *(She takes the cake out of the box. It is a magical moment.)* Gosh, it's a pretty cake.

MEG: *(Handing her some matches.)* Here now. You can go on and light up the candles.

BABE: Alright. *(She starts to light the candles.)* I love to light up candles. And there are so many here. Thirty pink ones in all plus one green one to grow on.

MEG: *(Watching her light the candles.)* They're pretty.

BABE: They are. *(She stops lighting the candles.)* And I'm not like Mama. I'm not so all alone.

MEG: You're not.

BABE: *(As she goes back to lighting candles.)* Well, you'd better keep an eye out for Lenny. She's supposed to be surprised.

MEG: Alright. Do you know where she's gone?

BABE: Well, she's not here inside—so she must have gone on outside.

MEG: Oh, well, then I'd better run and find her.

BABE: Okay 'cause these candles are gonna melt down.

(Meg starts out the door.)

MEG: Wait—there she is coming. Lenny! Oh, Lenny! Come on! Hurry up!

BABE: *(Overlapping and improvising as she finishes lighting candles.)* Oh, no! No! Well, yes—yes! No, wait! Wait! Okay!

(Lenny enters. Meg covers Lenny's eyes with her hands.)

LENNY: *(Terrified.)* What?! What is it?!! What?!!

MEG AND BABE: Surprise! Happy Birthday! Happy Birthday to Lenny!!

LENNY: Oh, no! Oh me!!! What a surprise! I could just cry! Oh, look, "Happy Birthday to Lenny—A Day Late!" How cute! My! Will you look at all those candles—it's absolutely frightening.

BABE: *(Spontaneous thought.)* Oh, no, Lenny, it's good! 'Cause —'cause the more candles you have on your cake, the stronger your wish is.

LENNY: Really?

BABE: Sure!

LENNY: Mercy.

(They start the song. Lenny, interrupting the song.)

LENNY: Oh, but wait! I—I can't think of my wish! My body's gone all nervous inside.

MEG: For God's sake, Lenny—come on!

BABE: The wax is all melting!

LENNY: My mind is just a blank, a total blank!

MEG: Will you please just—

BABE: *(Overlapping.)* Lenny, hurry! Come on!

LENNY: Okay! Okay! Just go!!

(Meg and Babe burst into the "Happy Birthday Song." As it ends Lenny blows out all of the candles on the cake. Meg and Babe applaud loudly.)

MEG: Oh, you made it!

BABE: Hurray!

LENNY: Oh, me! Oh, me! I hope that wish comes true! I hope it does!

BABE: Why? What did you wish for?

LENNY: *(As she removes the candles from the cake.)* Why, I can't tell you that.

BABE: Oh, sure you can—

LENNY: Oh, no! Then it won't come true.

BABE: Why, that's just superstition! Of course it will, if you made it deep enough.

MEG: Really? I didn't know that.

LENNY: Well, Babe's the regular expert on birthday wishes.

BABE: It's just I get these feelings. Now come on and tell us. What was it you wished for?

MEG: Yes, tell us. What was it?

LENNY: Well, I guess, it wasn't really a specific wish. This—this vision just sort of came into my mind.

BABE: A vision? What was it of?

LENNY: I don't know exactly. It was something about the three of us smiling and laughing together.

BABE: Well, when was it? Was it far away or near?

LENNY: I'm not sure, but it wasn't forever; it wasn't for every minute. Just this one moment and we were all laughing.

BABE: What were we laughing about?

LENNY: I don't know. Just nothing I guess.

MEG: Well, that's a nice wish to make.

(Lenny and Meg look at each other a moment.)

MEG: Here, now, I'll get a knife so we can go ahead and cut the cake in celebration of Lenny being born!

BABE: Oh, yes! And give each one of us a rose. A whole rose apiece!

LENNY: *(Cutting the cake nervously.)* Well, I'll try—I'll try!

MEG: *(Licking the icing off a candle.)* Mmmm—this icing is delicious! Here, try some!

BABE: Mmmm! It's wonderful! Here, Lenny!

LENNY: *(Laughing joyously as she licks icing from her fingers and cuts huge pieces of cake that her sisters bite into ravenously.)* Oh, how I do love having birthday cake for breakfast! How I do!

(The sisters freeze for a moment laughing and catching cake; the lights change and frame them in a magical, golden, sparkling glimmer; saxophone music is heard. The lights dim to blackout, and the saxophone continues to play.)

END OF PLAY

AM I BLUE

DEDICATED TO
STUART WHITE, MY LOVE

John Tillitson and Marci Glaser
in Southern Methodist University's 1974 production of
Am I Blue.

photo by Ann Miller

ORIGINAL PRODUCTION

Am I Blue was presented by the Circle Repertory Company, in New York City, on January 10, 1982, as part of a triple bill entitled "Confluence." It was directed by Stuart White; the set was by Bob Phillips; costumes were by Joan E. Weiss; the lighting was by Mal Sturchio; sound was by Chuck London and Stewart Werner; and the production stage manager was Kate Stewart. The cast was as follows:

John Polk Richards . . . . Jeff McCracken
Ashbe Williams . . . . June Stein
Hilda . . . . Pearl Shear
The Barker . . . . Jimmie Ray Weeks
The Bum . . . . Edward Seamon
The Hippie (Clareece) . . . . Ellen Conway
The Whore . . . . Katherine Cortez

Am I Blue was written in 1972, and premiered at Southern Methodist University in 1974.

THE CAST

JOHN POLK: 17
ASHBE: 16
HILDA: 35, a waitress
STREET CHARACTERS: BARKER, WHORE, BUM, CLAREECE

THE SETTING

A bar, the street, the living room of a run-down apartment

THE TIME

Fall, 1968

The scene opens on a street in the New Orleans French Quarter on a rainy blue bourbon night. Various people: a whore, bum, street barker, Clareece appear and disappear along the street. The scene then focuses on a bar where a piano is heard from the back room playing softly and indistinctly "Am I Blue?" The lights go up on John Polk, who sits alone at a table. He is seventeen, a bit overweight and awkward. He wears nice clothes, perhaps a navy sweater with a large white monogram. His navy raincoat is slung over an empty chair. While drinking, John Polk concentrates on the red-and-black card that he holds in his hand. As soon as the scene is established, Ashbe enters from the street. She is sixteen, wears a flowered plastic rain cap, red galoshes, a butterfly barrette, and jeweled cat eyeglasses. She is carrying a bag full of stolen goods. Her hair is very curly. Ashbe makes her way cautiously to John Polk's table. As he sees her coming he puts the card into his pocket. She sits in the empty chair and pulls his raincoat over her head.

ASHBE: Excuse me…do you mind if I sit here please?

JOHN POLK: *(Looks up at her—then down into his glass.)* What are you doing hiding under my raincoat? You're getting it all wet.

ASHBE: Well, I'm very sorry, but after all it is a raincoat.
      (He tries to pull off coat.)

ASHBE: It was rude of me I know, but look I just don't want them to recognize me.

JOHN POLK: *(Looking about.)* Who to recognize you?

ASHBE: Well, I stole these two ashtrays from the Screw Inn, ya know right down the street. *(She pulls out two glass commercial ashtrays from her white plastic bag.)* Anyway, I'm scared the manager saw me. They'll be after me I'm afraid.

JOHN POLK: Well, they should be. Look, do you mind giving me back my raincoat? I don't want to be found protecting any thief.

ASHBE: *(Coming out from under coat.)* Thief—would you call Robin Hood a thief?

JOHN POLK: Christ.

ASHBE: *(Back under coat.)* No, you wouldn't. He was valiant—all the time stealing from the rich and giving to the poor.

JOHN POLK: But your case isn't exactly the same, is it? You're stealing from some crummy little bar and keeping the ashtrays for yourself. Now give me back my coat.

ASHBE: *(Throws coat at him.)* Sure take your old coat. I suppose I should have explained—about Miss Marcey. *(Silence.)* Miss Marcey, this cute old lady with a little hump in her back. I always see her in her sun hat and blue print dress. Miss Marcey lives in the apartment building next to ours. I leave all the stolen goods, as gifts on her front steps.

JOHN POLK: Are you one of those kleptomaniacs? *(He starts checking his wallet.)*

ASHBE: You mean when people all the time steal and they can't help it?

JOHN POLK: Yeah.

ASHBE: Oh, no. I'm not a bit careless. Take my job tonight, my very first night job, if you want to know. Anyway, I've been planning it for two months, trying to decipher which bar most deserved to be stolen from. I finally decided on the Screw Inn. Mainly because of the way they're so mean to Mr. Groves. He works at the magazine rack at Diver's Drugstore and is really very sweet, but he has a drinking problem. I don't think that's fair to be mean to people simply because they have a drinking problem— and, well, anyway, you see I'm not just stealing for personal gain. I mean, I don't even smoke.

JOHN POLK: Yeah, well, most infants don't, but then again, most infants don't hang around bars.

ASHBE: I don't see why not, Toulouse Lautrec did.

JOHN POLK: They'd throw me out.

ASHBE: Oh, they throw me out too, but I don't accept defeat. *(Slowly moves into him.)* Why, it's the very same with my pickpocketing.
(John Polk sneers, turns away.)

ASHBE: It's a very hard art to master. Why, every time I've done it I've been caught.

JOHN POLK: That's all I need is to have some slum kid tell me how good it is to steal. Everyone knows it's not.

ASHBE: *(About his drink.)* That looks good. What is it?

JOHN POLK: Hey, would you mind leaving me alone—I just wanted to be alone.

ASHBE: Okay. I'm sorry. How about if I'm quiet?
(John Polk shrugs. He sips drink, looks around, catches her eye, she smiles and sighs.)

ASHBE: I was just looking at your pin. What fraternity are you in?

JOHN POLK: S.A.E.

ASHBE: Is it a good fraternity?

JOHN POLK: Sure, it's the greatest.

ASHBE: I bet you have lots of friends.

JOHN POLK: Tons.

ASHBE: Are you being serious?

JOHN POLK: Yes.

ASHBE: Hmm. Do they have parties and all that?

JOHN POLK: Yeah, lots of parties, booze, honking horns, it's exactly what you would expect.

ASHBE: I wouldn't expect anything. Why did you join?

JOHN POLK: I don't know. Well, my brother—I guess it was my brother—he told me how great it was, how the fraternity was supposed to get you dates, make you study, solve all your problems.

ASHBE: Gee, does it?

JOHN POLK: Doesn't help you study.

ASHBE: How about dates? Do they get you a lot of dates?

JOHN POLK: Some.

ASHBE: What were the girls like?

JOHN POLK: I don't know—they were like girls.

ASHBE: Did you have a good time?

JOHN POLK: I had a pretty good time.

ASHBE: Did you make love to any of them?

JOHN POLK: *(To self.)* Oh, Christ—

ASHBE: I'm sorry—I just figured that's why you had the appointment with the whore—'cause you didn't have any one else—to make love to.

JOHN POLK: How did you know I had the, ah, the appointment?

ASHBE: I saw you put the red card in your pocket when I came up. Those red cards are pretty familiar around here. The house is only about a block or so away. It's one of the best though really very plush. Only two murders and a knifing in its whole history. Do you go there often?

JOHN POLK: Yeah, I like to give myself a treat.

ASHBE: Who do you have?

JOHN POLK: What do you mean?

ASHBE: I mean which girl.

(John Polk gazes into his drink.)

ASHBE: Look, I just thought I might know her is all.

JOHN POLK: Know her, ah, how would you know her?

ASHBE: Well, some of the girls from my high school go there to work when they get out.

JOHN POLK: G. G., her name is G.G.

ASHBE: G.G.—Hmm, well, how does she look?

JOHN POLK: I don't know.

ASHBE: Oh, you've never been with her before?

JOHN POLK: No.

ASHBE: *(Confidentially.)* Are you one of those kinds that likes a lot of variety?

JOHN POLK: Variety? Sure, I guess I like variety.

ASHBE: Oh, yes, now I remember.

JOHN POLK: What?

ASHBE: G.G., that's just her working name. Her real name is Myrtle Reims, she's Kay Reims' older sister. Kay is in my grade at school.

JOHN POLK: Myrtle? Her name is Myrtle?

ASHBE: I never liked the name either.

JOHN POLK: Myrtle, oh. Christ. Is she pretty?

ASHBE: *(Matter-of-factly.)* Pretty, no she's not real pretty.

JOHN POLK: What does she look like?

ASHBE: Let's see…she's, ah, well, Myrtle had acne and there are a few scars left. It's not bad. I think they sort of give her character. Her hair's red only I don't think it's really red. It sort of fizzles out all over her head. She's got a pretty good figure—big top—but the rest of her is kind of skinny.

JOHN POLK: I wonder if she has a good personality.

ASHBE: Well, she was a senior when I was a freshman; so I never really knew her. I remember she used to paint her fingernails lots of different colors—pink, orange, purple. I don't know, but she kind of scares me. About the only time I ever saw her true personality was around a year ago. I was over at Kay's making a health poster for school. Anyway, Myrtle comes busting in screaming about how she can't find her spangled bra anywhere. Kay and I just sat on the floor cutting pictures of food out of magazines while she was storming about slamming drawers and swearing. Finally, she found it. It was pretty garish—red with black and gold sequined G.'s on each cup. That's how I remember the name— G.G.

(As Ashbe illustrates the placement of the G.'s, she spots Hilda, the waitress, approaching. Ashbe pulls the raincoat over her head and hides on the floor. Hilda enters through the beaded curtains spilling her tray. Hilda is a woman of few words.)

HILDA: Shit, damn curtain. Nuther drink?

JOHN POLK: Mam?

HILDA: *(Points to drink.)* Vodka coke?

JOHN POLK: No, thank you. I'm not quite finished yet.

HILDA: Napkins clean.

(Ashbe pulls her bag off the table. Hilda looks at Ashbe then to John Polk.

She walks around the table, as Ashbe is crawling along the floor to escape.
Ashbe runs into Hilda's toes.)

ASHBE: Are those real gold?

HILDA: You again. Out.

ASHBE: She wants me to leave. Why should a paying customer leave? *(Back to Hilda.)* Now I'll have a mint julep and easy on the mint.

HILDA: This preteen with you?

JOHN POLK: Well—I—No—I—

HILDA: I.D.'s.

ASHBE: Certainly, I always try to cooperate with the management.

HILDA: *(Looking at John Polk's I.D.)* I.D., 11-12-50. Date 11-11-68.

JOHN POLK: Yes, but—well, 11-12 is less than two hours away.

HILDA: Back in two hours.

ASHBE: I seem to have left my identification in my gold lamé bag.

HILDA: Well, boo hoo. *(Motions for Ashbe to leave with a minimum of effort. She goes back to table.)* No tip.

ASHBE: You didn't tip her?

JOHN POLK: I figured the drinks were so expensive—I just didn't—

HILDA: No tip!

JOHN POLK: Look, Miss, I'm sorry. *(Going through his pockets.)* Here, would you like a—a nickel—wait, wait, here's a quarter.

HILDA: Just move ass, sonny. You too, Barbie.

ASHBE: Ugh, I hate public rudeness. I'm sure I'll refrain from ever coming here again.

HILDA: Think I'll go in the back room and cry.

(Ashbe and John Polk exit. Hilda picks up tray and exits through the curtain tripping again.)

HILDA: Shit. Damn curtain.

(Ashbe and John Polk are now standing outside under the awning of the bar.)

ASHBE: Gee, I didn't know it was your birthday tomorrow. Happy birthday! Don't be mad. I thought you were at least twenty or twenty-one, really.

JOHN POLK: It's O.K. Forget it.

(As they begin walking various blues are heard coming from the nearby bars.)

ASHBE: It's raining.

JOHN POLK: I know.

ASHBE: Are you going over to the house now?

JOHN POLK: No, not till twelve.

ASHBE: Yeah, the pink and black cards—they mean all night. Midnight till morning.

(At this point a street barker beckons the couple into his establishment. Perhaps he is accompanied by a whore.)

BARKER: Hey, mister, bring your baby on in, buy her a few drinks, maybe tonight ya get lucky.

ASHBE: Keep walking.

JOHN POLK: What's wrong with the place?

ASHBE: The drinks are watery rot gut and the showgirls are boys.

BARKER: Up yours, punk!

JOHN POLK: *(Who has now sat down on a street bench.)* Look, just tell me where a cheap bar is. I've got to stay drunk, but I don't have much money left.

ASHBE: Yikes, there aren't too many cheap bars around here and a lot of them check I.D.'s.

JOHN POLK: Well, do you know of any that don't?

ASHBE: No, not for sure.

JOHN POLK: Oh, God, I need to get drunk.

ASHBE: Aren't you?

JOHN POLK: Some, but I'm losing ground fast.

(By this time a bum who has been traveling drunkenly down the street falls near the couple and begins throwing up.)

ASHBE: Oh, I know! You can come to my apartment. It's just down the block. We keep one bottle of rum around. I'll serve you a grand drink, three or four if you like.

JOHN POLK: *(Fretfully.)* No thanks.

ASHBE: But look, we're getting all wet.

JOHN POLK: Sober too, wet and sober.

ASHBE: Oh, come on! Rain's blurring my glasses.

JOHN POLK: Well, how about your parents? What would they say?

ASHBE: Daddy's out of town and Mama lives in Atlanta; so I'm sure they won't mind. I think we have some cute little marshmallows. *(Pulling on him.)* Won't you really come?

JOHN POLK: You've probably got some gang of muggers waiting to kill me. Oh, alright—what the hell, let's go.

ASHBE: Hurrah! Come on. It's this way. *(She starts across the stage, stops, and picks up an old hat.)* Hey, look at this hat. Isn't it something! Here, wear it to keep off the rain.

JOHN POLK: *(Throwing hat back onto street.)* No, thanks, you don't know who's worn it before.

ASHBE: *(Picking hat back up.)* That makes it all the more exciting. Maybe it was a butcher's who slaughtered his wife or a silver pirate with a black bird on his throat. Who do you guess?

JOHN POLK: I don't know. Anyway what's the good of guessing? I mean you'll never really know.

ASHBE: *(Trying the hat on.)* Yeah, probably not. *(At this point, Ashbe and John Polk reach the front door.)* Here we are.

(Ashbe begins fumbling for her key. Clareece, a teeny-bopper, walks up to John Polk.)

CLAREECE: Hey, man, got any spare change?

JOHN POLK: *(Looking through his pockets.)* Let me see—I—

ASHBE: *(Coming up between them, giving Clareece a shove.)* Beat it, Clareece. He's my company.

CLAREECE: *(Walks away and sneers.)* Oh, shove it, Frizzels.

ASHBE: A lot of jerks live around here. Come on in.

(She opens the door. Lights go up on the living room of a run-down apartment in a run-down apartment house. Besides being merely run-down the room is a malicious pig sty with colors, paper hats, paper dolls, masks, torn up stuffed animals, dead flowers and leaves, dress up clothes, etc., thrown all about.)

ASHBE: My bones are cold. Do you want a towel to dry off?

JOHN POLK: Yes, thank you.

ASHBE: *(She picks a towel up off of the floor and tosses it to him.)* Here.

(He begins drying off, as she takes off her rain things then she begins raking things off the sofa.)

ASHBE: Please do sit down.

(He sits.)

ASHBE: I'm sorry the place is disheveled, but my father's been out of town. I always try to pick up and all before he gets in. Of course he's pretty used to messes. My mother never was too good at keeping things clean.

JOHN POLK: When's he coming back?

ASHBE: Sunday, I believe. Oh, I've been meaning to say—

JOHN POLK: What?

ASHBE: My name's Ashbe Williams.

JOHN POLK: Ashbe?

ASHBE: Yeah, Ashbe.

JOHN POLK: My name's John Polk Richards.

ASHBE: John Polk? They call you John Polk?

JOHN POLK: It's family.

ASHBE: *(Putting on socks.)* These are my favorite socks, the red furry ones. Well, here's some books and magazines to look at while I fix you something to drink. What do you want in your rum?

JOHN POLK: Coke's fine.

ASHBE: I'll see do we have any. I think I'll take some hot Koolade myself. *(She exits to the kitchen.)*

JOHN POLK: Hot Koolade?

ASHBE: It's just Koolade that's been heated, like hot chocolate or hot tea.

JOHN POLK: Sounds great.

ASHBE: Well, I'm used to it. You get so much for your dime it makes it worth your while. I don't buy presweetened, of course, it's better to sugar your own.

JOHN POLK: I remember once I threw up a lot of grape Koolade when I was a kid. I've hated it ever since. Hey, would you check on the time?

ASHBE: *(She enters carrying a tray with several bottles of food coloring, a bottle of rum, and a huge glass.)* I'm sorry we don't have Cokes. I wonder if rum and Koolade is good? Oh, we don't have a clock either. *(She pours a large amount of rum into the large glass.)*

JOHN POLK: I'll just have it with water then.

ASHBE: *(She finds an almost empty glass of water somewhere in the room and dumps it in with the rum.)* Would you like food coloring in the water? It makes a drink all the more aesthetic. Of course, some people don't care for aesthetics.

JOHN POLK: No thank you, just plain water.

ASHBE: Are you sure? The taste is entirely the same. I put it in all my water.

JOHN POLK: Well.

ASHBE: What color do you want?

JOHN POLK: I don't know.

ASHBE: What's your favorite color?

JOHN POLK: Blue, I guess.

(She puts a few blue drops into the glass—as she has nothing to stir with, she blows into the glass turning the water blue.)

JOHN POLK: Thanks.

ASHBE: *(Exits. She screams from kitchen.)* Come on, say come on cat, eat your fresh good milk.

JOHN POLK: You have a cat?

ASHBE: *(Off.)* No.

JOHN POLK: Oh.

ASHBE: *(She enters carrying a tray with a cup of hot Koolade and Cheerios and colored marshmallows.)* Here are some Cheerios and some cute little colored marshmallows to eat with your drink.

JOHN POLK: Thanks.

ASHBE: I one time smashed all the big white marshmallows in the plastic bag at the grocery store.

JOHN POLK: Why did you do that?

ASHBE: I was angry. Do you like ceramics?

JOHN POLK: Yes.

ASHBE: My mother makes them. It's sort of her hobby. She is very talented.

JOHN POLK: My mother never does anything. Well, I guess she can shuffle the bridge deck okay.

ASHBE: Actually, my mother is a dancer. She teaches at a school in Atlanta. She's really very talented.

JOHN POLK: *(Indicates ceramics.)* She must be to do all these.

ASHBE: Well, Madeline, my older sister, did the blue one. Madeline gets to live with Mama.

JOHN POLK: And you live with your father.

ASHBE: Yeah, but I get to go visit them sometimes.

JOHN POLK: You do ceramics too?

ASHBE: No, I never learned…but I have this great potholder set. *(Gets up to show him.)* See I make lots of multicolored potholders and send them to Mama and Madeline. I also make paper hats. *(Gets material to show him.)* I guess they're more creative but making potholders is more relaxing. Here would you like to make a hat?

JOHN POLK: I don't know, I'm a little drunk.

ASHBE: It's not hard a bit. *(Hands him material.)* Just draw a real pretty design on the paper. It really doesn't have to be pretty, just whatever you want.

JOHN POLK: It's kind of you to give my creative drives such freedom.

ASHBE: Ha, ha, ha, I'll work on my potholder set a bit.

JOHN POLK: What time is it? I've really got to check on the time.

ASHBE: I know. I'll call the time operator. *(She goes to the phone.)*

JOHN POLK: How do you get along without a clock?

ASHBE: Well, I've been late for school a lot. Daddy has a watch. It's 11:03.

JOHN POLK: I've got a while yet.

(Ashbe twirls back to her chair, drops, and sighs.)

JOHN POLK: Are you a dancer too?

ASHBE: *(Delighted.)* I can't dance a bit, really. I practice a lot is all, at home in the afternoon. I imagine you go to a lot of dances.

JOHN POLK: Not really, I'm a terrible dancer. I usually get bored or drunk.

ASHBE: You probably drink too much.

JOHN POLK: No, it's just since I've come to college. All you do there is drink more beer and write more papers.

ASHBE: What are you studying for to be?

JOHN POLK: I don't know.

ASHBE: Why don't you become a rancher?

JOHN POLK: Dad wants me to help run his soybean farm.

ASHBE: Soybean farm. Yikes, that's really something. Where is it?

JOHN POLK: Well, I live in the Delta, Hollybluff, Mississippi. Anyway, Dad feels I should go to business school first; you know, so I'll become, well, management-minded. Pass the blue.

ASHBE: Is that what you really want to do?

JOHN POLK: I don't know. It would probably be as good as anything else I could do. Dad makes good money. He can take vacations whenever he wants. Sure it'll be a ball.

ASHBE: I'd hate to have to be management-minded.

(John Polk shrugs.)

ASHBE: I don't mean to hurt your feelings but I would really hate to be a management mind. *(She starts walking on her knees, twisting her fists in front of her eyes, and making clicking sounds as a management mind would make.)*

JOHN POLK: Cut it out. Just forget it. The farm could burn down and I wouldn't even have to think about it.

ASHBE: *(After a pause.)* Well, what do you want to talk about?

JOHN POLK: I don't know.

ASHBE: When was the last dance you went to?

JOHN POLK: Dances. That's a great subject. Let's see, oh, I don't really remember it was probably some blind date. God, I hate dates.

ASHBE: Why?

JOHN POLK: Well, they always say that they don't want popcorn and they wind up eating all of yours.

ASHBE: You mean, you hate dates just because they eat your popcorn? Don't you think that's kind of stingy?

JOHN POLK: It's the principle of the thing. Why can't they just say, yes, I'd like some popcorn when you ask them. But, no, they're always so damn coy.

ASHBE: I'd tell my date if I wanted popcorn. I'm not that immature.

JOHN POLK: Anyway, it's not only the popcorn. It's a lot of little things. I've finished coloring. What do I do now?

ASHBE: Now you have to fold it. Here…like this. *(She explains the process with relish.)* Say, that's really something.

JOHN POLK: It's kind of funny looking. *(Putting the hat on.)* Yeah, I like it, but you could never wear it anywhere.

ASHBE: Well, like what anyway?

JOHN POLK: Huh?

ASHBE: The things dates do to you that you don't like, the little things.

JOHN POLK: Oh, well, just the way they wear those false eyelashes and put their hand on your knee when you're trying to parallel park, and keep on giggling and going off to the bathroom with their girlfriends. It's obvious they don't want to go out with me. They just want to go out so that they can wear their new clothes and won't have to sit on their ass in the dormitory. They never want to go out with me. I can never even talk to them.

ASHBE: Well, you can talk to me and I'm a girl.

JOHN POLK: Well, I'm really kind of drunk and you're a stranger…well, I probably wouldn't be able to talk to you tomorrow. That makes a difference.

ASHBE: Maybe it does. *(A bit of a pause and then extremely pleased by the idea she says.)* You know we're alike because I don't like dances either.

JOHN POLK: I thought you said you practiced…in the afternoons.

ASHBE: Well, I like dancing. I just don't like dances. At least not like—well, not like the one our school was having tonight…they're so corny.

JOHN POLK: Yeah, most dances are.

ASHBE: All they serve is potato chips and fruit punch, and then this stupid baby band plays and everybody dances around thinking they're so hot. I frankly wouldn't dance there. I would prefer to wait till I am invited to an exclusive ball. It doesn't really matter which ball, just one where they have huge, golden chandeliers and silver fountains, and serve delicacies of all sorts and bubble blue champagne. I'll arrive in a pink silk cape. *(Laughing.)* I want to dance in pink!

JOHN POLK: You're mixed up. You're probably one of those people that live in a fantasy world.

ASHBE: I do not. I accept reality as well as anyone. Anyway, you can talk to me remember. I know what you mean by the kind of girls it's hard to talk to. There are girls a lot that way in the small clique at my school. Really tacky and mean. They expect everyone to be as stylish as they are and they won't even speak to you in the hall. I don't mind if they don't speak to me, but I really love the orphans and it hurts my feelings when they are so mean to them.

JOHN POLK: What do you mean—they're mean to the orpheens? *(Notices pun and giggles to self.)*

ASHBE: Oh, well, they sometimes snicker at the orphans' dresses. The orphans usually have hand-me-down drab ugly dresses. Once Shelly Maxwell wouldn't let Glinda borrow her pencil, even though she had two. It hurt her feelings.

JOHN POLK: Are you best friends with these orphans?

ASHBE: I hardly know them at all. They're really shy. I just like them a lot. They're the reason I put spells on the girls in the clique.

JOHN POLK: Spells, what do you mean, witch spells?

ASHBE: Witch spells? Not really, mostly just voodoo.

JOHN POLK: Are you kidding? Do you really do voodoo?

ASHBE: Sure, here I'll show you my doll. *(Goes to get doll, comes back with straw voodoo doll. Her air as she returns is one of frightening mystery.)* I know a lot about the subject. Cora, she used to wash dishes in the Moonlight Cafe, told me all about voodoo. She's a real expert on the subject, went to all the meetings and everything. Once she caused a man's throat to rot away and turn almost totally black. She's moved to Chicago now.

JOHN POLK: It doesn't really work. Does it?

ASHBE: Well, not always. The thing about voodoo is that both parties have to believe in it for it to work.

JOHN POLK: Do the girls in school believe in it?

ASHBE: Not really, I don't think. That's where my main problem comes in. I have to make the clique believe in it, yet I have to be very subtle. Mainly, I give reports in English class or Speech.

JOHN POLK: Reports?

ASHBE: On voodoo.

JOHN POLK: That's really kind of sick, you know.

ASHBE: Not really. I don't cast spells that'll do any real harm. Mainly, just the kind of thing to make them think—to keep them on their toes.

(Blue drink intoxication begins to take over and John Polk begins laughing.)

ASHBE: What's so funny?

JOHN POLK: Nothing. I was just thinking what a mean little person you are.

ASHBE: Mean! I'm not mean a bit.

JOHN POLK: Yes, you are mean— *(Picking up color.)* and green too.

ASHBE: Green?

JOHN POLK: Yes, green with envy of those other girls; so you play all those mean little tricks.

ASHBE: Envious of those other girls, that stupid, close-minded little clique!

JOHN POLK: Green as this marshmallow. *(Eats marshmallow.)*

ASHBE: You think I want to be in some group…a sheep like you? A little sheep like you that does everything when he's supposed to do it!

JOHN POLK: Me a sheep—I do what I want!

ASHBE: Ha! I've known you for an hour and already I see you for the sheep you are!

JOHN POLK: Don't take your green meanness out on me.

ASHBE: Not only are you a sheep, you are a NORMAL sheep. Give me back my colors! *(Begins snatching colors away.)*

JOHN POLK: *(Pushing colors at her.)* Green and mean! Green and mean! Green and mean! Etc.

ASHBE: *(Throwing marshmallows at him.)* That's the reason you're in a fraternity and the reason you're going to manage your mind, and dates—you go out on dates merely because it's expected of you even though you have a terrible time. That's the reason you go to the whorehouse to prove you're a normal man. Well, you're much too normal for me.

JOHN POLK: Infant bitch. You think you're really cute.

ASHBE: That really wasn't food coloring in your drink, it was poison!

(She laughs, he picks up his coat to go and she stops throwing marshmallows at him.)

ASHBE: Are you going? I was only kidding. For Christ sake it wasn't really poison. Come on, don't go. Can't you take a little friendly criticism?

JOHN POLK: Look, did you have to bother me tonight? I had enough problems without—

(Phone rings. Both look at phone, it rings for the third time. He stands undecided.)

ASHBE: Look, wait, we'll make it up. *(She goes to answer phone.)* Hello— Daddy. How are you?…I'm fine…Dad, you sound funny…what?… Come on Daddy, you know she's not here. *(Pause.)* Look, I told you I wouldn't call anymore. You've got her number in Atlanta. *(Pause, as she sinks to the floor.)* Why have you started again?…Don't say that. I can tell it. I can. Hey, I have to go to bed now, I don't want to talk anymore, O.K.? *(Hangs up phone, softly to self.)* Goddamnit.

JOHN POLK: *(He has heard the conversation and is taking off his coat.)* Hey, Ashbe—

(She looks at him blankly, her mind far away.)

JOHN POLK: You want to talk?

ASHBE: No. *(Slight pause.)* Why don't you look at my shell collection? I have this special shell collection. *(She shows him collection.)*

JOHN POLK: They're beautiful, I've never seen colors like this.

(Ashbe is silent, he continues to himself.)

JOHN POLK: I used to go to Biloxi a lot when I was a kid...one time my brother and I, we camped out on the beach. The sky was purple. I remember it was really purple. We ate pork and beans out of a can. I'd always kinda wanted to do that. Every night for about a week after I got home, I dreamt about these waves foaming over my head and face. It was funny. Did you find these shells or buy them?

ASHBE: Some I found, some I bought. I've been trying to decipher their meaning. Here, listen, do you hear that?

JOHN POLK: Yes.

ASHBE: That's the soul of the sea. *(She listens.)* I'm pretty sure it's the soul of the sea. Just imagine when I decipher the language. I'll know all the secrets of the world.

JOHN POLK: Yeah, probably you will. *(Looking into the shell.)* You know, you were right.

ASHBE: What do you mean?

JOHN POLK: About me, you were right. I am a sheep, a normal one. I've been trying to get out of it, but now I'm as big a sheep as ever.

ASHBE: Oh, it doesn't matter. You're company. It was rude of me to say.

JOHN POLK: No, because it was true. I really didn't want to go into a fraternity, I didn't even want to go to college, and I sure as hell don't want to go back to Hollybluff and work the soybean farm till I'm eighty.

ASHBE: I still say you could work on a ranch.

JOHN POLK: I don't know. I wanted to be a minister or something good, but I don't even know if I believe in God.

ASHBE: Yeah.

JOHN POLK: I never used to worry about being a failure. Now I think about it all the time. It's just I need to do something that's—fulfilling.

ASHBE: Fulfilling, yes, I see what you mean. Well, how about college? Isn't it fulfilling? I mean, you take all those wonderful classes, and you have all your very good friends.

JOHN POLK: Friends, yeah, I have some friends.

ASHBE: What do you mean?

JOHN POLK: Nothing—well, I do mean something. What the hell, let me try to explain. You see it was my "friends," the fraternity guys that set me up with G.G., excuse me Myrtle, as a gift for my eighteenth birthday.

ASHBE: You mean, you didn't want the appointment?

JOHN POLK: No, I didn't want it. Hey, ah, where did my blue drink go?

ASHBE: *(As she hands him the drink.)* They probably thought you really wanted to go.

JOHN POLK: Yeah, I'm sure they gave a damn what I wanted. They never even asked me. Hell, I would have told them a handkerchief, a pair of argyle socks, but, no, they have to get me a whore just because it's a cool ass thing to do. They make me sick. I couldn't even stay at the party they gave. All the sweaty T-shirts, and moron sex stories—I just couldn't take it.

ASHBE: Is that why you were at the Blue Angel so early?

JOHN POLK: Yeah, I needed to get drunk but not with them. They're such creeps.

ASHBE: Gosh, so you really don't want to go to Myrtle's?

JOHN POLK: No, I guess not.

ASHBE: Then are you going?

JOHN POLK: *(Pause.)* Yes.

ASHBE: That's wrong. You shouldn't go just to please them.

JOHN POLK: Oh, that's not the point anymore, maybe at first it was, but it's not anymore. Now I have to go for myself—to prove to myself that I'm not afraid.

ASHBE: Afraid? *(Slowly, as she begins to grasp his meaning.)* You mean, you've never slept with a girl before?

JOHN POLK: Well, I've never been in love.

ASHBE: *(In amazement.)* You're a virgin?

JOHN POLK: Oh, God.

ASHBE: No, don't feel bad, I am too.

JOHN POLK: I thought I should be in love—

ASHBE: Well, you're certainly not in love with Myrtle. I mean, you haven't even met her.

JOHN POLK: I know, but, God, I thought maybe I'd never fall in love. What then? You should experience everything—shouldn't you? Oh, what's it matter, everything's so screwed.

ASHBE: Screwed? Yeah, I guess it is. I mean, I always thought it would be fun to have a lot of friends who gave parties and go to dances all dressed up. Like the dance tonight—it might have been fun.

JOHN POLK: Well, why didn't you go?

ASHBE: I don't know. I'm not sure it would have been fun. Anyway, you can't go—alone.

JOHN POLK: Oh, you need a date?

ASHBE: Yeah, or something.

JOHN POLK: Say, Ashbe, ya wanna dance here?

ASHBE: No, I think we'd better discuss your dilemma.

JOHN POLK: What dilemma?

ASHBE: Myrtle. It doesn't seem right you should—

JOHN POLK: Let's forget Myrtle for now. I've got a while yet. Here, have some
    more of this blue-moon drink.

ASHBE: You're only trying to escape through artificial means.

JOHN POLK: Yeah, you got it. Now come on. Would you like to dance? Hey,
    you said you liked to dance.

ASHBE: You're being ridiculous.

JOHN POLK: *(Winking at her.)* Dance?

ASHBE: John Polk, I just thought—

JOHN POLK: Hmm?

ASHBE: How to solve your problem—

JOHN POLK: Well—

ASHBE: Make love to me!

JOHN POLK: What?!

ASHBE: It all seems logical to me. It would prove you weren't scared and you
    wouldn't be doing it just to impress others.

JOHN POLK: Look, I—I mean I hardly know you—

ASHBE: But we've talked. It's better this way, really. I won't be so apt to point
    out your mistakes.

JOHN POLK: I'd feel great stripping a twelve-year-old of her virginity.

ASHBE: I'm sixteen! Anyway, I'd be stripping you of yours just as well. I'll go
    put on some Tiger Claw perfume. *(She runs out.)*

JOHN POLK: Hey, come back! Tiger Claw perfume, Christ.

ASHBE: *(Entering.)* I think one should have different scents for different moods.

JOHN POLK: Hey, stop spraying that! You know I'm not going to—well, you'd
    get neurotic, or pregnant, or some damn thing. Stop spraying, will you!

ASHBE: Pregnant? You really think I could get pregnant?

JOHN POLK: Sure, it'd be a delightful possibility.

ASHBE: It really wouldn't be bad. Maybe I would get to go to Tokyo for an
    abortion. I've never been to the Orient.

JOHN POLK: Sure, getting cut on is always a real treat.

ASHBE: Anyway, I might just want to have my dear baby. I could move to
    Atlanta with Mama and Madeline. It'd be wonderful fun. Why, I could
    take him to the supermarket, put him in one of those little baby seats to

stroll him about. I'd buy peach baby food and feed it to him with a tiny golden spoon. Why, I could take colored pictures of him and send them to you through the mail. Come on— *(Starts putting pillows onto the couch.)* Well, I guess you should kiss me for a start. It's only etiquette, everyone begins with it.

JOHN POLK: I don't think I could even kiss you with a clear conscience. I mean, you're so small with those little cat eyeglasses and curly hair—I couldn't even kiss you.

ASHBE: You couldn't even kiss me? I can't help it if I have to wear glasses. I got the prettiest ones I could find.

JOHN POLK: Your glasses are fine. Let's forget it, O.K.?

ASHBE: I know, my lips are too purple, but if I eat carrots, the dye'll come off and they'll be orange.

JOHN POLK: I didn't say anything about your lips being too purple.

ASHBE: Well, what is it? You're just plain chicken I suppose—

JOHN POLK: Sure, right, I'm chicken, totally chicken. Let's forget it. I don't know how, but, somehow, this is probably all my fault.

ASHBE: You're darn right it's all your fault! I want to have my dear baby or at least get to Japan. I'm so sick of school I could smash every marshmallow in sight! *(She starts smashing.)* Go on to your skinny pimple whore. I hope the skinny whore laughs in your face which she probably will because you have an easy face to laugh in.

JOHN POLK: You're absolutely right, she'll probably hoot and howl her damn fizzle red head off. Maybe you can wait outside the door and hear her, give you lots of pleasure, you sadistic little thief.

ASHBE: Thief—was Robin Hood—oh, what's wrong with this world? I just wasn't made for it is all. I've probably been put in the wrong world, I can see that now.

JOHN POLK: You're fine in this world.

ASHBE: Sure, everyone just views me as an undesirable lump.

JOHN POLK: Who?

ASHBE: You for one.

JOHN POLK: *(Pause.)* You mean because I wouldn't make love to you?

ASHBE: It seems clear to me.

JOHN POLK: But you're wrong, you know.

ASHBE: *(To self, softly.)* Don't pity me.

JOHN POLK: The reason I wouldn't wasn't that—it's just that—well, I like you too much to.

ASHBE: You like me?

JOHN POLK: Undesirable lump, Jesus. Your cheeks, they're—they're—

ASHBE: My cheeks? They're what?

JOHN POLK: They're rosy.

ASHBE: My cheeks are rosy?

JOHN POLK: Yeah, your cheeks, they're really rosy.

ASHBE: Well, they're natural, you know. Say, would you like to dance?

JOHN POLK: Yes.

ASHBE: I'll turn on the radio. *(She turns on radio. Ethel Waters is heard singing "Honey in the Honeycomb." Ashbe begins snapping her fingers.)* Yikes, let's jazz it out.
(They dance.)

JOHN POLK: Hey, I'm not good or anything—

ASHBE: John Polk.

JOHN POLK: Yeah?

ASHBE: Baby, I think you dance fine!
(They dance on, laughing, saying what they want till end of song. Then a radio announcer comes on and says the 12:00 news will be in five minutes. Billie Holiday or Terry Pierce, begins singing, "Am I Blue?")

JOHN POLK: Dance?

ASHBE: News in five minutes.

JOHN POLK: Yeah.

ASHBE: That means five minutes till midnight.

JOHN POLK: Yeah, I know.

ASHBE: Then you're not—

JOHN POLK: Ashbe, I've never danced all night. Wouldn't it be something to—to dance all night and watch the rats come out of the gutter?

ASHBE: Rats?

JOHN POLK: Don't they come out at night? I hear New Orleans has lots of rats.

ASHBE: Yeah, yeah, its got lots of rats.

JOHN POLK: Then let's dance all night and wait for them to come out.

ASHBE: Alright—but, but how about our feet?

JOHN POLK: Feet?

ASHBE: They'll hurt.

JOHN POLK: Yeah.

ASHBE: *(Smiling.)* Okay, then let's dance.
(He takes her hand and they dance as lights black out and the music soars and continues to play.)

END OF PLAY

THE WAKE OF JAMEY FOSTER

FOR MAYPOE AND CHARLIE

Susan Kingsley, Belita Moreno, Adam LeFevre,
Amanda Michael Plummer, and Patricia Richardson
in Hartford Stage's 1982 production of
The Wake of Jamey Foster.

photo by Lanny Nagler

ORIGINAL PRODUCTION

The Wake of Jamey Foster was presented on Broadway by FDM Productions, Francois De Menil/Harris Maslansky, Elliot Martin, Ulu Grosbard, Nan Pearlman and Warner Theatre Productions Inc. at the Eugene O'Neill Theatre, in New York City, on October 14, 1982. It was directed by Ulu Grosbard; the setting was by Santo Loquasto; costumes were by Jennifer von Mayrhauser; lighting was by Jennifer Tipton; sound was by David Rapkin; and the associate producer was Arla Manson. The cast, in order of appearance, was as follows:

Marshael Foster	Susan Kingsley
Leon Darnell	Stephen Tobolowsky
Katty Foster	Belita Moreno
Wayne Foster	Anthony Heald
Collard Darnell	Patricia Richardson
Pixrose Wilson	Holly Hunter
Brocker Slade	Brad Sullivan

The Wake of Jamey Foster had it's world premiere at Hartford Stage Company, Hartford, Connecticut, 1981.

SYNOPSIS OF SCENES
ACT I
  Scene I: Morning
  Scene II: Supper Time
ACT II
  Scene I: Late that night
  Scene II: Throughout the night
  Scene III: The following morning

THE CAST

MARSHAEL FOSTER: 33, Jamey's widow
LEON DARNELL: 25, Marshael's brother
KATTY FOSTER: 29, Wayne's wife
WAYNE FOSTER: 29, Jamey's brother; Katty's husband
COLLARD DARNELL: 30, Marshael's sister
PIXROSE WILSON: 17, Leon's friend; an orphan
BROCKER SLADE: 53, Marshael's friend

THE SETTING

The entire action of the play takes place at Marshael Foster's house. The rooms that are visible are: the parlor; the front hall with stairs leading to the upstairs hall; Marshael's bedroom; and an outside area along the right side of the house. The house is an old rambling country home that is in distinct disrepair with faded drapes, peeling paint, old furniture, worn-out rugs, and so on. Throughout the house books, papers, journals, and so forth are scattered about, as evidence of Jamey's excessive though incomplete historical research. In the front hall there is a grandfather clock, a love seat, and a card table with chair that has been temporarily set out for the occasion. There is a front door Up Center. There is also a door that leads to the parlor. The furniture in the parlor has been rearranged to leave a vacant space for the expected coffin. Several funeral wreaths and flower arrangements surround this area. The second door in the front hall, which is stage left, is a dining room door that leads to the rest of the downstairs. Upstairs the hallway has one exit leading to Marshael's bedroom. The bedroom is by far the most cluttered room in the house. There is a bed, a vanity with stool, a chaise lounge, a table with a world globe, a sewing machine, a dress dummy, a clothes rack with pink and gold drill team outfits on it in different stages of completion, and several boxes of household improvement items that are stacked against the wall. There is also a closet, a door leading to the bathroom, an Upstage window, and a balcony stage right. The Upstage window looks out onto the front yard. The balcony looks over the side yard. In the outside area there is a tree that grows at least as high as the balcony.

THE TIME

Spring

ACT I
SCENE I

The lights go up on stage. It is morning. Upstairs, Marshael Foster, thirty-three, is sitting on her bed. She is thin with shoulder length, curly hair and deep set haunted eyes. She wears a black dress. Marshael pulls a chocolate Easter rabbit out of an Easter basket and bites off the top of its ears. She has another bite, then rises, picks up a ladies' magazine and drops back down onto her bed. She lies glancing through the magazine, gnawing on the ears of the chocolate rabbit.

KATTY'S VOICE: *(Offstage.)* Go on and set them in there with the other flowers.
(Leon Darnell, twenty-five, enters the front hall from the dining room. Leon is tall and gangly. He wears a white shirt and a dark skinny tie with black Sunday pants that are a bit high-waisted. He carries two large flower arrangements that he is swinging haphazardly about.)

LEON: Where?!
(Katty Foster, twenty-nine, follows him into the room carrying a small arrangement of flowers in a basket. Katty is pretty in a baby-doll-matron sort of way. She is still wearing a beehive hairdo that was popular when she was in college.)

KATTY: I'll arrange them myself. You just set them down there. In the parlor.

LEON: *(As he moves into the parlor.)* Alright! Fine. 'Cause my angel is arriving today!

KATTY: *(Setting her basket down.)* These'll look real nice right out here on the card table by the memorial book—don't you think?

LEON: *(Swinging the baskets of flowers around the parlor.)* 'Cause she's riding in to see me.

KATTY: Do you think that we should serve the mourners any refreshments?

LEON: Riding in on the Greyhound express!

KATTY: Do you suppose just assorted beverages will do? I don't know what's called for—I've never done all this before—Oh no, Leon; not there! We have to leave some room. *(She moves the flowers away from the area reserved for the coffin.)*

LEON: Well, look, I'm going. I gotta get those soda bottles cashed in—got a car load.

KATTY: Oh, wait, Leon! Has anyone heard further from your sister, Collard?

LEON: Due in yesterday; that's the latest. Ah! *(He steps on a large tack and sits down to pull it out of his shoe.)*

KATTY: *(Arranging the flowers.)* Oh, mercy, I hope she's alright. Heaven knows, she should be used to driving up and down the highways of this state. But life is so full of unknown horror—

LEON: *(Pulling out a tack with a pocket knife.)* Collard's coming, she said she's coming—she always comes home when anybody dies. Wow! Look at the size of that tack!

KATTY: Why, here, let me throw that thing away! Where'd it come from, anyway?

LEON: *(Pondering his shoe.)* It's Pixrose I'm anxious on.

KATTY: Why, she's not due in till twelve noon? *(About the tack.)* Maybe it dropped out of one of these folding chairs.

LEON: It's just—it's just I love her so much! I do. I love her. Oh, and she loves me too. She does. Is my hair looking funny down in front where Margarite Roper yanked out that handful?

KATTY: It could stand a comb.

LEON: *(Pulling out his comb.)* See, we're exactly alike. Pixrose and me. We're exactly the same. Both of us enjoy public transportation and both of us have bumps right here on our heads. *(Showing her.)* Look! We do! We do!

WAYNE'S VOICE: *(Offstage.)* Katty! Katty! Katherine!

(Wayne Foster appears on the upstairs landing, as Katty and Leon move into the front hall. Wayne, twenty-nine, is an attractive man with cold, nervous eyes.)

KATTY: *(Overlapping.)* What?! Yes, darling! What?!

WAYNE: *(Running on.)* My cuff links—the silver ones with the monograms. Did you forget to pack them?

KATTY: Why, I hope not. Did you check your little jewel case.

WAYNE: I've checked everything—all the luggage! Look, here, my cuffs are totally undone!

KATTY: Well, now, I'll go take a look myself.

WAYNE: And nobody's doing a thing about Marshael's children. She's supposed to be getting them dressed! One's got gum all stuck in its ears and hair—

KATTY: Oh, dear, Leon, quick, you bring me those scissors from in there.

(Leon goes to get scissors from the parlor.)

KATTY: *(As she straightens his collar.)* Now just hush down, Honey Lamb. Why we're all gonna do every little bitty thing we can do to unburden poor, old Papa Sweet Potato.

LEON: *(Slinging the scissors.)* Here, catch!

WAYNE: My God!

KATTY: *(Overlapping.)* Leon!

WAYNE: And just what is he doing inviting strange house guests over, as if we don't have misery enough to deal with?!

KATTY: She's not a house guest, Angel Cake, she's a homeless refugee.

LEON: She's my girl!

WAYNE: I don't care what she is. I need my time of grief. I need my solitude. God.

KATTY: I know. Of course, you do. It's awful. But try to be charitable, darling. Two entire wings of that orphanage were destroyed, and it seems Leon is the only obliging friend that child has.

WAYNE: Friend?! Ha! He hardly knows her.

LEON: Hardly know her?! Ha! Why, I've kissed her!

KATTY: Oh, please, now, honey, go on and force yourself to eat some breakfast. It'll do you good. I'll go up and check on those children and find your cuff links for you. *(On her way upstairs.)* I know I packed them. They gotta be there. *(She exits down the upstairs hall.)*

LEON: *(Turning back to face Wayne.)* And guess what? We both hate Dr. Peppers and Orange Crushes are our favorite beverage. Both of us.

WAYNE: Forget it, Leon. I'm sorry. I'm on the edge here. You understand. It's been a blow.

LEON: Yeah. I'm lucky. I never had a brother. Well, gotta go cash in them bottles.

WAYNE: Leon, would you wait here a minute?

LEON: What is it?

WAYNE: I just wanted to know what all went on with Marshael yesterday afternoon over at the funeral parlor? I mean what all did she decide on?

LEON: Well, not much. 'Cept she said for me to handle it, and so I did. I handled it all.

WAYNE: You mean, she left the arrangements entirely in your hands? She let you settle on everything—all by yourself?

LEON: —Yeah. 'Cept for the coffin. She pointed at it and said, "That's the one." Then she tells me she needs to get home and dye up some Easter eggs; so I'm supposed to handle it all. And I did too. Precisely that.

WAYNE: Well, I certainly would have hoped that the details and arrangements of my only brother's funeral would have concerned his wife more than coloring up a batch of goddamn Easter eggs!

(Upstairs, Marshael puts down the bunny, leaves the bedroom, and exits up the hall.)

LEON: Now look here, Willie Wayne, I handled it all. Picked out a nice cheerful suit for Jamey to be wearing here today. Took down a dress shirt and matching tie. Why, I even signed him up for a shave, shampooing, and manicure. He's gonna look his best.

WAYNE: It's just I—I want it done proper. He's my brother. I want things done with class and dignity and respect.

LEON: Well, I'm the one you want in charge then. See, I ordered this memorial book here and a solid blanket of roses for the coffin. Why, tomorrow we've got us a limousine being escorted by a policeman on a motorcycle. I even got us black arm bands to pass out and black veils for the ladies, I got the works! No need to worry, Willie Wayne. No need at all.

COLLARD'S VOICE: *(Offstage.)* Hello! Wooh! Hey, I made it! I'm home! How's Marshy?! *(The front door flies open and Collard Darnell enters in a muddy red evening gown and a pair of men's cowboy boots that are several sizes too large. She carries a large straw bag. Her hair is wild and her face is dirty. She is thirty years old.)*

LEON: *(Overlapping.)* Collard! You?! Collard Greens! Collard Greens!!

COLLARD: *(Overlapping as she hugs him.)* Leon! Baby boy! Baby boy!

LEON: I told you she'd make it! I told ya!

COLLARD: *(Stopping.)* Well, hi ya, Willie Wayne! Let's see, car exploded; suitcase stolen; and shoes stuck in the Memphis mud. It's funny, Willie Wayne, but I always know just what you're gonna say even before you open your mouth.

WAYNE: I wasn't gonna say anything, Collard. Nothing you do surprises me much less your lack of concern for your bereaved sister. Excuse me, but I've got to go see if I can force some breakfast down this lump in my throat. *(He exits out the dining room door.)*

COLLARD: How do people get like that? How the hell do they do it?

LEON: Must be born to it.

COLLARD: I suppose he's not even gonna acknowledge the Get Well Soon card I sent t'Jamey. Pompous little pig. Shit. Well, home again, home again, jigady jig. *(Pause.)* So Jamey's really dead?

LEON: Looks like it.

COLLARD: How's Marshy taking it?

LEON: Seems t'be doing alright.

COLLARD: Well, shit. So how'd it happen? Willie Wayne's giving me this song and dance about some sorta head injury. Didn't sound all that serious when I got the call last Sunday.

LEON: Well, I guess it was pretty serious cause by Wednesday noon he's dead.

COLLARD: Jesus.

LEON: Seems that head injury he'd acquired caused him to have a stroke Tuesday evening, paralyzing one half of his entire body. Then Wednesday 'bout noon time...

COLLARD: *(Finding her cigarettes.)* Lord. So how'd he get this head injury? He run into some wood post?

LEON: No, he's kicked in the head by a cow.

COLLARD: He's what?!

LEON: Right out in the field over by Cambden on Highway 17. I suppose he'd had quite a load t'drink.

COLLARD: Out boozing in a field and gets kicked in the head by a cow. What the hell was he doing out there?

LEON: Chasing cows, I guess.

COLLARD: Holy Church of the Lord. You got a light?

LEON: *(Moving into the parlor.)* In here. There are matches galore right here in this dish—

COLLARD: *(Entering the parlor.)* What's all this? What's happening here? What's all the crap? Jesus!

LEON: They're setting up for the exhibition of the body—for the wake.

COLLARD: A wake? Here? In this house? Aren't they going to use a funeral home like most decent, civilized folks?

LEON: Jamey's mother wanted it here. She says that's how it's been done for generations in her family up in north Mississippi 'round Tubler.

COLLARD: God. Poor Marshy. She must be going to pieces 'bout now.

LEON: Well, I'm seeing that she's gonna have some close personal relatives and friends t'help t'get her through this long and desolate night.

COLLARD: *(Looking around slowly at the flowers.)* Close relatives? Swell, like Willie Wayne and his bee-hive wife.

LEON: Well, yeah, there's them and there's you and also I've called in Mr. Brocker Slade.

COLLARD: Who's he?

LEON: Close personal friend of Marshael's. He built her them new red kitchen chairs. You'll like him for sure. He's done it all. Everything. He's eaten certified dog meat in China and he's got tattoos up and down his arms and legs both.

COLLARD: *(Still dazed by all the flowers.)* Sounds remarkable t'me.

LEON: Oh, he's absolutely your style of person. I told him to please come over and help stand guard over the body here tonight. Just by chance peculiar things start t'happening.

COLLARD: *(With a shudder.)* Well, I'll just bet our Mama and Daddy are rolling over in their sweet graves right about now at the thought of those North Mississippi dirt farmers bringing a rotting old carcass right into our very home.

LEON: Well, it ain't our home anymore.

COLLARD: No, not since Jamey Foster took it over lock, stock, and barrel with his dusty books and pamphlets and idiotic papers. Imagine, we used to play dominoes right down here on this torn up rug.

LEON: You and me live other places now.

COLLARD: Oh, I know it. It's these bright flowers here giving me the jumping jitters. They make the whole place look morbid and scary. Now look here, I'm practically on the verge of tears.

LEON: Why, Collard. Collard Greens, what's wrong? I'll save ya.

COLLARD: *(Crying.)* Oh, it's nothing. Just I—I really could have been here earlier to help Marshy out with things—I told her I'd be here, but it's my Easter vacation, you know, and I didn't want t'spend the time watching some man die in a hospital. Shit. I already tried doing that with Daddy.

LEON: Well, nobody was for sure he'd die. Nobody guessed it.

COLLARD: *(Wiping her eyes with her red skirt.)* But even after I knew he was already dead, I went on up t'Memphis for a wild party. That's why I didn't make it home yesterday. I'm a shit. A hopeless shit! Oh, but you should see the car G.W. Porter lent me t'get down here in—a beautiful, white, Cadillac convertible.

LEON: No kidding?

COLLARD: Go on and take a look at it. It's parked out there in the street. See it?

LEON: Wow!! A cloud! Why, it looks just like a big, fat white cloud! Can I— Could I go out—

COLLARD: No, you can't! Don't even touch it! I can't afford t'get it all smudged up.

LEON: But I could sit in it, couldn't I? Just sit in it. I mean, when my girl comes—my girl! Oh, brother, I gotta go get those bottles turned on in. *(Racing to the front hall.)*

COLLARD: What girl? What bottles? What're you talking? *(She follows him into the front hall.)*

LEON: My girl, Pixrose, she's arriving at twelve noon. I gotta get those empty bottles turned on in so I can afford t'get her a precious remembrance.

COLLARD: *(In the front hall.)* Jesus, are you back t'gathering up those goddam Coke bottles?! What happened to your paper route?

LEON: Why, Collard Greens, you're not up-to-date. I have me a permanent full-time job now. Them bottles are strictly sideline. Well, I gotta run, Marshael wants me back before they arrive with—well, with the body. See ya!

COLLARD: Yeah.

(Leon exits slamming the door, Katty enters through the upstairs hallway. She carries the cuff links.)

KATTY: Wayne?! Baby, I found your silver— *(Spotting Collard as she comes down the stairs.)* Why, Collard! Honey, when did you arrive? We were so anxious for your safety—why, my, you're—all dressed in red.

COLLARD: It's the only stitch I got, Katty. Rest a' my clothes was filched up in Memphis.

KATTY: Filched? How utterly astounding. How astounding. What were you doing up in Memphis?

COLLARD: *(Uncomfortable.)* Oh, on a visit.

KATTY: Well, I just don't know what you're gonna wear. The people will be arriving from ten this morning on. Do you think you could find something of Marshael's that might be suitable? You see, the only clothes I brought are strictly organized. I mean, I'm wearing this outfit all day today, and then tomorrow I'm wearing my navy blue suit with my navy pumps and my navy dress hat with the white piping.

COLLARD: Forget it Katty, I'll manage.

KATTY: But, of course now, if you feel you could fit into my navy outfit, I suppose you could wear it today. I mean, you're welcome to try it.

COLLARD: *(Going into the parlor.)* It's alright.

KATTY: *(Following her.)* I could wash and iron it out tonight so I could still wear it tomorrow morning for the funeral. That is if Marshael has all the cleaning apparatus that I'll be needing.

COLLARD: Look, Katty, I don't want to wear your navy suit. I don't like navy. It reminds me too much of blue.

KATTY: Well, pardon me, I'm sure. I was just trying to be gracious. *(Pause.)* We're all overwrought. *(Pause.)* Reverend Rigby says sudden violent deaths are the most difficult to deal with. *(Pause.)* So, how's your job going?

COLLARD: Swell, I'm on vacation from it.

KATTY: Oh, right. How stupid of me. How could you be taking school portraits of the children when they're all out for their Easter holidays.

COLLARD: It'd be hard.

KATTY: *(Laughing.)* Oh, it would be. I tell you. I've always envied your job. How you get to travel all over the state—going to all the public and parochial schools—taking pictures of those precious children—thinking up amusing tricks to make them smile—driving in a company car—seeing the world.

COLLARD: Right.

KATTY: Oh, by the by, Mother Foster asked me to see if I could implore you to take some memorial pictures for her of, well, of Jamey. Since you're the professional in the family, we thought you could do them really nicely.

COLLARD: Well, I didn't bring my photographic equipment home with me—

KATTY: Oh, that's alright. We've got a camera right here that's got a flash attachment for the indoors and everything. You could take the shots as soon as the body arrives—before we open up the room for all the mourners.

COLLARD: I'm sorry, Katty. I—I just don't like t'look at dead people. Look, I gotta go change. I'm tired. I gotta lie down.

KATTY: Oh, Collard, wait! Wayne and I are staying in your old room.

(Collard stops.)

KATTY: We moved James Jr. in with his sisters. 'Course the children are all going over to your Aunt Muffin's for tonight. That way they won't have to be here with the wake and all going on. It might could frighten little children.

COLLARD: It might could.

KATTY: Anyway, this friend of Leon's coming in and she's gonna stay up in the children's room. That means you'll be sleeping with Marshael in her room for tonight. I'm sure she can use the company.

COLLARD: Fine.

KATTY: *(Trying to grab hold of Collard's straw bag.)* Here, let me help you with your bag? You look tired.

COLLARD: I got it.

KATTY: No, really—I'll get it—

COLLARD: Katty—

(A few things fall from the bag, among them a small pink sack.)

KATTY: Oh, mercy, here—some things dropped out. Here you go. Just call me butter fingers.

COLLARD: *(About the sack.)* Oh, well, that's for you anyway, if you want it.

KATTY: For me? How thoughtful. *(She opens the sack.)* Why, look, it's a pair of spring booties with sweet, little yellow ribbons.

COLLARD: I saw 'em in a store window. I thought with the baby coming in the winter—maybe it'd be able to wear 'em by next spring.

KATTY: *(Shaken.)* Oh, well, thank you, Collard. But I lost the baby. It's not gonna be coming. I don't know what t'do with the present I—I guess I'll just give it back t'you.

COLLARD: Katty.

KATTY: I gotta go see to Marshael's kids. I gotta go get 'em ready. *(She exits down the upstairs hall.)*

COLLARD: Katty— *(Slinging the booties back in her bag.)* Jesus! *(She takes a deep breath and opens the door to Marshael's room.)* Marshy?
(She is intensely relieved to find no one is there. She takes a moment to notice the rack of marching costumes, sighs, then drops her bag down and sinks onto the bed. There is a knock at the front door. Collard pulls a boot off and slings it against the wall. A second knock is heard. Collard slings off her other boot. After a third knock Wayne enters from the dining room carrying a cloth napkin and a half eaten piece of toast.)

WAYNE: What's wrong around here? Doesn't anyone have the good manners to open a door? Must I do it all? Everything?!
(He opens the door. Pixrose Wilson, seventeen, stands on the other side holding a small torn up suitcase. Pixrose wears red stockings and a long-sleeved dress. She has sunken eyes, long, stringy hair and white, white skin.)

WAYNE: Hello. Oh. Won't you come in.

PIXROSE: Much obliged.

WAYNE: I'm Wayne Foster, the, ah, brother of the deceased.

PIXROSE: I'm Pixrose Wilson from the Sacred Heart Orphanage Asylum.

WAYNE: Yes, well, we're glad to have you, Prissrose.

PIXROSE: It's Pix. Like fix.

WAYNE: Oh, of course, Pix. Here, let me take your luggage for you.

PIXROSE: Thank you, sir. That's very obliging.

WAYNE: Well, why don't you come into the parlor and take a seat.
(They start into the parlor.)

WAYNE: I don't believe Leon was expecting you till about twelve noon.

PIXROSE: Well, I started early and got myself a ride on back of a milk truck. That way I was able to save my bus fare in its entirety.

WAYNE: That's very economical of you. They do say "A penny saved is a penny earned."

PIXROSE: Is this where they're gonna be setting down the body?

WAYNE: Why, yes. I, ah, hope you don't find it too upsetting.

PIXROSE: What's that?

WAYNE: A, well, a body. The presence of a body in the house.

PIXROSE: *(With a slight, slight shrug.)* It won't be going nowhere.

WAYNE: Well, ah, it is regrettable, Pixrose, that your, ah, stay falls at what is a time of grave personal tragedy for our family. I do hope that you'll be able to bear with us through our grief. Won't you have a seat? *(Pause.)* Leon should be returning any minute. Probably very soon. He'll be back. Would you like some breakfast?

PIXROSE: No, sir.

WAYNE: How about some coffee?

PIXROSE: I appreciate it, sir, but I don't believe I'm feeling thirsty.

WAYNE: Hmm. Well, we were all very distressed to hear about the fire over at the orphanage. It appears the damage was quite extensive.

PIXROSE: Yes. It's a terrible crime—arson.

WAYNE: Arson? Was it actually arson?

PIXROSE: Oh, no doubt in my mind.

WAYNE: Arson. How loathsome, inflicting misery and terror on a group of helpless children.

PIXROSE: Well, fortunately, I was able to drop some of the small infants out from the windows and down into the azalea bushes below.

WAYNE: It must have been quite a terrifying episode for you.

PIXROSE: Why, it certainly was. Particularly as I've been afflicted by fire most of my entire life.

WAYNE: How do you mean?

PIXROSE: Well, it started out my mama hating the house we lived in. She used t'say it was trashy. She'd sit around in the dark holding lit matches—always threatening to burn this trashy house down—and one day she did it. She lit up the dining room curtains, loosing flames over the entire house and charcoaling herself to death as a final result.

WAYNE: My God.

PIXROSE: It's a terrible crime, arson. Caused me t'get burns all over the lower parts of my body.

WAYNE: *(Rubbing his forehead.)* That's horrible.

PIXROSE: *(Pulling at her stockings.)* Well, I can cover up the scars by wearing these leg stockings.

WAYNE: I see.

PIXROSE: I just wish my arms hadn't caught on fire in that automobile explosion. I used t'like to look at them. But, of course, my daddy, he died an instantaneous death, and my brother, Franky, suffered permanent brain damage; so I guess I was just lucky t'be flung burning from outta the car. That explosion was also diagnosed as deliberate arson.

WAYNE: I don't feel well. My nose—

PIXROSE: Arson…It's a terrible, terrible crime.

WAYNE: Excuse me. I'm bleeding. I apologize. *(About his nose.)* This damnable business. How disturbing. This is extreme.

(The phone begins ringing, as he runs out of the room bringing the napkin up to his massively bloody nose. Upstairs Collard throws a pillow over her head. As he exits out the dining room.)

WAYNE: I can't get it now—I can't do everything! My nose…it's—It's sickening.

(The phone stops ringing. Pixrose goes to look at the drops of blood that have fallen from Wayne's nose. Marshael appears on the upstairs landing. Pixrose gently presses the drops of blood into the carpet with the toe of her shoe then goes to sit down on the sofa. Marshael goes into her bedroom. Collard turns to see her.)

MARSHAEL: Collard! Coll, you're home! You're here! You're home!

COLLARD: *(Overlapping as she jumps out of bed.)* Marshy! Marshy! Marsh! Are you doing alright? How are you doing?

MARSHAEL: *(Opening her mouth.)* Look—look, here—canker sores! All over my mouth! I'm in pain; I'm not kidding: I'm about to die! Do you see 'em? They're all purple and swollen.

COLLARD: God. Well—well, get yourself some salt water and start t'gargling. That looks awful!

MARSHAEL: Oh, hell, I've been gargling my mouth raw, but just to no avail. Well, so you're looking awfully fine. I see ya came dressed for the occasion.

COLLARD: *(Uncomfortable.)* Yeah, well, I gotta borrow something a' somebody's. *(Getting up to get a cigarette.)* Hey. I'm sorry I'm late. I don't mean t'keep relentlessly letting everyone down. Some unavoidable circumstances.

MARSHAEL: Doesn't matter.

COLLARD: Now that I'm here I'll try to help out. What needs to be done?

MARSHAEL: Nothing.

COLLARD: I could order some flowers or call up a church or something.

MARSHAEL: It's all taken care of.

COLLARD: Well, I'll try not to screw things up. *(About the costumes on the clothes rack.)* God, what the hell's all this?

MARSHAEL: Oh, my costumes. I'm making the marching dresses for all of next year's Prancing' Ponies.

COLLARD: Jesus, they're still using those same awful colors. And look, they've still got the same tacky tassels and vests to go with 'em. Praise God, I always had sense enough to stay out of that fascist organization. How many of these ya gotta make?

MARSHAEL: Oh, this is only the beginning you see right here. I've got about twenty more t'cut out.

COLLARD: Well, you're mighty industrious.

MARSHAEL: You're telling me. *(Kicking a sealed box.)* Look, here, I've even taken to selling household improvement ornaments.

COLLARD: What're they?

MARSHAEL: Oh, you know; things like wall light fixtures and decorative place mats—salt and pepper shakers shaped like crocodiles. A load of junk.

COLLARD: When'd you start doing all this?

MARSHAEL: Been at it a long while. Gotta keep busy. I, ah, can show you the catalogue if you want— *(She gets catalogue.)*

COLLARD: No, that's alright. I don't use place mats.

MARSHAEL: Oh…Sure.

COLLARD: *(Pause.)* So. Well. Gosh. I'm sorry.

MARSHAEL: Yeah. Well. Heck.

COLLARD: He was a real smart man. I know he would have been able to publish his work in time. He was just so awfully young.

MARSHAEL: You think? Nah, he's thirty-five. He'd put on plenty of weight and started losing his hair. He'd even developed this sorta rash all over his knuckles. He'd always get nervous and start t'rubbing it. He wasn't that young. Everyone's saying he died so young. He wasn't really. He'd changed alot.

COLLARD: Well, I didn't mean to imply he was a spring chicken or anything.

MARSHAEL: No. *(Pause.)* Oh, do you hear those birds chirping outside?

COLLARD: Yeah.

MARSHAEL: They're right out my window. They've made a nest down there on the ledge. Go on and look.

(Collard goes to the window.)

MARSHAEL: See it. I saw some eggs in their nest. They were speckled.

COLLARD: Oh…I see it. Yes. Your very own bird's nest.

(Katty comes down the hall and knocks at Marshael's door. She carries a blue satin ribbon.)

KATTY: Marshael, honey?

MARSHAEL: Yes?

KATTY: *(Entering the bedroom.)* Hi. Listen, Mr. Mommett called from the funeral home. He said the hearse is on its way. They should be arriving any minute.

MARSHAEL: Alright.

KATTY: I'll go downstairs to greet them.

MARSHAEL: That's good.

KATTY: Oh, one more thing. Do you mind me twisting Cherry Lee's braids up into a bun on top of her head? She said she likes the way it looks.

MARSHAEL: No, I appreciate it, Katty. It's real nice of you.

KATTY: Good. Then I'll go on and put the bow in it. 'Bye-'bye now.

(Katty exits. Collard starts to pull at her hair.)

COLLARD: *(In a whisper.)* God. Rip out my soul.

MARSHAEL: What?

COLLARD: Tear out my heart with jagged glass.

MARSHAEL: What—

COLLARD: Oooh, I just gave Katty baby booties—for her new baby.

MARSHAEL: Oh, God, no one told you? She lost the baby about three weeks ago. It makes her third miscarriage.

COLLARD: It does?

MARSHAEL: She keeps going out to that fertility clinic, but it never seems to work out for her.

COLLARD: I could die.

MARSHAEL: Oh, it's not your fault. You didn't know. I should have called you.

COLLARD: But you know, the funny thing is, Marshy...I sensed it. For some reason I sensed she'd lost it. But I just gave her the booties anyway.

MARSHAEL: Why would you do that?

COLLARD: I don't know. I'm a black sheep. A black, black soul.

(A car is heard pulling up.)

MARSHAEL: *(Rushing out onto the balcony.)* God, that's probably them. Oh, it is! I don't believe it! Look at that horrible black car. This whole thing's a joke! I could just about eat fire! So this is how he finally returns to the house. It's so humiliating. So cheap.

COLLARD: *(Overlapping.)* What are you saying? Marshy, what's wrong?

MARSHAEL: Oh, he'd abandoned me. Four months ago. Abandonment.

COLLARD: He did? But you never said. You never called me. I wish you'd call me.

MARSHAEL: Well, I just kept thinking if the blood ever dried he'd be back home. Foolish notion. I got over it. Filed for divorce not two weeks ago. Now he pulls this little stunt. Thinks he can leave it all in my lap to sort out and make right. Well, as you can see, I've got mixed emotions about the entire event.

COLLARD: I don't wonder you do.

(Leon enters from the dining room below.)

LEON: Pixrose? Pixrose! I heard you'd arrived! They told me you'd arrived!

PIXROSE: I have, Leon! I'm here! Right here!

MARSHAEL: *(Hanging over the balcony railing.)* Look, there it comes—the box he's in. They're lifting it out of the car.

COLLARD: My God, they are!

LEON: *(Finding her in the parlor.)* Why, you've finally arrived.

PIXROSE: I know—I have.

(They stare at each other.)

COLLARD: I hope they're careful. It looks awfully flimsy.

MARSHAEL: It oughta be. It was the cheapest pinebox they had.

(Lights fade to blackout.)

SCENE II

It is evening. The door to the parlor is closed. Pixrose's suitcase has been removed. A cheap pine lift-lid coffin has been set up inside the room. The upper half of the lid has been removed from the case and left leaning against a nearby wall. Thus part of the corpse is visible. It wears a bright orange and yellow plaid jacket.

Marshael sits on the stairway in the front hall drinking a glass of gin and eating jellybeans that she carries in her dress pocket. After a moment, she throws a jellybean at the umbrella stand. It lands inside. She tries two more jellybeans that miss. She pauses a moment—looks at the closed parlor door and throws a jellybean at it. She goes back to drinking her gin.

Leon enters from the dining room left, carrying a plate and some silverware.

LEON: How ya doing?

MARSHAEL: Fine.

LEON: I brought out your food for you. You didn't touch nothing on your whole plate.

MARSHAEL: I'm not hungry.

LEON: I know, but ya need t'try and eat something. I swear, I haven't seen ya eat or sleep for three days now. Your eyes are blood red.

MARSHAEL: I feel fresh.

LEON: Just try some of your ham. It's awfully good. Annie Hart sent it over. Go on have a bite. Try it. You're gonna like it. *(A pause as he looks at her waiting for her to eat.)*

MARSHAEL: I can't eat with you watching over me. Go on back to the kitchen and finish your supper. Go on now, Leon. I'll eat it.

LEON: Alright. *(He starts to leave, then stops.)* Hey, Marshael?

MARSHAEL: What?

LEON: Do you like Pixrose?

MARSHAEL: She's a real nice girl. Go on now, Leon. I'm gonna eat this ham. *(He exits. She waits a moment then begins messing the food around on her plate. Collard enters from the front door. She has changed into one of Leon's shirts and a pair of rolled up jeans. She has washed her face, but her hair is still a mess.)*

COLLARD: Hi.

MARSHAEL: Hi. Get the kids off okay?

COLLARD: Oh, sure. Aunt Muffin had frozen Coca-Colas waiting for them and she's letting them watch TV till ten o'clock.

MARSHAEL: That's good.

COLLARD: *(Getting a cigarette from the carton that she has brought in with her.)* Oh shit, you know I forgot t'ask Aunt Muffin if I could borrow something of hers for the funeral. Jesus, I'm so unreliable it's almost perfect.

MARSHAEL: Oh, well. Never matters. We'll make do. So did the children really enjoy the ride over in the convertible?

COLLARD: Sure. I'll say. Lucy had a sack full of rocks she kept throwing out at cows as we passed by. She said she hates cows now and she wants to kill them all! I love that child. She reminds me of me.

MARSHAEL: Well, I hope she didn't hurt any of the poor animals.

COLLARD: Oh, no. Missed 'em by a mile. She just had to blow off steam, that's all. Don't blame her for that. Some miserable day, huh?

MARSHAEL: Sure was.

COLLARD: Lordy, Lord.

MARSHAEL: Katty kept going around pretending like we were giving some sort of ghastly tea party. "Here's a coaster and a fresh napkin for your drink. Do you need some more ice cubes? Oh, by the by, the deceased is residing in the parlor."

COLLARD: He's the one in the yellow plaid coat.

MARSHAEL: Agony, agony, agony.

COLLARD: 'Course now, Katty is a Windsor from North East Jackson. That makes her real quality folk.

MARSHAEL: Did you see the way Willie Wayne started tap dancing around when her daddy and uncles arrived to pay their respects?

COLLARD: I expected him to start passing out his business cards at any moment.

MARSHAEL: The thing I love about Willie Wayne is I can just totally despise him.

COLLARD: She's got him monogrammed from top to toe—wearing those three-piece business suits—

MARSHAEL: Don't forget his genuine cow leather briefcase—

COLLARD: He's moving up at the bank—

MARSHAEL: He ain't trash no more!

COLLARD: Speaking of trash—

MARSHAEL: Who?

COLLARD: Mother Foster and her humpbacked brother!

MARSHAEL: Please! If I hear the tale about—

COLLARD: What?

MARSHAEL: How she was just like her brother, Wilbur, had a hump growing in her back—but she prayed to God and He straightened up her back and at the same time made all her dandruff disappear.

COLLARD: Oh, no!

MARSHAEL: Yes!

COLLARD: What are you drinking?

MARSHAEL: Gin.

COLLARD: Where's the bottle?

(Suddenly a loud commotion is heard coming from the kitchen off left. Smoke comes pouring in from the kitchen. As she exits right.)

COLLARD: What the hell is that? What's all this smoke?

(Marshael takes a sip of her drink, Wayne enters in an uproar from upstage center.)

WAYNE: She's a firebug, a menace, a pyromaniac lunatic!

(Katty follows him into the room.)

KATTY: Hush up! Hush up!

WAYNE: I don't wonder she's a third-degree burn victim!

KATTY: Will you please hush up!

MARSHAEL: What happened?

KATTY: Nothing. Little grease fire in the kitchen.

WAYNE: I haven't even finished my dinner. That smoke'll never clear!

KATTY: *(Calling off left.)*
Just bring your plates on in here! We'll eat in here! The dining room table's already set for tomorrow's buffet!

WAYNE: And she stays out of the parlor! There's flammable material in there. She stays away from it!

(Pixrose and Leon enter carrying their supper plates.)

PIXROSE: I'm so sorry. I'm so sorry. I'm so sorry.

LEON: *(Overlapping.)* It's nobody's fault. That rag just burst into flames. Why, it's no more your fault—

(Katty exits to the kitchen. Collard enters with the bottle of gin and two red kitchen chairs.)

PIXROSE: *(Overlapping; to Wayne and Marshael.)* I'll pay for all the damages. Here, you can have my grandmama's garnet brooch. It's a priceless brooch. See— *(While trying to show the brooch, she manages to drop her plate and break it.)* Oh, no! Oh, no!! Now my supper plate is shattered! Look at the pieces! It's broken for life!

MARSHAEL: It's an old plate, Pixrose. For Heaven's sake! It doesn't even matter—

WAYNE: That girl is a menace! A total menace!

PIXROSE: *(Overlapping, as she tries to pick up the pieces.)* OH, oh, oh, oh, oh—

LEON: *(Overlapping.)* Look, here, you're making Pixrose unhappy! You're making her cry!! Don't cry!

PIXROSE: I'm just picking up the pieces. I've never been in people's homes.

COLLARD: Here, sit down, Pixrose. Sit down. Have some gin. Take a swallow.

WAYNE: Will somebody sit her down before she tears this place apart!? What's this I'm stepping on?! Looks like jellybeans! It's jellybeans! Oooh!! What next?! What next?!!

(Wayne scrapes jellybeans off his shoes as Katty enters from the dining room with a tray of supper plates, glasses, etc.)

KATTY: Here, everyone. We'll just finish our supper in here. We'll have a nice quiet supper in here. Oh, was there another accident?! For Heaven's sake!

MARSHAEL: It's alright, Katty—it's nothing at all. Just a stupid plate.

KATTY: Fine then. Just fine. Wayne, why don't you come sit down over here and finish your supper.

(Leon throws the broken pieces into a garbage can with a loud crash. There is a long moment of silence.)

KATTY: I heard a very interesting piece of information this afternoon.

(Leon surreptitiously throws an English pea at Wayne. Wayne looks around.)

KATTY: Mattey Bowen informed me that when you're buying canned stewed tomatoes the cheapest brand is actually preferable to the most expensive.

(Leon throws another pea at Wayne.)

KATTY: You see, those cheaper brands move off the shelves at a much faster rate and, therefore, they're the fresher product.

(Leon throws a third pea.)

WAYNE: Are you throwing food at me?

(Leon throwing a pea at him.)

WAYNE: He's throwing food at me!

(Leon slings a pea.)

WAYNE: Look at this! English peas!

(Leon is now openly throwing peas.)

KATTY: Leon, really!

WAYNE: You'd better stop that! He'd better stop that! I mean it, by God!

COLLARD: For Heavens sake, Willie Wayne, it's just vegetables!

WAYNE: I don't care! I won't have it! This is a serious night! Give me that plate!

KATTY: *(Overlapping.)* Leon, please!

COLLARD: *(Overlapping.)* I don't believe he's having a conniption fit about a few vegetables!

WAYNE: I'll jerk you bald headed, boy! Give me that plate!

LEON: *(Throwing the rest of his food in Wayne's face.)* Here! I'm finished anyway. I cleaned my plate!

WAYNE: *(Taking the plate.)* What a brainless imbecile! I'm surprised they don't send him off to the moon!

LEON: He's always disliked me, ever since I was alive.

WAYNE: It's no surprise to me that you've never held down a job—have to live in a shack—

KATTY: Hush, now, honey—

WAYNE: Goes around picking up trash just for the fun of it. It near t'killed him when they brought out those no deposit bottles—cut his income clean in half. Isn't that so, Leon?

KATTY: Hush up, now, Wayne, darling. Leon has himself a permanent job now. Don't you dear?

COLLARD: Well, now, that's just wonderful.

WAYNE: First I've heard of it.

COLLARD: So, what do you do?

LEON: I work over at the chicken factory. I'm a turkey jerker.

COLLARD: A what?

LEON: A turkey jerker. They send them old turkey carcasses by on this conveyor belt, and I jerk out the turkey innards and put 'em in a sack. Have me an apron I wear and everything.

WAYNE: Classic! That is too classic! Suit the man to the job, that's what I always say! Make a turkey jerker out of a jerky turkey! Classic!

(Leon is hurt.)

COLLARD: Oh, cute, Willie Wayne. You've always been so cute. Remember how cute Willie Wayne used to be when we'd wrap him up in white surgical bandages—make him into a mummy and roll him down the hill? He made the best damn mummy!

PIXROSE: How could he breathe?

WAYNE: For a girl who flunked out of Co-lin College you're awfully smart. 'Course everyone knows Collard is a real live genius. Her and her high IQ.

MARSHAEL:	COLLARD:	KATTY:
Just, please, don't start—	Yes, we all have beautiful histories— don't we now?	Now, if we can't say something nice, let's not say anything at all.

MARSHAEL: Owww!!!

LEON: What?

MARSHAEL: I bit down on that damn sore in the side of my mouth.

KATTY: Anyway, we've got all sorts of pressing issues to debate. For instance, we've got to make a decision about who all is going to ride out to the graveyard tomorrow in the limousine.

COLLARD: What limousine?   LEON: I hired it.

(The phone begins to ring.)

KATTY: I'm sorry to have to bring it up, but Mother Foster is very concerned about it. Will you be a papa sweet potato and get that?

WAYNE: Alright.

LEON: Why does she talk to him in that funny voice?

(Collard shrugs. Wayne answers the phone.)

WAYNE: Hello...Hi, Mama, what's going on?

KATTY: *(Overlapping.)* Now Mother Foster and you and Wayne and I are supposed to all ride out in the limousine, but Mother Foster sincerely desires for James Jr. to ride along with us.

LEON: I'm going to get those Rice Krispie bars out from the kitchen. *(He exits upstage center.)*

KATTY: *(Running on.)* She feels, although he is the youngest of the children, he is the only son and Jamey's namesake.

(Collard gets up and pours some more gin.)

KATTY: Of course, I don't mind where I ride. It makes no never mind to me. But Mother Foster just thought— *(To Wayne.)* Who was that, darling?

WAYNE: Mother Foster.

KATTY: What'd she want?

WAYNE: Ah, well, it seems that, ah, Uncle Wilbur spilt some gravy on his good suit; so, ah, he'll need to get something of Jamey's to wear tomorrow. Mama says they're close to the same size in a lot of ways.

KATTY: Well, I'll pick something out for him. Marshael's been real busy.

WAYNE: She, ah, said she'd prefer the blue pinstriped suit. I don't know which one she means.

MARSHAEL: Well, it's okay. I know which one it is.

WAYNE: *(Uncomfortable.)* And she mentioned something about you picking out a few suits for Uncle Wilbur to take on back up to Tubler with him tomorrow; seeing as, well, as you won't have much future use for them.

MARSHAEL: Whatever she wants. I've no objections.

WAYNE: She's a very practical old bird.

COLLARD: Sure and there's some silverware in the sideboard and coffee in the cupboard while she's at it!

WAYNE: Look, don't make fun of my mama.

COLLARD: Why not?

WAYNE: It's just too easy to poke fun at a poor, old farm woman who had to move down here and sell mattresses just so her two small boys could eat. *(Collard makes like she's crying.)*

WAYNE: Oh, sure, she's just some rednecky hick to you! But what makes y'all so high and mighty? Just 'cause your father was some drunken lawyer. You never learned a damn thing! Why, just look at the way this funeral is being run. I've never stood and witnessed such a tawdry affair in all my born days. *(Leon enters with a plate of Rice Krispie bars.)*

LEON: Who sent the Rice Krispie bars? They sure are good!

WAYNE: Why, look at him!! He's got Jamey wearing a plaid sports jacket, for Christ's sake! It's—it's a mockery to decorum!

LEON: You don't like that jacket? I thought it was cheerful.

WAYNE: A red nose is cheerful! And that coffin in there! It is a disgrace! You may as well of sent off for a mail-order job, or just picked up a couple of orange crates over behind the A&P! What could have possessed you, Marshael? What in the world could have possibly possessed you?

COLLARD: Well, what with all the insurance and savings and trust funds Jamey left her—

WAYNE: I'm not talking about that! Why, the way you've refused to go in that room all day long shows me how ashamed you are of the way Jamey's been laid out on display—looking like some penniless clown in a box.

MARSHAEL: *(Rising to her feet.)* Willie Wayne, I'm getting awfully tired of listening to you talk—I'm getting awfully sick and tired of listening to one white man talk!

KATTY: Reverend Rigby says we all have to learn to face our own finiteness—

MARSHAEL: I mean all this sudden deep show of concern and respect when you never even liked Jamey! You never even cared for him at all. It made you happy watching him struggle and fail!

WAYNE: It never did—

MARSHAEL: I remember clearly how you gloated with joy last Christmas Eve giving us that colored TV set when all we could give y'all was a double book of Life Savers! You never wanted him to succeed! You never wanted him to make good!

WAYNE: I never wanted! Hey, listen, Missy, you're the one who saddled him with those three children and that job he despised. You're the reason he never got his damn Master's degree.

MARSHAEL: Don't you talk to me about his Master's degree! You could have lent him the money. When I came to you—

WAYNE: I wanted to talk to him, not to you. It was a business arrangement! I needed to talk to him!

MARSHAEL: You needed to humiliate him! You needed to make him beg and plead and give up his pride!

WAYNE: What pride? You destroyed any pride he ever had! Why, by the time you were finished with him he was nothing but a broken alcoholic slob!

MARSHAEL: What the hell do you know about anything?

WAYNE: I know about you sneaking his incompleted manuscript off to that New York publisher and them telling him it was superficial and sophomoric and what were some of those other adjectives they used?

COLLARD: How 'bout noxious, putrid, stinking, balless, rotten, lousy junk? And I never even read it!

MARSHAEL: I had to see. I needed to see.

WAYNE: *(Continuing after a moment's pause.)* I don't blame him for walking out on you, after you showed him that letter! I don't blame him for that at all!! It was cruel and vicious and mean!

MARSHAEL: I couldn't let us keep on lying and hoping. It was like slow poison! I never wanted him to leave. I didn't mean for him to leave.

WAYNE: Besides, I wanted him to have that TV set! I didn't care what he gave to us. We enjoyed those Life Savers. We did.

(There is a tense pause.)

KATTY: Look, I—I brought my Sunday school pamphlets with me and my Bible and my Bible dictionary. Whatever you'd like to use.

MARSHAEL: I'm going upstairs. I'm tired. I'm going upstairs. I've gotta polish Lucy's shoes. I'm going upstairs. *(She goes up the stairs and walks into her bedroom.)*

WAYNE: *(After a moment.)* Anyway, he must have left her some money; some insurance.

COLLARD: Not a dog's dime.

PIXROSE: It says on this tag Mrs. R.K. Miller sent the Rice Krispie bars.

LEON: Are they your favorite dessert?

PIXROSE: So far.

LEON: They're mine too.

PIXROSE: It doesn't mean anything. 'Cept we like 'em.

WAYNE: *(About Marshael's plate.)* Look at this; she just messed the food around on her plate. She's thirty-three years old and she's still messing the food around on her plate.

LEON: Pixrose is gonna be a dog bather when she graduates from high school. They've already got her placed at a dog hospital and everything.

KATTY: Well, how nice for you.

WAYNE: He was my brother. Of course you love him. She needs professional help.

LEON: Maybe I'll be moving up to Jackson and become her assistant or something.

PIXROSE: It's not that easy a job.

LEON: But I could do it. I could! I know I could!

(Pixrose gets up to leave the room.)

LEON: Where are you going?

PIXROSE: To watch the moon.

(Leon rises to go with her.)

PIXROSE: By myself.

(Leon stops in his tracks, as Pixrose turns and leaves out the door.)

LEON: I've loved her ever since we first met at Monkey Island.

KATTY: *(To Leon, who is on his way out.)* Where are you going?

LEON: To watch her watch the moon. *(He exits.)*

WAYNE: It's funny how, even after she showed him that rejection letter, he never stopped belittling my job at the bank.

KATTY: *(After a moment of silence.)* My. What a night. *(Pause.)* Well, the silences are alright too. Here, let me just clear these plates. *(She exits upstage center with some dishes.)*

WAYNE: *(About the gin.)* Do you mind?

COLLARD: Never.

WAYNE: *(Pouring himself a glass.)* You know, even without combing your hair, you're still very pretty.

(Collard looks at him. There is a knock at the front door.)

WAYNE: Who do you think—

COLLARD: I don't know.

(Wayne opens the door for Brocker Slade. Brocker Slade, fifty-three, enters holding a beat-up hat in his hands and wearing a ten-year-old brown suit that he seems to be breaking out of. He carries two wooden spoons in his coat pocket. Brocker is big, tired, and worn-out. Yet sometimes when he smiles, he will look like a confused child.)

WAYNE: Yes?

BROCKER: 'Evening, I'm Brocker Slade. I hear you're having a wake.

WAYNE: Oh, yes, well, please do come in. I'm Wayne Foster, the younger brother of the deceased. And, ah, this is Collard Darnell. She's the sister to the widow.

BROCKER: Mighty pleased to make your acquaintance.

COLLARD: *(Immediately attracted.)* Likewise, I'm certain.

WAYNE: Perhaps you'd, ah, like to pay your respects?

BROCKER: Oh…yeah.

COLLARD: Here, I'll show Mr. Slade to the parlor. I've yet to pay my own respects.

WAYNE: Why don't you then—

COLLARD: *(Taking her ham sandwich and drink with her.)* This way, Mr. Slade.

BROCKER: Brocker's fine.

COLLARD: Brocker then.

(They go into the parlor.)

COLLARD: *(Trying to avoid looking at the coffin.)* He's over there.

BROCKER: I see.

(Collard moves away from the coffin and eats a bite of her sandwich. In the hallway Wayne's drinking gin. Upstairs Marshael spins the world globe around. She stops it with her finger.)

BROCKER: So you're Marshael's sister?

COLLARD: Right. I don't live in this part of the state any longer. Generally, I just get back home for deaths; and Christmas occasionally.

BROCKER: Oh.

COLLARD: I don't like to affiliate myself with the rest of this menagerie. *(Upstairs Marshael looks at her violin. Katty enters the front hall from upstage center.)*

KATTY: *(As she stacks the dishes onto a tray.)* Where's Collard?

WAYNE: In the parlor.

KATTY: Oh, really? Well, at least she finally decided to go in!

WAYNE: Ah well, some visitor's in there with her—a Mr. Slade.

KATTY: No! Not that horrible man whose pigs all exploded.

WAYNE: *(Totally in the dark.)* I don't know.

KATTY: That old man who painted Marshael's kitchen chairs red. Terrible man—he told little Lucy she was an animal. She cried all day because of it.

WAYNE: *(In an annoyed whisper.)* Talk a little louder, why don't you?

KATTY: I'm sorry—but he's a barbarian, an absolute barbarian. *(She exits upstage center with the tray.)*

WAYNE: *(Whispering after her.)* Twat.

BROCKER: *(Staring at the corpse.)* Wonder why she married him? I do. I often wonder why.

COLLARD: Did you know him?

BROCKER: Met him when I moved here 'bout two years ago. Saw him off and on; here and there.

COLLARD: What did you think of him?

BROCKER: He appeared to me to be a miserable, bewildered man.

COLLARD: I never liked him. He had a genius IQ and all the promise in the world, but he was a lazy coward with no guts and never finished a thing he'd start. He lied to himself and to everyone else.

BROCKER: Still he had that woman.

COLLARD: Oh, he deluged her with gifts and things when they were young. Bought her barbecued chicken every Saturday night. And he could tell stories and paint up dreams real pretty. She was sincerely mad for him. *(Setting her drink down.)* Oh, hell, I may as well have one last look at the son of a bitch. *(She moves up to the coffin carrying her ham sandwich. Totally amazed.)* God. When did he get so fat? He's downright fat.

BROCKER: Beats the hell out of me.

COLLARD: And his glasses. They've got him wearing his glasses. Oh— *(A piece of her ham falls onto the corpse.)*

BROCKER: Watch out here. *(Picking up the ham slowly, and offering it to her.)* You dropped some ham.

COLLARD: I don't want it.

BROCKER: *(After a moment of indecision.)* Ah, hell.

(He eats it. Katty enters upstage center with a dishrag.)

KATTY: Wasn't it sweet of Uncle Ben and Uncle Walter to make the trip up from Jackson?

WAYNE: Yeah.

KATTY: *(Wiping up crumbs.)* Uncle Ben likes you a lot. He said you were very poised. His opinion means a lot at the bank. Better move that glass, the napkin's soaked through and through.

WAYNE: Stop acting like my mother.

KATTY: What?

WAYNE: You remind me of my mother.

KATTY: *(Hurt.)* Oh. *(She goes back to cleaning.)*

COLLARD: Well, shit.

BROCKER: Huh?

COLLARD: If this fool can get through dying, anyone should be able to do it. I mean, look, here—he's doing it right. No questions asked. Shit, so what's the big deal?

BROCKER: I'd like t'know.

(Leon racing into the front hall.)

LEON: Hi! Where's Brocker? Is he here? I saw his dog out back—

WAYNE: He's in the parlor.

LEON: Great! I'll go get Marshy— *(He starts up the stairs.)*

BROCKER: Think we've been in here long enough?

COLLARD: Sure. *(She goes to get her glass.)*

KATTY: *(Quietly to Wayne.)* If we only could have a child. You'd see I had so much to give.

LEON: *(Knocking at Marshael's bedroom door.)* Marshy. Hey, Marshael—

MARSHAEL: *(Still holding her violin.)* Yeah?

LEON: *(Opening her door.)* Come on downstairs. There's someone here to see you.

MARSHAEL: Leon, I'm done in here—

LEON: Please, I know you'll be glad to see him. It'll ease your mind.

MARSHAEL: Who is it?

(Downstairs, Collard and Brocker move into the front hall.)

LEON: You'll see; come on; please—

MARSHAEL: *(Moving to the upstairs landing.)* It better not be— *(Spotting Brocker.)* Brocker Slade.

BROCKER: Hi M. It's good to see you.

MARSHAEL: Well, I guess, you don't mind coming here tracking mud all over my feelings.

LEON: What's wrong?

BROCKER: Look, I came here for the wake. I hope to be of some meager help.

MARSHAEL: Help?

KATTY: She's upset 'cause he let her children eat Gravy Train. He told little Lucy she was an animal.

BROCKER: For God's sake, lady, she is an animal! The kid's a mammal!

KATTY: See! He's crazy!

MARSHAEL: *(Coming down the stairs.)* Look, Brocker, there is no reason to concern yourself with my vulgar travail; so just take that flea-bitten mongrel of yours and get off a' my place.

BROCKER: Hey, now, M. I'm telling ya I'm sorry about that night but frankly—

MARSHAEL: Go home, Brocker! I'm telling you to go home!

BROCKER: No ma'am, I'm staying here tonight. I'll sleep in a ditch; but I'm not leaving here, not till the last dog is dead.

(Pixrose enters upstage center with a pie.)

PIXROSE: Marshael, a lady just brought over this pie for you. She says it's blueberry.

MARSHAEL: What lady?

PIXROSE: A yellow-haired lady.

MARSHAEL: *(Standing on the middle of the stairs.)* Give me that pie.

WAYNE: Don't give her the pie.

MARSHAEL: It's my pie. Bring it here.

KATTY: Look, I'll just take the pie—

MARSHAEL: Don't you dare take that pie!

WAYNE: Won't you please just—let me take the pie.

MARSHAEL: Give me that Godamn blueberry pie!!

(Pixrose takes the pie to Marshael.)

WAYNE: Go on and give her the pie.

MARSHAEL: *(Tearing off the card.)* "With deepest love and condolence, Esmerelda Rowland." She sent me one of her pies.

COLLARD: Who's Esmerelda Rowland?

WAYNE: Ssshush up.

MARSHAEL: *(Walking up and down the stairs.)* She actually went and sent me one of her pies. 'Course they must be pretty good. Jamey got awfully fat eating them. Why, he must of put on twenty-five pounds in just four months they were living together.

COLLARD: Jamey was living with another woman?

MARSHAEL: You didn't know? Why, it's been noised all over Madison County—Jamey Foster and his twenty-two-year-old, twice divorced, yellow-haired, sweet shop baker!

COLLARD: I never heard.

MARSHAEL: *(Still pacing.)* Oh, sure, she was right out there in the field with him on the fatal night of his demise. So, who wants some pie? Who wants a big piece of blueberry pie? It's Jamey's favorite kind! It oughta be really good!

WAYNE: Come on, now, put the pie down.

MARSHAEL: *(Running to the top of the staircase.)* You'd better eat some. You'd better eat it all! I mean it now—

WAYNE: Come on, now, and give it to me—Marshael, just calm down and hand me that pie.	KATTY: Your nervous system's just all shocked—

MARSHAEL: *(Screaming as she waves the pie back and forth and over her head.)* Ooooooh!! Oooooooohhh!!

PIXROSE: *(Overlapping.)* She's gonna smash it.	KATTY: It's all so trying. Why, Reverend Rigby always says—
COLLARD: *(Overlapping the scream.)* No, she's not—	BROCKER: *(Overlapping.)* Oh, Lord, she's hot as a firecracker now!

MARSHAEL: *(Throwing the pie from the upstairs landing down to the floor below.)* You shitty pie!!

COLLARD: She did it!	WAYNE: All over the rug!
PIXROSE: She sure did!	KATTY: Look at that mess!

MARSHAEL: *(Totally still.)* I don't know how I'm gonna get through this night.

LEON: I never seen her scream out like that.

MARSHAEL: I can't imagine ever seeing the morning.

(The lights fade to blackout.)

END OF ACT I

ACT II
SCENE I

The setting is the same. The blueberry pie has been cleaned up. Marshael and Pixrose are upstairs in the bedroom. Marshael is working on one of the drill team costumes that is on the dress dummy. She wears the same black dress that she wore throughout Act I. Pixrose is dressed in a long cotton night-gown. She is polishing a small black patent leather shoe. Downstairs, Wayne is sitting at the card table that has been cleared. He is studying a camera and its flash attachment. He is also drinking gin. Leon is pacing back and forth in the front hall. From time to time he glances into the parlor to look at the casket that has now been closed.

LEON: *(After several moments of pacing.)* We just stand here? Is that all there is to it? This is it? This is a wake?

WAYNE: That's right.

LEON: Well, then I gotta go get me a drumstick! *(He exits upstage right center.)*

PIXROSE: Marshael, I've finished the first coat on Lucy's shoe. I'm gonna set it down here by Jamey Jr.'s and do the other one while it dries. *(She puts the shoe down on a sheet of newspaper and starts on the second one.)*

MARSHAEL: You're a big help. I appreciate it.

(The phone rings. Marshael starts.)

MARSHAEL: God, I hate it when that phone rings. It scares me. *(She picks up the phone.)* Hello?…Well, how're you doing? How're your sisters?…Well, that's good…What?…Why, sure I remember the cut-out bunny you made at school—It's green, right?…Well, I don't know, Jamey, Jr., maybe you could—just give it to someone else…Sure…No, Daddy wouldn't mind…No, honey, he wouldn't mind a bit. I'm sure…Well, that's a good idea. I know Uncle Leon would just love it. It's an awfully fine bunny…Alright then, you sleep tight and don't let the bedbugs bite. I love you, boy. 'Bye-'bye. *(She puts down the phone.)* My little boy's calling. He's only six. Gee. Thank God he's not crying or anything. That's the worst thing for me, watching my children cry.

PIXROSE: That's exactly how I feel about my brother, Franky. I can't bear t'watch him cry.

MARSHAEL: Oh, I didn't know you had a brother.

PIXROSE: Well, he's out at Ellisville.

MARSHAEL: Oh. I'm sorry.

PIXROSE: He does alright. They've got him wearing this football helmet all day and all night just in case he starts banging his head into walls. Seems he's got some sorta brain damage.

MARSHAEL: Do you see him much?

PIXROSE: Once a year 'bout Christmas time I'll visit him and take him his gift—soap on a rope. He loves the soap on a rope to wear in the shower. But other than my brother, Franky, I have nobody.

MARSHAEL: Well…how do you feel about Leon?

PIXROSE: I don't know. He's probably just in love with love, and he's something of a misfit. Still we did kiss each other at Monkey Island. No, it will never, never be.

MARSHAEL: Why do you say that?

PIXROSE: *(Putting the shoe down to dry.)* I'd just rather keep him like a jewel in my mind. That way I will always have him. *(Picking up the violin.)* My, this is a fine looking instrument. Do you play it?

MARSHAEL: Sort of. Jamey always left the house when I started to play it though. He said it sounded screechy.

(Pixrose picks up the bow and plays a weird array of notes.)

PIXROSE: Sounds lovely t'me.

(Katty enters into the upstairs hall. She is wearing a pink robe and fluffy slippers. She leans over the banister and whispers down to Wayne.)

KATTY: Psst, Papa Sweet Potato? Honey Pie? I've laid out all your night clothes for you, if you decide you want to retire.

WAYNE: *(Looking up at her.)* Why do you talk to me in that funny voice?

KATTY: *(Stung.)* I don't know. I just do. Excuse me, I've got to go and floss my teeth.

WAYNE: You sure do keep yourself clean.

(Katty hears this last jab as she exits down the hallway. Wayne goes back to drinking his gin.)

MARSHAEL: *(After staring at the closet.)* Oh, well…Lord. I'd better go on and get those suits out for Uncle Wilbur while I'm thinking about it, leastwise I'll never do it. *(She opens closet and gets his suits out.)* There. Here it is. His blue pinstriped suit. I liked it best, and here I am holding it, but somehow I don't feel a tear in this world. It's like a hole's been shot through me, and all my insides have been blown out somewhere else.

PIXROSE: Well, I know from my own experience that it ain't ever gonna be worth it feeling all that love for somebody.

MARSHAEL: *(She gets a brush and starts brushing the suit.)* Feeling love for somebody? I just wish I knew what I felt for Jamey. First one thing, I guess, and then another, I sure wish I knew. It haunts me not to know.

PIXROSE: Well…was he nice?

MARSHAEL: *(Continues to brush suit.)* He could be, I suppose…He did things different. I remember one time he brought this huge, ugly, fat boy home with him about supper time. Jamey whispered that he'd found the fat boy crying in the road 'cause his only pet bird had flown away and could I please fix blueberry muffins for dessert. He kissed my fingers when I said I would. *(Cross to hall door—hang up suit.)* He had dreams though. And it's hard being involved with a man whose dreams don't get fulfilled.

PIXROSE: What dreams did he have?

MARSHAEL: Oh, he wanted to be a great worldwide historian. He used to have all sorts of startling revolutionary ideas about the development of mankind that he kept trying to write into books and theories.

PIXROSE: Well, he must a' been a real smart man.

MARSHAEL: Oh, he was. And fun too. Why, the way he laughed was so big and so strong—like the world was going to crack open and there'd be beautiful treasures all inside. We sometimes played this game where we'd spin this globe around. *(Spin.)* Saying like, "We're gonna go…there!" *(She yells out the name of the country her finger actually lands on.)* Or, "We're taking a banana boat *(Spin.)* to…here!" *(She looks down and reads the name.)* Then we'd imagine how it would be when we arrived. *(Sits on chest.)* It was a fun game, but we stopped playing after he had to take that awful job in real estate. *(She spins the globe around and around. She stops the globe with her finger and says the name of the country it lands on.)* I was afraid to ask him for anything. I never wanted him to know how scared I was. I just kept on telling him how, until all his theories were finished and started selling, that real estate was fine with me.

PIXROSE: And real estate's when you sell other people's homes for 'em?

MARSHAEL: Right. Except he didn't sell much of anything. I wanted so badly for things to be right for us. My parents fought all the time when I was little. Yelling and crying in the night. I wanted a different kind of life; but it didn't work out.

PIXROSE: He started yelling at you?

MARSHAEL: Oh, all the time. Stupid things like, "This mayonnaise jar is too damn small! Don't you know you save more money with the large economy size!" Slam! Break the jar! It was ridiculous.

PIXROSE: You musta cried a lot.

MARSHAEL: Oh, yeah. It seemed the harder I tried the less he cared. The more he blamed me and the children for his dreams not coming true, I thought maybe it would help, if we just knew one way or the other about his work. That's why I sent it off to the publisher. When he found out, he was gone. Went off to live with that fat yellow-haired woman. And now he's really gone. He's out of the whole deal; and I don't even know what we felt for each other. Stupid. Lord. My mouth aches.

(Collard runs into the outside area right, carrying two bottles of gin.)

COLLARD: *(Calling off right.)* Hey! Hey, last one here's a rotten egg! You're a rotten egg, Brocker! A goddamn rotten egg! Marshy! Marshy!

MARSHAEL: *(Going out onto the balcony.)* What? Don't shout.

COLLARD: Look! We got it! We got a load of gin! Here, I'll throw ya up a bottle.

MARSHAEL: No!

COLLARD: *(Swinging the bottles around and around in a circle.)* You ready?! Get ready!!

MARSHAEL: Stop! Don't be stupid, Collard! It's gonna break!!

COLLARD: Right! *(She stops swinging the bottles.)* Don't be stupid. That's kind of hard for me, huh? What with my low IQ—my bovine mind!

MARSHAEL: Oh, please! Look, just come on up here.

COLLARD: Why? You don't need things from me. You handle it all yourself.

MARSHAEL: Oh, please, I can't tonight. My mouth hurts.

COLLARD: That's right! Don't talk to me! Just run off carrying the world on your lonely shoulders.

MARSHAEL: Look, Collard, don't you talk to me about running off! You're the one who ran off and left me to keep care of Mama the six months she was sick, and then later, when Daddy was dying, you were here just long enough to upset everyone, then you ran off again!

COLLARD: He didn't wanna see me! He didn't need my help and neither did you! Nobody asked me to stay, 'cause I'm just too stupid! Just too damn stupid to live!

MARSHAEL: Shut up saying you're stupid! I'm so sick of that excuse I could retch up blood! Ooh!!! *(She goes back inside.)*

PIXROSE: What's wrong with Collard?

MARSHAEL: She thinks she's stupid. She took some idiotic test twenty years ago that said she was dumb, and she believed them; so I guess she must be dumb. I don't know. My eyes ache. I'm gonna go put a cold rag over them.

(She exits into the bathroom. Brocker enters, downstage right carrying a bottle of whiskey. He is shaken.)

BROCKER: Where the hell were you going to, a fire?

COLLARD: I only wish.

BROCKER: You hit something in the road, you know?

COLLARD: When?

BROCKER: That's what that large thud was that bumped us five feet out of our bucket seats.

COLLARD: It was probably just some old armadillo or coon crossing the road.

BROCKER: Well, there's blood and fur all stuck to your front fender!

COLLARD: It's okay; I never liked having solid colored cars.

BROCKER: Well, you don't.

COLLARD: Have a drink, Brocker. Calm yourself down. What's the matter with you? Don't you like plowing up the fields, raising some hell, dancing with glee?

BROCKER: Look, love, I don't need crazy. I've had crazy. I'm an old man.

COLLARD: You look mighty appealing to me. *(Moving in on him.)* I don't think much of men, ya understand, I just can't live without 'em.

BROCKER: Honey…

COLLARD: Look, I just want somebody who's fun and crazy and mean as me.

BROCKER: Well, I'm none of those.

COLLARD: What's the matter, Brocker, honey…you gonna leave me forever unravished?

BROCKER: Look, it's just I—I like Marshael. I mean, God help my feeble soul, but—I do.

COLLARD: Oh, Marshael. Right, Marshael. Well, that's alright then. 'Course she's nothing like me. She doesn't caress death and danger with open legs. *(She takes a long, slow slug of gin.)*

BROCKER: *(Not accusing.)* Are you really this tough?

COLLARD: No, darling, I'm pretending to be tough. But if you pretend really hard, it amounts to about the same thing. Here, now, I'll call your lady love out for you. Marshael! Hey! Come on out here! An old troll wants to woo you!

(Pixrose goes out on the balcony as Collard exits.)

PIXROSE: What is it? Marshael's putting water on her eyes.

BROCKER: It's not a thing. Sorry for the disturbance. Go back to sleep.

PIXROSE: Hey, listen, you need to dip that skinny black dog of yours. He's practically more flea than dog.

BROCKER: I don't own that old junkyard dog. It's not my dog. I never feed it. I got no idea how it even stays alive—chews on the same damn piece of wood all winter long. It's not my dog. I got no use for it!

(Marshael comes out of the bathroom with a washcloth.)

MARSHAEL: *(Moving out to the balcony.)* Who's that? Is that Brocker? Is that Brocker Slade?

PIXROSE: *(Moving out of the way.)* It is.

MARSHAEL: You lily-livered man! When I needed you where were you? I'm sick of betrayal! Sick!

BROCKER: Look, I'm sorry, M. I'm sorry about last Tuesday night, but I'm a fifty-three-year old jackass, and I hadn't even kissed a woman in close on to two years—

MARSHAEL: You're no good, Brocker! No damn good! I don't even like laying my eyes on you.

BROCKER: God, M., honey, you're breaking my heart. I'm about ready to run jump into the Big Black River.

MARSHAEL: Well, don't forget to hang a heavy stone around your scrawny old neck.

BROCKER: Lordy, lord, is there no redemption in your heart?

MARSHAEL: It's in mighty short supply.

BROCKER: What do you want from me? What?

MARSHAEL: *(It comes to her.)* Triumph! It's a feeling I'm sadly lacking. Give me some triumph: some glory: some exaltation!

BROCKER: So what do you want me to do? Climb up the side of the house and carry you up to the moon on a cloud?!

MARSHAEL: Yes! Try it! At least you can try it!

BROCKER: I'd break my scrawny old neck!

MARSHAEL: Then why don't you use some ingenuity!

BROCKER: Ingenuity?! Hell! Here goes— *(He makes a feeble attempt to climb up the side of the house and falls back down to the ground.)*

MARSHAEL: You call this ingenuity?!

PIXROSE: He might make it, he might.

MARSHAEL: No, he won't, he'll never—ow!

BROCKER: What's wrong?

MARSHAEL: My mouth! Those sores!

BROCKER: Christ! Oh, my back!

MARSHAEL: You stupid old fool! Oh, I'm through with it! Through with it all! *(Marshael leaves the balcony and slams into the bathroom. Pixrose looks out on the ledge as Brocker gathers himself together.)*

PIXROSE: Hey, there's a bird's nest out here. It has little blue speckled eggs in it waiting to be born.

BROCKER: I'm falling on my butt for a woman with sores in her mouth. Hell, I think I'm gonna go 'round and kick that stupid dog till he dies!

(Brocker hobbles off as Collard enters the front door. The lights in the front hall are dim. Collard is brooding: her shoulders are slumped. She carries a bottle of gin under each arm.)

COLLARD: *(To Wayne.)* Hello.

WAYNE: Hey, Collard. Say, could you come take a look at this camera? Have I got this on right?

(She walks over to the table. He hands her the camera.)

COLLARD: Hmm. Sure, it's right. It's perfect. Now all you do is look through here and click this button and you'll have a pretty picture.

WAYNE: Thanks.

COLLARD: *(Setting a bottle of gin down on his table.)* Here's your gin.

WAYNE: Thanks, Charlotte.

COLLARD: Huh?

WAYNE: Charlotte. That's your name isn't it? I like it better than Collard. Charlotte. *(As he lifts her chin with his fingers.)* It suits a certain side of you. Charlotte.

COLLARD: What are you doing?

WAYNE: Huh?

COLLARD: Lifting my chin up like that—you're making me feel like some sort of goddamn horse—I'm not a horse!

WAYNE: *(As he backs her against the red chair.)* You are a horse! A goddamn horse! Come here—come here—

COLLARD: *(Overlapping.)* Oh, so you do like your women dirty?

WAYNE: *(Grabbing her.)* I like you—I like you—Charlotte! Oh, Charlotte!!

(They manage to knock a chair over as Katty appears on the upstairs landing. She is winding a clock.)

KATTY: *(Coming down the stairs.)* What's this? Wayne? What's going on here?! Excuse me, please, but what's going on?!

(Leon enters upstage right center with a plate of chicken.)

LEON: You know, that green dish detergent really does feel softer on your hands…What's going on?

COLLARD: *(After a tense moment.)* Oh, Willie Wayne was just giving me an extremely good chance at nothing.

KATTY: It is becoming more and more painfully apparent that you have no affection or regard for me, whatsoever!

WAYNE: Go on up to our room, Katty. We'll talk up there.

KATTY: Just because my daddy gave you a decent job there's no reason to resent me!

(Marshael comes out of the bathroom upstairs.)

MARSHAEL: Who's fighting?

(Pixrose shrugs her shoulders. Marshael goes and opens the bedroom door.)

WAYNE: We'll discuss it all in our room—

KATTY: Just because I lose those babies is no reason to treat me viciously—no reason at all! You know I can't help it!

WAYNE: You're crazy now, Katty—totally crazy!

KATTY: And I'm nothing like that redneck mother of yours! I wouldn't be caught dead wearing those broad, bright-colored stripes! Especially if I was as fat as she is!!

WAYNE: Go to our room, Katty! Now!

KATTY: I won't! I won't! I won't! *(Katty starts up stairs and rushes past Marshael into the bedroom.)*

MARSHAEL: Katty— *(Marshael follows her into the bedroom.)*

KATTY: *(Runs to bathroom.)* She should be wearing dark clothes with vertical stripes!! *(Katty slams the bathroom door shut and locks it. As she continues yelling she bangs her fists on the door.)* Everyone knows that!! Everyone!!!! Everyone but that stupid, fat, old redneck!

(Brocker opens the front door—shuts it—looks around at everyone.)

BROCKER: *(Gesturing with his whiskey bottle.)* What'd I miss?

(The lights fade to blackout.)

SCENE II

The lights go up on the bedroom. Three large Easter baskets are out around the room. Most of the candy from these baskets has been devoured. Pixrose is pulling through the green grass in one of the baskets looking for more candy. Marshael is fooling with her violin and drinking gin. She still wears the black dress but has taken off her shoes and stockings. Collard is pounding on the bathroom door.

PIXROSE: Look, here's another marshmallow chicken—who wants it?

MARSHAEL: I'll take it!

COLLARD: How long you think she's gonna stay in there.? All night or what? Katty?! Hey, Katty!

KATTY'S VOICE: *(She speaks from inside the bathroom.)* Look, please, I'll be out soon. Really.

COLLARD: When? You've been in there over an hour and a half already. Now, when?

KATTY'S VOICE: Soon. I—I just can't come out now.

COLLARD: For Christ's sake, why not?

KATTY'S VOICE: I don't know. I'm too ashamed. I can't forget it. My life has ended. I can't forget it.

COLLARD: *(Turning back to Marshael and Pixrose.)* So what am I supposed to do, go down to East Peace Street and throw myself in front of cars or what?! Oh, shit! I'm just leaving then. Going back up the Natchez Trace and stop stirring up trouble for everyone here. What'd I do with G.W.'s boots? Where the hell are those stupid boots?

MARSHAEL: Oh, damn it, Collard.

PIXROSE: Oh, Collard, wait. Here, wait. Hey, Katty? Katty? This is me, Pixrose Wilson. And, well, I'm really sorry you're feeling so badly upset. But you just need to, ah—come on out a' the bathroom.

KATTY'S VOICE: I just can't face it. I can't. Why, none of y'all have suffered the cruel humiliation I have. None of y'all.

PIXROSE: Oh, sure. We've all had cruel, sad, unbearable things happen to us in this life.

COLLARD: No kidding.

PIXROSE: Look, here's one just happened recently to me. It's when Laurie Crussy said she would set the Sacred Heart Orphanage Asylum on fire, if I wouldn't give to her my grandmama's garnet brooch which is my only cherished possession.

COLLARD: What?

MARSHAEL: Really?

PIXROSE: That's right and she did it too. Burned down two entire wings 'cause she knows how fiercely and dreadfully afraid I am of fires.

COLLARD: My God! That's awful! Did you tell someone? Did you report that little monster?

PIXROSE: Well, 'course I did, but old Sister Daniel said I told lies out of jealousy over Laurie's pink, satin skin. Now I know my skin is ugly, but it wasn't a lie.

(Moment of stunned silence.)

PIXROSE: So Collard? What about you? Do you have one?

COLLARD: Yeah. Well...the one that keeps coming to my mind is about Daddy.

KATTY'S VOICE: What? I can't hear it?

COLLARD: *(Moving to the bathroom door.)* Daddy—our daddy—how I used to be his favorite. We'd always talk and discuss life and politics. He wanted me to come join his firm—be a lawyer with him. Then when I was twelve we took these stupid IQ tests. Mine, well, mine said I was below average; ninety-two or something.

KATTY'S VOICE: But Collard, honey, those tests aren't accurate. You should have taken it again.

COLLARD: I did. Twice more! It got lower each time! I ended up with an eighty-three. That's twenty-one points lower than Leon, for Christ's sake! Twenty-one points below Leon!! Oh, God! I was nothing in his eyes from then on! Just dumb and stupid and nothing! So, Katty, you coming out now?

KATTY'S VOICE: I don't know. I'm starting to feel better. Oh, I don't know.

MARSHAEL: Hey, Katty—I went to see Jamey Tuesday afternoon over at the hospital and Esmeralda was there. She was all dressed up in a flowered dress and a flowered hat. I didn't look very good; so I thought, "Well, I'll just say, Hello, and leave." But Jamey, he kept talking to me and making conversation and all the time he was holding Esmeralda's hand, or putting his arm around her waist to give it a squeeze. He said, "Hey, Marshael, why don't you try one of those delicious caramel pecan balls Essey brought? You could stand some weight on those saggy bones." It fiercely hurt me and my pride—like I wasn't even a woman.

KATTY: *(Coming out of the bathroom.)* Oh, Marshael, honey, you are a woman. A beautiful woman. Don't let anyone tell you different from that.

MARSHAEL: Oh, Katty. Katty. *(Then realizing.)* Katty!! You're out of the bathroom!!

COLLARD: Praise God! You're out!

PIXROSE: Bravo!

(Pixrose showers Katty with a handful of eggs in silver foil, as the lights go down in the bedroom and come up in the front hall below. Wayne is sitting on the stairs drinking and fooling with the camera. Brocker is sitting at the card table drinking the last of his whiskey. His sleeves are rolled up. You can see his tattoos. Leon is sitting, looking at a deck of dirty cards.)

LEON: Wow! Great! Great! Hey, look, Willie Wayne! Brocker's got a deck of playing cards with pictures of necked women on 'em! Well, well, some of 'em are wearing like aprons or tropical flowers, or looks like garden hoses—just take a look! They're spectacular!

WAYNE: Then *you* keep them. I'm gonna go and get those photographs taken for Mama. *(He goes into the living room.)*

LEON: Think he's still upset about his wife?

BROCKER: Who knows? He left his bottle though. I'll grab it while he's gone. *(He jumps up to get the bottle. The bones in his body crackle.)*

LEON: Gosh! Will you listen to all them bones cracking away under your skin!

BROCKER: Well, Christ. I'm an old man. What the hell do you expect?

LEON: Shoot. Yeah. So what's it like being old?

BROCKER: Pure D-shit. That's what. The highs are never as high. The lows get lower. Hangovers'll last ya ten days. Your back aches; your butt hurts; you can't smell spring...Hey, how 'bout a game of Bid Whist?! *(Wayne returns.)*

WAYNE: I'll do it later. I'll get to it later, that's all. It's too dark in there now. Where's my gin?

BROCKER: *(Brocker holds up the bottle.)* Here.

WAYNE: Oh. Well, go ahead. Have a drink. Sure, help yourself. So, Mr. Slade, what's all this about pigs? I hear you, ah, raise pigs.

BROCKER: *(As he shuffles the cards and proceeds to deal out four hands.)* Right. That's right. I came down here for that distinct purpose. Came down here with a wild-haired, big-thighed woman—she's the one who supposedly knew all about this hog raising business. I was just backing her with my cash and affection, but, by the by, she runs off and leaves me holding the fuckin' bag. Seems we had some sort of run-in over a dog I'd kicked. She leaves me out in that old shack saddled with twenty-seven hogs. Only three of which remain, a good fifteen of 'em having exploded, the other nine got loose or died mysteriously. Hey, do you play Bid Whist?

WAYNE: Poorly.

BROCKER: Have a seat. Now we've got this one extra hand to deal with...hell, I'll just bid 'em both. No problem. *(They start picking their cards up.)*

WAYNE: So what about these hogs exploding? Was it a munitions accident, or what?

BROCKER: Hell no. They just got bigger and fatter, and, of course, they were eating like pigs, and one day their bellies would be dragging along the ground, and the next day their skin would be all stretched out and they'd explode and die.

WAYNE: Jesus. Amazing. This man's amazing.

BROCKER: Well, before it was all over I discovered a good many of 'em had these deformed damn butt holes and that was the major cause of it all. I mean, it certainly was the crux of it. Hey, Leon! Your bid, boy! Your bid! *(The lights black out downstairs and go up on the women in the bedroom.)*

KATTY: *(Pulling at her hair with glee.)* Oh, it's so awful! It's too horrible! You won't think I'm sweet anymore!

COLLARD: We don't care! We don't care!

PIXROSE: No, we don't care! Tell us!

KATTY: Oh, alright. See, I was always rich, you know, and people always hated me for it. And one Easter Sunday I was walking to church with my maid, Lizzie Pearl. Well, I was all dressed to kill for in my white ruffled dress and my white Easter bonnet and carrying my white parasol. Well, we had to pass by the Dooleys' house, and the Dooleys were always known as white trash, and that bunch really despised me. Well, Harry and Virginia Dooley came up and shoved me down into a huge mud-hole, spoiling my entire Easter outfit! I cried, I tell you, I cried!

COLLARD: For God's sake, Katty! This is supposed to be a story about the cruelest thing *you've* ever done, not that's been *done to you!*

KATTY: I haven't finished yet! Will you let me finish! See later on in the day, when the Dooleys were all in for their dinner, Lizzie Pearl and I sneaked back over to their backyard and yanked the chirping heads off of every one of their colored Easter chicks—we murdered them *all* with our bare hands! Those brats cried for weeks! I swear it was weeks!

COLLARD: Great! Katty, that's rotten. That is really rotten!

PIXROSE: *(Overlapping.)* Yes, that's cruel, Katty! That's very cruel!

KATTY: I know, that's why I told it. Who's got one now? Collard, I bet you've got one. I bet you do.

COLLARD: Oh, yeah—I've slept with married men, I've slept with priests, I've stolen from stores, I've killed animals in the road, lied and cheated just to win at a game of cards.

PIXROSE: Oh, but what I did was worse than that.

COLLARD: Yeah?

PIXROSE: See, after I was burned and had to be in bandages, I bandaged up all my dolls, put methiolade on the bandages and kept 'em down in the cellar. I kept 'em wearing slings and using crutches and some of 'em were even blind. See, just 'cause I was scarred, I wanted them to be too. It was not fair.

MARSHAEL: Well, listen to this one. After Jamey'd had that stroke and the left half of his body'd gotten paralyzed, I went in to see him, and he asked me to bring him some of his papers from home. I told him he'd have to hobble home on his good side and get them himself 'cause I'd just sold our car t'pay for these ridiculous hospital bills. That's the last night I ever saw Jamey. He'd always made me feel so ashamed for being stronger and for getting our house and feeding the kids. Well, now he was gonna be weaker and more dependent than ever and I just wanted him t'pay for it.

KATTY: Oh, Marshael, I know Jamey was grateful to you for all the help you gave him.

MARSHAEL: No, he hated me for it. 'Cause when I left he said to me, "Fine, then when I die you just stick me in a pine box. Don't you dare go making five hundred drill team suits so that you can bury me in something nice, 'cause I won't be taking any more favors from you."

COLLARD: If Jamey didn't want your damn favors, he shouldn't of taken them.

MARSHAEL: No, 'cause after his work never came to anything again and again, we both got to resenting each other so bad. It seemed like the house and the children became mine and something else was his. It wasn't always awful but somehow it got to be. I don't know when it changed. I don't know when we changed. But I still remember the first time he said he loved me 'cause we were lying under the purple trees.

(The lights slowly fade out in the bedroom then go up immediately in the hall below. The men are all drunk. Brocker is playing the spoons. Leon is making loud, weird sounds. Wayne is singing a sad song.)

LEON: OOH AHHH BREAKAAAAA!!!

BROCKER: *(Overlapping.)* Yes sir! Let the good times roll!

LEON: BREAKAAAWOOSHAA!!! Whoo! Sometimes I just like to make noises. Stimulates the old brain.

WAYNE: *(Coming out of some sort of stupor.)* You know, people just get deader and deader each day they live!

LEON: *(Impressed.)* Wow. He's right. He's absolutely correct.

WAYNE: See I too can say sensitive, provocative things. Sir Jamey is not the only one among us with a brain which is what my dear Mama would have us all believe.

BROCKER: My dear old Mamee!

WAYNE: Get this. Get this! I'm pulling in fifty-five thousand bucks a year. Fifty-five thousand, and she's telling me how Jamey's the smart one, the creative one, the special one; and I'm just good in arithmetic! Just good in arithmetic, too classic! And now—now she wants me to take some farewell pictures of Saint Jamey so she can build him up a goddamn shrine! Well, screw her pictures! Screw her! and screw that stinking bastard in there!!! *(His nose begins bleeding.)* God, my nose. My nose. Lord Jesus! I've never known love. Never will. Oh, my nose. My nose. *(He exits upstage center.)*

LEON: *(After a moment.)* People get deader and deader every day they're alive. That's deep.

BROCKER: Hell, anything's deep if you think about it long enough. A man's best friend's his dog is deep if you give it any thought.

LEON: *(Realizing that a man's best friend is his dog, is deep.)* Yeah.

BROCKER: People are always saying, "Life is this!"—"Death is that!" They think they'll clear everything up for themselves if they can just hone it all down to a small twist of phrase. Poor idiots!

(The lights fade downstairs and go on upstairs. The women have settled in under blankets, pillows, etc. They are all drinking gin. It is darker now. All but one of the lights have been turned off.)

KATTY: *(As she rubs lotion all over her face, and arms.)* I hate the me I have to be with him. If only I could have the baby it would give me someone to love and make someone who'd love me. There'd be a reason for having the fine house and the lovely yard.

MARSHAEL: God. I wanted children so badly. I was like some giant sea turtle looking for a place in the warm sand to lay my eggs. I felt all fertile inside. I wanted a home and babies and a family. But Jamey never wanted all that. Still I really thought I had to have it. I really thought I did.

COLLARD: Not me. No way. No how. After my abortion I went out and ate fried chicken. Got a ten-piece bucket filled with mashed potatoes and gravy, coleslaw, and a roll. First it tasted good and greasy and gooey. Then I felt like I was eating my baby's skin and flesh and veins and all. I got so sick—all there in the car. Now I—I never eat chicken. I take the pill and use a diaphragm too. It'll never happen again. *(Dipping a stick into a bubble jar. Waving her hand, making bubbles.)* Wooh, look at those…beautiful. *(She can't resist popping one.)*

PIXROSE: I've never actually been pregnant. I guess 'cause I'm, well, I'm still a virgin. But I was pregnant one time in a dream. And when the child was born he was half human and half sheep and they said he was to be sold as a slave. But before they took him, I was allowed to hold him in my arms. His body was so warm and soft. I felt his heart beating against my heart. Then I looked down at his small sheeplike face, and he was crying. Then they took him away to become a slave.

KATTY: *(She rises.)* Well…hum. We'll just be exhausted tomorrow. That's all there is to it, just totally exhausted. *(Twisting an alarm clock, heading for the door.)* Come on, Pixrose, I'll help you get settled into the children's room. Good night, all.

MARSHAEL: Katty. Ah, what are you gonna do tomorrow—'bout Willie Wayne and all?

KATTY: Why, nothing. That's all I can do. I don't have children or a career like you do. Anyway I don't like changes. My hair's still the same as I wore it in college. Come on, Pixrose, it's late.

(Pixrose and Katty leave the bedroom and exit down the hall.)

COLLARD: God, I feel so old and tired.

MARSHAEL: It's late. You try and get some sleep. It'll be morning soon.

(The lights dim upstairs as they rise downstairs. Leon and Brocker are in a deep discussion. Brocker is playing with the wooden spoons.)

LEON: It's strange.

BROCKER: I know.

LEON: I mean she used to sing and whistle all the time when you were around painting those kitchen chairs red.

BROCKER: It's strange.

LEON: She loved listening to you playing them spoons.

BROCKER: Yeah. Hey, look, I've got a thought. Why don't we get those snapshots taken for Willie Wayne? Do him a favor? After all, he's a bleeding man.

LEON: You mean it?

BROCKER: Sure. We got flash cubes; what the fuck.

LEON: Fine with me.

(As they move into the parlor.)

LEON: So anyway, what happened with Marshael? I mean, you used to make her laugh. I asked you over here 'cause you knew how t'make her happy.

BROCKER: Look, Leon, I can't make my ownself happy; so how the hell am I gonna make her happy?

LEON: *(As he removes the lift lid from the coffin.)* Well, I just don't understand what could have happened between you two. *(Noticing the corpse.)* Boy, I wonder what it's like really being dead.

BROCKER: Don't look like much. Smile! *(He takes the picture.)*

LEON: So what about Marshael? Why does she hate you now?

BROCKER: *(He takes pictures through the following.)* Who knows. She, ah, called me to come pick her up from the hospital Tuesday night. We were driving home. It was raining. She was upset, but, ah, but she still looked, you know, good. And for some reason, I started telling her how the first time I'd seen her was, when she was playing her violin at the pancake supper. I said she looked like some sort of wild, frightened angel, ripping up that violin with her black eyes blazing. Then, ah, she started crying. She told me to pull the car over. I did. Well, I don't know. Nothing had ever happened, that way, between us before, and I felt funny with my tongue down her throat holding onto her hair. You know, with her husband there paralyzed in the hospital and with her all in distress. Seemed like maybe I was taking advantage of a situation or something; and so I left. I just took off. Walked home in the storm. Stepped in some goddamn horseshit, leaving her there in the car—alone—wanting somebody; needing something. God. What an asshole. Jesus, no wonder she hates me.

(Upstairs Marshael walks out onto the balcony.)

BROCKER: I leave the one woman I love alone in a great, unrelenting deluge. I give her nothing. Nothing. Not one thing. God, help us all. Listen, Leon; I gotta go. *(He heads for the front door.)*

LEON: Go where?

BROCKER: To find it. To get it.

LEON: What? To get what?

BROCKER: Exaltation! Love! Rapture! Glory! That's all there is! That's all that's left.

(He exits. As the lights go down, Leon returns to the parlor to put the lid back on the coffin. The moonlight drifts into the bedroom. Collard is sleeping in the bed. Marshael is standing on the balcony, talking to herself.)

MARSHAEL: I won't sleep. My eyes are red. I'm afraid to sleep. It's not like my nerves are raw, you know. It's like—like they've been stripped, leaving nothing but cold, cold bones.

(Pixrose enters the upstairs hall in her nightgown. She is terrified, distraught.)

PIXROSE: I can't stay there. I can't. I can't.

LEON: Pixrose? What's wrong? Are you alright?

PIXROSE: I don't like sleeping in the children's room. All the toys and dolls look at me and scare me—

LEON: Here, now, here. Don't be scared. Don't be.

PIXROSE: See, it's not fair how my folks were trying to burn Franky and me up too. They were afraid of things. Thought life was evil and burned themselves up. But—but they shouldn't a' tried burning me and Franky away with them. First at home and then in that car. Still though, we survived. We survived—Oh, Leon. *(Then as she leaps down the stairs into his arms.)* Hold me quick!

LEON: Here, now, here. *(Leon picks her up in his arms. Then, after a moment, starts to carry her out.)* I'll get you a glass of milk. There's a cot on the back porch. You can drink the milk out on the cot. Out where Brocker's dog is sleeping.

(He carries her out through the dining room. The lights focus back on

Marshael's room. She is talking to herself and putting Jamey's clothes in a sack.)

MARSHAEL: All these ties. You never wore even half of 'em. Wasted ties. God, loose change. Always pockets full of loose change. And your Spearmint chewing gum sticks. Damn, and look—your lost car keys. Oh, well, the car's gone now. Damn you, leaving me alone with your mess. Leaving me again with all your goddamn, gruesome mess t'clean up. Damn, you, wait! You wait! You're not leaving me here like this. You're gonna face me! I won't survive! You cheat! I've got t'have something…redemption… something. *(She leaves the room, goes down to the parlor and walks in. The coffin is closed. She begins to circle it.)* There you are. Coward. Hiding. Away from me. Hiding. *(Moving in on him.)* Look, I know I hurt you something bad, but why did you have to hold her fat, little hand like that? Huh? Treating me like nothing! I'm not…nothing. Hey, I'm talking. I'm talking to you. You'd better look at me. I mean it, you bastard! *(She pulls the lid off the coffin.)* Jamey. God, your face. Jamey, I'm scared. I'm so scared. I'm scared not to be loved. I'm scared for our life not to work out. It didn't, did it? Jamey? Damn you, where are you? Are you down in Mobile, baby? Have you taken a spin t'Mobile? I'm asking you—shit—Crystal Springs? How 'bout Scotland? You wanted to go there…your grandfather was from there. You shit! You're not…I know you're not…I love you! God. Stupid thing to say. I love you!! Okay; okay. You're gone. You're gone. You're not laughing. You're not…nothing. *(She moves away from the coffin, realizing it contains nothing of value.)* Still I gotta have something. Still something… *(As she runs out of the parlor then out the front door.)* The trees. Still have the trees. The purple, purple trees—

(The front door is left open. There is a moment of silence before Brocker appears in the side yard carrying wild flowers and a ladder. He is very drunk. He wears some of the flowers in his hair.)

BROCKER: Hey! Love! My, love! I'm carrying you off to the moon! To the stars! To the shining planet of Mars! *(He now has the ladder up and is making his way to the top.)* Exaltation!!! Where angels aspire to glory! Exaltation!!!

COLLARD: *(Overlapping, as she comes out of her sleep.)* Who's there? Shut up. My aching head. God! Who is it?! Stay away! *(She runs out onto the balcony and starts throwing colored Easter eggs at Brocker.)* Who's there? Stay away! Go away! I mean it. Get out of here! God. Take that.

BROCKER: *(Overlapping.)* Hey, love! I'm carrying you in my arms to paradise! Remember?! Exaltation?!! Hey, watch it! OW! Look out, that's my chest!

COLLARD: *(Running on.)* It's Brocker! You lunatic! You raving imbecile!

BROCKER: *(Overlapping.)* Collard, you bitch!

COLLARD: *(She is at the ledge now and throws the real eggs out of the bird's nest.)* Take that! You stinking drunkard! You broken dog. Take that!!

BROCKER: *(Overlapping.)* AAH!!! YUK!! Help! Help!

COLLARD: Oh, God! Look at this! Look! Now you've made me murder these baby eggs! I've done murder! What else is left? What else?! OOOHH!! *(She collapses back down onto the bed.)*

BROCKER: Jesus! YUK!!! It's a madhouse. There's nothing more but to go sleep in a ditch with my dog. Here, Pooch! Hey, Pooch!
(Brocker whistles. A dog's bark is heard in the distance.)

BROCKER: Pooch, come here—Pooch, Pooch!
(He walks off looking for the dog, as the lights fade to blackout.)

SCENE III

It is the following morning. The coffin and the flower arrangements have been removed. The blue pinstriped suit is also gone. The visible rooms in the house are empty. Pixrose is outside. She wears a pink dress with long white gloves and white stockings. She has on a hat with cherries. She is humming a song and spinning around and around in circles as the lights go up. Brocker enters right. He looks like he has been sleeping in a ditch.

PIXROSE: *(Still spinning.)* Hi Brocker! Good morning!!

BROCKER: Yeah, morning. Hey, what's going on?

PIXROSE: Just spinning around! Trying to make myself dizzy— *(Laughing as she staggers to the ground.)* It's fun. You wanna try it?

BROCKER: No, thanks. I don't need to spin t'get dizzy anymore. I'm just blessed with it.

PIXROSE: Hey, Leon and me washed your dog for you this morning.

BROCKER: *(Picking up the ladder.)* Well...thanks.

PIXROSE: What's his name anyway?

BROCKER: He's called Blacky. That's his name, Blacky.
(Brocker walks away carrying the ladder as Collard comes out of the upstairs bathroom. She is dressed in an ill-fitted dress with ridiculous shoes and a funny-looking hat. The outfit should be the exact opposite of the image Collard likes to present of herself. She wobbles out of the bathroom and stares at herself in the mirror.)

COLLARD: You look preposterous. Absolutely and totally. I'm not going. That's all. I'm just not going.

(*Leon and Katty enter from the dining room. Katty is dressed in her navy blue outfit. Leon has on his suit and tie. He carries a corsage and boxes containing the armbands and veils. He sets the boxes down on the card table.*)

KATTY: But did you see her at all this morning?

LEON: No, I ain't seen her at all.

KATTY: Are you sure she didn't go with Wayne to deliver the suit?

LEON: No, she didn't go with him. I spoke to him before he left—

KATTY: You did? What did he say? Was there anything interesting that was said?

(*Wayne enters through the front door. He is dressed in a three-piece suit.*)

WAYNE: Leon! Is she back? Has Marshael come back?

LEON: No, no one's seen her at all.

WAYNE: Well, we've got to find her!

LEON: Look, I gotta give Pixrose this precious rememberance. Marshael'll get back if she wants to.

(*Leon exits to the kitchen. There is a tense moment of silence between Katty and Wayne.*)

WAYNE: I, ah, took Uncle Wilbur his suit.

KATTY: That's good.

WAYNE: Look, things have really been tense for me. Losing my only brother and all. It's been a shock.

KATTY: I know, Wayne, I know. Here, I'll ah, make some eggs up for you and heat the coffee. You gotta keep your strength up, Angel Pie. You know that? You really do.

(*They exit through the dining room door, as Leon comes around the house, right, to find Pixrose sitting in the grass.*)

LEON: Hi.

PIXROSE: Hi.

LEON: You look pretty. That's a pretty dress...the hat too.

PIXROSE: Thanks. It's my Easter outfit.

LEON: Well...Here's a gift for you.

PIXROSE: For me?

LEON: Them's purple violets. It's my favorite kind of flowers. But—but that don't mean that they have to be your favorite kind too!

PIXROSE: They smell pretty. (*Holding the flowers up to Leon.*) Here, smell them. They're pretty.

LEON: Good. Hey, you wanna go 'round to the front and wait for the limousine? It's due to arrive directly.

PIXROSE: Sure! I've never seen a limousine before!

LEON: You think I have?

(They exit to the front of the house. Suddenly Marshael, Wayne, Katty, and Brocker all enter the front hall from upstage center. They are in an uproar. Marshael starts up the stairs; the rest follow her.)

KATTY: Really, Marshael, I think, for your own sake, you should go—

BROCKER: *(Overlapping.)* Will you stop hounding the woman! For Christ's sake—

WAYNE: *(Overlapping.)* But you've got to go! You can't not go! Why won't you go?

MARSHAEL: Because I'm tired! I'm finally tired. I think I can sleep. And what's that horrible smell?!!

KATTY: I know! It's like—rotten eggs! What could it be?

WAYNE: But it's a disgrace, if you refuse to go to your own husband's funeral! A selfish, foolish disgrace!

(They are upstairs by now. Marshael enters her bedroom. The rest follow.)

MARSHAEL: Look, I'm not going to go and put that rotting mess of formaldehyde in the ground, and that's all there is to it!

WAYNE: You're totally irreverent! Totally! There ought to be some sort of law—

BROCKER: *(Overlapping.)* The woman needs rest, you asshole!!

COLLARD: *(Overlapping.)* What's all this?! Don't bring him in here!!!

BROCKER: Oh, what do *you* know!

COLLARD: Lunatic!

WAYNE: *(To Marshael.)* Look, just comb your hair, and we'll go. It's getting late!

MARSHAEL: What's that rotting smell? It's making me sick.

KATTY: Collard, are you wearing that?

COLLARD: No!

(Suddenly Leon rushes in the front door.)

LEON: *(Yelling up to them.)* Hey. Hey, everyone! It's here! The limousine! It's here! (He runs back out and right.)

WAYNE: The limousine?!

KATTY: Oh my, it's finally arrived.

(They start down the stairs.)

WAYNE: Well, I'd better go check on it.

KATTY: Here, I'll go too. You might need some help.

WAYNE: Make sure things are all in order.

KATTY: Make sure they have the directions straight.

WAYNE: Make sure the headlights are all working.

(Katty and Wayne exit the front door.)

MARSHAEL: It's you, Brocker. That smell; it's you.

BROCKER: I know it. I know.

MARSHAEL: Well, it's making me dizzy.

BROCKER: Sorry. Look, I'll go change. I'll just go change. (He leaves the room and goes downstairs. In the front hall he starts to take his shirt off. He picks up his hat and coat and the two wooden spoons and then walks out the front door. It is alright if his actions overlap somewhat with the scene that is going on upstairs in the bedroom.)

COLLARD: Look, Marsh, I can't go to the funeral. I just look too preposterous. I don't even have on clean underwear. I'm not gonna go.

MARSHAEL: But you gotta go. I—told the kids you'd go. I had breakfast with them over at Aunt Muffin's this morning. They wanna ride in the white convertible. They said they wanna ride with you.

COLLARD: But who are you gonna go with?

MARSHAEL: I don't need to go. Shit, Collard. I'm asking you to go!

COLLARD: (A moment.) Alright then. I'll go. I'd be glad t'go.

MARSHAEL: Good. I told them you'd bring their shoes when you came.

COLLARD: Alright. Here, I can put 'em in here. God. You need rest bad, Marshy. Look here, your hands are shaking.

MARSHAEL: Right. Yes. I'm gonna try and get some sleep soon. Stop my eyes aching.

COLLARD: (Picking up the children's shoes.) Good then you rest. I gotta go. Don't worry. I'll see they get their little shoes. I'll take care of it all. You sleep.

(Wayne, Katty, Leon, and Pixrose all come in the front door. Pixrose is wearing the violet corsage.)

WAYNE: I don't believe they've got Jersey Crow driving our limousine in that stupid hat.

COLLARD: That's them.

LEON: Look, if she doesn't want to go, I don't see why she should have to go. (Handing Wayne a black arm band.) Now here, Willie Wayne, this is for you.

PIXROSE: Hey, Collard, look! Honeysuckle!

(She waves the honeysuckle to Collard who is coming down the stairs. Katty and Pixrose both start struggling with their veils. Katty is also putting on her gloves and getting her handbag.)

WAYNE: Get Marshael, Collard, we've got to go immediately!

COLLARD: She's not going.

WAYNE: What is this? She's got to go! It's required!

COLLARD: Look, just because you'll always have the taste of leather in your mouth, doesn't mean the rest of us have to.

LEON: Collard, here's your veil.

PIXROSE: *(Overlapping.)* Am I wearing this right?

(Katty goes to her assistance.)

COLLARD: *(Overlapping as she takes the veil with a new sense of command and warmth.)* Thanks. I'm gonna take the kids in the convertible. Look, you and Pixrose go in the limousine. *(She tries putting her veil on over her hat.)*

LEON: Great!

WAYNE: *(As he leaves.)* I wash my hands of it! I wash my hands of it entirely!

KATTY: Remember then, Collard. It's Grace Episcopal Church right on East Peace Street! Do you have that!

COLLARD: *(Putting her veil directly on her head then triumphantly putting the hat on over it.)* Yeah, I got it! I'll be there. I got it.

(They all exit out the front door. Upstairs Marshael rises. She has taken off her black dress and stands only in a white slip. She sits down on the bed and takes hold of a pillow. Brocker appears around the side of the house. He is wearing his hat and his dark suit coat without his shirt. He looks at the window, then starts playing a song on the spoons. Marshael wraps a blanket around herself and goes out onto the balcony.)

MARSHAEL: Brocker—

BROCKER: Hi. Just dropped by. Thought you might need something. I don't know. Thought I'd see.

MARSHAEL: Thanks. I'm just gonna rest. Lord, you look awfully funny.

BROCKER: I do?

MARSHAEL: Sorta. What's that on your chest?

BROCKER: *(Opening his coat.)* A ship. *(Then making the ship move by moving his muscles.)* It's on a troubled sea.

MARSHAEL: *(Bursting out laughing.)* Oh, Lord! Look at that! A troubled sea!!

BROCKER: I like it when you laugh. I love to hear you laugh!

MARSHAEL: Really? I don't even know what my laugh sounds like.

BROCKER: It sounds…happy.

MARSHAEL: Hey, look, you could do one thing for me.

BROCKER: I could?

MARSHAEL: I need some more Easter candy for my kids. You know, things like bunnies and chickens and eggs and stuff.

BROCKER: Oh, sure, sure. I saw a whole bunch of that junk over at Ben Franklin's Dime Store. I'll, ah, get it for you right away. I'll buy a whole load of stuff! I'll run go and get it now! *(He starts to go right.)*

MARSHAEL: Brocker, wait!

(He stops.)

BROCKER: What? What is it?

MARSHAEL: I don't know. Play something for me. Will you? Just till I go to sleep. Play something on the spoons. Would you?

BROCKER: Alright. Sure. I'll play you a tune. Wanna hear, "This Old Man?" I do it real well. Why—why, you won't be able to keep your eyes open.

MARSHAEL: Play it. Yes, play that one.

(Brocker sits on the stump. He starts playing the spoons and singing "This Old Man.")

BROCKER: *(Singing.)* This old man
He played one
He played knick-knack
On my drum.
With a knick-knack paddy whack
Give a dog a bone
This old man comes rolling home.
This old man
He played two

MARSHAEL: That's nice.

BROCKER: *(Continuing.)* He played knick-knack
On my shoe.

MARSHAEL: That's a nice song. *(She starts slowly into the bedroom.)*

BROCKER: *(Continuing.)* With a knick-knack paddy whack
Give a dog a bone
This old man comes rolling home.

MARSHAEL: *(Getting into bed.)* I like it.

BROCKER: *(Continuing.)* This old man
He played three
He played knick-knack
On my knee

MARSHAEL: *(Almost asleep.)* I do…

(She falls asleep as he continues to play the spoons.)

BROCKER: *(Continuing.)* With a knick-knack paddy whack
Give a dog a bone
This old man comes rolling home.
This old man
He played four
He played knick-knack
On my door
With a knick-knack paddy whack
Give a dog a bone
This old man comes rolling home.
(The lights fade to blackout.)

END OF PLAY

THE MISS FIRECRACKER CONTEST

WITH LOVE AND STARS TO STEPHEN

Budge Threlkeld, Mark Linn-Baker, Holly Hunter,
Patricia Richardson, Belita Moreno, and Margo Martindale
in Manhattan Theatre Club's 1984 production of
The Miss Firecracker Contest.

photo by Garry Goodstein

ORIGINAL PRODUCTION

The Miss Firecracker Contest was presented by the Manhattan Theatre Club, in New York City, on May 1, 1984. It was directed by Stephen Tobolowsky; the scenery was designed by John Lee Beatty; the costumes were designed by Jennifer von Mayrhauser; the lighting was designed by Dennis Parichy; the sound was designed by Stan Metelits; and the production stage manager was Wendy Chapin. The cast was as follows:

Carnelle Scott	Holly Hunter
Popeye Jackson	Belita Moreno
Elain Rutledge	Patricia Richardson
Delmount Williams	Mark Linn-Baker
Mac Sam	Budge Threlkeld
Tessy Mahoney	Margo Martindale

The Miss Firecracker Contest had it's world premiere at Victory Theatre, Burbank California, 1980.

THE CAST

CARNELLE SCOTT: 24, the beauty contestant
POPEYE JACKSON: 23, Carnelle's seamstress
ELAIN RUTLEDGE: 32, Carnelle's first cousin; a beauty
DELMOUNT WILLIAMS: 28, Carnelle's first cousin; Elain's brother
MAC SAM: 36, the balloon man
TESSY MAHONEY: 23, the beauty contest coordinator

THE SETTING

The action of the play takes place in Brookhaven, Mississippi, a small southern town.

THE TIME

The ending of June and the beginning of July.

AUTHOR'S NOTE: It is strongly suggested that the actress playing Carnelle dye her hair bright red instead of opting for a wig.

SYNOPSIS OF SCENES

ACT I

Scene I: The living room of Ronelle Williams' house in Brookhaven, Mississippi—about five o'clock Monday afternoon on a hot day at the end of June. There is something dreary and suffocating and frightening about the room with its dark oak furniture, its heavy, bright curtains and the endless clutter of knickknacks. An old spinning wheel sits in a far corner of the room. There are three entrances and exits: a front door, a door leading to the kitchen, and a staircase leading to the upstairs rooms.

Scene II: The same setting. About eight o'clock in the evening, on the following Saturday.

ACT II

Scene I: The carnival grounds—about three o'clock in the afternoon on the Fourth of July. We see the outside area behind a large carnival tent and the inside of a backstage dressing room. There is simply a bench and a garbage can in the outside area. To get to this area the characters enter from right. It should be established that when entering from down right the characters are coming from a different part of the carnival then when entering from up right. The characters can get to the dressing room from this outside area by taking a step up and entering through a doorway. Inside the dressing room there is a dressing table, a chair, a stool, and a clothes rack. There is a curtain in the dressing room at left. This entrance and exit leads to the backstage area of the beauty contest.

Scene II: The same setting. Several minutes later.

Scene III: The same setting. That evening.

ACT I
SCENE I

The lights go up onstage. Carnelle Scott, twenty-four, stands with her back to the audience looking into a mirror. Carnelle is tallish with an oddly attractive face, a nice figure, and very bright dyed red hair. She wears purple leotards, tights, and tap shoes.

Carnelle turns away from the mirror with a glint in her eyes. She pushes the rolled up rug back even farther, then rushes to place the needle back on the record spinning on the record player. A sung version of "The Star Spangled Banner" begins playing loudly.

Carnelle checks a notebook, then rushes madly back to the kitchen. She quickly returns with wooden spoons and stainless steel knives. She leaps into her talent routine that requires tap dancing, marching, and baton twirling, none of which she is extremely adept at. When the record comes to "And the rockets red glare…," she picks up a wooden spoon that she uses as an imaginary roman candle. She says, "Pow," each time she imagines it goes off. For the final "Oh, say does that…," she puts down the spoons and picks up two knives that she uses as imaginary sparklers. She twirls them about. When the record is over Carnelle goes to remove the needle, as she repeats part of her routine to herself.

CARNELLE: Let's see, that was, "And the rockets red glare— *(Then as the imaginary Roman candle goes off.)* Boom!—The bombs bursting in air— Boom!—gave proof—Boom!—through the night—Boom!—that our flag was—Boom!—there—Boom! Boom! Boom!" *(She goes to mark down the ideas in her notebook.)* Hmm. I don't know. I think that'll work. I think it will.

(There is a knock on the door.)

CARNELLE: Coming. Coming—! Coming!

(Before going to the door Carnelle shakes her head of red hair back and forth, takes a towel from a chair and slings it carelessly around her neck. She begins panting deeply as she goes to open the door for Popeye Jackson. Popeye, twenty-three, is a small, glowing person. She wears a homemade dress with many different size pockets and thick glasses with heavy black rims. She does not carry a purse.)

CARNELLE: Oh, hello, Popeye. Come in. Come on in.

POPEYE: Thanks.

CARNELLE: *(Still breathing heavily.)* Wheew! Just make yourself at home. Oh, and please excuse the way I look, but I've been practicing my routine. It's something, I tell you, hard work. But it's coming along. It's coming right along.

POPEYE: Good.

CARNELLE: *(After an awkward moment.)* Well. I guess what I should do is show you the sketches so you'll have some idea of what I want.

POPEYE: Alright.

CARNELLE: *(Getting the sketches.)* They're right over here, I believe. Yes, here they are. *(Turning around.)* What's that thing?

POPEYE: *(Who has removed a magnifying glass from her pocket.)* It's my magnifying lens.

CARNELLE: A magnifying lens? You need that thing to see with?

POPEYE: Well, up close I do.

CARNELLE: Goodness gracious. Well, here're the sketches. Of course, now, I'm not an artist or anything; so the drawings aren't much. *(Pause.)* But I think you'll get the general idea.

POPEYE: *(Looking at the sketches through the lens.)* Oh, that's pretty.

CARNELLE: *(As if someone has given her a gift.)* You think so?

POPEYE: I like them stars.

CARNELLE: Well, I wanted to go with something really patriotic. Kinda traditional. You know, noble, in a sense.

POPEYE: And this costume's for a dance contest?

CARNELLE: Well, no; it's not a dance contest; it's for the Miss Firecracker Contest.

POPEYE: *(In the dark.)* Huh?

CARNELLE: The Miss Firecracker Contest?

(Popeye shakes her head.)

CARNELLE: It's the beauty contest. They have it in Brookhaven every Fourth of July. It's a tradition. It's a big event. It's famous. Why, Representative Louis Pooley's gonna be here this very year to put the crown on the winner's head. It's a famous contest.

POPEYE: Well, I guess, I just don't know nothing about it.

CARNELLE: Well, it's odd to me. It's really odd to me.

POPEYE: 'Course I haven't been here in town but a short while. Only 'bout three weeks.

CARNELLE: *(Relieved.)* Oh! Oh, well, that explains it! That explains it all!!

POPEYE: Yeah.

CARNELLE: Anyway, this outfit is what I'm gonna be wearing in the talent section of the contest.

POPEYE: Oh.

CARNELLE: What I do's kind of a tap-dance-march-type-a-thing. It's gonna be done to, "The Star Spangled Banner." I'm gonna end up spinning these lit up sparklers around and around—one in each hand. *(She twirls the imaginary sparklers.)*

POPEYE: Gosh!

CARNELLE: And before that Roman candles going off— *(As she shoots off imaginary roman candles.)* Boom! Boom! Boom! Like that—right out over the top a' the crowd!

POPEYE: Really?

CARNELLE: Oh, sure.

POPEYE: Boy.

CARNELLE: Well, so you think you'll be able to make up a pattern following these drawings?

POPEYE: I expect so.

CARNELLE: Well, then…the job is yours.

POPEYE: Thank you.

CARNELLE: You're welcome.

POPEYE: Maybe I should go on and get your measurements off you right now if ya don't mind.

CARNELLE: Oh, no, no. Fine. Go ahead. Alright.

POPEYE: *(Getting her measuring tape from her pocket.)* I just need a few.

CARNELLE: Take all you want. I'll just stand right here. *(She strikes a dramatic pose.)* Just natural. Is this okay with you? This stance right here?

POPEYE: Sure. *(She begins measuring, looking at the measurement through her glass, writing it down, then starting a new measurement.)*

CARNELLE: My, I feel like a model or something. Very elegant. Of course, that's exactly what I should be doing. Modeling, that is. People have told me that. They say, "Carnelle, why do you keep slaving away at Slater's Jewelry Shop? You should be up in Memphis working as a model. You really should."

POPEYE: *(Trying to get Carnelle to relax her tightly tucked in stomach.)* You can just relax.

CARNELLE: What? Oh, I'm fine. Just fine.

POPEYE: Alright. *(She finishes with the waist measurement, looks at it through the glass, writes it down, than goes on.)*

CARNELLE: You know you do this very well. Expertly, in fact. Of course, you come highly recommended to me from Miss Celia Lily. She says you've done some really fine work in her shop. She says you seem really experienced to her.

POPEYE: Well, I'm that for sure. See, I been making clothes practically all my life. Started out when I was four years old.

CARNELLE: Oh, really?

POPEYE: Used to make little outfits for the bullfrogs that lived out around our yard.

CARNELLE: Bullfrogs! Yuk!

POPEYE: They was funny looking creatures.

CARNELLE: But why didn't you design clothes for your dolls?

POPEYE: We din't have no dolls.

CARNELLE: Oh; how sad.

POPEYE: Them frogs was okay.

CARNELLE: But what kind of clothes could you design for a frog? They'd look ugly in anything.

POPEYE: Well...one thing was a nurse's suit. Oh, and I remember a queen's robe and a cape of leaves. Different things.

CARNELLE: (With a giggle.) Well, I certainly hope you don't think of me as any bullfrog.

POPEYE: Huh?

CARNELLE: I mean, think I'm ugly like one of those dumb bullfrogs of yours.

POPEYE: Oh, I don't.

CARNELLE: Well, of course, you don't. I was just joking.

POPEYE: Oh.

CARNELLE: (Suddenly very sad and uncomfortable.) Are you about done?

POPEYE: Mostly. This here's all I need.

(Carnelle stares forlornly into space as Popeye measures her head.)

POPEYE: There. Done.

CARNELLE: Well, I've got to stretch a minute. (She stretches from her waist, then kicks her leg up high.) There! And, kick! And...kick!

POPEYE: You sure do kick high!

CARNELLE: Well, I work at it daily.

POPEYE: I could never kick like that.

CARNELLE: I don't know, maybe you could with practice. Want to try it? Come on and try it. Go ahead! And kick! And kick! And kick! And kick! (Popeye kicks feebly in the air.)

CARNELLE: Not bad. Keep on working at it. That's the only way to improve. Listen, I have a snack made up for us in the kitchen. Would you like it now?

POPEYE: Sure.

CARNELLE: I hope you don't mind, it's just ice tea and saltine crackers.

POPEYE: I love saltines.

CARNELLE: Alright then, I'll go get the snack.

> *(Carnelle exits to the kitchen. Popeye looks around. She goes over to the spinning wheel and spins it around. She watches it. She pretends to prick her finger on the needle. Carnelle comes back in carrying the snack tray. She now has an apron on over her leotards. Popeye turns around startled.)*

POPEYE: This sure is a scary house.

CARNELLE: You don't like it?

POPEYE: It's scary.

CARNELLE: Well, it's just like my Aunt Ronelle fixed it up. It's got her special touch: this old spinning wheel; these lace doilies; these old pictures in frames here. I'd prefer something more modern and luxurious, but— that's just me.

POPEYE: You live here with your aunt?

CARNELLE: Oh, no. She died. She had cancer.

POPEYE: I'm sorry.

CARNELLE: It happened just a few weeks before last Christmas. We were very close. It was a tragedy.

POPEYE: I'm sorry.

CARNELLE: *(As she pours Popeye's tea.)* You may of heard about her; Ronelle Williams? It was a famous medical case—ran in all the newspapers.

POPEYE: No.

CARNELLE: Well, see what it was—do you take lemon?

POPEYE: Please.

CARNELLE: Anyway, she had this cancer of the pituitary gland, I believe it was; so what they did was they replaced her gland with the gland of a monkey to see if they could save her life—just help yourself to the sugar—

POPEYE: *(Moving to sit on the floor.)* Thanks.

CARNELLE: And they did, in fact, keep her alive for a month or so longer than she was expected to live.

POPEYE: Well, that's good.

CARNELLE: *(Pouring herself some tea.)* Of course, there were such dreadful side effects.

POPEYE: Mmm.

CARNELLE: She, well, she started growing long, black hairs all over her body just, well, just like an ape.

POPEYE: Gracious, Lord.

CARNELLE: It was very trying. But she was so brave. She even let them take photographs of her. Everyone said she was just a saint. A saint or an angel; one or the other.

POPEYE: It gives me the shivers.

CARNELLE: It was awfully hard on me losing my Aunt Ronelle—although I guess I should be used to it by now.

POPEYE: What's that?

CARNELLE: People dying. It seems like people've been dying practically all my life, in one way or another. First my mother passed when I was barely a year old. Then my daddy kinda drug me around with him till I was about nine and he couldn't stand me any longer; so he dropped me off to live with my Aunt Ronelle and Uncle George and their own two children: Elain and Delmount. They're incredible those two. They're just my ideal. Anyhow, we're happy up until the time when Uncle George falls to his death trying to pull this bird's nest out from the chimney.

POPEYE: He fall off from the roof?

CARNELLE: That's right. Tommy Turner was passing by throwing the evening paper and he caught sight of the whole event. Boom.

POPEYE: How awful.

CARNELLE: Anyhow, my original daddy appears back here to live with us looking all kinda fat and swollen. And after staying on with us about two years, he suddenly drops dead in the summer's heat while running out to the Tropical Ice Cream truck. Heart failure, they said it was. Then this thing with Aunt Ronelle dying right before Christmas. It's been hard to bear.

POPEYE: (After a moment.) I had a brother who was bit by a water moccasin down by the Pearl River, and he died.

CARNELLE: Well; you know, they say everyone's gonna be dying someday. I believe it too.

POPEYE: Yeah. May as well. (She finishes a cracker and wipes her lips with a napkin.) That sure was tasty.

CARNELLE: Well…thank you much. Would you like to see the material I've chosen to make my costume with?

POPEYE: Why, yes.

CARNELLE: Good. Then I'll just run get it.

POPEYE: Oh, Carnelle?

CARNELLE: Yes?

POPEYE: Do you mind if I look at these pictures in frames here?

CARNELLE: Oh, no. That's what they're there for.

(Carnelle exits upstairs to the bedrooms. Popeye goes over and picks up her magnifying glass. She then goes and looks at the pictures. She looks at one, then another, then suddenly, at the third picture, she is struck. She picks it up and looks at it, studying it closely with her lens.)

POPEYE: My. Oh, my.

(Carnelle comes back down carrying a sack.)

CARNELLE: Who are you looking at?

POPEYE: A man. This man here.

CARNELLE: Oh, that's my cousin, Delmount.

POPEYE: What eyes. Look at his hair—it's wild, wouldn't you say? It's wild.

CARNELLE: Well, I suppose, Delmount is rather a romantic figure.

POPEYE: Really?

CARNELLE: He was always writing sheets and sheets of poetry to the women he loved then he'd set them all afire and bury the ashes.

POPEYE: *(Swooning.)* How sad!

CARNELLE: Yes, Delmount's very odd. He can do this trick where he wiggles his ears.

POPEYE: *(Totally sold that this is the man for her.)* He can!?

CARNELLE: Sure.

POPEYE: *(Impulsively.)* Where's he live now?

CARNELLE: Well, it's strange…see, Delmount, he's had kind of a checkered past.

POPEYE: Checkered?

CARNELLE: Right. And about the first of the year a Louisiana judge sentenced him to a—well, to a mental institution.

POPEYE: Is he mad?

CARNELLE: No. Not really. He hit a man in the face with a bottle; so his lawyer got him put there instead of jail.

POPEYE: Oh.

CARNELLE: *(Upset.)* He was released in the spring, but he hasn't been home since. I don't know where he is now.

POPEYE: I hope he's alright.

CARNELLE: Here, let's look at the material.

POPEYE: Alright.

CARNELLE: *(Taking the red material from the sack.)* Here's the red.

POPEYE: Ooooh, that's pretty. *(Touching it.)* Silky too.

CARNELLE: And, of course, the blue.

POPEYE: *(Looking at the material through her glass.)* It's just like a midnight sky. I love blue.

CARNELLE: And then, the most expensive, the most elegant of all—silver for the stars.

POPEYE: Why, you went all out on this material—I can see that.

CARNELLE: Well, yes. I hope it's gonna be okay. Not having any white. I mean, I hope red, blue, and silver will be patriotic enough.

POPEYE: Well, I just can't wait to—

ELAIN'S VOICE: Carnelle! Carnelle, Honey!

(Elain Rutledge, thirty-two, enters through the front door. She is dressed in elegant pastels but appears somewhat wilted in the summer's heat. Elain could most definitely be described as beautiful, but her looks are now more strained and anxious than they once were. She carries expensive luggage, a cosmetic case, and a gift.)

CARNELLE: *(Running to hug her.)* Elain!! It's Elain!!!

ELAIN: *(Hugging her.)* Why, hello, my little Carnation! How are you doing?!

CARNELLE: *(Overlapping.)* Oh, Elain! Elain! I'm just fine!

ELAIN: Why, you really did dye your hair, didn't you?

CARNELLE: Do you like it?

ELAIN: Well, it's just as red as it can be!

CARNELLE: That's what I wanted, crimson red.

ELAIN: Well, then, it couldn't be more perfect! Will you help me with these bags, here? My arms are just falling off!

CARNELLE: *(Taking the biggest bags.)* Of course! I'm sorry! Goodness, I thought you weren't coming in till the weekend.

ELAIN: Oh, I know, I know. I suddenly decided to cut my stay off short with my mother-in-law. I decided just to drive by Hollybluff and beep twice.

CARNELLE: *(With a giggle.)* Oh, you crazy thing!

ELAIN: No, really, I'm sorry, dar'lin, I should a' called you up but— *(Suddenly noticing Popeye.)* Why, hello, Honey!

CARNELLE: Oh, this is my friend, Popeye Jackson. Popeye, this is my cousin, Elain Rutledge, the one I—

ELAIN: *(Overlapping.)* Why, hello, Popeye, so nice to meet you. What a smashing outfit!

POPEYE: Thank you.

CARNELLE: Elain knows everything about clothes. She just adores them.

ELAIN: Oh you crazy dear! Look, here's a little something I picked up for you at a shop in the Quarter. *(Handing Carnelle a gift.)*

CARNELLE: What! Oh, you shouldn't have! Really, you shouldn't have. *(She opens the box and takes out a very strangely decorated Mardi Gras mask.)* Why, look! It's beautiful! Isn't that beautiful!

ELAIN: I just thought of you when I saw it. You'll have to wear it to a masked ball.

CARNELLE: *(Holding the mask in front of her face.)* How elegant! How simply elegant! Look, Popeye!

POPEYE: May I hold it too?

CARNELLE: Why, of course.

(She hands Popeye the mask. Elain and Carnelle hug then turn back to Popeye. There is a moment of silence as Popeye holds the mask over her eyes and slowly moves her head from side to side. Perhaps she makes a strange sound.)

ELAIN: *(Taking off her dangling, shimmering earrings and handing them out to Popeye.)* Oh, here, Popeye, these are for you.

POPEYE: What?

ELAIN: Please, they're a gift to you. Here, put them on.

POPEYE: Oh, no.

CARNELLE: Oh, Elain! Elain!

ELAIN: *(Overlapping.)* Yes, yes! I insist! They're just right for you; they're just your color. Here, I'll put them on for you. *(She puts the earrings on Popeye.)* Oh, stunning! They look just simply stunning!

POPEYE: *(Slowly shaking her head back and forth.)* Why, thank you.

CARNELLE: Isn't she wonderful, Popeye! Isn't she just perfectly perfect!

ELAIN: Oh, how I wish I were!

CARNELLE: Don't be silly; you are!

POPEYE: *(Shaking her head.)* I never had me no earbobs.

ELAIN: Well, I'm glad you have them, Popeye. They look dazzling on you.

POPEYE: Well. I think I better be going. It's getting toward dark. Let me get all this rounded up. *(She starts getting the materials together.)*

CARNELLE: Popeye's going to be using this material to make my costume for the Miss Firecracker Contest.

ELAIN: You mean, you went on and signed up for that?

CARNELLE: Yes, I registered today.

ELAIN: I don't see why you're so interested in being Miss Firecracker; there's nothing to it.

CARNELLE: Well, not for you. See, Elain was Miss Firecracker way back when she was just eighteen.

ELAIN: Well, seventeen, actually.

CARNELLE: Anyway, it was way back that first year when I came to live with them. She was a vision of beauty riding on that float with a crown on her head waving to everyone. I thought I'd drop dead when she passed by me.

ELAIN: All that was ages ago. It's silly to think about.

CARNELLE: Anyway, I just thought I'd give it a whirl. I'm twenty-four. Twenty-five's the age limit. I just thought I'd give it a whirl while I still could.

ELAIN: *(Powdering her nose.)* They ought to change that name to—well, to something like, Miss Fourth of July. Miss Firecracker sounds so trashy.

CARNELLE: 'Course, I don't expect to win—that's crazy. I'm just in it for the experience—that's the main thing.

POPEYE: Well, I think you'd be perfect for a Miss Firecracker—with your red hair and all.

CARNELLE: Oh, well, that's actually why I dyed my hair red; I thought it'd be more appropriate for the contest.

POPEYE: It's a nice dye job too. I don't see no roots or nothing.

CARNELLE: I try to do a careful job on it.

POPEYE: Well, I got it all together here.

CARNELLE: Good, well here're the sketches.

POPEYE: And when will you be needing your costume by?

CARNELLE: Oh. Well, the audition'll be this very Saturday; so could you have it by Wednesday afternoon or Thursday at the latest?

POPEYE: Tuesday's fine.

CARNELLE: Alright, I'll see you on Tuesday.

(Carnelle and Popeye are at the front door now.)

POPEYE: Alright. 'Bye.

CARNELLE: 'Bye-'bye.

POPEYE: *(To Elain.)* And I love my earbobs!

ELAIN: *(From the sofa.)* Oh, good!

POPEYE: Well, alright, 'bye. *(She exits.)*

CARNELLE: 'Bye-'bye. *(Turning and coming back to Elain.)* Oh, Elain! That was so sweet what you did—giving Popeye those earrings. It meant so much to her. You're so generous!

ELAIN: *(Meaning it.)* Don't talk about it, please. It was nothing. Oh, mind if I have a glass of this delicious looking ice tea? I'm about ready to drop dead from the heat.

CARNELLE: Oh, of course! Please! Here, I'll run get you a fresh glass out from the kitchen.

(Carnelle picks up the tray and exits. Elain takes off her hat and fans herself.

She looks sadly around the room. Carnelle returns with a glass with a small umbrella in it.)

CARNELLE: Here, now—

ELAIN: Bless you.

CARNELLE: There you are.

ELAIN: Why, Carnation, you're saving my life. This is heaven. Sheer heaven!

CARNELLE: *(Running to Elain's clothes bag.)* Oh, Elain, did you bring that dress along with you that I asked about on the phone? You know, the beautiful red antebellum dress that you wore at the Natchez Pilgrimage the first year you got married. See, it's gonna be perfect for me to wear in the contest. I'm trying to make crimson red my thematic color. *(Opening the bag: She discovers the dress is not there.)*

ELAIN: I see—but I thought you said you weren't gonna be needing a formal dress for the audition this Saturday.

CARNELLE: I know, that's true. We'll just need them in the actual contest for the opening Parade of Firecrackers.

ELAIN: So, why don't we just wait till after the audition and see if you make it to the pageant.

CARNELLE: Why? Don't you think I'll make it?

ELAIN: Well, I hope so, Carnelle, but they only pick five girls.

CARNELLE: Well…I've thought about it, and I, frankly, can't think of five other girls in town that are prettier than me. I'm speaking honestly now. 'Course I know there's Caroline Jeffers, but she has those yellow teeth—

ELAIN: *(Not wanting to get into it.)* My, this mint is delicious! Did you grow it yourself?

CARNELLE: Aunt Ronelle planted it before she died.

ELAIN: Well, it's quite refreshing.

CARNELLE: I know why you're worried. You think I've ruined my chances, 'cause—'cause of my reputation.

ELAIN: I don't know what you mean—you're perfectly sweet.

CARNELLE: Well, everyone knew I used to go out with lots of men and all that. Different ones. It's been a constant thing with me since I was young and—

ELAIN: Let's not discuss it in all a' this heat.

CARNELLE: I just mention it 'cause it's different now, since Aunt Ronelle died and since—I got that disease.

ELAIN: Please, Carnelle, nobody's profiting by this information!

CARNELLE: Anyway, I go to church now and I'm signed up to where I take an orphan home to dinner once a week or to a movie; and—and I work on the cancer drive here just like you do in Natchez.

ELAIN: That's all very admirable, I'm sure.

CARNELLE: My life has meaning. People aren't calling me, Miss Hot Tamale anymore like they used to. Everything's changed. And being in that contest—it would be such an honor to me...I can't explain the half of it.

ELAIN: Well, if you don't make it to the finals, just try to remember that Mama was at her most noblest when she was least attractive.

CARNELLE: I wish you had about a drop a' faith in me. I'm not all that ugly.

ELAIN: And I wish you would stop fishing for compliments—'cause I'm sick and worn out with giving people compliments about themselves!

CARNELLE: (Overlapping.) I'm sorry. I'm so, so sorry, I make such stupid blunders. I know you don't think I'm ugly.

ELAIN: (Overlapping.) I'm not myself—I'm just not myself.
(She begins brushing her hair. The phone rings. Elain freezes. Carnelle goes to answer it.)

ELAIN: If it's for me—say—say, I'm resting.

CARNELLE: Hello...Oh, hello, Franklin...Yes, she's here...Well, I think she decided not to stop by there...No, she's asleep now. She's gone on to sleep...Well, wait just a minute, I'll go see. (She puts her hand over the phone.) He wants me to go wake you up.

ELAIN: (In a whisper.) He what! Oh, how inconsiderate can he be! Why, I've been driving all day long in this blazing heat and he doesn't even care if I get my rest. You tell him I'm out dead with exhaustion and you absolutely cannot wake me.

CARNELLE: (She waits a few beats and then says breathlessly into the phone.) Franklin...I absolutely cannot wake her. She's out dead with exhaustion...Alright, I'll tell her. 'Bye-'bye. (She hangs up the phone.) He says for you to please call him when you wake up.

ELAIN: Oh, he does, does he? Well, he can just sit and wait, 'cause I'm not calling him—not ever.

CARNELLE: Why not?

ELAIN: Listen, Carnation, I think you should know something—I'm not just here on a visit.

CARNELLE: You're not?

ELAIN: No. (Then after a moment.) I've left Franklin.

CARNELLE: What?!

ELAIN: Now, remember, it's a sworn secret and not a living soul is to find it out.

CARNELLE: I won't say a word to anyone. I swear.

ELAIN: You see, I haven't told Franklin yet and he actually still believes everything is—bearable between us.

CARNELLE: I just can't believe all this. You were so in love. It seemed like Franklin loved you so much. I thought I wanted a man to love me that much.

ELAIN: Yes; he did love me. But it just caused him to follow me around asking, "Do you love me? How much do you love me? Tell me how you love me," till I could shake him till he rattled.

CARNELLE: Then you don't love him anymore?

ELAIN: *(Taking off her jewelry.)* No. He makes me ill.

CARNELLE: How awful.

ELAIN: Yes.

CARNELLE: But what about your two little boys. They need a mother.

ELAIN: Oh, children manage in this world. Don't ask me about them.

CARNELLE: Gosh, Aunt Ronelle said you had it all up there in Natchez; everything—just like a queen in a castle.

ELAIN: I know. I did. I only hope I can stand to give it all up. *(Deeply moved.)* We had such beautiful clocks. I must have a bath. *(She rises.)*

CARNELLE: Elain.

(Elain stops.)

CARNELLE: What was it like—when you had it all?

ELAIN: Ah, Carnation! The abundance of treasures merely serves to underline the desperate futility of life. *(She exits upstairs to the bedrooms.)*

CARNELLE: Oh—tell me more—please! Tell me more!

(She picks up all of the bags and follows Elain out of the room. The stage is empty for a few moments. Suddenly, the front door opens, Delmount Williams enters. Delmount, twenty-eight, is tall and thin with piercing blue eyes and a sallow complexion. He wears a white shirt and a pair of worn-out pants. He carries a brown paper bag containing all of his belongings. Leaving the front door ajar, Delmount enters the room. He finds something about the atmosphere loathsome. He sits down and lights up a pipe. He sits smoking for a few moments, taking in the room. Popeye peeps in the front door.)

POPEYE: *(As she enters.)* Carnelle? Carnelle— *(Spotting Delmount.)* Oh!

DELMOUNT: Hello.

POPEYE: Hi. Are you—you're—

DELMOUNT: Delmount Williams. I'm Carnelle's cousin.

POPEYE: Yeah.

DELMOUNT: Well, I don't know where Carnelle is right now.

POPEYE: Oh.

DELMOUNT: You're a friend of hers, I suppose?

POPEYE: Yes. I just met her recently. I'm Popeye Jackson.

DELMOUNT: Popeye? That's an unusual name.

POPEYE: Oh, well…It's not my original name. I wasn't born with it. *(Embarrassed she begins to run on.)* See, what happened was my brother Lucky, he threw a handful a gravel in my eyes and they started stinging and then he give me this brown bottle a' drops t'put inside my eyes and telling me it's eye drops but, in fact, it's drops for the ears and then this burning sensation come into my eyes, causing me t'scream out and cry like the devil and after that I got me a pair a' glasses and my eyes was bulged out a bit; so folks was calling me Popeye and the name just stuck with me—Popeye. That's how I got the name.

DELMOUNT: *(After a moment.)* Well, that's a mighty tragic tale.

POPEYE: Ah, no. Actually, the fortunate part is I can now hear voices through my eyes.

DELMOUNT: Through your eyes.

POPEYE: Well, now and then I hear 'em—laughing and—carrying on.

DELMOUNT: Yeah. Well, I think I'll see if I can rustle up Carnelle for you. Carnelle! Honey! Are you home?! Carnelle! Carnelle!

POPEYE: Oh, no! No! I just forgot these measurements and I see 'em right here on the side table!

(Carnelle enters from the bedrooms.)

CARNELLE: Delmount! No! No, it isn't you! Why, I can't believe my eyes! Oh, Popeye, this is my cousin, Delmount! He's come back at last! How are you? Are you doing alright? You look tired.

DELMOUNT: I'm fine. Is that a wig?

CARNELLE: What? Oh, no; it's real.

DELMOUNT: My, God, Child, are you trying to look like a bareback rider in the Shooley Traveling Carnival Show?

CARNELLE: You don't like it?

DELMOUNT: Hardly, Honey. Hardly.

CARNELLE: Maybe you'll grow accustomed to it. I have more and more myself. First I didn't like it at all—thought it was loud, in fact. Ah, did you meet my friend, Popeye?

DELMOUNT: *(Sitting down to smoke his pipe.)* We've spoken.

(Carnelle looks over to Popeye. Popeye manages to smile but stands frozen.)

CARNELLE: *(Turning back to Delmount.)* Why, look at you! When did you start smoking a pipe?

DELMOUNT: Don't be silly. I've *always* smoked a pipe. Good Lord and butter. *(After a moment to the women.)* Why don't you sit down?

POPEYE: *(Making her exit in a flurry.)* No. I—really have to be going. I just forgot these measurements here. Now I got 'em.

CARNELLE: Well, alright. I'll be seeing you. 'Bye!

(Popeye is gone. Carnelle turns back to Delmount.)

CARNELLE: So, what have you been doing?

DELMOUNT: Not much. Had a job scraping up dead dogs from the road.

CARNELLE: We were—concerned about you.

DELMOUNT: I was alright. 'Course the dogs were a rotting mess.

CARNELLE: *(After a moment.)* So, what brings you back home to Brookhaven?

DELMOUNT: Business.

CARNELLE: Oh.

DELMOUNT: I don't know if you realized this but my mamma the monkey left the whole of this house to me.

CARNELLE: I realized it.

DELMOUNT: Well, I'm going to sell it. I'm going to sell this house and every stick of furniture in it. And I don't want to hear anything from you about it. It's mine; it's been given to me. And I'm not going to feel sorry for you just 'cause you went and dyed your hair fire engine red!

CARNELLE: Well, alright, Delmount! You don't have to get mean about it! If you want to sell the house, it's your house to sell; so go on and sell it!

DELMOUNT: I will! I'm through working at disgusting job after disgusting job. I hate working! I loathe it!

(Elain appears on the staircase in a flowing robe.)

ELAIN: Carnation, Honey, where'd you put the—

DELMOUNT: Oh—No!!

ELAIN: Delmount!

DELMOUNT: You bitch! You!

ELAIN: What!?

DELMOUNT: How could you betray me like that!?! Your own flesh! Your own blood!

ELAIN: What's wrong with you? Are you still insane?

DELMOUNT: Ooh! Ooh! I'm not speaking to you! I'm not speaking to you!!

CARNELLE: *(Overlapping.)* What's going on? What is it?

ELAIN: Don't ask me! Don't ask me!

DELMOUNT: No! No! Don't ask her! She could never tell. She could never tell that the beautiful, the sweet, the perfect, Elain Rutledge refused to help her own brother get out of a dirty lunatic asylum!

ELAIN: Why, it was clean, it was cheerful, it was the most expensive money could buy! Oh, but you've always lied—even as a child we could never believe a word you said!

CARNELLE: *(Overlapping.)* Oh, what's wrong? What happened? Tell me! Please!!

DELMOUNT: It's all quite simple, child a mine. They would have released me after two months time into Mrs. Rutledge's loving custody, 'cause, you see, she is my next a' kin, but she wouldn't have me. She wouldn't sign the papers.

ELAIN: *(Overlapping.)* Please, Delmount. I'm sorry, but we thought you needed the professional help. You were so upset about Mama dying—

DELMOUNT: Oh, Lord! She knows I wasn't upset 'cause of that! She knows that!

ELAIN: And Franklin just thought, 'cause of the children—

DELMOUNT: *(Under his breath.)* Franklin—that sheep pussy.

ELAIN: *(Angry.)* I mean, after all, Delmount, you did commit a violent act— hitting that poor man in the face with a bottle—

DELMOUNT: *(To Carnelle.)* Do you actually think I'm of such base character? I challenged that man to a duel! A duel! I can't help it if the weapons he chose were broken bottles! It was an honorable act in defense of a woman with beautiful, warm, bronze skin. I do not regret it.

ELAIN: *(Trying to break in between Carnelle and Delmount.)* Well, besides all of that, you know good and well, you've always had a checkered past!

DELMOUNT: What checkered past?

ELAIN: For one thing, you tried to choke Carnelle's poor father to death right in there at the dining room table!

DELMOUNT: Why, I never!

ELAIN: You did! It was right on New Year's Day!

CARNELLE: That's right, 'cause I found the dime in the black-eyed peas—

DELMOUNT: Alright, I did! I did it! But he was boring me to death! I just wanted to shut him up!

ELAIN: Now, see! See! That is not reasonable behavior! It's just not reasonable. And how you almost got run out of town on a rail 'cause of what happened with T.S. Mahoney's two young virgin daughters! It's no wonder you have bad dreams! It's no wonder!!

DELMOUNT: Rub my face in it, why don't you! You're so damn perfect and I'm such a no-account failure! Rub my face in it!

ELAIN: I'm sorry, Delmount. I'm sorry. Oh, you bring out the worst in me. You always have. You always have!

(Elain exits in a flurry. Carnelle and Delmount look after her for a moment then Carnelle goes to pick up the crackers and Delmount goes back to his pipe.)

DELMOUNT: The irony of it. The intense irony.

CARNELLE: What irony?

DELMOUNT: Mahoney's two ugly daughters. I went up there thinking all they wanted was for me to see their box of newborn kittens. Well, when we got up in the attic, I saw most all of the kittens had swollen heads and crippled bodies. It was nothing but a cardboard box full of deformed damn cats. That's all there was to it. Well, I felt sorry for those two ugly daughters with their deformed box of cats. And they were dying for it. Hell, I was doing them a favor. There's the irony. You just can't go around obliging other people in this world. That's one thing I've learned.

CARNELLE: *(Sticking a dirty cracker into her mouth.)* I feel sorry for ugly girls. I really do.

DELMOUNT: Yeah. Ah, listen, little child a mine. About selling the house and all, I was planning on giving you half of what I make. That way you can get out of this town for good and always. How about it?

CARNELLE: Well, Delmount. I don't know! I've never thought about leaving Brookhaven.

DELMOUNT: Well, think about it. There's never been anything here for you but sorrow.

CARNELLE: Yes, that's true. Still...I don't know. *(After a moment.)* Maybe if I could, if I could leave in a blaze of glory. Yes! That's what I'd like to do—leave this town in a blaze of glory!

DELMOUNT: How do you mean?

CARNELLE: Well, if I won the Miss Firecracker Contest—see, I'm a contestant in it and if I could just win first prize then I would be able to leave this town in a crimson blaze of glory!

DELMOUNT: The Miss Firecracker Contest—Hell and damnation! *(He gets up.)*

CARNELLE: *(Following after him.)* Where are you going?

DELMOUNT: For a walk! *(He exits out the front door.)*

CARNELLE: *(Yelling after him.)* Delmount! Well, what in the world is eating you?! *(After a moment.)* Hmm, yes...a crimson blaze of glory!
(She performs with solemn beauty as the lights begin to fade.)

CARNELLE: "And the rockets red glare—Boom!—the bombs bursting in air—Boom!—gave proof through the night—that our flag was—Boom!—there!" Boom! Boom! Boom!
(Blackout.)

SCENE II

The lights go up on the living room. It is about eight o'clock in the evening on the following Saturday. Several cold, formal arrangements of long-stemmed roses have been placed around the room. Most pieces of furniture now have price tags tied onto them. Delmount stands smoking a pipe, and spinning the spinning wheel around as he listens to it creak.

DELMOUNT: Hmmm…

(He gives the spinning wheel a kick. It wobbles. He goes to the desk to fill out a price tag. Elain enters carrying a silver tray with a decanter of wine and three glasses on it. One of the glasses has already been poured. Elain is somewhat tipsy.)

ELAIN: Hello, Delly, I've brought you out a cool glass of Japanese plum wine.

DELMOUNT: No, thank you.

ELAIN: *(Setting the tray down.)* It's really exquisite wine. I just love things that are Japanese.

(He doesn't respond.)

ELAIN: Sure you don't want a glass?

DELMOUNT: Yes. *(He goes to put a price tag on the spinning wheel.)*

ELAIN: How much are you asking for the spinning wheel?

DELMOUNT: Five dollars.

ELAIN: Five dollars! Why, that is just wildly ridiculous! I mean, that's an actual antique you've got before you!

DELMOUNT: If you don't mind, Miss Priss, this is all my affair!

ELAIN: Ooh. And I thought you weren't mad at me anymore.

DELMOUNT: What made you think that?

ELAIN: Yesterday afternoon when we were sitting out back snapping green beans for supper you started laughing and telling your stories—I thought we were friends again. Please, you know you're just being hard-hearted about the whole thing.

DELMOUNT: I don't know what I'm being. I had bad dreams last night. I always have them. They never stop. Every night I have them.

ELAIN: *(Fanning herself.)* Must a' been the heat.

(The phone rings. They look at each other.)

ELAIN: Get it!!

(Delmount dashes for the phone. Carnelle appears at the door with a dish rag in her hand. It is obvious that she has raced to get there.)

DELMOUNT: *(Answering the phone.)* Hello?…This is he speaking…Yes…

What?…No, I would not consider giving it away…I'm sorry but I happen to need the profit…

(Carnelle goes and picks up Delmount's dinner tray that is sitting on the desk.)

DELMOUNT: Well, it'll be up for auction at the July Fourth Carnival, if you want it so badly you can bid for it there…Yes…Fine. Good-bye. *(He hangs up the phone.)* That was Mrs. J.R. Biggs. Imagine! She wanted me to donate that old spinning wheel to the D.A.R. How ludicrous! As though that entire organization couldn't afford to bid five dollars for it! What presumption! It's most maddening!

CARNELLE: Well, I guess, I better go and finish up the dishes. That—ah, that tuna nood'll really stick t'your plates. *(She exits to the kitchen, holding back tears.)*

DELMOUNT: Dammit! When were they supposed to have called by?

ELAIN: Six o'clock. It's after eight now.

DELMOUNT: I hate this. So she didn't even make it to the stupid finals.

ELAIN: I guess not.

DELMOUNT: God.

ELAIN: Not only that—Ruby Kay told me this year they had the worst turn-out in history. Ever since they had to integrate the contest she says the turnout's been decreasing and the quality of the entire event has gone down, down, down.

DELMOUNT: Oh, stop it, please! I don't want to hear about it. Jesus God.

ELAIN: I know, I know.

DELMOUNT: *(Frantically.)* I don't know what to do. I mean, she actually thinks she's tap-dancing. *(He imitates her.)* She's moving around like this, or something and she thinks she's tap-dancing. Remember how Uncle Willie just dropped her off here and left her with nothing but a pillowcase full of dirty rags? I'd never seen anything so pathetic. Had ringworms in her head.

ELAIN: Uh. Mama had to shave off all of her hair and put ointment on those sores in her head—I don't know, seemed like several times a day.

DELMOUNT: God, she was an ugly sight.

ELAIN: Wasn't she though. She always went around wearing that yellow wool knit cap pulled down over her head even in the summer's heat. Mama told her people would just think she had short yellow hair.

DELMOUNT: Mama was such a brilliant woman.

ELAIN: Well, from a distance it kinda looked like that.

DELMOUNT: I do doubt it. Anyway, she never did attain any self-esteem. Had to sleep with every worthless soul in Brookhaven trying to prove she was attractive.

ELAIN: *(Finishing another glass of wine.)* Please! It was just some sort of degrading stage she was going through. I'm certain she's over it now.

DELMOUNT: Well, I wish she was back in it.

ELAIN: Delmount!

DELMOUNT: I do! Least then she wasn't putting herself into stupid, miserable contests and publicly getting kicked in the face. Least for the disease she just privately took some shots.

ELAIN: Don't talk about it! I can't bear that side of life! It's repulsive to me. So shut up your mouth for once!!

DELMOUNT: Well, don't have a hissy fit!

(The phone rings.)

ELAIN: My, God.

DELMOUNT: You think it's them?

ELAIN: No. I don't know.

(Carnelle appears at the door with a brownie in her hand.)

CARNELLE: Here, I'll get it. I'll go on and—get it. *(She picks up the phone.)* Hello?…Oh. Yes, just a minute. It's for you Elain. It's Franklin.

ELAIN: Thanks.

(Carnelle exits to the kitchen, stuffing the brownie into her mouth.)

ELAIN: Hello…Yes, Dear, I got them…Oh, they're beautiful; they're—very fragrant; they're—I-I don't want to come home…I mean not ever, or for awhile, or for not ever…I feel like I'm missing my life…I don't know about the children. They'll manage…Oh, for God's sake, Franklin, no one's going to bake them into a pie!…Oh, please! I don't want to discuss it anymore. I'm tired of it all, I'm through with it all. Good-bye! *(She hangs up the phone. She is stunned and shaken by what she has done.)*

DELMOUNT: *(Who has been listening to all of this while pretending to work with the price tags.)* Did you mean it? You're gonna leave him?

ELAIN: Yes.

DELMOUNT: By God, Swayne. By God. I love ya, Honey! How I do love ya! Now are you sure you meant it?

ELAIN: Uh huh.

DELMOUNT: Don't just tell me you meant it, then later take it all back. You've done that before, you know.

ELAIN: I haven't.

DELMOUNT: What do you mean you haven't?!? It's a personality trait with you. It's your trademark! You tell me you're gonna do something one way and then you go back on it 'cause of what Mama said or what Franklin said or what some other fly-by-night-fool-idiot said!

ELAIN: Don't pick on me!

DELMOUNT: Ooh! I knew it! You didn't mean it! I knew it!

ELAIN: I meant it! I said it!

DELMOUNT: All you want is for everyone to think you're perfect. Well, perfect is dull!

ELAIN: Don't you dare call me dull. Just because I'm not insane and obsessed and possessed by dreams.

DELMOUNT: *(Overlapping.)* Shut up, Elain. Shut up your red blood lips!

ELAIN: You are a selfish human being! Mama always loved you ten times better than me.

DELMOUNT: Oh God.

ELAIN: I had to win contests and be in pageants before she'd give me any notice at all. When I graduated junior college she said, "You've had your spoonful of gravy now go out and get a rich husband"; so I did.

DELMOUNT: You're a fool to let Mama ramshackle your life. Mama was nothing but mean.

ELAIN: Not to you. She was sweet to you.

DELMOUNT: She pretended to be sweet.

ELAIN: Well, everyone always thought she was. Till the day she died, people were saying she was a blessed angel on earth.

DELMOUNT: Yeah, an angel in ape's clothing.

ELAIN: You are so cruel.

DELMOUNT: Well, hell, she just turned herself into a monkey to get at us—just to be mean. I always knew Mama was mean.

ELAIN: No. She wasn't always. Things change. She wasn't always.

DELMOUNT: Why, I remember when I was a child a' three how she tortured our favorite dog, White Face, right before my very eyes.

ELAIN: Wha'd she do to White Face?

DELMOUNT: Well, remember how White Face would always stand out by the back porch door hoping somebody would throw him some measly scraps?

ELAIN: I guess so.

DELMOUNT: Well, one day she was making a lemon pie and she says to me, "Ha! Let's see how he likes *this!*" and she slings a lemon rind right out to White Face and he jumps up and bites into it then runs off howling. And she's just standing there—laughing.

ELAIN: *(Stunned.)* Oh my God. So, Mama's always been mean. G'me a drag off a' your pipe.

(He hands her the pipe. She takes a long drag.)

DELMOUNT: Are you really gonna leave him?

ELAIN: *(Handing back the pipe.)* I said I would.

(The phone rings. They look at each other.)

DELMOUNT: I can't stand it. *(He grabs the phone angrily.)* Yeah!?…Oh. Yes, just a minute. Carnelle? Carnelle, telephone!! Carnelle!

ELAIN: *(Overlapping.)* Carnelle! Honey! Phone!

(Carnelle appears. Her face is beet red.)

CARNELLE: For me?

DELMOUNT: Uh huh. *(He hands her the phone.)*

CARNELLE: *(Into the phone.)* Hello…Oh, Ronnie…No, I don't think so…'Cause, I don't go out riding around like that anymore. I got other interests now…You just don't understand anything about me…Now don't you call me that…I said don't call me that. So long. *(She hangs up the phone and stands totally still.)*

ELAIN: Who was it?

CARNELLE: Nobody. Just that creep Ronnie Wayne I used to date. He's calling me Miss Hot Tamale. Listen, I guess, I won't be needing that red dress of yours. It looks like I didn't make the Miss Firecracker Contest after all.

DELMOUNT: Ah well…count yourself lucky—that type a' false pageantry; it's way beneath you.

ELAIN: Yes, it is. Why-why since it's been integrated the quality of the contest has really gone down, down, down.

DELMOUNT: Why, it's nothing but a garish display of painted-up-prancing pigs! That's all there is to it.

CARNELLE: Well, the main thing is—it was gonna be—I don't know—visible proof. And I would a' liked to ride on a float and wave out to people.

ELAIN: Why, all this is gonna help build up your character! Remember, the more Mama suffered the more divine she became.

(There is a knock at the door.)

CARNELLE: That must be Popeye. I told her I'd pay her tonight for sewing my costume. Tell her I'll be right back with the money. *(She exits up the stairs, holding back tears.)*

DELMOUNT: Popeye—that's all we need. Did she lose her brains or what?

ELAIN: I like Popeye. She's a nice girl.

DELMOUNT: Then you talk to her. I'm gonna go get my dessert. *(He exits to the kitchen, mumbling to himself.*) So, it's over. It's finished. She lost. Good. I'm glad!

ELAIN: (*As she opens the door for Popeye.*) Hello, Honey. Come on in.

(*Popeye enters. She is wearing the earrings.*)

POPEYE: Hi.

ELAIN: Well, it looks like our little Carnation didn't make the beauty pageant after all.

POPEYE: (*Shocked.*) She didn't?

ELAIN: No.

POPEYE: I can't believe it.

ELAIN: Well, here, Honey, let me get you a glass of cool, plum wine.

POPEYE: I just knew she was gonna make it—with her red hair and her dancing and those roman candles shooting off right up into the sky.

ELAIN: (*Handing her some wine.*) I know. She put a lot of work into it. It's a disappointment. But life is hard and it's never easy to lose anything.

POPEYE: No, I suppose not. (*After a moment.*) I once knew these two midgets by the names of Sweet Pea and Willas. I went to their wedding and they was the only midgets there. Rest a' their family was regular-size people. But they was so happy together and they moved into a little midget house where everything was mite size like this little old desk they had and this little ole stool. Then Sweet Pea got pregnant and later on she had what they called this Cesarean birth where they slice open your stomach and pull the baby out from the slice. Well, come to find out, the baby's a regular-size child and soon that baby is just too large for Sweet Pea to carry around and too large for all a' that mite-sized furniture. So Sweet Pea has to give up her own baby for her Mama to raise. I thought she'd die to lose that child. It about crushed her heart.

ELAIN: (*Finishing off her glass of wine.*) I don't feel that way about my two boys. I don't want to spend time teaching them manners. I don't like them.

POPEYE: Y'don't?

ELAIN: No. My husband either.

POPEYE: What's wrong with him?

ELAIN: (*Gaily, as she pours herself some more wine.*) He smells of sweet cologne and wears three rings on every finger.

POPEYE: (*Pretending she has three rings on every finger.*) Gosh. They must feel heavy.

ELAIN: It's such a burden trying to live up to a beautiful face. I'm afraid I'm missing everything in the world.

(*Delmount enters from the kitchen.*)

DELMOUNT: What happened to all of those brownies?

ELAIN: They're right in there on that blue china tray.

DELMOUNT: All of them?

ELAIN: Yes, Delly, the whole batch.

    (Delmount exits to the kitchen.)

POPEYE: *(Whispering hoarsely.)* What's the matter? He can't find the brownies?

ELAIN: I'm sure they're right under his nose.

    (Delmount enters, carrying an empty tray.)

DELMOUNT: They're all gone! The whole batch!

ELAIN: My, goodness! Well, I guess Carnelle ate them up. She's a compulsive eater when she's unhappy.

DELMOUNT: Dammit! I wanted a brownie! *(Then he stops, embarrassed.)* Ah, hello, Popeye. How're you?

POPEYE: Fine.

DELMOUNT: *(Smoothing down his wild hair.)* Well…good. Ah, lovely earrings you're wearing.

POPEYE: Thank you. They was a present t'me from Elain. She give 'em to me.

DELMOUNT: Oh, right. Carnelle mentioned it…Well, maybe we—have some ice cream in the freezer. *(He exits to the kitchen.)*

POPEYE: *(Weakly.)* Oh. Oh. Oh. *(She begins fanning her heart and blowing air onto it.)*

ELAIN: What's the matter? Are you alright?

POPEYE: My heart—it's—hot. It's hot. It's burning. *(Blowing air onto her heart.)* Puff, puff, puff. *(She puts the wineglass against her heart.)* There. Ah. It's better now. It's better.

ELAIN: My word, you look faint.

POPEYE: Tell me, when your heart gets hot, does that mean you're in love?

ELAIN: Dar'lin, are you in love?

POPEYE: I reckon.

ELAIN: Not—not with Delmount?!

POPEYE: Yes. *(Puff puff.)* Yes.

ELAIN: How astonishing! Why, his complexion's so sallow—and he's got a rude, irritable disposition.

POPEYE: It does seem like it.

ELAIN: How utterly odd. Tell me, Popeye, have you ever been in love before?

POPEYE: Well, my heart's never been hot or nothing, but I did have me a boyfriend once.

ELAIN: And what was he like?

POPEYE: Not much. He like t'pet me like I was a cat or something. He's asking me to purr and meow. Like, "meow, meow, purr, purr, purr." I don't know, he's crazy. I's expecting him t'give me a box a' cat nips for Christmas.

ELAIN: What did he give you?

POPEYE: ...Nothing.

ELAIN: *(Pouring them both more wine.)* Well, if you want my opinion, that is just about what Delmount will give you. He's an unstable character and he's had a very checkered past.

POPEYE: I know 'bout that.

ELAIN: Well, did you know about his strange, obsessive eye for beauty?

(Popeye shakes her head.)

ELAIN: How he's been known to follow a normal-looking woman through the streets all day and all night because he finds the mere shape of her nose exotic or beautiful; or perhaps he finds the texture of her lips to be unusually soft and smooth. You don't want anything to do with him. I worry about him. He's not right. He's obsessed. *(She finishes her drink. She is uncomfortable and upset.)* What in the world is keeping Carnelle? She must be up in her room crying. I'd better go get her.

(Elain exits up the stairs. Popeye sits alone sipping wine. She begins shaking her head back and forth. After a moment she makes a solemn toast to the voices inside her eyes.)

POPEYE: Cheers.

(Delmount enters from the kitchen. He is eating a dish of vanilla ice cream.)

DELMOUNT: Oh. Hello. Where's Elain?

POPEYE: She's getting Carnelle.

DELMOUNT: *(Smoothing down his hair.)* Oh. *(He sits at the desk and begins writing.)*

POPEYE: Are you writing poems?

DELMOUNT: What?

POPEYE: Carnelle said you write poems.

DELMOUNT: Oh. Well, on occasion I have.

POPEYE: I'd like to read 'em.

DELMOUNT: *(Embarrassed.)* They're personal.

POPEYE: Oh. *(She starts to run on.)* 'Course, I never read many poems before. There weren't all that many poem books you could get off a' the traveling bookmobile. Most books I got was about animals. Farm animals, jungle animals, Arctic animals and such. 'Course they was informative, I learned some things; they's called: a gaggle a' geese, a pride a' lions, a warren a' rabbits, a host a' whales. That's my personal favorite one: a host a' whales!

(They look at each other.)

POPEYE: Carnelle says you can wiggle your ears.

DELMOUNT: Does she?

POPEYE: Yes.

DELMOUNT: *(Straightening his hair.)* It's an old trick.

POPEYE: I would liked t'have seen it.

DELMOUNT: I don't do it anymore. *(He straightens his hair again.)*

POPEYE: What d'ya dream about at nights?

DELMOUNT: *(Taken aback.)* Why do you ask?

POPEYE: I don't know, your face looks tired. I thought maybe you was having bad dreams.

DELMOUNT: What are you saying? You make me uncomfortable. A gaggle of geese! What's that?! What are you talking about? This whole night has been unbearable! Ooooh! Now the ice cream has given me a headache. Lord Jesus! A gaggle of geese! Oh, my head! My head!

(He exits to the bedroom, holding his head. Popeye watches him leave then she puts both of her hands over her heart and starts to sob.)

POPEYE: Oh. Oh. Oh. I must be stupid. I must be.

(Carnelle enters from the bedrooms. Her nose is red. She carries a wad of Kleenexes and a change purse. She spots Popeye crying.)

CARNELLE: Popeye! What is it? What's the matter?

POPEYE: *(Sobbing.)* Oh, I'm stupid. I'm stupid.

CARNELLE: Why? What happened? What?

POPEYE: It seems—it seems I love him. *(Pointing to the door.)* I love Delmount.

CARNELLE: Oh, no! I knew it. I knew it.

POPEYE: But I don't know what to say. I don't know how to come to say it. I just say, "Carnelle says you can wiggle your ears." He doesn't love me. I've lost him!

CARNELLE: *(Starting to cry.)* Oh, oh. Dear, little Popeye. I've lost too. I've lost too.

POPEYE: What?

CARNELLE: The contest! I lost the Miss Firecracker Contest!

POPEYE: Oh, right.

CARNELLE: I didn't even make the finals! They don't want me. I'm a failure!

POPEYE: Oh! There, there.

CARNELLE: I'm ugly, Popeye! My thighs are fat! No one loves me!

POPEYE: *(Overlapping.)* Oh, he'll never love me! Never! Never!! Oh, I hope I don't scream out—aaahh!!!

CARNELLE: *(Overlapping as she pulls at her hair.)* I hate my hair! I hate it!

(Elain enters from the bedroom. She spots them crying.)

ELAIN: My, God! What is it? What's wrong?! Did someone die?!

CARNELLE: *(Falling across the couch.)* Oh, don't ask! Don't ask!

ELAIN: What happened?! Please! What?!

POPEYE: *(Wiping away tears.)* Well...well, she's crying 'cause she lost the beauty contest—and, and I'm crying 'cause he—he—he doesn't care about me! *(Popeye breaks down crying.)*

ELAIN: Oh, I see. You poor dears. You poor dears. There, there now. Here, here, now. There, there.

(Popeye and Carnelle whimper softly.)

ELAIN: You don't have to worry anymore. Things'll get better. Your lives aren't over, not like mine is. No, neither of you have to face the sort of tragedy I'm facing. Neither of you is starting life all over again, feeling nothing but terror and fear and loneliness!

(Popeye and Carnelle sob loudly.)

ELAIN: Oh, God. Oh, God. I can't believe I've left him. I've left him! Oh, my, dear God! There'll be no more roses! No more! *(She caresses an armful of roses.)*

CARNELLE: What? You've really left Franklin?

ELAIN: Yes! *(Weeping as she throws a handful of roses.)* Good-bye!

CARNELLE: You've told him?

ELAIN: *(Throwing another handful of roses.)* Yes! Farewell!

CARNELLE: Oh, Elain! Elain!

ELAIN: *(Throwing roses.)* No more! No more!!

POPEYE: Roses! Look! Roses!

ELAIN: *(Throwing roses.)* I don't know what to do! I don't know what I can do!

CARNELLE: Me neither; me neither. Oh, life!

POPEYE: *(Holding roses.)* Roses! Roses! Roses!

(Pause. The phone rings. All throw roses at the phone as they continue weeping.)

POPEYE: *(Pointing to the phone with a rose.)* It rings!

ELAIN: Oh, let it ring! Just let it ring!

POPEYE: Yes, ring!

(The phone rings four more times.)

CARNELLE: *(Suddenly alive.)* Wait. I'll get it. Quick! Here, I'll get it! *(She grabs the receiver.)* Hello...Yes, this is she...What?...Oh, I'm so sorry...Oh, no. How sad. How tragic...What?...Yes, alright...Thank you. 'Bye-'bye. *(She puts down the phone.)* That—That was Miss Blue and, well, do you remember her little dog, Turnip?

ELAIN: The brown and white one—

CARNELLE: *(Breathlessly.)* Yes, well, Turnip was hit by a van and he died; so Miss Blue was late in notifying the five finalists but—oh my God.

POPEYE: Huh?

CARNELLE: Oh my God.

ELAIN: What?

CARNELLE: I made. I made it! By God I made the pageant!!! I did! I did! I made it! AAAHHH!!!!!

ELAIN: *(Overlapping.)* Praise God! Praise God! Some victory!

POPEYE: *(Overlapping.)* Oh you made it! You made it! Hurray!

ELAIN: *(Running on.)* Oh, Carnation! Carnation, what a triumph for you! Of course, I always knew you'd make the pageant! I never doubted it for one minute!

CARNELLE: They're—they're gonna be taking my picture for the newspaper at ten o'clock in the morning at the Courthouse square. I'll be famous!

ELAIN: It's just stupendous! Here; here let's have a toast!

CARNELLE: A toast for *me?* Make a toast for *me?*

ELAIN: Yes! Yes! *(She starts to pour the glasses.)*

POPEYE: Yes, a toast! A toast!

ELAIN: Quick, call Delmount! I'll pour out these glasses.

CARNELLE: Delmount! Delmount, come quick! We're having a toast! We're having a toast to me!

ELAIN: *(Overlapping.)* Here you go, Popeye. And for our Carnation. *(Delmount enters from the bathroom. He is in his bathrobe and wears a towel wrapped around his head.)*

DELMOUNT: What is it? What? I'm right in the middle of my hot oil treatment!

ELAIN: *(Handing him a glass.)* Here, Delmount, we're having a toast!

DELMOUNT: Huh?

ELAIN: Well, no more glasses. I'll just have to drink from the bottle. A toast, everyone! To Carnation! May she win first prize in the Miss Firecracker Contest!

DELMOUNT: What?!

ELAIN: *(She raises the bottle.)* Cheers!

POPEYE: *(Raising her glass.)* Cheers!

CARNELLE: *(Raising her glass.)* Cheers!

DELMOUNT: *(As he clinks each of their glasses.)* Oh—my—miserable—God! *(They go about clinking each other's glasses as Delmount downs his drink and the lights black out.)*

END OF ACT I

ACT II
SCENE I

The lights go up on an empty stage. Mac Sam, the balloon man, enters up right carrying a bunch of colored balloons, and coughing painfully. Mac Sam is in his mid-thirties. He is amazingly thin, stooped shouldered, and in drastically poor health. Yet there is something extraordinarily sensual about him. His eyes manage to be magnetic and bloodshot at the same time. He walks slowly over to the doorway of the dressing room.

MAC SAM: Hey, Carnelle. Hey, beautiful. *(He sees that no one is inside.)* Hmm. *(He finishes his cigarette and tosses it to the ground and spits up a lot of blood. He wanders off up right, coughing and whistling a tune. Carnelle enters left into the dressing room with Tessy Mahoney. Tessy is the uglier of T.S. Mahoney's two ugly daughters. She has a large nose, a weak chin, tiny eyes, and bad posture. She covers up her bitterness by being as sweet as she can be. Carnelle is wearing a simple button-down shift but she has applied lavish makeup and elaborately styled her hair in preparation for the contest. Both women are carrying armloads of beauty contest paraphernalia: the red antebellum dress; a hoop for the skirt; pantaloons; the red, silver, and blue costume; a robe, a makeup case; shoes; stockings; roman candles; etc.)*

TESSY: *(As she enters the dressing room carrying only the tap shoes.)* It's over here. It's this way. It's this way, here!

CARNELLE'S VOICE: Oh. Oh, I see. I see!

TESSY: Can you make it?

CARNELLE: *(Making her way into the dressing room.)* Yeah. I got it. Here, I got it. *(Dropping her belongings where she can.)* Wheew! Brother. Thanks very much for the help.

TESSY: Sure. It's what I'm here for.

CARNELLE: Oh, look! Is this my dressing room? Is this mine?

TESSY: *(Picking up her clipboard and taking a pencil from behind her ear.)* Uh huh. It's the only one left. The good ones have all been taken. *(Looking at her watch.)* You're running late, you know.

CARNELLE: *(Struggling with her belongings.)* Yes, I know. I was sewing on my dress. Things aren't going smoothly at all today. Oh, look! Now my hair piece is falling out. I worked all morning on that. So, is your sister nervous?

TESSY: Not really. I guess she knows she doesn't have a chance.

CARNELLE: *(As she straightens up her things.)* What makes you say that?

TESSY: Well, she's not at all attractive. I'm amazed she ever got in the contest. I'm sure it's just 'cause the judges think she's some sort of concert pianist. But she just knows that one opus by Johann Sebastian Bach. I swear that's all she knows.

CARNELLE: Hmm, I suppose that talent part of the contest will count quite a bit.

TESSY: Well, she looks like a tank in her swimsuit.

CARNELLE: She does?

TESSY: She's hump shouldered from practicing that one Johann Sebastian Bach opus on our piano all day long.

CARNELLE: What a shame.

TESSY: This is strictly confidential, but the word is out that the only real contenders for the Miss Firecracker crown are you and Caroline Jeffers.

CARNELLE: *(Overcome.)* Oh, gosh, I don't know—

TESSY: It's the truth. Everyone's saying it. We're all agreed.

CARNELLE: Of course Caroline's really a lovely girl…

TESSY: Yeah, except for those yellow teeth.

CARNELLE: Well, I hear she took medicine for seizures that she had as a child and it scraped off most of her tooth enamel.

TESSY: I heard that too, but it doesn't matter.

CARNELLE: It doesn't?

TESSY: I really don't think the judges are interested in sentimentality—just the teeth themselves. *(Referring to the red dress.)* That's such a beautiful red dress. It's really very fine.

CARNELLE: Yes, it's beautiful. I'm just a little worried though. It just arrived from Natchez yesterday and, well, it didn't seem to fit me exactly right.

TESSY: What's wrong with the fit?

CARNELLE: Well, the waist was a little snug. But I worked on it this morning and added in this extra bit of material. *(She shows that a large strip of pink material has been awkwardly added to the bodice of the red dress.)*

TESSY: *(Disdainfully.)* Oh. Well.

CARNELLE: 'Course, I know it's not the exact matching color. Actually, my cousin Elain's gone to get my seamstress, Popeye Jackson, and see what she can do. We couldn't find her last night. She'll fix it right up. This is just temporary.

TESSY: Well, I hope so. It looks a little funny.

CARNELLE: *(Looking outside.)* Oh, I know Elain'll bring Popeye; she promised she would. She's never let me down in her life. Gosh, I think I'm starting t'sweat. My makeup is melting right down my face. *(She starts fixing her face.)*

TESSY: *(Looking at her watch.)* Hmm. Actually, you don't have much time. It's only twenty-eight minutes till the opening Parade of Firecrackers. *(Tessy blows her whistle.)*

CARNELLE: Oh, my word! Well, I'm ready except for my dress. I mean, my head is ready.

TESSY: *(Removing schedule from her clipboard.)* Well, anyway, here's your schedule.

CARNELLE: Thanks.

TESSY: Oh and have you seen the Grand Float they've made for Miss Firecracker to ride at the head of the Independence Day Parade?

CARNELLE: Oh, yes, I saw it—it's…beautiful.

TESSY: Why, yes, it's very fine. Well, I'd better go let Miss Blue know you're checked in. *(After glancing at herself in the mirror.)* Oh. Mind if I borrow some of your hairspray?

CARNELLE: No, go ahead.

TESSY: Thanks. *(As she sprays her already rock hard hair.)* I, ah, hear your cousin Delmount's back in town.

CARNELLE: Yes, he's back.

TESSY: *(Still spraying.)* Well, you can tell him for me that I've forgiven him. I understand now that some men just don't have any self-control. Just none at all. Think that'll hold?

CARNELLE: Uh huh.

TESSY: Anyway, tell him my Uncle Ferd's given us a new litter of Siamese kittens if he wants to drop by and see them. I know he always enjoyed animals.

CARNELLE: I'll tell him.

TESSY: Well, good luck. I'll be standing by backstage running the contest. Let me know if any emergencies arrive.

CARNELLE: Alright.

TESSY: Give 'em H.

CARNELLE: I'll try.

(Tessy exits left. Carnelle turns back and looks in the mirror. She stares at herself as she wipes sweat off the back of her neck.)

CARNELLE: Oh, Lord. *(She tries a big friendly smirk. It falters.)* Oh, Lord. *(She begins fooling with her hair and makeup. Mac Sam enters from the carnival grounds upstage right. He stops, looks at the dressing room, ties his balloons to the bench, and goes toward the dressing room.)*

MAC SAM: *(Looking inside the dressing room.)* Hi, ya!

CARNELLE: AAH!

MAC SAM: Admiring y'physiognomy?

CARNELLE: *(Catching her breath.)* Mac Sam. What are you doing here?

MAC SAM: Just came t'wish you well. Heard you were in the beauty contest and came by t'wish you well.

CARNELLE: *(Breathlessly.)* Thanks. I'm nervous.

MAC SAM: Sure y'are. Well, good luck. I wish y'well.

(He leaves the dressing room. She follows.)

CARNELLE: I—didn't think I'd be seeing you again.

MAC SAM: Yeah, well, wonders never do quite cease. *(He looks at her with his magnetic eyes then starts to leave again.)*

CARNELLE: I tried to notify you. After I found out. Couldn't…locate you though.

MAC SAM: Oh, "that." Yeah, well, I'm enjoying—"that." Find it most fascinating.

CARNELLE: But didn't you get the shots?

MAC SAM: Nah.

CARNELLE: But all you do is—they give you these shots and you're cured. It cures you.

MAC SAM: I don't care t'be cured.

CARNELLE: What do you mean? You've got to be.

MAC SAM: *(Taking out a cigarette.)* Listen, Honey, this life a' mine is strictly on the house. Strictly a free roll a' the eternal dice. I was almost choked to death by my mama's umbilical cord at birth. Spent three days purple and gasping for breath. I'm tired out of gasping. *(He lights his cigarette and blows out the match.)* Mmm. Your hair looks really nice. I like that color. It looks good on you.

CARNELLE: It doesn't seem too loud?

MAC SAM: *(Smelling her hair.)* Not a bit. No, Sugar, not a bit.

DELMOUNT'S VOICE: Carnelle!? Carnelle, are you about?!

CARNELLE: *(Yelling.)* Delmount! Is that you? *(To Mac Sam.)* It's my cousin, Delmount.

DELMOUNT'S VOICE: Carnelle!!

CARNELLE: I'm over here!

MAC SAM: Well, I'll be ambling along. It was good seeing you.

CARNELLE: *(Impulsively.)* Will ya come back by?

MAC SAM: *(His eyes becoming magnetic.)* Oh, yeah. *(He exits right.)*

DELMOUNT'S VOICE: Carnelle!

CARNELLE: I'm over here!!!

(Delmount enters excitedly from the carnival grounds downstage right. His hair is wild; he carries a stuffed dog.)

DELMOUNT: Oh! Well, there you are! Sounded like your voice was coming from over there by the snow cone stand.

CARNELLE: No, I'm here.

DELMOUNT: Well…well, look, here's an artificial dog I won pitching dimes onto plates. Take it; it's for you if you want it.

CARNELLE: Why, thank you, Delmount. *(She kisses him.)* Oh my lips. *(Carnelle hurries into the dressing room to fix her lips. Delmount follows.)*

DELMOUNT: Things are going very good over at the auction. I mean, the furniture, it all seems to be selling like hot cakes. Why, it looks to me, child a mine, that our lives may actually be on the verge of being fine.

CARNELLE: Gosh, everything feels so all of a sudden. Selling the house and all of the belongings and…leaving…It makes it much more important that I win the contest. I mean, the main thing is I gotta leave in the blaze of glory. *(She leaves the dressing room and starts pacing back and forth.)* Let's see, I know I'll beat Saphire Mendoza just 'cause she's the token Negro and Mexican. I'm not trying to be mean about it, but it's the truth. Then there's Joe Anne Jacobs.

DELMOUNT: Frank Jacob's sister's in the pageant?

CARNELLE: Uh huh.

DELMOUNT: She's a shrimp.

CARNELLE: Well, sorta. Then there's Missy Mahoney—

DELMOUNT: Oh, my God! Is she in the pageant?

CARNELLE: Yeah.

DELMOUNT: Why, next to her sister Tessy, Missy's the ugliest girl in the whole town!

CARNELLE: Sssh! Sssh! *(Pointing to the dressing room.)* Tessy's in charge of the pageant coordination. She may hear you.

DELMOUNT: Oh, Jesus. Keep me away from those two. They are trouble.

CARNELLE: Well, Tessy was asking about you just now.

DELMOUNT: She was? Holy cow; holy cow. Where's my pipe? I've got to lay low; that's all. Lay low till I can get out of this town for good and always.

CARNELLE: Let's see, then there's Caroline Jeffers. She is awfully pretty except…Oh, I don't know! I don't know! *(She begins chewing her nails.)* Have you seen Elain?

DELMOUNT: Not since this morning.

CARNELLE: She was gonna go find Popeye to help sew up that red dress. It looks funny the way it is.

DELMOUNT: Well, I haven't seen Popeye since that night you got into this blessed contest.

CARNELLE: *(Biting her nails.)* Oh, shoot! I said I wasn't gonna chew on my nails! *(She takes a nail file from her dress pocket and begins filing.)*

DELMOUNT: She's strange anyway…that Popeye. She's very strange. A strange bird.

CARNELLE: *(Working on her nails.)* I guess so. I guess she is. Still…well, I guess, I shouldn't tell you. No, never mind.

DELMOUNT: Oh, that's fine. That's just fine. You start to say something and then you don't. Very nice, Carnelle, very nice.

CARNELLE: Well, it's just…it's just, well, she said she liked your hair and—

DELMOUNT: What? My hair? She said she likes my hair?!

CARNELLE: Yes, and how you can wiggle your ears and write poetry.

DELMOUNT: Wiggle my ears!? Good Lord and butter.

CARNELLE: Oh, I may as well tell you…she's in love with you.

DELMOUNT: What!?! No, she's not. I don't believe that. Who told you that?

CARNELLE: Well, she said it. And she was crying over you. It's the truth, Delmount. She was in the living room crying over you.

DELMOUNT: No, I don't believe it. Crying?

CARNELLE: I know. But I didn't have the heart to tell her about your obsessive eye for beauty. You know; that one you have.

DELMOUNT: Oh. Yes, I have acquired a weakness for the classical, exotic beauty in a woman. I've been a fool for it. It's my romantic nature.

CARNELLE: And I guess you don't think that Popeye's exactly classical? *(Delmount looks forlornly at her.)*

CARNELLE: Well, I've got to at least go put on my pantaloons and hoop. I've got to at least do that.

DELMOUNT: This tobacco is too sweet. It's making my head spin. Anyway, my hair's an unruly mess!

ELAIN'S VOICE: Carnelle! Carnation, Honey!?!

CARNELLE: *(Stopping.)* Elain—
(Elain enters right in a flowing summer dress. She looks radiant and fresh. She carries the Mardi Gras mask in a paper sack.)

ELAIN: Oh, Da'lin, there you are!

CARNELLE: Oh, Elain, I knew you'd come!

ELAIN: Why, hello, Delly!

DELMOUNT: Hello, Swaney.

ELAIN: Will you just look up at that sky! It's as blue as the mighty sea! Oh, I feel like a child today! I swear, I do! You'll never believe it, but Miss Blue has asked me to come up and give a speech before the contest starts. She wants me to talk on, "My Life as a Beauty." Isn't it too exciting!

CARNELLE: Oh, yes, yes. But—but where's Popeye? The dress—I couldn't make it look right.

ELAIN: Oh, Carnation, I went over to Miss Lily's Dress Shop and heard the most disheartening news: poor, little Popeye was fired yesterday afternoon. They said she was giving away the merchandise.

CARNELLE: Oh, no!

DELMOUNT: Well, where'd she go?

ELAIN: No one knows. They haven't seen her. But anyway, I came up with the most creative idea to save the day. You can wear this lovely Mardi Gras mask in the opening parade. That way you can just hold it up to your face like this, covering the side of your dress where the extra material is with your arm and elbows, plus adding some mystery and elegance to— well, to your total look. Just walk around like this. *(She moves around making dips and swirls, alternately moving the mask from in front of her face to the side of it with flip of her wrist, as she makes her dips.)* And scoop! And scoop! And scoop! You think you can manage it?

CARNELLE: *(Taking the mask.)* I'll try. I'll really try. *(She begins practicing.)* And scoop! And scoop. And scoop, etc.

ELAIN: That's it. Now just flip out your wrist. Make it crisp! That's good. Just keep at it. That's the only way to improve. *(Turning to Delmount.)* It's amazing but everyone recognizes me. They say I'm still exactly the same as I was. "Just in full bloom like a rose!" That's what one dear man said. I wish Mama were here. She'd love all of this!

CARNELLE: *(Still practicing.)* I know. She'd be so surprised if she could see me. I'm totally changed from when she knew me. Totally new. I think I got it. *(Tessy sticks her head into the left side of the dressing room.)*

TESSY: Carnelle?

CARNELLE: Out here, Tessy! I'm here!

CARNELLE AND ELAIN: Tessy!

DELMOUNT: Tessy! *(He leaps under the tent.)*

TESSY: *(Entering the dressing room left carrying a shoe box with a rubber band around it and holes punched in it.)* Carnelle?!

CARNELLE: I'm over here!

TESSY: Oh! *(As she steps out of the dressing room to the outside area.)* Why, Elain! Hello! How're you doing?

ELAIN: Why, if it isn't Tessy Mahoney! I'm doing fine. Just fine.

TESSY: Will you look at you. If you aren't the most beautiful thing in the whole wide world!

ELAIN: Oh, you silly, dear!

TESSY: *(Handing Carnelle the shoe box.)* Here, Carnelle. Some man brought this as a gift to you.

CARNELLE: Why, thank you. Who could have sent it?

TESSY: I just can't get over how beautiful you are. I just can't.

ELAIN: Why, how sweet can you be?

CARNELLE: *(Reading the scrawled message.)* "Thought you'd enjoy this. Good luck always. Mac Sam."

ELAIN: So, what's in the box?

CARNELLE: I don't know. But I—I think it's alive.

ELAIN: What? Let me see— *(She opens the box.)* AAH!!! *(She slams the top back on the box and drops it to the ground.)*

CARNELLE: What is it?

ELAIN: It's a horrible little frog in a pink outfit!

CARNELLE: Oh, my lord. *(She picks up the box and looks inside.)* Oh, lord. *(To Tessy.)* Where'd he go? Where'd the man go?

TESSY: I don't know. He gave me the box up front.

CARNELLE: Show me. Quick! Show me!

TESSY: *(As she hurries back through the dressing room and runs off left.)* Well, it's this way. But you better hurry up; it's only seventeen minutes till the opening Parade of Firecrackers—

CARNELLE: *(Overlapping as she follows Tessy out.)* Come on, Elain! Come on! He'll know where Popeye is! He'll know!

ELAIN: *(Following Carnelle off left, overlapping.)* But why? What do you mean? What's all this about? What an awful gift! Some friend you must have! *(They all exit left. Delmount comes out from under the tent. He is dusting off his pants when Popeye suddenly enters from down right dancing, humming, and eating blue cotton candy. She is wearing her earbobs and a pretty summer dress.)*

DELMOUNT: Popeye.

POPEYE: *(Stopping her dancing.)* Hello. *(She fans herself with the blue cotton candy as they stare at each other for a moment.)* I was looking for Carnelle.

DELMOUNT: Oh. Well. I don't know. I think she went looking for you. Found some sort of frog in a suit.

POPEYE: Was it a pink suit?

DELMOUNT: I think it was.

POPEYE: Oh, well, I sold me about ten different outfits out at a booth this morning. But I only had me that one frog in the pink suit, kinda there on display; case you didn't have no dolls.

DELMOUNT: I see.

POPEYE: Well. So why was Carnelle a'hunting for me?

DELMOUNT: Oh. Well, she, ah, she needed you to help sew on this red dress she has for the contest. She's been looking for you since last night.

POPEYE: Oh. Well, I rode the bus up to Jackson last night. Went to visit the observatory. They had the telescope aimed up on the moon. Thought I'd take a look.

DELMOUNT: How'd it look?

POPEYE: Big. Orange. Kinda shiney and sparkley.

DELMOUNT: Sounds nice.

POPEYE: It was.

DELMOUNT: *(There is an awkward pause. He begins smoothing down his hair.)* Hmm. Gosh. *(He stops smoothing. Looks at her.)* Oh. *(Suddenly messing his hair all up.)* I prefer it unruly. Don't you?

POPEYE: I don't much know. *(A pause.)* Ah, where's the dress? Maybe I should go take a look at it.

DELMOUNT: Oh, well, it's in here. It's right in here.

(They go inside the dressing room. He shows her the dress.)

DELMOUNT: It's ah, too small right here in the waist.

POPEYE: Hmm. Let me take a look.

DELMOUNT: Well, here, I'll hold your cotton candy.

POPEYE: Thanks. You can finish it, if you want.

(At that moment Carnelle, Mac Sam, and Elain are heard coming from the carnival from down right. They are in an uproar.)

MAC SAM'S VOICE: But I told you, I took the thing from some small kid who was tired of it! How do I know where he got it!?!

ELAIN: *(Overlapping.)* Well, in my opinion, it's a tasteless sort of gift!

(By now they are all on stage.)

MAC SAM: I thought it was festive!! A unique gift for a unique girl! Who are you anyway?!

ELAIN: Who are *you*?!?

DELMOUNT: Wait! It's them! *(Stepping outside the dressing room.)* She's here! She's inside! Popeye! She's looking at the dress!

CARNELLE: She is?!

ELAIN: She's here!?

MAC SAM: Who is this Popeyed anyway?

(They all rush into the dressing room. The following dialogue goes at a rapid pace.)

CARNELLE: Popeye! You're here!

POPEYE: Hello. I need scissors.

ALL: Scissors. Scissors.

CARNELLE: Scissors. Scissors. Let me look. Let me look! *(She begins searching through her makeup case.)*

DELMOUNT: Listen, Bub, those balloons don't fit in here.

MAC SAM: Is that Popeyed?

ELAIN: Popeye! It's Popeye!

CARNELLE: Oh, I don't think I have any scissors! They're none here!

TESSY'S VOICE: *(Coming from off left.)* Elain! Oh, Miss Elain!

DELMOUNT, ELAIN, CARNELLE: Tessy!

DELMOUNT: Quick! Hide me behind those balloons. *(Delmount jumps behind Mac Sam's balloons.)*

MAC SAM: Watch it, Sonny!

TESSY: *(As she enters from the left side of the dressing room.)* Miss Blue says it's only five minutes till she introduces you for your speech on beauty.

ELAIN: Oh, thank you, Darlin. Thank you. *(Looking in the mirror.)* For heaven's sake, my face isn't even on!

MAC SAM: Her face?

TESSY: Why, Carnelle, you'd better hurry and get dressed! All the other beauty contestants are already in their gowns and ready to go!
(She exits left, blowing her whistle. All scream. Delmount reappears.)

CARNELLE: What can I do? There're no scissors. What can I do?!

ELAIN: *(Sitting at the dressing table, putting on her makeup.)* Just wear the mask; you'll be fine, really.

CARNELLE: Oh, will somebody, please, take this frog!?

MAC SAM: Here, Honey, Mac Sam'll take care of it. *(He takes the box from her.)*

CARNELLE: Quick, now my pantaloons! Oh, God, I'm hot. I'm sweating. I stink.
(Someone throws her the pantaloons.)

DELMOUNT: I believe I mentioned your balloons don't fit!

MAC SAM: I'm holding the frog!

CARNELLE: *(Struggling with her pantaloons.)* Oh! Oh, which is the right end?! Look, I can't even find the right end of my pantaloons! It's hopeless!! It's hopeless!! It's utterly hopeless!! *(She throws the pantaloons into the air, collapses on the floor then starts crawling around on the floor searching for her pantaloons.)*

ELAIN: Now just try to be calm, Carnation, Honey. Try to enjoy yourself; it's all going to go as smooth as silk! I promise you—I give you my word of honor!

DELMOUNT: You'll do alright, child a mine—it's a stupid, idiotic contest, you'll do fine!

MAC SAM: You're beautiful, Baby—just beautiful!

POPEYE: *(About the pantaloons.)* Here. Here, now. You step in 'em like this.

MAC SAM: Yeah, put your foot in there.

CARNELLE: *(Trembling.)* In there? Right in there?

POPEYE: Uh huh.

DELMOUNT: Come on, child, you can do it.

CARNELLE: *(Gritting her teeth.)* Well, alright. *(She grabs the pantaloons and furiously starts to put them on.)*

MAC SAM: That's it!

ELAIN: Good. Good.

DELMOUNT: You've got it now!

CARNELLE: Hey! Hey, look, they're on me! My pantaloons are on!!

(General applause, sighs of relief, etc. Mac Sam raises Carnelle's hand in victory. Fast blackout.)

SCENE II

The setting is the same. Several minutes have passed. The red dress, the hoop, the pantaloons, and the Mardi Gras mask are gone. Mac Sam sits on the bench smoking a cigarette and drinking whiskey from a flask. His balloons are tied to the bench. Delmount is pacing back and forth in front of the bench.

DELMOUNT: Wonder how it's going?

MAC SAM: Why don't ya take a look?

DELMOUNT: Not interested.

MAC SAM: Oh.

DELMOUNT: She look alright to you in that big, red thing?

MAC SAM: Oh, yeah.

DELMOUNT: God. How she can put herself through this I'll never understand. Never.

MAC SAM: Well, women are funny about their looks. My granpapa used to say to me, "Sammy, all ya have to do is tell a woman she's beautiful and she goes like that!" *(He makes a horizontal victory sign with his fingers.)*

DELMOUNT: How pithy.

MAC SAM: Well, of course I try not to abuse the knowledge but it has come in handy in some borderline cases.

DELMOUNT: Well, fortunately, I have yet to make advances to any woman who did not possess at least one classically, beautiful characteristic. It's sort of a romantic notion I've had. I don't know. Perhaps, it's caused me to be fragmented in love. Perhaps, it's been obsessive. What do you think?

MAC SAM: Well, what I like is a woman who can take it right slap on the chin. That's what I like. *(He begins to cough, spreading germs all over his flask. He takes a slug, relieving his cough, then he says.)* Care for a slug?

DELMOUNT: *(Aghast.)* No, thank you.

(Popeye and Elain enter in a flurry from up right. Popeye carries a half-eaten hot dog.)

POPEYE: Ooh! Ooh, me! Ooh!

ELAIN: *(Overlapping.)* It's a travesty! A travesty! An utter Godforsaken travesty!

DELMOUNT: What's going on? Is it going alright? How's it going?

ELAIN: Air! Air! I must have some air!

(She falls back onto the bench as Delmount and Mac Sam fan her furiously.)

POPEYE: *(Acting it out.)* See, see, she tripped on that big ole red skirt and fell down flat on her face! Whoops! *(She falls to the ground.)* And people was laughing. "Ha, ha, ha, ha, ha!"

DELMOUNT: *(Overlapping.)* Laughing! Oh, my God! Laughing!

POPEYE: They was laughing out loud!

ELAIN: *(Coming out of her faint.)* There—there's a group of hoodlums out there yelling, "Miss Hot Tamale! Miss Hot Tamale!!" It's a disgrace. It's a humiliation! And that horrible Ronnie Wayne is actually throwing peanuts and trash and ice right up there on the stage in front of everyone!

DELMOUNT: At her? Is he throwing them at her?

ELAIN: Well, a peanut caught her right between the eyes!

DELMOUNT: What? What! He dies!! DIES!!!! Ronnie Wayne! Ronnie Wayne!!

(Delmount exits upstage right. as Carnelle enters left into her dressing room. The red dress, which was quite lovely and seductive when Elain wore it eleven years ago, now looks like a whore's gown on Carnelle. It is faded and ill-fitted and totally askew. She slings down the torn and broken Mardi Gras mask furiously. There are peanuts and trash on her dress and in her hair.)

CARNELLE: AAAAH! OOH! It's awful! It's so awful! They never forget! They never do!

(Elain and Popeye start for the dressing room. Mac Sam stays on the bench. He lights up another cigarette.)

ELAIN: *(Overlapping.)* It's her! She's there!! *(Stepping inside the dressing room.)* Carnation—

POPEYE: *(Stepping inside.)* Hi.

CARNELLE: Did you hear them? Oh, did you hear them? They were laughing and calling me, "Miss Hot Tamale." Did you hear it?

ELAIN: Why, look at you, you're dripping wet…let me help you out of this gown before you perish. *(She starts to unbutton the gown.)*

CARNELLE: Oh, if only the dress had come sooner. I could have fixed it right. I wouldn't of needed that fancy mask. I felt so foolish wearing it.

ELAIN: *(Defensively, as she tries to get the dress over Carnelle's head.)* I'm sorry, but I thought it would do—I just didn't realize that, well, that you were so big boned! Anyway, the color's all wrong—it was just too loud.

CARNELLE: But I love the color red. I love how it blazes!! Oh, I've got a pushing sensation right between my eyes as though it like to crack open my brains! Ooh!!

ELAIN: Now, listen, Carnation, if you don't calm down, you're headed for a clear-cut nervous breakdown! Just try to remember how Mama was enlightened by her affliction. Why, remember what she was always telling you, "Pretty is as pretty does."

(Carnelle collapses in despair.)

POPEYE: You want this hot dog? I ain't enjoying it.

CARNELLE: Thanks.

(Carnelle takes the hot dog and stuffs it into her mouth, as Tessy enters left. She is in an uproar.)

TESSY: Will you stop him! Will you please try and stop him!! He's messing up Missy's whole opus. He's out there in the audience causing a horrible, horrible scene!!

CARNELLE: *(Overlapping.)* Who? What? Stop who?!

TESSY: Delmount, that's who! He's smashing Ronnie Wayne's head into the dirt! And everyone's hollering!

CARNELLE: Oh, Lord, I've got to stop him— *(She starts to leave left.)*

TESSY: No! Don't go through the stage!

CARNELLE: Oh— *(She turns and runs out the right side of the dressing room.)*

ELAIN: Wait! Carnelle! You're in your hoop!

CARNELLE: *(Who is now in the outside area.)* Oh, no! I'm in my hoop!

MAC SAM: Well, you don't have to tell me!

CARNELLE: *(Covering herself.)* Oh, please, run around there and stop Delmount! He's out there in a fight—he's stirring up trouble!

MAC SAM: Alright, Baby. I'm going. *(About his balloons.)* Hey, see that no one steals my capital! *(He exits up right.)*

CARNELLE: Thanks, Mac Sam! Thanks a lot! *(She goes back into the dressing room.)* It's alright. It'll be fine. Mac Sam's gone to stop him.

TESSY: That Delmount is just wild. He is just recklessly wild!

ELAIN: *(Sitting down on a stool, fanning herself.)* Well, as we all know, he's had a very checkered past.

(Tessy looks to Elain who turns away with a grimace.)

TESSY: I suppose, Missy's whole opus is just ruined. Well, be that as it may, the show must go on. *(Looking at her clipboard.)* Let's see…let me get this straight. Joe Anne Jacobs follows Missy with her comedy pantomime to, "Take Me Out to the Ball Game," then there'll be Caroline Jeffers' dramatic interpretation from, *Gone With the Wind*. Then, of course, there's Saphire's hula hoop act and finally, last but not least, is your tap dance routine to, "The Star Spangled Banner." Alright, do you have that order?

CARNELLE: *(Who has removed her hoop and put on a robe.)* Uh huh.

TESSY: Since you go on last, it looks like you'll have to really rush to get into that bathing suit for the final crowning.

CARNELLE: It doesn't matter. It's all over. It's all ruined.

ELAIN: Don't worry, we'll help her out. It won't be a problem.

TESSY: Why, thank you, Elain. You're probably the most admirable person I've ever met. Truly you are! Oh my! *(She exits left.)*

ELAIN: It's sweltering in here. Let's get some air. *(She steps from the dressing room to the outside area.)*

CARNELLE: *(Following her.)* Alright.

POPEYE: Good. Maybe we can catch a breeze. *(She steps outside the dressing room.)*

CARNELLE: I hope so, Popeye. Oh Lord, I do.

DELMOUNT'S VOICE: I showed them! I showed them all!! Those cold-blooded swine!!

(Mac Sam and Delmount appear from upstage right. Mac Sam is supporting Delmount who is dragging his leg and has blood on his face.)

POPEYE: Oh!!

CARNELLE: Delmount!

ELAIN: Delly, are you alright?!

CARNELLE: What's happened?

MAC SAM: They started throwing rocks at him. They hit him there on the leg.

CARNELLE: Oh, Lord, are you hurt? You're not hurt are you?!

DELMOUNT: They don't make um hard enough.

ELAIN: Well, you look dreadful. I'll run get that disinfectant from the car! *(She exits downstage right.)*

POPEYE: Well, I'll—I'll get ya some ice. You can put it on your swolled up leg! *(She exits down right.)*

CARNELLE: *(Sinking to the ground.)* This is awful. Throwing rocks. They were throwing rocks. I'm about to cry.

DELMOUNT: It's alright, child a mine. Nobody's hurt. We enjoyed it.

MAC SAM: Yeah. *(Cough, cough.)* Yeah. *(Cough, cough, cough, cough, cough. He spits up blood.)*

CARNELLE: Mac Sam, what's wrong? Are you choking?

MAC SAM: Nah. I'm just spitting up clots of blood.

CARNELLE: What?

MAC SAM: It's nothing. Happens all the time. Look at that clot there; it's a nice pinkish-reddish sorta color.

CARNELLE: You're making me sick, here. Sick.
(Tessy enters left into the dressing room. She is holding a record.)

TESSY: Carnelle?! Oh Carnelle!

CARNELLE: It's Tessy.

DELMOUNT: Christ, I'm too weak to move.

TESSY: *(Stepping outside, spotting Delmount.)* Why, will you look at you! I just hope you're proud of yourself. Causing all of that racket! Here, Carnelle, Tommy Turner wants you to show him which song on this record you want played for your routine.

CARNELLE: Alright. *(She takes the record, goes through the dressing room, and exits left.)*

TESSY: So how's life been treating you?

DELMOUNT: Oh, fair.

TESSY: Well, I just thought you should know that I'm still bearing emotional scars because of the time you took unfair advantage of me up in the attic. They're deep scars, Delmount. They hurt.

DELMOUNT: *(Quietly as he squirms.)* Have a little mercy. I'm bleeding here. Look: blood. *(He mops off his head with a handkerchief.)*

TESSY: Well, you don't have to worry. I've already forgiven you. It's my religion: First Presbyterian. And to show you I mean it, tonight I'll let you take me to watch the fireworks.

DELMOUNT: What—

TESSY: *(She starts to leave.)* I'll even trust you to sit by me all alone in the dark! See you back here at 7:45 P.M. on the nose!

DELMOUNT: No, wait— *(He tries to get up but flinches in pain.)*

TESSY: *(As she exits through the dressing room and out left.)* I've got to run now! There's a show on!

DELMOUNT: *(Overlapping, he crawls after her.)* Please—don't forgive me! Don't forgive me! Don't! It was rotten behavior! I stink, I tell ya! I stink! *(Dropping to the ground.)* Christ.

MAC SAM: *(After a moment.)* Classically—beautiful—characteristics?

DELMOUNT: She was an exception.

MAC SAM: I'll say.

DELMOUNT: It was a long time ago.

MAC SAM: You don't have to make excuses to me. I've done nearly as bad myself. 'Course, now, Alligator Woman did have a way with her tongue. *(He helps Delmount to the bench as Popeye enters from downstage right. She carries a purple snow cone.)*

DELMOUNT: Alright! Alright! So I'm confused about women. I'm an idiot! A fool!

MAC SAM: Relax, chump. I'm just enjoying the day.

POPEYE: Here! Here, I got ya some ice. It oughta help take down that swelling.

DELMOUNT: But that's purple ice!

POPEYE: Well, they was out a' cherry.

MAC SAM: Hmm. That's pretty good, Popeye! Pretty good! Here, pull up the pants. *(He jerks up Delmount's pants leg.)*

DELMOUNT: AAH!

MAC SAM: *(Taking the snow cone and dumps it down on Delmount's leg.)* Now slap down that ice!

DELMOUNT: Jesus Christ, Man!!

MAC SAM: Feel better?

(Elain enters from downstage right. She carries a can of medicated spray.)

ELAIN: I'm back, Delly! I'm back! You can just relax now! You're gonna be fine! Let me just put on this medicated spray—

DELMOUNT: Look, it's alright. I'm fine. I don't need anything *else.*

ELAIN: Oh, my God! Your leg's turned purple! I think I'm gonna faint!

DELMOUNT: No, it's ice! Purple ice! *(Holding up the paper cone.)* Ice!

ELAIN: Oh! Well, you had me going. For awhile there, you did have me going. Now let me just apply this spray—

DELMOUNT: Look, I'm fine! I don't need anything else; so just leave me alone. Okay?

ELAIN: Well, alright. Alright. You can't do anything with him when he gets like this. *(Her eyes meet Mac Sam's.)* Hello.

MAC SAM: *(Saying everything with his magnetic eyes.)* Hello.

ELAIN: *(Nervously.)* So, Popeye, we hear you, ah, lost your job.

POPEYE: Well, I was fired from it.

ELAIN: It's such a shame.

DELMOUNT: Yeah. It is.

ELAIN: *(Primarily for Mac Sam's benefit.)* So, what transpired? I mean, what all happened? Do tell!

POPEYE: Oh, well, I reckon what it was was when I was sewing up there in the front a' the big store. This little child walked in and she started looking in at all that shiny jewelry behind the glass counter. I saw her looking and I said, "My, what lovely eyes you have. Them's pretty eyes. What color are them eyes?" And she looks up at me and says, "I don't know. I don't have no idea."

ELAIN: Imagine, not knowing the color of your own eyes. Amazing. Continue, please.

POPEYE: Well, I gets out this compact case from behind the glass counter. It's covered with the most beautiful colored sea shells in all the world. And I give it to her and says, "Look in there and tell me what color your eyes is." She takes a long look and says, "Them's blue eyes." And that was the truth, she was right about it. So I give her the sea-shelled compact case to take on with her, just by chance she forgets what color her eyes is and needs to take a look. Well, Miss Celia Lilly comes looking for that compact case later on in the day. I told her what happened and that's when she give me the news, "Popeye, you're fired."

MAC SAM: Hey. I like this Popeye character. She's hep.

DELMOUNT: Hep? She isn't hep.

ELAIN: Well, it's a shame, Popeye. They should have given you a second chance.

POPEYE: Oh, I don't mind it. I like traveling.

(About Mac Sam who is casually blowing out smoke rings.)

POPEYE: Hey, look! He's blowing smoke rings out from his mouth! Watch him! Wooh! What a trick!

MAC SAM: *(Taking the cigarette out of his mouth.)* Oh, that—that's nothing. Here, take a look at this! *(As he sticks the lit part of his cigarette into his mouth.)* Enter the infernal jaws of hell! *(With the backwards cigarette in his mouth, he blows out smoke.)*

POPEYE: Oh, look! Smoke! He's blowing out smoke! He's gonna burn up his throat!!!

MAC SAM: *(Taking out the cigarette. To Popeye.)* Ta-da! How'd ya like that, Beautiful?

(Delmount's eyes go crazy.)

POPEYE: It was wonderful! It was!! Do you know any more?

DELMOUNT: Here! I know one! I can do one. Just watch! Now I'm going to wiggle my ears!

ELAIN: Oh, that's right! Delmount can do the most stupendous trick where he wiggles his ears!

POPEYE: Oh, let's see it!

(They all watch as Delmount makes a facial grimace, while trying to wiggle his ears.)

MAC SAM: *(After a moment.)* I don't see 'em wiggling.

ELAIN: No, they're not wiggling.

POPEYE: Nah, they ain't.

DELMOUNT: Well, I—guess I'm out of practice.

(Mac Sam laughs cheerfully.)

POPEYE: *(Disappointed.)* Ooh.

DELMOUNT: But here, I can do this trick where my thumb comes off. Like this! *(He does the trick where his thumb comes off.)*

POPEYE: Oh, I know that one too! *(She takes off her thumb.)*

ELAIN: That's an old one. *(She takes off her thumb.)*

MAC SAM: Yeah. *(He takes off his.)*

DELMOUNT: Well, perhaps I should just go!…I don't know. I don't know.

(He wanders away from the group. Carnelle enters left into the dressing room.)

CARNELLE: *(Mumbling to herself, as she sinks down at the dressing table.)* "I'll never be hungry again. I'll never be hungry again. As God is my witness…As God is my witness…"

POPEYE: *(Spotting Carnelle through the doorway.)* Carnelle! Is it time for your act to go on? *(Running inside the dressing room.)* Do you need some help?

CARNELLE: Oh, Popeye, I was just watching Caroline Jeffers do that heartbreaking speech from *Gone With the Wind*—I tell you, that's what I should have done: a dramatic interpretation piece. See, because I could break down and cry real tears right now if I wanted to. It's acting like I was laughing or happy or something—that's what'd be hard.

POPEYE: I like your act. It's beautiful. Them roman candles shooting off. Here, put on your suit. *(She hands Carnelle the red, blue, and silver costume.)*

ELAIN: *(To Mac Sam.)* So, Mr. Mac Sam, what sort of day have you been having?

MAC SAM: Oh, not bad. Just been sitting here rotting away in the July sun.

DELMOUNT: *(Walking up to them.)* Excuse me. I believe I need to apply some medical spray to my wounds. *(He takes the spray and moves away.)*

POPEYE: *(About Carnelle's costume.)* Oh, that looks so good. Them silver stars really shine.

CARNELLE: I don't know, Popeye. I'm afraid it's a lost cause.

POPEYE: But I love it when you twirl them sparklers all around. I practically lose my breath. Here're your tap shoes.

ELAIN: Nice assortment of balloons you've got—and in a variety of colors.

MAC SAM: And which, may I ask, is your favorite color?

ELAIN: Pink. I adore pink.

MAC SAM: Ah, pink. I once knew a woman whose skin was awfully pink and pretty looking.

DELMOUNT: *(Sticking his head into the dressing room.)* Hey, what does that guy do? He looks like a corpse. How does he look like that?

CARNELLE: He's sick.

DELMOUNT: I'll buy that. *(He leaves.)*

POPEYE: Gosh. I've been trying so hard t'forget him.

CARNELLE: You mean Delmount?

POPEYE: Uh huh.

CARNELLE: How's it going?

POPEYE: Well, today I found out he'd forgotten how t'wiggle his ears. But it don't matter.

TESSY'S VOICE: Carnelle! *(Tessy enters the dressing room left.)* They're voting on Saphire's hula hoop act right now! You better get out there. You're on next! *(She blows her whistle and exits left.)*

CARNELLE: Oh, my God, I'm on next. I'm next.

POPEYE: *(Running outside.)* Hey, everyone! Carnelle's on next! She's gonna be doing her dancing routine to "The Star Spangled Banner!"

MAC SAM: *(Getting up and making his exit upstage right.)* I'm on my way!

CARNELLE: I don't know if I can go back out there.

POPEYE: Here's your sparklers and your roman candle.

CARNELLE: Do I look okay?

POPEYE: Just right.

CARNELLE: Let's go.

(They exit left.)

ELAIN: Well, aren't you going?

DELMOUNT: I don't think I can watch it. I mean, she thinks she's tap-dancing and she's just clomping her feet around. It makes me very anxious.

ELAIN: Poor Carnation. She wants to be beautiful without understanding the limitations it brings.

DELMOUNT: Well, it'll all be over soon. Carnelle will go up to Memphis; I'll start my life in New Orleans and you'll go—wherever the winds take you. *(He looks over at Elain who seems somber.)* Hey, don't worry, Swayne. You're free. You're finally gonna find out just why you're alive.

(Tessy enters left. She carries a box of long-stemmed roses and brings them out to Elain.)

TESSY: Elain! Oh, Elain! Look, here's a box of flowers that were sent to you. Isn't it exciting! Oh, here's the card; it dropped off. *(She hands the card to Delmount because Elain is holding the box.)* Well, I've got to rush back! Got a show on! Don't forget the fireworks! *(She exits through the dressing room and off left.)*

DELMOUNT: I thought he stopped sending the roses.

ELAIN: He did.

DELMOUNT: Mind if I take a look at this card?

ELAIN: Go ahead.

DELMOUNT: "My Dear Elain, I've been very, very happy since your phone call this morning. How I do need to hear how much you love me. I'll be by for you tomorrow morning at eleven A.M. You're adoring husband, Franklin." *(After a moment.)* What kind of idiot am I? What kind of dupe? You would think that after you left me in that lunatic asylum I would know not to trust you.

ELAIN: Be fair! You always had everything! Mama left the whole of the house to you and all of the furniture and all of the silver and even the hand-made quilts! She left nothing to me! Nothing at all!

DELMOUNT: You can have it. You can have all of the money that's made! Just leave him.

ELAIN: *(Overlapping.)* I don't want it. Stop planning my life! I'm used to better things now...my face cream...my clocks. And he adores me. I need someone who adores me.

(Mac Sam enters upstage right, in excitement.)

MAC SAM: *(Throwing a handful of confetti.)* Stupendous! Ravishing! A little bit of sheer heaven!

ELAIN: What—

(Carnelle and Popeye enter the dressing room left. They are elated. Carnelle twirls a burning sparkler.)

CARNELLE: I don't believe it! I don't believe it! They were all clapping! It was a hit!

POPEYE: *(Overlapping, as she shoots off imaginary Roman candles.)* Pow! Pow! Pow!

MAC SAM: She was out there just dancing and marching and the music was swelling—

POPEYE: *(Overlapping.)* She was so beautiful!

CARNELLE: *(Overlapping as she tap dances and twirls her baton.)* Yes sir! Yes sir!

MAC SAM: *(Running on.)* And everyone started cheering when the Roman candles went off—

POPEYE: Pow! Pow! Zoweey!

CARNELLE: They were cheering for me!

MAC SAM: Brilliant performance! And can she dance!
    (Delmount looks dumbfounded.)

ELAIN: *(Running to join Carnelle and Popeye in the dressing room.)* Did it really go well? Did it really?

POPEYE: Oh brother! I about died!

CARNELLE: Quick! Let's go, girls! I gotta change into my bathing suit! I don't have much time.

MAC SAM: *(Sitting down.)* Boy, *(Cough, cough.)* so beautiful, *(Cough, cough, cough.)* so fine!

DELMOUNT: *(Accusingly.)* Tell me, just exactly what do you mean when you're telling Carnelle how beautiful she is?

MAC SAM: I mean she's…beautiful.

DELMOUNT: You're a liar.

MAC SAM: Yeah, well, I do work the carnivals. *(He spits up a clot of blood.)*

CARNELLE: *(Pulling up her bathing suit.)* Lord, is this tight! Come on. There! There, I got it. I hope this French bra'll help. How do my thighs look?

TESSY: *(Sticking her head into the room left.)* Quick! Get out there! They're starting the lineup! *(She exits left blowing her whistle.)*

CARNELLE: Oh, my God. It's time for the final crowning. It's time! Hey, let me wave good-bye to the boys. *(Carnelle waves good-bye.)* Good-bye, boys! I'm going. I'm going out to the final crowning!

MAC SAM: Hey—good luck! We'll be right there cheering!

DELMOUNT: You look good, Child!

ELAIN: Do your best.

CARNELLE: *(Hugging them.)* Oh, Elain! Oh, Popeye!

TESSY: *(Sticking her head in.)* Come on! They're moving out on the stage!

CARNELLE: Farewell, Everyone! Farewell! *(Carnelle exits left.)*

POPEYE: Quick! We've got t'run around and see her! *(She starts out.)*

MAC SAM: I'm moving out!

(Elain pauses a moment to exchange a look with Delmount. She then turns and exits. Delmount looks after them. He paces around for several moments. He glances into the empty dressing room.)

DELMOUNT: I'll never understand it. Never. It lacks sense. It makes me ill. I mean, for Christ's sake, who would want to ride in a parade? It's so piti- ful. Man parading his ridiculous pomposity down his pathetic little streets, cheering at his own inane self-grandeur. *(He looks at himself in the dressing room mirror.)* Oh, God, I hope she comes in first! I hope she does. I do. I do. I swear I hope she beats them all!!

(Mac Sam enters upstage right.)

MAC SAM: Wooh. Amazing. Unbelievable.

(Delmount looks at him.)

MAC SAM: She lost. I don't know what for.

DELMOUNT: Holy cow. Holy cow.

(Elain and Popeye enter upstage right.)

ELAIN: Oh! I just don't understand it. She tries so hard. I guess, they really just took those "Miss Hot Tamales" to heart. *(To Delmount.)* Did you hear the results?

DELMOUNT: I heard.

ELAIN: 'Course everyone knew Caroline Jeffers would come in first. And I suppose, in a way, it's understandable that Joe Anne came in second.

DELMOUNT: The shrimp?

ELAIN: But, I mean, when Missy Mahoney came in third!

DELMOUNT: Third!

ELAIN: Well, I nearly died! But to me the crowning blow was having Saphire Mendoza come in ahead of our Carnation! That was the crowning blow!

DELMOUNT: Holy cow. What are we gonna say to her? What are we gonna say?

(Carnelle enters the dressing room left. They all stare at her. She wears a fifth place banner. She looks at herself in the mirror, then she bravely turns to face her family and friends, hoping for acceptance.)

DELMOUNT: Well, it was a stupid meaningless contest.

MAC SAM: Completely laughable.

ELAIN: Mama always said that what's really important in life is—

CARNELLE: I—don't—want—to—hear—it!! I wanted to win that contest. I cared about it. It was important to me. *(To Delmount.)* And I don't care how stupid and meaningless you think it was!! *(To Elain.)* And what are you looking at?! You never wanted me to win! You think I'm ugly, that's why you told me to wear that stupid mask over my face! I can't believe I ever wanted to be like you or that mean old monkey either!

(Mac Sam starts to cough. Carnelle turns to him.)

CARNELLE: And why don't you get well!?! You make me *sick* you're so *sick!!* You look like shit!!! I tell you, I'm so mad I could spit! *(Spit.)* There! *(Spit, spit.)* There, I spit! *(Spit.)* Die you monkey! Die!

TESSY: Carnelle!! *(She enters the dressing room left carrying a large American flag on a pole.)* Carnelle, come on! You and Saphire are gonna follow along behind the Grand Float carrying these American flags. You better get out there; everyone's waiting. *(She holds out the large American flag.)*

CARNELLE: *(Grabbing the flag.)* Thanks!

DELMOUNT: Wait. You don't have to do that. You don't have to follow that float.

CARNELLE: Look, if you come in last, you follow that float. I took a chance and I came in last; so, by God, I'm gonna follow that float!! *(She exits right carrying the American flag.)*

MAC SAM: Hey! You're beautiful when you're mad. Beautiful, Baby!

DELMOUNT: She's gonna fall flat on her face carrying that big ole flag.

ELAIN: *(Straight front.)* I'm not like Mama. I'm not.

TESSY: *(Checking her stopwatch.)* Only four hours and forty-nine minutes till tonight's colorful display of fireworks.

(She hurries back into the dressing room and exits left. Delmount looks after her, then looks forlornly to Mac Sam. Mac Sam offers his flask—Delmount takes a long slug. Meanwhile, Popeye slowly turns her head upward to look toward the coming fireworks.)

(Quick fade to blackout.)

SCENE III

The setting is the same. It is now early evening and darkness is beginning to fall. The stage is empty for a moment then Elain enters the dressing room left. She carries her purse and a half-empty bottle of red wine. She is weary and a bit drunk.

ELAIN: Carnelle? Good; not here. *(She looks around the empty dressing room then goes and sits down at the dressing table. She gazes at her face in the mirror. She straightens her hair.)* You're not yourself today. Not yourself.

DELMOUNT'S VOICE: Carnelle! Carnelle, you here? Honey? *(He enters left and spots Elain.)* Oh. Has Carnelle come back yet?

ELAIN: I don't know. I haven't seen her since she ran off and hid after the parade.

DELMOUNT: Think she'll be alright?

ELAIN: I doubt it.

DELMOUNT: Lord, you waiting here for her?

ELAIN: No. I just came by to get my dress. *(She rises and starts gathering up the red dress.)* I don't think she's that interested in seeing me. Looks like she doesn't admire me so much anymore.

DELMOUNT: I don't understand you. I know you're probably a kind person. You gave Popeye your earrings; you have a need to be excited by life. So why do you go back to being what Mama wanted? You know she was mean!

ELAIN: *(Turning to him angrily.)* Yes, I know she was mean and you know it too. So why do you straighten your wild hair? Why do you have horrible, sickening dreams about pieces of women's bodies? Some all beautiful; some all mutilated and bloody! I hate those dreams. I wish you didn't tell me about them. They scare me.

DELMOUNT: I'm sorry. I'm sorry.

ELAIN: It's okay.

DELMOUNT: I—I don't have those dreams anymore. I've stopped having them.

ELAIN: You have?

DELMOUNT: Yes.

ELAIN: Well, good. That's good. Do you want some wine?

DELMOUNT: Sure. Give me some wine.

(She hands him the bottle—he takes a drink. He hands the bottle back to her—she takes a long drink.)

ELAIN: You know about those earrings I gave Popeye…

DELMOUNT: Yeah?

ELAIN: I hated the damn things. They pinched my ears. I was glad to get rid of them.

DELMOUNT: *(After a moment.)* Swayne.

ELAIN: What?

DELMOUNT: You're incredible.

ELAIN: Well, you've always forgiven me.

DELMOUNT: Yeah. I always have.

ELAIN: So I better be going.

DELMOUNT: Where're you going?

ELAIN: *(Referring to the red dress.)* To take this out to the car. Then on out to have some real fun before I drop dead off this planet. I've got myself a date for the fireworks. I'm meeting him in the grove down under the wisteria trees.

DELMOUNT: Well, Honey, I hope you have yourself a real good ole time.

ELAIN: Don't you worry. I'm gonna be a reckless girl at least once in my dreary, dreary life. 'Bye-'bye now.

(She leaves the dressing room. He follows her to the doorway.)

DELMOUNT: 'Bye.

ELAIN: *(As she exits down right, carrying the red dress.)* Be seeing you!

DELMOUNT: 'Bye. *(He stands looking after her.)*

(Popeye enters left from the dressing room. She wears binoculars around her neck and is eating peanuts from a sack.)

DELMOUNT: *(Turning to see her.)* Popeye—

POPEYE: Hi.

DELMOUNT: Hello.

POPEYE: Is Carnelle come back?

DELMOUNT: No. I'm waiting here for her.

POPEYE: Oh.

DELMOUNT: I'd like to see her.

POPEYE: Yeah.

DELMOUNT: 'Course, I'm not even sure if she's coming back here or what.

POPEYE: Oh. *(Uneasy, she starts to leave.)*

DELMOUNT: Would you like to wait here too?

POPEYE: *(Stopping.)* Sure. Alright. Peanut?

DELMOUNT: Thanks. *(A pause.)* So you'll be leaving Brookhaven?

POPEYE: I reckon.

DELMOUNT: It's funny 'cause I'm leaving here too.

POPEYE: You is? Where was you planning to go?

DELMOUNT: I thought I'd be going to New Orleans—get back to the University and learn to be a philosopher. That way, after I have time to study and think it all through, I'll be able to let everyone know why we're living. It'll be a great relief...I believe. And where are you going to go?

POPEYE: Well, I don't know the particulars. But I heard a' this place name of Elysian fields.

DELMOUNT: Elysian fields?

POPEYE: Right. See, they got this ambrosia t'eat and wine and honey t'drink and all sorts of people carrying on. Do you know what state it's located in?

DELMOUNT: It—isn't in a state.

POPEYE: It ain't?

DELMOUNT: No. It isn't even in the world. It's—it's fictional. It's a made-up place. Why, it's only in books and stories.

POPEYE: Oh. Well, shoot. Guess I won't be going there.

(Tessy enters left into the dressing room. She is wearing a big straw hat.)

TESSY: Oh, Delmount!! Are you here? Delmount?! *(She steps from the dressing room to the outside area.)* Oh, there you are! *(Looking at her watch.)* Right on the nose! You punctual thing! Do you like this hat?

DELMOUNT: It becomes you.

TESSY: Isn't he sweet. Well, do come on. Well. Tell your friend good-bye and let's head to the fireworks.

DELMOUNT: Ah, Tessy...

TESSY: Yes?

DELMOUNT: Well, I—I can't go with you to the fireworks.

TESSY: Oh, you can't?

DELMOUNT: No, I—I promised Popeye I'd go with her. I'm sorry. I tried to tell you this afternoon.

TESSY: I see. I see. I try to turn the other cheek and you slap it too. You're ungrateful and unworthy and low and dirty and mean! Why, I'm never gonna forgive you again! Never! I hope you rot in H!! *(She exits down right.)*

DELMOUNT: Brother.

POPEYE: Why did you lie t'her?

DELMOUNT: Huh?

POPEYE: You told her you was promised t'go t'the fireworks with me.

DELMOUNT: Oh. Well, I just didn't want to go out to the fireworks with her and...And you can't go around obliging other people in this world.

POPEYE: Oh.

DELMOUNT: Of course I do want to go watch the fireworks. They always have a nice, colorful display. You weren't planning to—I don't know, go to the fireworks yourself?

POPEYE: Sure. It's why I brung my binoculars. Had me a place picked out and everything.

DELMOUNT: Oh. Hmm. Well, I guess you…

POPEYE: Huh?

DELMOUNT: No, nothing. I'll be seeing you. 'Bye.

(He exits down right. Popeye sits on the bench and stares ahead. She reaches into her peanut bag. There are none left.)

POPEYE: *(Miserably.)* Guess that's the last of 'em.

(Delmount reappears abruptly from downstage right.)

DELMOUNT: Popeye, would you mind going to watch the fireworks with me tonight?

POPEYE: No. I wouldn't. Sure. Alright.

DELMOUNT: *(Overlapping.)* Good. Good then. Good. Let's go!

(They exit downstage right. The stage is empty for a moment before Carnelle sneaks on from under the tent. She is wearing a short trench coat over her red bathing suit. She looks around, sees no one, and heads into the dressing room. Mac Sam suddenly appears out of the darkness.)

MAC SAM: Hey! Red! Where ya going?

CARNELLE: Mac Sam! Dammit! I didn't want anyone to see me.

MAC SAM: Well, I saw ya. How ya been?

CARNELLE: Oh, alright.

MAC SAM: Hey, you sure blew up this afternoon.

CARNELLE: I know it.

MAC SAM: Well, you really did explode.

CARNELLE: I know. I'd never been so mad as I was. And I spit out at everyone. I just spit at them. Oh! That's so awful it's almost funny!

MAC SAM: Hell, it was the best part of it!

CARNELLE: Oh, I don't know. I better get my stuff out of here.

MAC SAM: You know, I went looking for you after the parade. Where'd you get off to?

CARNELLE: Oh, nowhere. Just out walking by the railroad tracks.

MAC SAM: What were you doing down there?

CARNELLE: *(As she gathers up her belongings.)* Kicking rocks. Thinking. I thought maybe I was a victim of broken dreams but then I thought maybe I wasn't. I was trying so hard t'belong all my life and…I don't know. Oh, looks like Elain came for her red dress. Anyway, I just don't know what you can, well, reasonably hope for in life.

MAC SAM: Not much, Baby, not too damn much.

CARNELLE: But something—

MAC SAM: Sure. There's always eternal grace.

CARNELLE: It'd be nice. *(Holding up the shoe box.)* Look, here, my frog's gone.

MAC SAM: Yeah. That Popeye set it loose.

CARNELLE: Oh, well, I still have the suit.

(She holds up the pink suit. They look at each other and smile.)

MAC SAM: God, you're beautiful. I wouldn't trade those times we had together not for anything.

CARNELLE: *(Throwing her arms around him.)* Really?

MAC SAM: Not for a golden monkey.

CARNELLE: But how about—I mean I gave you—

MAC SAM: Oh, the syph. Hell, I've got TB, alcoholics disease, rotting gut. I tell ya, I'm having fun taking bets on which part of me'll decay first: the liver, the lungs, the stomach, or the brain.

CARNELLE: *(Suddenly uneasy.)* It's getting late. I gotta go.

(Carnelle leaves the dressing room carrying all of her belongings. He follows.)

MAC SAM: Hey, listen, you want to go to the fireworks with ole Mac Sam? We could spend a fine night together.

CARNELLE: No. I—I just need some rest. You'd be tiring me out awful fast.

MAC SAM: Yeah.

CARNELLE: I gotta get this out to the car. Good-bye, Mac Sam. Good night.

(He doffs his cap to her. She exits downstage right.)

MAC SAM: Good-bye, Baby. I'll always remember you as the one who could take it on the chin. *(He looks after her a moment, spits up a clot of blood, wipes off his mouth, and starts to exit upstage right.)* Ah, well, on to the wisteria trees.

(He is gone. Suddenly Popeye and Delmount appear climbing out onto the roof of the tent from off right. Popeye is leading, she carries a box of popcorn. Delmount follows nervously.)

POPEYE: This way. That's right. Hold on, now.

DELMOUNT: Holy Christ.

POPEYE: There. Aren't these seats great?

DELMOUNT: Oh, yeah, wonderful.

POPEYE: And we can keep an eye out for Carnelle—case she comes back by.

DELMOUNT: Yeah. Great.

POPEYE: Here. Take a look through the binoculars. See how the sky looks.

(Delmount looks through the binoculars.)

POPEYE: Well, how's it look?

DELMOUNT: *(Becoming interested.)* Hmm. Not bad.

POPEYE: *(As she throws handfuls of popcorn in front of the binoculars.)* Watch out! It's snowing! Look! It's snowing! See it! See it snowing!

DELMOUNT: *(Overlapping.)* Oh, great! Snow flakes! Yeah! I see it! *(Impulsively, as he takes the binoculars from in front of his eyes.)* Oh, Popeye, I just have to tell you about these beautiful dreams—I just have to—No, it's absurd! *(He turns away in anguish and spots Carnelle who has entered downstage right.)*

DELMOUNT: Why, Carnelle!

POPEYE: Oh, Carnelle! Hi!

CARNELLE: *(Taken aback.)* Why, look at you two! What in the world are you doing way up there?!

POPEYE: We're gonna watch the fireworks! Come on up!

DELMOUNT: Yeah, come on! Please, we've been missing you. It's great up here!

CARNELLE: No, I really don't care about the fireworks. I think I'm gonna just go on home.

POPEYE: Oh, please, they's so beautiful to see!

DELMOUNT: Come on, Child! Just for awhile. You can come up for awhile.

CARNELLE: No, really, I just left something in the dressing room; I'm gonna get it and go on home. *(She enters the dressing room.)*

DELMOUNT: Lord, I hope she's alright. She didn't even mention the contest. God, I wish she'd come watch the fireworks with us.

POPEYE: Me too.

(Carnelle pulls the artificial dog out from under the dressing table. She pats it.)

DELMOUNT: Here, you want to look through the binoculars for awhile?

POPEYE: Okay.

(Popeye takes the binoculars and looks through them. Carnelle sits at the dressing table and looks at herself in the mirror.)

POPEYE: Ooh, I love the heavens. I'd love to live up there. Do you think it's cold or warm up there?

DELMOUNT: Hmmm. I don't know. Cold maybe? Warm? I don't know.

CARNELLE: *(Looking at herself in the mirror.)* It used to be brown. I had brown hair. Brown.

POPEYE: The man at the observatory he's talking about things such as black holes in space, globular clusters, blue giant stars and other galaxies, he says, "If you can think of it; you've got it." My mind's about to burst just trying.

CARNELLE: *(Looking around the room.)* Grace. Eternal grace. Grace. Hey, hey. I wanna watch the fireworks. *(She picks up the dog and runs out of the dressing room ablaze with excitement.)* Hey! Hey, how do I get up there? I wanna come up!

DELMOUNT: *(Overlapping.)* Oh child, you're coming up?!

CARNELLE: Yes! Yes! I wanna come up! I've changed my mind! I'm coming up. How do I get up?!

POPEYE: *(Overlapping.)* Hurray! Hurray! It's easy! You just run around there and jump off of them piled up boxes and climb up the pole!

CARNELLE: Great! I'm on my way! I'm coming up! *(She exits upstage right.)*

POPEYE: WOW! She's coming up! I'm so happy! I'm happy!

DELMOUNT: Oh, Popeye! *(He grabs her and kisses her full on the mouth.)* I've been dreaming about you at night. I see you riding across the sea with a host of green whales. Popeye, I love you.

POPEYE: *(Past ecstasy.)* I feel like m'teeth is gonna fall out a' my head.

(Carnelle appears on the roof; she is carrying the dog.)

CARNELLE: Hey! I'm up here! I made it! I'm up.

DELMOUNT: That's right! Now just slide on out here. That's it. Good. You made it.

CARNELLE: Oh, will you look at all those stars in the sky.

POPEYE: Yeah.

DELMOUNT: Oh, yeah.

CARNELLE: Listen, I—I don't know what I was thinking about this afternoon—when I was screaming and all.

DELMOUNT: Please, it's alright. You don't have to say anything. Everything's alright.

CARNELLE: It's just I was upset about not being able to leave in the blaze of glory. Of course, I know it doesn't matter. I mean, the main thing is—well, the main thing is…Gosh; I don't know what the main thing is. I don't have the vaguest idea.

(Carnelle is laughing when the first firecracker explodes in the sky.)

DELMOUNT: Wait! It's started!

POPEYE: *(As gold light floods their faces.)* A gold one! Look, it's a gold one!

CARNELLE: *(Now red light.)* Why, it's bursting into red! Red! Crimson red!

POPEYE: Pow!! Pow! pow. *(And then silently mouthing it.)* Pow…

(The explosion is over. They sit in silence for a moment.)

CARNELLE: Gosh, it's a nice night.

DELMOUNT: As nice as they come.

(Hold a moment. Blackout.)

END OF PLAY

THE LUCKY SPOT

WITH LOVE TO SUSAN KINGSLEY
AND HER TWO KIDS ROXIE AND GAR

Mary Stuart Masterson and Amy Madigan
in Manhattan Theatre Club's 1987 production of
The Lucky Spot.

photo by Gerry Goodstein

ORIGINAL PRODUCTION

The Lucky Spot was presented by Manhattan Theatre Club (Lynne Meadow, Artistic Director; Barry Grove, Managing Director) at City Center Theatre in New York City on April 9, 1987. It was directed by Stephen Tobolowsky; the sets were by John Lee Beatty; the costumes were by Jennifer von Mayrhauser; the lighting was by Dennis Parichy; the sound was by Scott Lehrer; the production stage manager was Peggy Peterson; and the fight staging was by B. H. Barry. The cast, in order of appearance, was as follows:

Cassidy Smith	Mary Stuart Masterson
Turnip Moss	Alan Ruck
Reed Hooker	Ray Baker
Whitt Carmichael	Lanny Flaherty
Lacey Rollins	Belita Moreno
Sue Jack Tiller Hooker	Amy Madigan
Sam	John Wylie

The Lucky Spot had it's world premiere at the Williamstown Theatre Festival (Nikos Psacharopolous, Artistic Director), Williamstown, Massachusetts, 1987.

THE CHARACTERS

CASSIDY SMITH: 15, works at the Lucky Spot Dance Hall.

TURNIP MOSS: 20s, works at the Lucky Spot.

REED HOOKER: 40s, owner of the Lucky Spot.

WHITT CARMICHAEL: 30s, a wealthy visitor from New Orleans.

LACEY ROLLINS: 30s, a taxi dancer.

SUE JACK TILLER HOOKER: 30s, Reed Hooker's estranged wife, a former taxi dancer.

SAM: late 60s, a patron of the Lucky Spot.

THE SETTING

The entire action of the play takes place at the Lucky Spot Dance Hall in Pigeon, Louisiana, a small southern town about sixty miles west of New Orleans. The dance hall is located along the main road at the edge of town.

The dance hall is actually an old Victorian farmhouse. The main room of which has recently been converted into a ballroom with a dancing area, a bar, a jukebox, and a carousel horse that spins. A few tables and a lot of chairs are stacked up together against the wall.

There are four entrances and exits to the ballroom: a swinging door left that leads to the kitchen, a staircase leading to the upstairs, a front door, and a side door right, leading to an outdoor area.

The outdoor area consists of an old wood stump and a leafless tree.

THE TIME
Christmas Eve, 1934

MUSIC SUGGESTIONS
ACT I
    Music A: "We're in the Money" with Ginger Rogers vocal, 1931
    Music B: Ike "Yowse suh" Hatch and his orchestra's recording of "Some of These Days," London, 1935
ACT II
    Music A: "I Need a Little Sugar in My Bowl," Bessie Smith, vocal, 1931
    Music B: Valaida Snow's trumpet solo on "I Must Have That Man," London, 1937
    Music C: Fletcher Henderson's "Twelfth Street Rag," Crown Records, 1931
    Music D: Jimmie Noone and Earl Hines' recording of "King Joe," Chicago, 1928
    Music E: Jimmie Noone and Earl Hines' recording of "Sweet Lorraine"—Take 2, Chicago, 1928
    Music F: Coleman Hawkins' recording of "Honeysuckle Rose," London, 1934
    Music G: James Price Johnson, piano solo, "Cryin' For The Carolines," New York, 1930
    Music H: Jimmie Noone and Earl Hines' recording of "Sweet Lorraine"—Take 1, Chicago, 1928
    Music I: Louis Armstrong and his orchestra's recording of "On the Sunny Side of the Street," with Louis Armstrong 100 vocal, Paris, 1934

ACT I
SCENE I

Cassidy Smith, fifteen, sits behind the counter writing slowly on a piece of oatmeal carton. She wears a derby hat and loose-fitted, dull-colored garments. Music A plays on the jukebox. Turnip Moss enters the outdoor area, dragging a freshly cut pine tree. Turnip, twenties, is a wiry young man with deep watchful eyes. Turnip hauls the tree in through the side door to the ballroom.

TURNIP: 'Morning.

CASSIDY: Oh look! Look at this! You're bringing in a tree. We're gonna have a Christmas tree!

TURNIP: Think it's big enough?

CASSIDY: Why, it's bigger than me. *(Cassidy comes out from behind the bar. We see that she is about eight months pregnant.)*

TURNIP: Yeah; I guess. Wonder where it oughta go?

CASSIDY: Don't know. Never put a tree inside a room before.

TURNIP: Well, how 'bout…how 'bout…how 'bout…How 'bout we put it over here by the staircase? That way people can see it as they're sashaying down the stairs.

CASSIDY: Oh, yeah, that'd be good!

TURNIP: You think it looks good there?

CASSIDY: Uh-uh.

TURNIP: I think it looks good there too. Damn good.

CASSIDY: Yep. You heard anything from Hooker?

(Turnip goes to pour himself the last of the coffee.)

TURNIP: No. He's been out all night long. Sure hope he struck it lucky.

CASSIDY: Yeah. Hey, Turnip. *(Indicating writing on the oatmeal carton.)* How's that look to you?

TURNIP: *(Reading.)* "Cassidy Smith Hooker." What's this for?

CASSIDY: It's my name. I'm practicing writing it for when I sign the papers.

TURNIP: Sign what papers?

CASSIDY: My marriage papers.

TURNIP: Who're you marrying?

CASSIDY: *(Pointing to the paper.)* Hooker. See there?

TURNIP: What makes you think you're marrying Hooker?

CASSIDY: He tol' me. He give me this yellow piece a' rope for a engagement ring.

TURNIP: Let me see that. Hmm. *(Turnip looks at the rope ring then looks back to Cassidy.)* Well, I don't mean this t'hurt your feelings or nothing, Cassidy; but I think he was just kinda—kidding around with ya.

CASSIDY: No, I don't think he was.

TURNIP: Well, thing is Hooker, he—he's already got a wife.

CASSIDY: Yeah, I know. Sue Jack's her name. But I don't think he cares much for her.

TURNIP: Why not?

CASSIDY: Soon as she's released out from Angola State Penitentiary—he's divorcing her and marrying me.

TURNIP: Who told you that?

CASSIDY: He did. He promised me.

TURNIP: I don't believe it.

CASSIDY: Then don't. *(Cassidy gets a broom and starts sweeping up pine needles.)*

TURNIP: Cassidy…you think he's in love with you?

CASSIDY: *(Sweeping.)* I didn't say that. I don't care nothing 'bout that. I don't even believe in all that.

TURNIP: Well, when you get married to a person, you're supposed to be in love with the person you're getting married to. I know that much. And people have called me dumb.

CASSIDY: Just look at all these pine needles. It's a damn mess you've made hauling in that ole tree.

TURNIP: You better believe how he was in love with Sue Jack. She's beautiful, and smart, all full of laughing times. Why, she was a real lady. Always wore fine lace gloves on her hands so that she could keep her fingertips soft for playing cards.

CASSIDY: Yeah, well I went out this morning and talked to them dancing women out back. Some of 'em used to work with her at the dime-a-dance halls over in New Orleans. They tol' me she was a broken-down wreck. And they put her away for throwing some rich lady over a balcony railing.

TURNIP: That's right—that lady's named Caroline Carmichael. Sue Jack come in a found her lyin' in bed with Hooker and she don't like nobody messing with her man. See, she's very touchy. 'Specially when she drinks. Meanest damn drunk I ever heard of or saw.

(Reed Hooker, mid-forties, enters from the front door. His white shirt is torn and a bloody handkerchief is tied around one of his arms. There is a worn mournful look in his eyes that belies his dashing exuberance.)

HOOKER: Well, now top of the morning and a Merry Christmas Eve t'the both of ya.

CASSIDY: *(Overlapping)*   TURNIP: *(Overlapping)*
Hooker, you're back!   Did ya win any money?

HOOKER: *(Running on.)* What's this? A Christmas tree? Well, I do love the color green. It's the color of cash!

CASSIDY: What's all this blood?

TURNIP: Do ya like it by the stairway?

HOOKER: Knife wound. No, no, by the window so they can see it from the road.

CASSIDY: Who cut ya? Who done it?

HOOKER: Ah, self-inflicted misfortune.

TURNIP: *(As if this were obvious.)* Oh sure, from the road. They gotta see it from the road.

CASSIDY: Well, I'll get ya some cobwebs from out in the barn t'help staunch the bleeding.

(Hooker picks up Cassidy and twirls her around in his arms.)

HOOKER: Now aren't you the sweetest girl in the whole wide world and her with her six little toes.

CASSIDY: Don't talk about my toes.

HOOKER: She's got the prettiest little toes.

TURNIP: Six all on one foot. I've seen 'em.

CASSIDY: I said stop talking about my toes less you want me to slice your eyes out—I don't like to hear nothing about that. You're just making your fun outta me.

HOOKER: No, no, I ain't making my fun outta you. Why, I been out all night long bucking the tiger just to bring you back a Christmas gift.

CASSIDY: A Christmas gift for me?!

(Hooker gets a jug of whiskey, from behind the counter, and throughout the following downs a couple of belts.)

TURNIP: I bet she's never had a Christmas gift.

CASSIDY: I have, too.

TURNIP: Mr. Pete never gave her anything but a cat-o'-nine tails from what I hear.

CASSIDY: My mama used t'give us an orange and a peppermint candy every Christmas morning.

TURNIP: Your mama's been dead almost ten years.

CASSIDY: I remember it though. *(To Hooker.)* So what'd ya bring t'me?

HOOKER: Well, Saucer Eyes, I was gonna bring ya a solid gold hat with red ostrich plumes, and Turnip, I was gonna bring you a pocket full of Mexican jumping beans. Unfortunately, I got hooked up in a godless card game. Lost my luck late. Came outta there with nothing but the mist of the morning dew.

CASSIDY: Well, what in the world was I gonna do with another hat? I already got this one.

HOOKER: Ah, six months from now, we'll be eating outta hats. Soon as we get the Lucky Spot Dance Hall rolling.

TURNIP: Yeah, well, I sure hope the place goes over big tonight 'cause we're flat broke around here.

HOOKER: Hey, look, it's Christmas Eve. People are so lonely out there you can smell it rotting on 'em. Here at the Lucky Spot we'll be selling hot music, fine dancing, and sweet solace of kindhearted women.

CASSIDY: I can't wait to see it with all the lights and music and the women in their long shiny gowns dancing with all the lonely souls.

HOOKER: We're gonna make a fortune.

TURNIP: I just hope they don't tear down the doors fighting t'get in.

CASSIDY: It'll be more like a dream than something real.

HOOKER: Well, now enough gold bricking. Let's get up our Christmas tree. We got any coffee left?

CASSIDY: I'll make a new pot. And I'll fix ya some breakfast.

HOOKER: Fine, fine, but do me a favor and don't put that greasy gravy all over everything on the plate.

CASSIDY: I won't. I'll make it real good this time. Real good. I promise.

HOOKER: Yeah.

(*Cassidy exits to the kitchen. Throughout the following Hooker and Turnip make a wooden Christmas tree stand and put the tree into it.*)

HOOKER: She's not a bad kid but I swear to God she is the worst damn cook I ever knew.

TURNIP: Well, what can you expect? You won her in a poker game.

HOOKER: Yeah, well maybe I should have taken the chestnut mare.

TURNIP: Why didn't ya?

HOOKER: Oh, you know…her face.

TURNIP: What about it?

HOOKER: That woebegone countenance. I don't know. Anyway, it's done. Come on and help me with this tree.

TURNIP: Hooker?

HOOKER: Huh?

TURNIP: It's about Cassidy. I think she's suffering from some sort of grand delusion.

HOOKER: Hold this here. Hold it tight now.

TURNIP: See, 'cause she is claiming you told her you'd marry her.

HOOKER: Oh yeah?

TURNIP: Yeah, she seems to be counting on it.

HOOKER: Look, I'm already married. Remember? To the ditch digger's daughter.

TURNIP: Yeah, well, Cassidy said you were gonna divorce Sue Jack and marry her. She claims you promised her.

HOOKER: Christ, I never promised her. *(A beat.)* Maybe I intimated something about the faint possibility.

TURNIP: Why would ya do a thing like that?

HOOKER: I don't know, Turnip. Maybe I just got fed up with the way she kept rolling herself down the staircase and eating boxes of match heads and banging at her belly with a two-by-four.

TURNIP: Oh, ya mean she didn't want t'have no kid.

HOOKER: I don't think she did, no. *(Hooker gets a banner from behind the counter.)* Here, let's get up the sign.

TURNIP: *(A beat.)* Gosh, so what're ya gonna do about Sue Jack when she gets out of prison? Would you divorce her for real?

HOOKER: God, no. I'd just shoot the bitch on sight.

TURNIP: You ain't still mad at her about it all?

HOOKER: The hell I'm not.

TURNIP: She loved him same as you. After it happened she got all torn up inside.

HOOKER: Bullshit! She was glad to be rid of both of us. The night after they laid my kid in the ground she went out to a cockfight in a red tasseled dress and squandered away her wedding ring. She went on boozing and brawling and lavishing away everything decent we ever had together. Don't ever mention her to me! Don't ever mention her to me!

TURNIP: Okay, okay. I won't; I won't! So, ah, what's gonna happen with Cassidy, I mean concerning the predicament ya got her in.

HOOKER: Look, she'll have the kid. The Lucky Spot'll be in full swing. I'll send her off to some respectable school, let 'em teach her how t'cook. She'll find a nice guy—that'll be that.

TURNIP: *(A beat.)* What about your baby?

HOOKER: I'll just hang on to him.

TURNIP: How do you know she won't want it?

HOOKER: The sign's not even. Your side's too low.

TURNIP: So how're ya gonna tell Cassidy ya ain't marrying her? How're ya gonna spring it on her?

HOOKER: Stop dogging me. I'll spring it on her. I'll spring it on her.

TURNIP: I mean, look at the condition ya got her in. I wouldn't know what the hell t'tell her by now.

HOOKER: Goddamnit, Turnip! Now your side's too high. Bring it down.

TURNIP: I wonder if I'll ever have a girlfriend. My brothers told me I'd never have a girlfriend as long as I had the name Turnip. But I didn't know how to change my name 'cause folks was always calling me by it.

HOOKER: *(Looking up at the sign.)* I reckon that'll do.

TURNIP: I just wish I wasn't plagued by self-doubt. But I'm afraid of…I don't know what, but I bet it's something.

(Cassidy re-enters from the kitchen. She carries a tray with a breakfast plate, silverware, cup and saucer, and coffeepot.)

CASSIDY: Oh, look, ya got up the tree! And look at that. *(She points to the banner and tries to read it as she makes cowboy coffee.)* Let's see. "Well…welcome. Welcome to…"

TURNIP: *(Reading easily.)* "Welcome to the Grand Opening, Lucky Spot Dance Hall."

HOOKER: *(To imaginary guest.)* Welcome, welcome, welcome.

TURNIP: Yes, sirree, welcome one and all.

CASSIDY: Hooker.

HOOKER: Huh?

CASSIDY: I need to talk to you on a matter. It's kinda…pressing. Here's your breakfast for ya.

HOOKER: Thanks. *(Hooker takes the plate, looks at it, and smirks derogatorily, then shakes his head to Turnip.)*

CASSIDY: It look bad to you?

HOOKER: It looks like it always looks when you cook breakfast.

CASSIDY: I'll take it back.

HOOKER: No, no. I'll eat it.

(Cassidy reaches for the plate to take it and Hooker notices her hand.)

HOOKER: Don't you ever wash your hands?

CASSIDY: …Sure.

HOOKER: Well, you could plant a vegetable garden underneath those fingernails. Don't you ever clean them?

CASSIDY: Yeah, I just…when I'm working, well the dirt gets stuck there and I can't never get it out.

HOOKER: Try scraping it with a hairpin.

CASSIDY: I ain't got no hairpins.

HOOKER: Then use a nail or a fork or something, for Christ sake!

CASSIDY: *(Picking up Hooker's fork.)* Okay.

HOOKER: Not my fork, God damn it! Look, I don't mean to harp on you about this or anything. We're pals, right? Come on. I'll try and eat some of this slop. I'm sure it isn't too horrible. Jesus Christ, you're not gonna start t'cry just 'cause I tell you you should wash your filthy hands once a goddamn century?!

CASSIDY: No, I'll...I'll go wash 'em. I'm just needing to talk to you, that's all. I'll wash up and come on back.

(Cassidy exits up the stairs. Hooker turns to Turnip.)

HOOKER: Jesus. Women. They're all alike. Them girls out back. You stay ten miles clear of any whiff of 'em—that's my best advice.

(Whitt Carmichael, thirties, enters through the front door. He is a tall man with an imposing elegance. He wears an expensive but understated suit and carries an alligator attaché case.)

TURNIP: Howdy.

CARMICHAEL: Reed Hooker?

HOOKER: What can I do for you?

CARMICHAEL: Well now, I'd like to discuss with you briefly my involvement in the ownership of this property.

(Hooker stares at Carmichael, poker-faced.)

CARMICHAEL: The story is that you won it off my cousin, Davenport Fletcher, in a five-day card game down on the Gulf Coast.

HOOKER: Yes, well, that's how that story goes.

CARMICHAEL: This was my aunt's estate and she did leave it to Davenport. Now, the only problem I perceive is my cousin's three hundred and fifty-five dollar debt to me that he used this house as collateral against. Right here's a copy of the papers alerting you of the situation.

(Carmichael hands Hooker a document. Hooker takes it.)

CARMICHAEL: Of course, I can see you've made some...improvements.

HOOKER: Yeah, well, they're a lot of initial expenses you accrue when starting out a new business. And there's always a bit of difficulty with handing out the ready cash; so as I'm sure you can imagine, your request for payment in full is difficult for me at this time. However, if you're a hunch bettor, I believe I could finagle you some points in the Lucky Spot that could triple your money for you in about a year's time.

CARMICHAEL: Then you honestly think this place is going to make money?

HOOKER: I'm afraid it's bound for glory. The Lucky Spot will be the first genuine taxi dance hall set in an isolated rural area. The glamour, magic, and music of the city sporting life will now be available to the simple country folk who secretly ache for such dazzling companionship on so many of these lonely moonless nights.

TURNIP: Yeah, we got the flyers up all over town. Everyone's talking the place up big.

HOOKER: Yes, all of our dance teachers have been hired directly out of New Orleans. They split their take fifty-fifty with the hall. We also get all of the door and, of course, the extras.

TURNIP: *(Holding up a hanger of old neckties.)* Yeah, like these neckties you can rent for ten cents at the door in case, say, you forgot your own necktie…or in case, say, you never had no neckties at all.

HOOKER: Of course, the real saving grace, economically speaking, is the jukebox. Isn't she a beauty? See, we won't have to pay a nickel to any local musicians for playing their lousy marshmallow music. Why, we've got twenty-six of the newest tunes, played by the hottest bands, right at our fingertips. So what d'ya say, pal? Are you a hunch bettor?

CARMICHAEL: As a matter of fact, Mr. Hooker, I am somewhat of a gambler and I believe I'm going to have a bet against this depressing little monkey hop and the fool-hearted ex-rumrunner who doesn't have a Chinaman's chance of making a business out a racket.

HOOKER: Well, now, would anybody care to add to that; or maybe subtract?

CARMICHAEL: I'll make it simple: Give me the cash or I close down the hall.

HOOKER: How long do I have?

CARMICHAEL: I believe that order the sheriff signed allows you 'til January one. Time's almost up.

HOOKER: You're a real sport. But I'm too many miles down the road t'turn back now. *(Hooker produces a deck of cards.)* Here, let's cut for it. Double or nothing.

CARMICHAEL: Afraid not.

HOOKER: *(With a forced grin.)* Look…it's Christmas.

CARMICHAEL: Well, I'm not Santa Claus.

(Cassidy comes running down the stairs excitedly. She carries a comb.)

CASSIDY: *(About her fingernails.)* Look! Look here, I scraped out every scrap of dirt from underneath there using the teeth on this here comb.

HOOKER: Ah, great work.

CASSIDY: Thanks. *(Extending her spotless hand to Carmichael.)* Hi, Mister!

TURNIP: This man's trying t'close down the Lucky Spot. Says Hooker owes him a lot a money.

CASSIDY: Well then, Hooker'll just have t'have himself another lucky streak. Just like he did that time down in Gulfport when he won me and this place and the Chevy motor car.

CARMICHAEL: All that. Well now, Mr. Hooker, you do seem to be quite a lucky man. But then I guess you did pick up a few gambling tips from your very talented wife.

CASSIDY: How d'you know his wife?

HOOKER: What d'ya know about her?

CARMICHAEL: Hmm. Well. I've played cards with her on occasion. And then there was a time when I was bringing my sister, Caroline Carmichael, back and forth from the hospital every day to testify against Mrs. Hooker at her trial.

HOOKER: Good Christ, he's Caroline Carmichael's brother!

TURNIP: No wonder he hates your damn guts.

HOOKER: Yeah, well, he can hate my guts as much as he wants to, but it wasn't me who shoved Caroline over that goddamn balcony railing! Sue Jack did it all on her own. *(To Carmichael.)* So you stop harassing us 'cause of that no-good wife of mine?! God, I'd love t'break her rotten neck and shut her up for good!

CARMICHAEL: Lucky you didn't shut her up before you mastered all of her card-playing pointers.

HOOKER: What pointers do you mean?

CARMICHAEL: Your wife was an expert card sharp: had great hands, knew all about shaved cards, hold outs…ringing in a cold deck.

HOOKER: What are you inferring?

CARMICHAEL: I'm not inferring.

HOOKER: Look, like you say, Sue Jack had the hands. You gotta have the hands. I never did. Nah, there's only one thing I learned from Sue Jack that ever did me any good.

CARMICHAEL: Now what would that be?

HOOKER: A simple rule of thumb: Whoever throws the first punch in a fist fight has a twenty-to-one shot at aceing the match.

(The two men stare at each other.)

CARMICHAEL: Is that a fact?

(Hooker shrugs his shoulders and turns.)

HOOKER: Seems t'be. Hey!

(Hooker turns back and clobbers Carmichael in the jaw. Carmichael falls to the floor.)

HOOKER: Sorry I pasted him, but he was becoming insufferable.

CARMICHAEL: You're gonna regret this. Believe me, you're gonna regret this a lot. I'm calling in the Sheriff.

HOOKER: Hey, Turnip, help the man outa here.

(Turnip pulls Carmichael to his feet and ushers him toward the door.)

CARMICHAEL: You're outta here. You're through. Pack your goddamn bags! You're finished!

(Hooker yells after them as Turnip and Carmichael exit out the front door.)

HOOKER: *(Overlapping.)* Relax, Carmichael. I'll have that money for ya by January one! No damn problem with the Lucky Spot opening. No damn problem!

TURNIP: *(Offstage)* No damn problem!

HOOKER: Jesus!

CASSIDY: Looks like you got that man pretty riled up.

HOOKER: Looks like it.

CASSIDY: You reckon he's gonna get us kicked outta here for good?

HOOKER: Look, the Lucky Spot Dance Hall opens at 8 P.M. tonight; by 9:15 we'll be strolling on Easy Street; by January one, you'll be dancing in satin red shoes. Every day's gonna be like a goddamn holiday in Paris, France! Now do ya have that straight?

CASSIDY: Uh huh.

HOOKER: Well, good. 'Cause I'm sure as hell not standing here telling ya all this crap just t'get your rotten hopes up for nothing.

CASSIDY: No, I—I sure I don't wanna get my rotten hopes up for nothing. 'Cause my hopes…well, sometimes, when they get way, way up there, I don't even know how t'get 'em back down without dying or not living or breathing or exploding. I don't know why. Sometimes.

HOOKER: Yeah. Sure. Well, I would never want t'get your hopes up for nothing.

CASSIDY: Thanks. I appreciate it.

(They look at the floor for a moment.)

CASSIDY: Hooker?

HOOKER: Yeah?

CASSIDY: I got this thing for you. *(Cassidy takes a dirty worn piece of paper out of her pocket.)*

HOOKER: What is it?

CASSIDY: Just a card. A birthday message.

HOOKER: Well, my birthday was way back in the damn summer.

CASSIDY: I know. I been carrying the card around since then.

HOOKER: Uh-huh.

CASSIDY: But I just never could find the right time t'…give it to ya.

HOOKER: Oh.

(Cassidy hands out the card then withdraws it.)

CASSIDY: Nah, maybe I should wait and go on and give it to you some other time.

HOOKER: Well, I may as well look at the thing.

CASSIDY: There's nothing particular about it.

HOOKER: Okay, if you don't want me t'have it…

CASSIDY: No, no. Go on. Here. It's for you. *(She hands him the card.)*

HOOKER: *(Hooker unfolds the paper and reads the message aloud.)* "To Reed Hooker. Happy Birthday. From Cassidy Smith." The *K*'s backwards. *(He hands the paper back to her.)*

CASSIDY: Well…okay.

HOOKER: I gotta go wash up. *(Hooker starts up the stairs.)*

CASSIDY: I'll, ah, I'll run iron ya your clean shirt.

(Hooker exits up the stairs. Cassidy exits out the kitchen door carrying the breakfast tray. Lacey Rollins, a shortish woman in her thirties, with peroxided hair and heavy rouge, appears outside dressed in a frilly, tattered robe and high heels. She stumbles across the yard and moves into the dance hall through the side door. She looks around, sees the room is deserted, spots the coffeepot, and starts looking for a cup. Turnip walks in through the front door. He eyes her nervously.)

TURNIP: Hi.

LACEY: *(Startled.)* I was just coming in from out back t'hunt me some coffee. I need t'have coffee every morning. Otherwise, my heart just won't start pumping and it's likely I'll drop into a dead heap right here on this floor.

TURNIP: Well, there's the coffeepot right there.

LACEY: I see it, but I'm gonna need me a cup. Do you know where there's a cup? Or even a bowl? I don't mind drinking outta bowls. I don't have t'be prissy.

(Turnip finds a cup.)

TURNIP: Here, use this.

LACEY: Thanks. I don't guess there's any sugar?

TURNIP: No.

LACEY: Oh, well. It's just I love sugar. You can't ruin sugar. I wish I could put it on every morsel I ever ate. Wouldn't it be wonderful poured all over your scrambled eggs, and your sausages and your grits?

TURNIP: I never thought t'give it a try.

(Lacey moves around the room.)

LACEY: Well, I've thought t'give it a try. I've thought and thought and thought and— *(Lacey trips on her robe and falls to the floor. On the verge of tears.)* Oh dear. Look here, I've tripped again. I'm always falling down. I've got very weak ankles. My ankle bones are practically the smallest bones in my body. It's a condition that I've had since early birth. *(Starting to cry.)* Oh Lord. I'm sorry if I seem t'be falling apart. My goodness, it's only Christmas Eve and already I'm emotional.

TURNIP: Is something wrong?

LACEY: Well, where am I supposed to go? What am I supposed to do? Tomorrow's Christmas Day, and I'm sure no one's even thought to get me a present. I'm stuck out here in this backwoods without a nickel in my stocking—

TURNIP: What're you talking about? You'll be dancing here at the Lucky Spot tonight. You'll clear some jack.

(Hooker comes down the stairs without wearing a shirt.)

HOOKER: Hey, Cassidy, where's the clean shirt? *(Noticing Lacey and Turnip.)* Oh, good morning, Lacey, right? Hope you girls had a good night's sleep. Ya'll all gotta look real beautiful for tonight.

LACEY: Don't you know?

HOOKER: Know what?

LACEY: The other girls have all gone. They're all catching the train back t'New Orleans. And not a stinking one of 'em would lend me the fare. They don't like me. I'm unpopular everywhere I go.

(Cassidy enters from the kitchen with a clean shirt.)

HOOKER: What're you saying? The girls aren't out back in the bungalows?

(Turnip runs out to check the bungalows.)

LACEY: Bungalows? He calls those bungalows! Why, every one of us recognized them to be authentic slave quarters. I don't care what fancy colors you paint them.

HOOKER: Look, what's happening here?

(Turnip enters.)

TURNIP: They're gone alright.

HOOKER: Why'd everyone go?

LACEY: They all heard she was coming back.

HOOKER: Who?

LACEY: Your wife, Sue Jack. They're all scared t'death of her—think she's dangerous.

HOOKER: For Christ sake, she's in prison. She's no more coming here than Santa Claus.

LACEY: Well, the kid in the derby hat seems to be differently informed.

HOOKER: *(To Cassidy.)* What do you know about Sue Jack coming here?

(Hooker takes the shirt from Cassidy and starts to put it on.)

CASSIDY: Well, it's just I been keeping in check with the lady over at Angola Penitentiary…

HOOKER: You what?

CASSIDY: Yeah. And she tells me there's a special order releasing some prisoners out early for Christmas time and Sue Jack's one of 'em.

HOOKER: Well, she sure as shit's not coming here for Christmas!

CASSIDY: Yeah, she is. 'Cause I told 'em where we was.

TURNIP: Oh Lord!

CASSIDY: And we wanted her to come on out here.

HOOKER: I oughta bust you, Cassidy. I oughta bust you good! Is this any of your goddamn business?! *(To Lacey.)* How long ago did the girls leave here for the train depot?

LACEY: I don't know. A while, I guess.

HOOKER: I gotta drive over there and stop them. *(To Turnip.)* Look, if she…if she comes here…

(Hooker shoves Cassidy, who is trying to stop him, into the door.)

HOOKER: God damn it!…you tell her to get out and stay out. She's not welcome ever.

CASSIDY: But you don't understand! She's gotta be here t'get her divorce so you can oblige your marriage t'me. Please. Then she can go away forever!

(Hooker pulls Cassidy up by her hair.)

HOOKER: Look, I don't want you getting involved with that woman. Stay clear of her! You understand me? Huh?!

CASSIDY: Uh-huh.

(He lets her go.)

HOOKER: Good. *(Hooker storms out the front door.)*

CASSIDY: He pulled my hair. He never done that before. He never shouted at me like that. I thought he was different, but he's just the same! Oooh! I hate him! I hate him! He's mean and awful! And I hate him forever!

TURNIP: Well, you should never have taken it on your own t'stick your nose in like you did, calling up the prison, telling them t'send Sue Jack here.

CASSIDY: *(Turning on him.)* Yeah, well, how else is she gonna get her divorce so I can get my marriage? Huh? Did you ever think of that?! See, 'cause he's just got to marry me soon. Otherwise, this thing will be born out a bastard. And everyone in the world will look down on it and it won't have no excuses at all. *(Breaking into tears of raging fury.)* Oh, he promised me he'd marry me. He promised! He wouldn't break his promise, would he? Oh, promise me, he wouldn't!! Promise me!!!

TURNIP: Sure, I promise. I promise. Just don't cry so much.

LACEY: That's right, sugar, all that crying's gonna use up your face. And you've only got this one little face t'get by on for your whole life long. Ya gotta use it up sparingly.

(Turnip gets a bucket of red berries and brings it over to Cassidy.)

TURNIP: Hey, you wanna start stringing up these berries? We gotta decorate the tree.

CASSIDY: We gonna string these berries then put 'em up on the tree?

TURNIP: Yeah.

CASSIDY: That'll look good.

TURNIP: And there's popcorn. I'll go make the popcorn. We'll string that up, too.

CASSIDY: Okay.

(Turnip exits to the kitchen. Cassidy takes a needle and thread out of her pocket and starts stringing the berries. Lacey watches Cassidy, who is contentedly stringing berries.)

LACEY: May I help?

CASSIDY: Okay. I got one more needle. *(Cassidy goes to get a needle and thread.)* Tell me.

LACEY: What?

CASSIDY: You reckon Hooker's gonna be able t'bring them dancing ladies back here for tonight?

LACEY: Well, I hope so. Otherwise, my life is simply at a complete loss for direction.

CASSIDY: I should never of spoken nothing about her coming back. I sure didn't guess it'd run 'em all off like that.

LACEY: Oh, those girls are all being horrible, silly, scaredy-cats. Why, back when she was dancing in New Orleans, everyone of 'em would of died to be just like her.

CASSIDY: They would of?

LACEY: Sure. Sue Jack Tiller was top girl at the Glitter Dance Palace. She was the most beautiful, the finest dancer, the funniest wit. She made a hobby of collecting diamond engagement rings. She was always fishing guys for silk gowns and mink furs. Why, she possessed this one floor-length white mink coat that all the girls stood dripping with envy over. 'Course it didn't bother me a lick as I've never had the slightest affection for rodents. Pass the berries.

(Cassidy passes the bucket of berries to Lacey.)

CASSIDY: Here.

LACEY: None of us could ever fathom why she hauled off and married an insane rumrunner like Reed Hooker. Oh not that he wasn't well-to-do. Prohibition was a very flush time for the rumrunners. Still she could have had anyone. After all she possessed a great many assets.

CASSIDY: Like what?

LACEY: Well now, her greatest asset, in my opinion, was her ability to hold a prolonged conversation with a man. My auntie always told me, if a man would hold a conversation with a woman, well, she was special. She had more than his grudging physical desire—she had his admiration and respectability.

CASSIDY: Well, me, I—I've talked to men. I say things t' 'em and mostly they talk right back.

LACEY: That's different, sugar. What I'm talking about is real conversation. Not things such as "Hi, cutie," or "Hot night," or "Where's my clean shirt?" See, a real conversation would be dealing in topics with much more depth and importance.

CASSIDY: Like what? What would be a real conversation?

LACEY: Hmm. It's hard t'say exactly. But more along the lines of a discussion as to how the sun is really a star and it's made up out of balls of burning fire and once there was an ice age and everything got frozen and died in the cold but then things began to thaw out and the sun came back out and people could start to living again but the dinosaurs were gone forever because they had become…extinct.

CASSIDY: Gosh. Well. I'd be confused speaking in a conversation like that.

LACEY: Sure. Most girls would be. Or say, for instance, one might have a conversation discussing deep, frightening things about living and dying that most people would never even mention because they're too stupid t' think 'em up in the first place.

CASSIDY: Like what deep frightening things 'bout living and dying?

LACEY: Oh…I don't know exactly. Just a very complicated sort of conversation. I don't get t'practice conversation that much. Most fellows won't pay any attention to me unless I'm being perky. But her…they'd have endless conversation with her.

CASSIDY: Still all an' all, I bet she's not one whit better'n me.

LACEY: Well…you're a good deal younger than she is. You've got the bloom of youth.

CASSIDY: Yeah; I hope.

LACEY: Does Hooker…does he ever tell you he loves you?

CASSIDY: *(Factually.)* Oh no. No person ever told me that. But one night, not long ago, I—I dreamed some furry animal said it loved me, but I don't remember what kind it was.

LACEY: Well, even though I've never really known it, I do believe in love. I don't think I could go on living if I didn't. Unfortunately, I've got a way of making any fellow I'm with so mad he'll haul off and hit me. The last one, he tried t'drowned me in the bathtub. Since then, it's been hard t'let myself trust a man. But I still keep trying. I still believe in love.

(Sue Jack Tiller Hooker, thirties, enters through the front door. She has the jarring presence of a ravaged beauty. She is tall and thin and wears a hand-me-down dress, a thin wool coat, and flat ugly shoes. She carries a large handbag.)

SUE JACK: Hi.

CASSIDY: Hi.

SUE JACK: Is this a dance hall?

CASSIDY: It is.

SUE JACK: Y'all opening tonight?

CASSIDY: We is.

SUE JACK: Oh. Well, good. Good. I—um, is Reed Hooker, is he around here anywhere?

CASSIDY: He's gone out.

SUE JACK: Oh. Well, how long do you think he'll be gone?

CASSIDY: Don't know. What d'ya want with him?

SUE JACK: Well…I'm his wife, Sue Jack Hooker…I've been away…awhile.

CASSIDY: Yeah. Yeah, I heard about you. But you don't look the same as I thought.

SUE JACK: No?

CASSIDY: Uh-huh.

SUE JACK: Um.

LACEY: Oh, hello. I'm sure you don't remember me but I worked at the Green Torch Dance Hall years ago when you were at the Glitter Palace down in New Orleans. My name's Lacey Rollins.

SUE JACK: Oh yeah, I remember you. You did cartwheels.

LACEY: Right. She's right.

SUE JACK: But your hair was much darker back then—it was jet black, almost a blue-black.

LACEY: Why, I'm flabbergasted! Who'd ever have thought you'd remember me? Tell me. Don't you think this new color is much more flattering? Doesn't it give me a much more perky look?

SUE JACK: Well, you were always very…perky. But I do, ah, like it a lot.

LACEY: Why, thanks, sugar. And your hair, it's all done…well, just completely differently.

SUE JACK: That's right. It's all different now.

(Turnip enters with the popcorn.)

TURNIP: Well, here's the popcorn.

SUE JACK: Turnip.

TURNIP: Sue Jack?

SUE JACK: Yeah, its me.

TURNIP: Gosh, you look—I mean, your face—

SUE JACK: I know, it looks like forty miles of bad road, all of it rained on. Well, hell, 'least I made it through three years at Angola, that's something.

TURNIP: Oh, sure.

LACEY: Sure.

TURNIP: Boy, I'm glad they set ya free when they did.

SUE JACK: Yeah, I got lucky. They decided to let some of us out early for Christmas. Probably so they could save on turkey dinners.

TURNIP: Well, gosh. Gosh, what was it like stuck in prison? Did y'all have any fun at all? I mean, what did they do on your birthday?

SUE JACK: Well…nothing.

TURNIP: Oh.

SUE JACK: Yeah. Nothing special. Just, you know, the same.

TURNIP: What's that like? The same?

SUE JACK: Oh, I can't really afford t'think about all that right now. I wanna try and make a good impression on Reed when he gets here. Tell me, do I really look plain ugly?

LACEY: No!

TURNIP: No, it's just…different.

LACEY: Different. *(Echoing Turnip.)*

TURNIP: I mean, from before. You don't—got on your gloves. But other than that…well, ya don't look ugly.

SUE JACK: Then will ya do me a favor?

TURNIP: What?

SUE JACK: Stop looking at me like that. You're starting t'get me scared.

TURNIP: What? No, there's nothing t'be scared for.

SUE JACK: I know. It's just I gotta see Reed. I haven't seen him in so long. And I'm standing here in these hand-me-down rags, with my hair all cropped off looking like something a cat dragged in.

TURNIP: You look okay.

SUE JACK: Thanks, I'm sorry. I'm just so jumpy today. I swear if somebody said boo t'me I'd cry.

TURNIP: Ain't nobody gonna say boo to ya.

SUE JACK: Sure. I'll be okay. I mean, I was just so surprised that he called for me.

TURNIP: Who called for you?

SUE JACK: Reed. He—he never visited me the whole time, and I thought I'd lost him for sure and here, outta the blue, he calls and leaves a message telling me t'come here for Christmas.

TURNIP: Oh…gosh.

SUE JACK: I've got all this hope welling up in me again. I swear my heart's spinning inside me like a runaway top.

TURNIP: Yeah, well, I don't know what t'say here. Umm. Here's the popcorn, Cassidy, if ya wanna start stringing it up.

CASSIDY: Thanks.

SUE JACK: This is a beautiful jukebox. Prettiest one I've ever seen.

TURNIP: It's Hooker's pride and joy. Says it's got all his favorite tunes on it.

SUE JACK: All these tunes are new. I don't recognize any of them.

CASSIDY: Look, there's some things of yours ya might be wanting.

SUE JACK: What things?

CASSIDY: Just belongings. I found 'em in one of the drawers in Hooker's trunk. I put 'em in a box for ya.

SUE JACK: Well, thanks.

CASSIDY: I'll go up and get 'em for ya. Ya might be needing 'em on your travels.

SUE JACK: Alright.

LACEY: *(To Turnip.)* Hey, what was it she called you?

TURNIP: Huh?

LACEY: Was it Turnip? Did she call you "Turnip"?

TURNIP: I guess.

LACEY: Turnip. That's hilarious. Whatever does it stand for?

TURNIP: Just stands for Turnip.

LACEY: But what's it short for?

TURNIP: My name, I guess.

LACEY: Well, what's your name?

TURNIP: …Turnip.

LACEY: Oh.

TURNIP: …Yeah.

(Whitt Carmichael enters through the front door. He doesn't notice Sue Jack who is seated in the window seat.)

CARMICHAEL: Hello. Is Hooker here?

TURNIP: No.

CARMICHAEL: Look, I just found out that all of your Gold Coast hostesses have run out in fear of the imminent arrival of Hooker's outlaw wife.

SUE JACK: Why, hello, Whitt.

CARMICHAEL: Sue Jack…Good Lord—I hardly recognized you.

SUE JACK: Yes, well, I guess I look kind of different without a frame around me.

CARMICHAEL: Well, well, so the never-miss girl has really returned. Tell me, how are those silk hands of yours? She had the prettiest hands. They never let her down.

SUE JACK: 'Least not to your level, anyway.

CARMICHAEL: You got close though. Back on Esplanade Avenue. You got awfully close. Let me see those hands.

SUE JACK: Oh, it's amazing what three years of raising hogs and picking cotton can do to a pair of hands. Feel for yourself.
(Sue Jack reaches up to rub her callused fingertips across Carmichael's face. He pulls away.)

SUE JACK: Oh Whitt, what's the matter? Don't you wanna see if I lost my touch?

CARMICHAEL: Look…I didn't come here to dwell on your hard luck or your felony conviction…I have a business proposition to discuss with your husband.
(Cassidy comes walking down the staircase carrying a cardboard box.)

SUE JACK: Tell me. Reed and I are partners.

CARMICHAEL: Well, in the light of the fact that your dancers have departed, I feel it is now painfully apparent that Hooker will not be able to settle his three-hundred-and-fifty-five dollar debt to me by January first. So, as a matter of convenience, I'd appreciate him signing this property over to me straight away. *(Carmichael hands a paper to Sue Jack. As she looks it over.)* Otherwise, I intend to inform all the people in town Hooker owes money to the distressing news that y'all are opening up your taxi dance hall with absolutely no taxi dancers. Believe me, it could make some of them rubes very, very angry.

SUE JACK: *(Handing the paper back to Turnip.)* I don't know where you get your information, Whitt, but someone just about pulled your leg completely off. Why, our only concern is that there will be so many beautiful ladies dancing here this evening that everyone strolling down this road will be made mindlessly drunk inhaling the intoxicating smell of all the sweet perfumes.

CARMICHAEL: Ah, Sue Jack, I do love it when you wax poetic but I saw all of your charity girls pulling out on this morning's train. They claimed they were escaping your villainous presence.

SUE JACK: That's pure sour grapes. They're just distressed because we rejected them for the dance hall. You see, we only want the creme de le creme working at the Lucky Spot.

(Lacey smiles broadly.)

SUE JACK: Come by tonight and see for yourself if you don't believe me.

CARMICHAEL: Don't worry, I'll be back. And so will a lot of other folks who have debts to settle.

SUE JACK: Wonderful. We need some big-time spenders. So long now. Merry Christmas.

CARMICHAEL: And a Merry Christmas to you, Miss Sue.

LACEY: Please do come back.

(Carmichael exits out the front door.)

SUE JACK: My God. Have all the dancers really gone?

LACEY: I'm afraid so. I'm the only one left.

SUE JACK: I can't believe people think I'm so horrible. I mean, maybe back when I drank I was something of a hothead.

LACEY: Well, Lola Dove was getting everyone all riled up, telling them about the time when you hit her with a brick just t'see if she would bleed.

SUE JACK: Oh, yeah, yeah, well surprisingly enough that cold, heartless bitch bled a whole lot. Reed's gonna hate me for this when he finds out.

TURNIP: He already knows.

SUE JACK: He does?

TURNIP: He went to try and stop the dancers at the train depot. Guess he didn't make it.

SUE JACK: Well, hell's fire, here he invites me for Christmas and I bring in this whole bag of trouble. What a goddamn mess. God, I'd kill for a drink. Haven't had one in three years.

TURNIP: Well, look. I think I better go try and find Hooker.

SUE JACK: Ooh! Just one straight shot of tequila.

TURNIP: See if he's got anything up his sleeve.

SUE JACK: Or gin, a jolt of gin.

(Turnip exits out the front door, slamming it behind him.)

SUE JACK: Okay, okay. I'm fine.

CASSIDY: Well, here's your box for ya. *(Cassidy hands Sue Jack the cardboard box packed with belongings from Sue Jack's past.)*

SUE JACK: Thanks. Thanks a lot. *(Sue Jack stares into the box a moment then takes out a hand mirror.)* Ha! Look here, my silver mirror's cracked. Well, now that's seven years bad luck. Hmm. Wonder when I broke it? God, look at me! How'd all of that sadness ever sink so deep into my face? Well, let's see what we can do to fix her up. *(Sue Jack takes out some melted rouge and smears it across her cheeks. She becomes disheartened by the effect. She tosses the mirror aside.)* Shouldn't be looking in mirrors. My mama, she shot herself while looking in a full-length mirror. 'Course I'm not like my mama. She went insane due to religious troubles. *(Sue Jack takes out an old bottle of hand lotion, opens it up, and smells it.)*

LACEY: Well, I don't know how my mother is; she's not speaking t'me. And I really don't even care 'cause when she was speaking t'me, she never got tired of telling me how I was swivel-hipped and I was never gonna be anything more than some poor man's pudding. Well, I've set out t'prove her wrong. *(To Cassidy.)* So how about your mama? What's she like?

CASSIDY: Well, it's hard t'say 'cause, well she's dead. All of 'em are except me.

SUE JACK: How'd they all die?

CASSIDY: Diptheria. Killed every one of 'em. Then they come out and burned our place down t'ashes. Said it was full of contamination.

LACEY: That's tragic. Having your whole family demolished.

CASSIDY: Of course, my paw, well, I don't know about him, 'cause see I never knowed him. He could be some rich lord living in a castle somewhere or maybe he's just some old bum standing in the breadlines. I'm hoping someday I'll meet him and find out.

SUE JACK: Well, I never met my daddy but if I did, I'd like nothing better than t'spit straight at him.

CASSIDY: Well, all men ain't so bad.

SUE JACK: No. How 'bout your husband? What's he like?

CASSIDY: I, well, I ain't exactly quite got no husband, yet.

SUE JACK: Oh.

CASSIDY: But I will. He's gonna marry me real soon.

SUE JACK: Well, that's good news. *(Pause.)* What sort of wedding you plan-ning?

CASSIDY: Oh, nothing much.

LACEY: Gosh, this sure is a stunning tree, and these berries are just gonna make it look so perky! Don't y'all think?

SUE JACK: Yeah. You know, you oughta do something special—dress up at least. Let me look through here. Maybe there's some things you can use. *(Sue Jack rummages through the box.)* God, I'll never forget our wedding.

It was St. Patrick's day and it was raining and Thumper Bell...Lacey, you remember Thumper Bell?...

LACEY: Oh yeh, yeh, the crazy drummer from the Palace.

SUE JACK: Why, he kept throwing rice all over us on the wet streets in the rain. Reed and I—we couldn't stop laughing...Doesn't that look pretty? *(Sue Jack takes off Cassidy's derby and puts on a fancy hat.)*

LACEY: *(In an attempt to change the focus.)* I've never been married. But I did get left at the church once. Well, actually, it was a home wedding. Oh, we had the house all decorated with colorful flowers and garlands and candlelight. I don't think they'll ever invent anything more romantic than candlelight. Anyway, it's a very funny story—all about how he never came by the house. I guess it makes me out t'look a little foolish. Afterwards, everyone remarked how I took it really well, coming down and joining the party like I did.

CASSIDY: But why didn't he come back t'marry you? What made him not come?

LACEY: I guess he just—Well maybe 'cause I...Oh, beats me.

SUE JACK: Here, try on this coat.

CASSIDY: I don't think I better be using your things.

SUE JACK: Look, didn't anybody ever tell you, it's better to give than to receive?

CASSIDY: No.

SUE JACK: Well, occasionally, it's true. *(Throwing the coat around Cassidy.)* There. Lacey, doesn't that look elegant?

LACEY: Now that does help! It hides a lot! In fact, I have a dress that'll be just the thing with that coat. I'll run and get it! *(Lacey exits out the side door.)*

SUE JACK: Here's some shoes.

CASSIDY: Why, them's red satin shoes. I always been longing t'have me a pair a them red satin shoes.

SUE JACK: Well, try 'em on.

CASSIDY: No, I, well, I got these different sort of feet. Would it be alright if I tried 'em on upstairs?

SUE JACK: Sure.

CASSIDY: Thanks.

(Cassidy takes the shoes and exits upstairs. Sue Jack goes back to the box. She finds an old deck of cards. She takes out a lace glove and puts it on her hand. She then spots an old teddy bear. She picks it up and holds it with a strange sad wonder. Hooker enters through the front door in a huff. He stops in his

tracks when he sees Sue Jack. Sue Jack feels his presence, she drops the toy bear back into the box and turns to face him.)

SUE JACK: Hi. I, well, I was gonna try and fix up.

HOOKER: No need.

SUE JACK: I'm sorry about running off the dancers.

HOOKER: Yeah.

SUE JACK: I'll try and...help out.

HOOKER: I don't think so.

SUE JACK: Well...whatever you'd like.

HOOKER: I'd like you outta here.

SUE JACK: I see.

HOOKER: You're like a bad luck charm around my neck. I keep trying t'rip you off and you keep burning my hand.

SUE JACK: I don't wanna burn your hand. I don't mean to.

HOOKER: Then just go.

SUE JACK: I'm not the same as I was, Reed. Go on and look at me. You see, I'm not the same. I'm not the same one who kept on hurting you by drinking, and brawling and gambling it all away. And I'm not the young, laughing girl you married with the rosy cheeks and pretty hands. I guess I'm not sure who I am. And, I tell you, it's been making me feel so strange. When I was in prison, the only belonging I had was this old photograph of myself that was taken just before I ran off from home. In it I'm wearing this straw hat decorated with violets and my hair's swept back in a braid and my eyes, they're just...shining...I used to take out that picture and look at it. I kept on pondering over it. I swear it confused me so much, wondering where she was—that girl in the picture. I could not imagine where she'd departed to—so unknowingly, so unexpectedly. *(A pause.)* Look, I won't drink or yell or fight or shoot pool or bet the roosters or—

HOOKER: Yeah, yeah, and I guess I've heard all that till it's frayed at the edges.

SUE JACK: Please, I don't wanna lose any more. I'm through throwing everything away with both fists.

HOOKER: I'm sorry. I just can't let you in on me ever again.

SUE JACK: Then why did you send for me? Why did you call for me t'come t'you?

HOOKER: ...I didn't. It was somebody else. It was somebody I'm in kinda a mess with.

SUE JACK: What sort of mess? What somebody?

HOOKER: Look, I really can't afford t'have you flying off the handle.

SUE JACK: I'm alright.

HOOKER: It's just something that happened and I think the best thing is if you just disappeared.

SUE JACK: What are you telling me? Just tell me what you're telling me.

(Cassidy enters at the top of the staircase wearing only one red shoe and holding the other one in her hand.)

HOOKER: Cassidy, get outta here!

CASSIDY: *(A beat.)* You tell her about us?

HOOKER: Move, do you hear me? Move! Move!

SUE JACK: What are you—what did you—this child?!

(Turnip rushes in the front door. He races behind the counter, grabs a shotgun and heads back toward the front door.)

TURNIP: Hooker, thank God, come quick! Carmichael's got the whole town riled up. Johnny Montgomery and some of the other guys ya owe money to are taking away everything: the Christmas hog, the Santy Claus mailbox, the Chevy car...

(Hooker grabs the shotgun from Turnip and leans it against the wall.)

HOOKER: Look, we don't need t'start killing people. I can handle Johnny Montgomery. He'll listen to reason.

(Hooker and Turnip exit out the front door.)

CASSIDY: *(Coming down the staircase.)* You want these things back?

(Sue Jack looks at her, then heads for the counter looking for some liquor.)

SUE JACK: I want a drink. The real world's getting much too potent. I gotta dilute it with some pure grain alcohol. *(Finding the bottle.)* Ahha! White mule. I knew I could depend on Mr. Hooker. *(Pouring a drink.)* There now. Let me just zing one back. *(She throws back a triple shot.)* Ah. So good ol' hooch is legal again. I like that. No more recooking extract, fermenting mash, drinking hair tonic. Wanna jolt?

CASSIDY: No thanks.

SUE JACK: Down the hatch. *(She throws back another big shot.)* So...the scum bastard made a play for ya? I mean, you're having his kid, right?

CASSIDY: That's right.

SUE JACK: You know, someone oughta notify the Children's Aid Society or maybe report that s.o.b. to the Morals court. I could do that. I think I'll do that. *(She has another drink.)*

CASSIDY: No, don't do that. He didn't do nothing bad.

SUE JACK: Maybe we'll just have to let the judge decide—like he decided about me. *(She has another drink.)* But personally, I believe that sexual

molestation of a young orphan child by a raving drunken idiot is suffi-
cient grounds for criminal prosecution.

CASSIDY: But it weren't like that. Please, ya can't send him off t'no jail!

SUE JACK: Oh, go on and cry all you want. Tears have never been precious to
me. Not my own or anybody else's.

CASSIDY: Lady, I'm just asking ya t'do what's right!

SUE JACK: Yeah and just what do you suggest is right?

CASSIDY: Well, it's a clear thing. He don't like you. He don't want you here.

SUE JACK: Did he tell you that?

CASSIDY: Yeah.

SUE JACK: Well, sometimes people don't mean—the things they say.

CASSIDY: I think he means it.

SUE JACK: I wager he doesn't. (She pours another drink.)

CASSIDY: Well, I ain't never had a kid by no man before and he tol' me he'd
marry me 'cause I ain't raising no stinking bastard.

SUE JACK: If he told you he'd marry ya, then he's a no good dirt-crawling liar.
See 'cause he's never gonna marry you. He can't. He's married to me.

CASSIDY: Well, he's divorcing you.

SUE JACK: He's what?

CASSIDY: That's right. He's divorcing you and marrying me.

SUE JACK: Oh, he's been dealing you out a very crooked hand.

CASSIDY: Why, you ain't even pretty. They all said how you was so beautiful
but you ain't even pretty. I got the bloom of youth and you ain't even
pretty.

SUE JACK: Listen to me, you greasy little runt. He's my husband. He loves me.
He can't help it. (Sue Jack picks up the shotgun and aims it in Cassidy's
direction.) And if I were you, I wouldn't go around spreading lies like
that. Understand, I'm never gonna get over loving Reed Hooker. 'Cause
even when I don't know who in this godless world I am, or was, or ever
will be—the one thing I know as sure as the smell of spring rain is that
I utterly, hopelessly love that rotten, worthless son of a bitch!
(Throughout the following, Sue Jack fires the shotgun shattering a mirror,
light fixtures, and the juke box.) I want, want, want him like a crazy
shrieking, howling dog. I can't live without him! I'll blow out my brains.
I'll shoot you to pieces. I'll rip this place t'the ground. But, by God, I
gotta have that miserable, lying, double-crossing, one and only love of
my broken life! (Sue Jack stops firing the gun. She looks around a moment
then stumbles across the room and gets the whiskey bottle.) Oh God, look
here. I've been misering the bottle. I didn't mean t'do that.

(Lacey runs in with the dress.)

LACEY: What in the world…? Are y'all alright? Oh, my Lord, look here.

(Lacey trips and falls as Turnip and Hooker come in together. They have been in a fight. Turnip is carrying Hooker; he is a bloody mess.)

TURNIP: Thank God, Sue Jack. Thank God for those shots. You scared those bastards away. They almost murdered Hooker.

(Turnip sits Hooker down.)

HOOKER: Yeah, thanks. Thanks a lot. *(Hooker looks up. He sees the damage, He sees the liquor bottle in Sue Jack's hand.)* What's all this? You've shot this place to shit. My jukebox. Look at my jukebox. *(Hooker rises, fury begins to blind him.)* Why, you stupid slut—

(What follows is an all-out, low-down, and rutty brawl. The other characters are all somehow thrust in and out and back in and out of this massive free-for-all battle that leaves the place in total shambles.)

SUE JACK: Don't you ever hit me.

HOOKER: Hit you? Hit you?! I'm gonna kill you! I'm gonna rip your head off your shoulders.

SUE JACK: Stay away. You stay away!

HOOKER: I'm sick of you ruining my life! You're not gonna ruin it anymore!

SUE JACK: I'm ruining your life? That's rich. That's damn rich. You're the worthless, two-timing bastard who messed out on me.

HOOKER: And what the hell else was I gonna do when you shut me out with you drinking for weeks on end, staying binged out of your goddamned mind, gambling away every nickel we ever had?!

SUE JACK: Yeah, well, at least I never messed out on you.

HOOKER: That's a damned lie!

SUE JACK: Don't call me a liar!

HOOKER: *(Running on.)* Why, you stayed for five weeks out in that trash can shack getting drunk and screwing your cousin, the undertaker.

SUE JACK: That was different! That was family!

HOOKER: Bullshit!

SUE JACK: You know good and well I never loved him. But I saw all those poems you wrote to Caroline Carmichael.

HOOKER: You read my poems?!

SUE JACK: That one about how she smelled!

HOOKER: I never said you could read my poems! I'm gonna butcher you for that!

SUE JACK: Go ahead! Poke out my red eyes. Tear out my dying hair. I'm a sickening, wretched, worthless glob of pulp. But at least I never crawled so low as t'mercilessly abduct and rape a poor runt of an orphan child!

HOOKER: Let me at her! I'm gonna shred open your face! I'm gonna tear out your decaying heart!

(Hooker catches Sue Jack. They struggle passionately.)

HOOKER: You bitch!

SUE JACK: You bastard!

HOOKER: I'm glad they stuck you in that jail. I pray you go back! I pray you get nothing but bread and water and blood-caked rot for the rest of your useless life!

(Hooker slings Sue Jack to the floor. Sue Jack gets to her feet and grabs the rifle. She comes toward him swinging it at him.)

SUE JACK: I'm glad I threw Caroline Carmichael over that balcony rail. I'm glad she broke both her arms and gashed up her face. Let that serve as fair warning to any other whore I find in your bed! Fair warning to all whores!

(Hooker grabs the rifle away from her. They start to strangle each other.)

HOOKER: I'm gonna kill you.

SUE JACK: I'm gonna kill you.

HOOKER: I hate your guts.

SUE JACK: I hate your guts.

HOOKER: You bitch.

SUE JACK: You bastard.

HOOKER: You bitch.

SUE JACK: You bastard. You—

HOOKER: You...

SUE JACK: You...

(They both collapse on the floor. It is a double knockout. Music B comes up as the lights fade to black.)

END OF ACT I

ACT II
SCENE I

The stage is dark. Music A: "I Need A Little Sugar In My Bowl"—a low-down, rinky-tink blues tune plays on a record player. It is about eight o'clock in the evening on the same day.

HOOKER'S VOICE: Okay, try the switch. *(A little toy village is lit up on the dark stage.)* It's working!

TURNIP: Yeah.

HOOKER: The whole village. *(A beat.)* All lit up. All aglow. Turnip?

TURNIP: Huh?

HOOKER: She gone yet?

TURNIP: Not yet.

HOOKER: Get her outta here. I don't wanna lay eyes on her ever again. *(A beat.)* You hear me?

TURNIP: Yeah. Can I get the lights now?

HOOKER: Go ahead.

(We see that Hooker has a bump on his head, a black eye, and his hand is wrapped in gauze. He is dressed in tails. Turnip wears a baggy suit and a skinny tie. The damage from this morning's brawl has basically been repaired or hidden under the decorations that have been put up for this evening's extravaganza. The record player and three or four large stacks of records sit on the counter top along with a huge punch bowl and coffeepot and a plate of cookies. A few empty chairs are lined up against the wall. Throughout the following Hooker and Turnip line the rest of the stacked up chairs up against the wall.)

TURNIP: Hooker.

HOOKER: Huh?

TURNIP: I don't think this is gonna work.

HOOKER: Well, then we'll toss it. There're plenty more swell ones. We've got stacks of 'em. *(Hooker removes the record and tosses it into a cardboard box.)*

TURNIP: I don't just mean these old records. I mean the whole thing. The whole opening of the Lucky Spot.

HOOKER: What about it?

TURNIP: I really think we oughta put off the Grand Opening. I mean we don't

have no music or no taxi dancers; our electric sign's all broke. Face it—
the cards are stacking up against us.

HOOKER: Look, we can't put off the Grand Opening. I owe too damn much
money. There're people out there who are waiting to break both my legs.
I need anything we can make tonight t'help fend off the wolves.

TURNIP: We're gonna be opening ourselves up to all sorts of ridicule.

HOOKER: Be that as it may.

TURNIP: I mean Cassidy can't be out here dancing around for ten cents a
ticket. *(Indicating a huge stomach.)* She's out t'here, for Christ sake.

HOOKER: Are you telling me how to run my affairs?!

TURNIP: No, it's just…well, ya oughtta think about her feelings sometimes.
She does have 'em.

HOOKER: Hey, I'm not a blind man. I know how I've treated her. I know I'm
a bilge bag. I hate my own goddamn guts.

TURNIP: I don't mean t'criticize you—

HOOKER: Go ahead! It's clear I'm culpable for the preposterous condition she's
in. I should have taken that chestnut mare, but I took Cassidy instead.
(A beat.) She had such a sad face; a woebegone countenance. I hoped I
could change that face. Instead I've made it worse.

TURNIP: The main thing is she doesn't want the kid to be born out a bastard.

HOOKER: Right. Right. So I'm supposed t'marry her.

TURNIP: Yeah. Well, listen, I don't know much about these things; so correct
me if I'm mistaken, but from the looks of it you and Sue Jack are kinda
on the outs—but even so if you needed someone to, well—about
Cassidy, I mean—I could take—
*(Cassidy comes walking down the stairs. She is dressed in the clothes Sue Jack
and Lacey helped her put together in Act I. Her hair is fixed in curls under
a hat.)*

TURNIP: Oh. Hi, Cassidy.

CASSIDY: Hi.

HOOKER: Hi.

CASSIDY: *(A beat.)* I look okay?

TURNIP: Yeah. Nice.

HOOKER: Your hair's kinda sticking out some around the sides. Come here
and let me fix it.
(Cassidy goes to Hooker. He starts working with her hair.)

HOOKER: Hold still. *(A beat.)* Does that pull?

CASSIDY: No.

HOOKER: *(Still working on her hair.)* So…Uh, you had any ideas about how t'do this wedding?

CASSIDY: *(A beat.)* No; just signing the papers.

HOOKER: You interested in a cake or a white dress or throwing rice or anything?

CASSIDY: I…no.

HOOKER: Maybe we could go out t'eat at a restaurant or something afterwards…if you wanted to.

CASSIDY: *(Nodding yes.)* Uh huh.

HOOKER: We'll do that then. There. That looks better—don't lose those hairpins. Gotta go out and…work on the sign.

(Hooker exits out the front door. Cassidy turns to Turnip. Both of them are white.)

CASSIDY: You hear that? He's talking about my marriage t'him. He remembered all about it. He's gonna marry me. He's gonna do it.

TURNIP: I reckon so.

CASSIDY: He's gonna keep his promise. Just like you said. Why, you're the one that promised me he'd keep his promise. You're the one! Oh, thank you, Turnip! *(Cassidy grabs Turnip and kisses him.)*

TURNIP: Well, don't kiss me about it! He's only marrying ya on the rebound.

CASSIDY: The what?

TURNIP: The rebound, the rebound, from Sue Jack. Ya don't just want him t'marry ya on the rebound, do ya?

CASSIDY: Yeah. I sure do. I sure do.

TURNIP: Yeah, I reckon so.

(Lacey sticks her head in from the kitchen door.)

TURNIP: Oh, Lacey, come on in! Come on in!

LACEY: *(Over her shoulder.)* The coast is clear.

(Lacey enters the room, Sue Jack follows behind her.)

TURNIP: *(Not noticing Sue Jack.)* We're just having the biggest celebration! Hooker's proposed marriage t'Cassidy. He's made a definite public proposal! Ain't life a boon!

(Turnip and Cassidy see Sue Jack.)

TURNIP: Oh I—

(Cassidy gasps at the sight of her and runs to hide under a table. Sue Jack wears makeup and has restyled her hair. She is dressed in a glamorous tight-fitted dress from her past. She has a bruise on her cheek. Lacey is dressed in an old evening gown with dirty hand prints around the waist.)

SUE JACK: It's alright. It's fine. *(To Cassidy.)* Hey, come on out from under there. I'm not gonna hurt ya. Look, I'm sorry I shot at ya this morning. Okay? I guess I just—stepped outta line a little bit.

TURNIP: So, any luck with the phone calling?

SUE JACK: Oh, sure. I've got several friends who want me t'spend Christmas with them. I've just got to decide if I'm looking for a real sophisticated kind of Christmas or a big warm family sort of time, or maybe I just want t'spend a quiet, peaceful Christmas with a few intimate friends.

TURNIP: Yeah. Well, it sounds pretty nice.

SUE JACK: I tell ya, I feel refreshed. All that stupid, miserable hope I've let eat at me for so long has finally been beaten t'death. Reed and I are disbanded. We were never quite right for each other. This morning we tried to...kill each other. *(A beat.)* I'm renewed. I'm free t'be a globe-trotter once again. T'live by my wits. Ah, how I love a changing panorama.

TURNIP: Yeah—well—you look real beautiful.

SUE JACK: Right. Gotta impress my old acquaintances. Oh, by the way, Turnip, do you have any idea whatever happened to Thumper Bell? I thought I might try and give him a call—make sure someone remembered to invite him up for Christmas.

TURNIP: No, I—well, Thumper, he died. I'm sorry t'tell ya. Happened last spring. He, ah, stopped in an alleyway t'pick up some change and got hit by a falling flower box.

SUE JACK: Oh. Rotten luck. Poor Thumper...Well, I'll get my things and be heading out.

TURNIP: Yeah.

(Sue Jack exits out the side door to the bungalows.)

TURNIP: She really get any of those folks she was calling?

LACEY: Didn't sound like it to me.

TURNIP: She's been on the phone all afternoon. Seems like somebody would've come through for her.

LACEY: It's so sad. She'll be spending Christmas all alone.

TURNIP: Sometimes life makes me wanna puke. One stroke of really bad luck and people just can't never seem t'recover.

LACEY: You mean about their little boy.

TURNIP: Yeah, after he died things went hateful crazy.

CASSIDY: Sue Jack and Hooker had some child together?

TURNIP: Yeah. His name was Andrew. *(A beat.)* They called him Andy.

CASSIDY: How old was he?

TURNIP: *(Indicating the height of a two- to three-year-old child.)* 'Bout this old. You know, small.

CASSIDY: And he died?

TURNIP: Yeah. Ran out in the road and got hit by some automobile. They say he was chasing after a hummingbird.

LACEY: Oooh! I'd just run and jump straight off a cliff if I didn't have a place t'go to on Christmas Day.

TURNIP: Hell, I might just do it anyway.

CASSIDY: *(A beat.)* Well, why don't she just stay on here for Christmas?

TURNIP: Here?

LACEY: You'd want her here?

CASSIDY: I wouldn't mind.

LACEY: Well, if you don't mind—

TURNIP: Hooker refuses t'ever lay eyes on her again.

CASSIDY: Maybe if we just explain—

LACEY: I mean after all, we certainly could use an extra taxi dancer.

TURNIP: Hooker ain't listening t'reason. He's trying t'open up this dance hall with two dancers and no music. Claims he needs the money. Why, we'd make more money selling apples on a street corner. But he can't see it. Ah, I don't care! What does any of it matter?! All these miserable people butting around. Trying so hard. For what?! Before it's all over every one of 'em's gonna be stone cold dead! Absolutely every one of 'em. *(Snapping his fingers.)* Dead! Dead! Dead! So what the hell are they all sweating?! That's what I'd relish t'know! Oooh!! What a low-down, rutty, rotten, little game we're all playing. It ain't like checkers. In checkers somebody wins and somebody loses. It's clear-cut. But playing this other—we're all big-time losers; every one of us. No ringing in the cold deck, no aces up the sleeves, no hold-outs. Just stacking up piles and piles of chips, t'give 'em all away. All losers! Every one of us—Christ, what a racket.

LACEY: *(A beat.)* Now there's conversation for ya. There's genuine, sparkling, earnest conversation.

CASSIDY: Well, it kinda makes me wanna go beat out all my brains.

LACEY: That's what real conversation'll do t'ya.

CASSIDY: Well, I don't like the feeling. Thinking about how this thing's gonna be dead here it ain't even been born yet. Why, it all just gives me goose chills straight up my thighs.

LACEY: I, on the other hand, appreciate a man who will converse with a lady. Tell me, Turnip, do you have any further conversation that I may partake in?

TURNIP: I, well, I do have things to say. Just generally I don't say 'em.

CASSIDY: Look, I'm going out front t'talk t'Hooker. I wanna explain t'him about that lady staying on here through Christmas Day. *(A beat.)* I'm going on out t'ask him.

(Cassidy looks uneasily at Turnip and Lacey who are staring at each other.)

TURNIP: Well…'Bye.

LACEY: 'Bye.

CASSIDY: Yeah. 'Bye.

(Cassidy exits out the front door. Lacey continues to look at Turnip with wet, listening eyes.)

TURNIP: …I'm not stupid. A lot of people think of me as stupid. My brothers they always called me stupid. But I wasn't. I thought a lot. Mostly about things they never even featured. Like don't always go around making fun of people with harelips 'cause it don't do no good and they can't help it no how.

LACEY: *(A pause.)* You know what you've got? Sensitivity. Real sensitivity.

TURNIP: You're probably right. What can I do about it?

LACEY: You're—You're asking me a vital question in a prolonged conversation. Oh my, oh my, oh my. *(Lacey stumbles around and manages to fall to the floor.)* See here! Didn't I tell ya? It's the bird bones in my ankles.

(Turnip helps Lacey to her feet as Sue Jack comes in carrying the dilapidated cardboard box with her belongings. She wears black lace gloves and a black hat with berries.)

SUE JACK: Hi.

LACEY: Oh hi.

TURNIP: Hi. *(A beat.)* Can you handle that?

SUE JACK: Sure. Look—I—Well, here's some Christmas things.

(Sue Jack sets down the box. She takes out some gifts wrapped in dirty tissue paper from the large handbag.)

SUE JACK: They're nothing, really. Just some things I made while I was in— there. I don't know; I thought somebody might want 'em. Turnip. *(Sue Jack hands a package to Turnip.)*

TURNIP: Thanks.

SUE JACK: Here, Lacey.

LACEY: Thanks, Sugar. I love Christmas presents.

TURNIP: Look, that box is falling apart. Let me go out back here and find you a flour sack or something t'make it easier for ya t'carry. *(Turnip picks up the box.)*

SUE JACK: Don't trouble yourself.

TURNIP: Ain't no trouble. Come on.

(Turnip and Sue Jack exit into the kitchen. Lacey quickly unwraps her gift. It is an embroidered Christmas bell.)

LACEY: A bell. *(A beat.)* Jingle, jingle, jingle.

(Hooker and Cassidy enter from the front door. Hooker carries a toolbox.)

HOOKER: Look, I'm about on my last leg around here and I refuse t'have her hanging around just t'kick it out from under me.

CASSIDY: But she ain't gonna kick ya. I swear she ain't.

LACEY: It's Christmas Eve. Give her one more chance.

HOOKER: No.

(Sue Jack and Turnip enter from the kitchen. Sue Jack's belongings have been transferred into a burlap flour sack.)

HOOKER: And what's all this crap? Who brought over these dirty Christmas presents?

SUE JACK: I did.

(Hooker turns to see Sue Jack.)

HOOKER: Oh. *(A beat.)* Well, we don't need 'em. We've got plenty of our own.

SUE JACK: Alright. *(Sue Jack takes the Christmas presents and slowly puts them in the burlap sack. To Hooker.)* Look, I'll write where I'm staying. You can send the divorce papers on and I'll sign 'em. *(A beat.)* Well, good-bye, everybody. Have a good Christmas.

TURNIP: Good-bye, Sue Jack. Merry Christmas.

LACEY: I—I love my bell. You have a real good Christmas now.

SUE JACK: Yeah, you, too. Good-bye now.

CASSIDY: Good-bye.

(Sue Jack exits out the front door. Cassidy, Lacey, and Turnip stare sadly after her, then turn and look at Hooker in stony silence.)

HOOKER: So enough goldbricking. Everyone back t'work. Tonight's our big night! *(Looking at his watch.)* Come on, everybody, as of now we're open for business!

(Turnip is opening the present Sue Jack gave him. Lacey and Cassidy gather around him.)

LACEY: So what'd she give ya?

TURNIP: Mittens with snowmen on 'em.

CASSIDY: Oh look, ain't it sad, one of 'em's melting.

(Hooker comes over to them; he grabs the mittens from Turnip.)

HOOKER: Let me see those! *(Hooker roughly puts one of the mittens on his hand, then pulls it off. He takes the mittens and throws them out the front door. He yells to Sue Jack, who is headed down the road.)* Hey, you got a lot of nerve walking outta here like this! You know damn good and well we only have two dancers for tonight! And it's all 'cause of you showing your face! But don't let it bother ya! Just run off t'your fancy Christmas parties. Forget about us! We'll do just fine all on our own!

(Hooker turns and comes back inside the room, slamming the front door shut. After a moment Sue Jack enters through the front door.)

SUE JACK: Alright, Hooker. I'll do the Lucky Spot this one favor. After all, it is Christmas.

HOOKER: Fine! But once we get squared—I don't even wanna remember your face.

(Music B—the trumpet solo from "I Must Have That Man"—comes up. Sue Jack slowly starts to remove her hat and gloves as the lights fade to blackout.)

SCENE II

The lights fade up. Music fades into Music C: "Twelfth Street Rag." It plays on the phonograph. Sue Jack sits in the window seat doing string tricks. Lacey and Cassidy dance awkwardly together. It is two to three hours later on the same evening.

LACEY: *(Instructing Cassidy.)* Don't look down. Up! Up! Smile! Look happy! Come on, be peppy! Get some zing! Bubble! Twirl out!

(Lacey twirls Cassidy out across the room. Cassidy crashes into the bar. Lacey removes the needle from the record.)

CASSIDY: It ain't much use. I don't know how t'move around t'this music.

LACEY: Don't worry, you'll get the hang of it. See 'cause, your main problem's not the dancing—it's simply that you're not used t'being in the lime-light.

CASSIDY: Nah, I ain't used t'being in no limelight.

LACEY: Well, being in the limelight's easy. All ya gotta do is learn how t'em-phasize your striking features. That way ya won't fade out.

CASSIDY: I don't wanna fade out.

LACEY: Well then, we'll emphasize your eyes. You've got very pretty eyes. Come here, we'll just darken 'em up some. *(Lacey gets an eyeliner pencil from her evening bag and starts darkening Cassidy's eyes.)* Take me. For a while I wasn't getting the dances; so I moved over and started in corner dancing. A place where I could really shine.

CASSIDY: What's corner dancing?

LACEY: Well, just dancing in a dark corner. You know, where you start allowing neck kissing, ear biting, and body pressing.

CASSIDY: Gosh, are they gonna be biting on my ears?

LACEY: Oh no, you've got years before ya have t'get into corner dancing. You've got the bloom of youth.

CASSIDY: That's good.

(From outside the front door we hear Hooker's voice calling through a megaphone in the distance.)

HOOKER: *(Offstage.)* Grand Opening! Lucky Spot Dance Hall! Come one! Come all!

SUE JACK: Oh God. Look at Reed out there calling to cars through that megaphone. He's making a laughingstock.

HOOKER: Free prizes! Come one! Come all!

LACEY: Well, we do need the business.

HOOKER: *(Offstage.)* Merry Christmas! Ho, ho, ho!

CASSIDY: I sure hope some people come.

SUE JACK: Would you come to a place with a madman standing out front yelling at ya through a megaphone?

(Turnip enters through the front door.)

TURNIP: Hey, Lacey, Hooker wants ya t'come out front and do your cartwheels.

SUE JACK: Oh good Christ.

TURNIP: He says maybe you can arrest the attention of some of them passing cars.

LACEY: Well, okay. But I better stretch out a little. *(Stretching.)* One and two and— *(She falls to the floor.)* Oops! My wayward ankles again.

TURNIP: Here, let me help ya up.

LACEY: *(To Turnip.)* Why, thank you, Turnip. You're such a lamb. I just can't keep my eyes off your eyes.

(Turnip escorts Lacey out the front door. Cassidy looks after them perturbed. Sue Jack goes back to playing with the string. Cassidy hikes her skirt up over her knees.)

CASSIDY: Look here, my knees got dirt all on 'em. I have real trouble keeping clean. *(She spits on her hand and starts scrubbing her knees.)* Mr. Pete, he used t' call me a godless bag a' stench. Mr. Pete's the man I was with before. He's the one Hooker won me offa. And that was a lucky day for me. See 'cause when I was with Mr. Pete practically all he'd ever give me t'eat was cow feed. Why, if fact be known, the man was downright feeble-minded. Look here where he branded me with his holy cross. *(Cassidy hikes up her skirt and reveals a cross branded to her inner thigh.)*

SUE JACK: My God.

CASSIDY: He's always telling me how all fired holy he is. Him being a member of the Church of Innocent Blood—and me being a godless bag a' stench. Lord, my life ain't never been no good till now. But here, well, we have supper together every night. It's the most I ever felt like a family.

SUE JACK: Yeah. Some people need that I guess.

CASSIDY: Uh huh. Look, I just wanted t'tell ya—it wasn't like what you was saying this morning. See Hooker, he wasn't all mean and drunk or nothing like that the night when it happened.

SUE JACK: Oh yeah?

CASSIDY: Well, used to be I'd hear him at night yelling out and gasping for air and such. I reckoned him t'be having bad dreams; so I started rushing down t'his room t'wake him up. I'd bring him water t'drink and wet down his forehead with a cool rag. Afterward he'd never go back t'sleep, but he'd send me back on t'bed telling me how I needed t'get my rest. Then one time he just up and says for me t'stop coming in with the water. Says for me just t'stay put and let him be. And I done that for some nights. I sure didn't like listening t'him, but I stood it. Then this one night I hear such crying, like it's coming from some sick, dying animal. Well, I can't find no control for myself, but t'run in with the water. I wake him up and I wash off his face and I hold him so hard and I say, "Don't be scared no more. I can make ya feel better. I know some ways t'make ya feel better." And I did too, from being out on the trail so long with Mr. Pete. Next day though he moves all my things up t'the attic. *(A beat.)* He locks me up there at nights now. Turnip, he'll come by and unlatch the door in the mornings. I'm hoping all that's gonna be changed once we're married. But I don't really know. Only thing I do know is this thing ain't being born out no bastard. See 'cause bastards they don't deserve nothing. Hooker'll be good to it. Once this skinny kid, he fell outta that mossy tree out front and split up his lip real good. Hooker done this trick with a nickel t'make him shut up crying then he let him keep the nickel.

SUE JACK: He did? He did that nickel trick?

CASSIDY: I ain't never seen anything like it.

SUE JACK: *(A pause.)* Yeah, well…sometimes I wonder…I really do wonder. *(A pause.)* The whole world's in trouble. So what's the use? Huh? *(Sue Jack gets up and starts pacing around the room with crazed exuberance.)* I mean, maybe ya gotta just toss in your hand, pay off your debts, stand up, and leave the goddamn table.

CASSIDY: Leave the table?

SUE JACK: Yeah. It's worth a go. Gotta go. Letting go! *(Sue Jack puts Music B on the record player. She starts dancing with a wild crazed passion.)*

CASSIDY: Gosh! Why're ya dancing around?

SUE JACK: *(Still dancing.)* I don't know. I just feel crazy and lighthearted. Like when you're standing on the very edge of a mountain cliff and you're kicking your legs up t'the sky. *(Sue Jack stands on the bar and starts kicking up her legs.)*

CASSIDY: I feel lighthearted too.

(The women dance around the room.)

CASSIDY: It's kinda like we're friends or something.

(Turnip enters carrying Lacey who is whining and laughing.)

LACEY: Ooh. Ooh. Ow

TURNIP: *(To Lacey.)* There, there, now.

LACEY: *(Gaily.)* I fell down again. I'm always falling—

(They stop and watch the women dance.)

TURNIP: Why are y'all so happy?

CASSIDY: We're dancing on the edge of a cliff.

(Hooker enters. He wears a silk hat and carries a megaphone. He stops the music.)

HOOKER: An extravaganza! This was supposed to be an extravaganza! Instead it's a farce, it's a flop. A dream so shattered I can't even remember what the pieces were.

CASSIDY: Oh, don't get discouraged. We still got a roof over our heads and tomorrow we're having ham for Christmas dinner. Things ain't so bad.

HOOKER: Right. Right. Sometimes I just have t'stop myself and take time out t'be grateful I'm not a one-eyed paraplegic with severe brain damage dancing in a cardboard hat. *(A beat.)* Damn. I didn't wanna have the Lucky Spot turning out t'be just like any other roadside attraction.

SUE JACK: I don't think you're in any danger of that!

HOOKER: That's right! Make fun! Laugh at me! You've always got all the smart answers.

SUE JACK: I was just joking.

HOOKER: I'm not a joke.

SUE JACK: Come on, Reed, the whole world's a joke. Consider yourself a real sucker when being taken seriously becomes any sort of goal at all.

HOOKER: Well now if this world is such a goddamn hilarious funny little joke, then please, you tell me, why the hell don't I feel like laughing?

CASSIDY: *(Looking out the window.)* Look, somebody's coming!

HOOKER: Hot damn! We're in business!

LACEY: Oh my God. He's coming up the walk.

HOOKER: Quick, get on some music.

(Turnip puts on Music C—"Twelfth Street Rag.")

CASSIDY: Where's my hat? I need my hat!

LACEY: Look on your head, silly.

HOOKER: Everybody line up over here. Look pretty!

LACEY: Get peppy, girls! Get peppy!

TURNIP: Okay, here're the ties. I've got the ties.

HOOKER: No, you sell the tickets; I'll sell the ties.

TURNIP: Okay.

HOOKER: No, no I'll sell the tickets, you sell the ties.

TURNIP: Okay, right.

CASSIDY: Here he comes!

(Carmichael enters through the front door. He is dressed in evening attire. At the sight of Carmichael everyone's energy drops except for Lacey who is too busy doing her cartwheels.)

SUE JACK: HOOKER, TURNIP. Shit.

LACEY: Dance? Dance? Wanna dance?

CARMICHAEL: Yes, I'll have a ticket. Just one, thanks. I'll pass on the neckties for now.

(Carmichael buys his ticket from Hooker, then walks over to the line of women. He scrutinizes them as he paces back and forth. He finally hands his ticket to Sue Jack. They start to dance.)

CARMICHAEL: So the place seems to be hopping. It's a shame about the jukebox. But you know these old race records of Davenport's aren't so bad.

(The record sticks.)

CARMICHAEL: Kinda scratchy. But not so bad.

(A beat as the record continues to repeat itself.)

CARMICHAEL: Not so bad. Not so bad. Not so bad.

(Turnip finally picks the needle up off the record. Sue Jack and Carmichael continue to dance in silence.)

CARMICHAEL: It's always such a pleasure dancing with you. It's like dancing with a dream.

(Hooker rings the bell.)

HOOKER: Okay, the dance is over. I said it's over. Look, you came by here to gloat; so you've gloated. Now get out.

CARMICHAEL: Listen to me a minute. You're a smart man. Try to keep a clear head. You know this place will never make it. Do yourself a favor, let me take it off your hands.

HOOKER: I don't get you, Carmichael. Just why are you so dead set t'get at this place?

CARMICHAEL: The truth is I promised my father I'd get it for him. As sort of a Christmas gift. *(Indicating Sue Jack.)* He couldn't stand the idea of her being here after that mess with Caroline. I don't blame him much. Here're the papers. If you sign 'em it'll let everyone off the hook.

HOOKER: I don't know. I'm not real keen on the idea.

CARMICHAEL: Believe me, it's a fair price.

SUE JACK: Well, now that worries me.

(Hooker takes the papers down to a table. He motions to Turnip to come with him.)

HOOKER: *(To Turnip.)* What d'you think?

TURNIP: Gosh, it's hard t'say. After all the bad-mouthing he's been doing about us around town I really don't know that we have a frank chance a' making it here.

CARMICHAEL: You don't have a blind chance.

HOOKER: I don't know. I got a strong feeling this place isn't realizing its full potential. I mean, look at that painted horse over there. Why it's—otherworldly.

CARMICHAEL: I think you're living in a rosy dream world.

SUE JACK: I smell fish.

CARMICHAEL: What?

SUE JACK: I said I smell fish.

CASSIDY: There's somebody out there. Somebody else is coming.

LACEY: A patron! It's a patron. A real live patron.

HOOKER: Turnip, music!

(Music D—"King Joe"—starts to play.)

CARMICHAEL: Look, this is a fair offer, but you'll have to accept it, right now.

HOOKER: I—No.

LACEY: How're my lips?

SUE JACK: Red, real red!

CARMICHAEL: Be reasonable. One patron's not going to change anything.

HOOKER: Excuse me now, I'm working.

LACEY: Get perky, everybody! Get perky!

CARMICHAEL: This price goes down three hundred dollars an hour.

HOOKER: No deal, Carmichael. No deal!

SUE JACK: That's a damn good tune.

HOOKER: It's a very pretty tune.

CARMICHAEL: Make that five hundred dollars an hour or fraction thereof.

HOOKER: I said, no deal.

SUE JACK: I do like that pretty tune.

LACEY: Dance. Dance. Wanna dance.

(Lacey turns cartwheels. The patron, Sam, enters. He is a thin shy man in his sixties dressed in clean simple clothes. His face and hands are weather-beaten from years of farming.)

HOOKER: Welcome, welcome, welcome.

SAM: 'Evening.

HOOKER: Come right in, sir. Come right on in. Now would ya like t'rent a necktie? I'm afraid they are required.

SAM: Alright.

HOOKER: That'll be fifteen cents.

TURNIP: *(Echoing.)* Fifteen cents.

HOOKER: No, that's twenty cents…

TURNIP: *(Echoing.)* Twenty cents…

SAM: *(After a beat.)* Alright.

HOOKER: How 'bout this red one. It's very festive. It's just your particular style. Turnip, help the gentleman out with his tie.

(Turnip puts the tie on Sam.)

HOOKER: Now how many dance tickets would you like?

SAM: How many ya reckon I'll need?

HOOKER: I don't know. Fifty? A hundred maybe?

SAM: How 'bout a dollar's worth. That's about all I got.

HOOKER: Alright. Fine. Here're your tickets. Now you go on and select any one of our beautiful dance teachers t'be your partner.

SAM: I pick?

HOOKER: Yes, you pick.

SAM: Which one do I pick?

HOOKER: Anyone you want. All of our girls make a wonderful partner. They all have very special qualities.

SAM: *(A beat.)* It's sure hard t'pick.

HOOKER: Well, just go on and point t'one of 'em. It's all the same. Go ahead. Point.

(Sam hesitates a moment then points to Cassidy.)

CASSIDY: He's pointing at me. Hey, mister, you're pointing at me.

SAM: What do I do now?

HOOKER: Give her your ticket and dance. Dance, quick, before the bell rings. *(Sam hands Cassidy his ticket. Cassidy and Sam make an awkward attempt at dancing.)*

SAM: I hope my hands ain't too clammy for ya.

CASSIDY: No, it's okay. *(A beat.)* I—

SAM: What?

CASSIDY: Nothing. I'm just glad I was picked. I ain't never been picked. *(Music D swells up then comes back down. Music E—"Sweet Lorraine"— comes up. The lights change indicating the passing of time. Sue Jack and Lacey are now dancing together. Hooker watches Sue Jack from the stairs. Cassidy and Sam continue dancing. Turnip stands by the record player. Carmichael goes outside and lights up a cigarette.)*

CASSIDY: *(To Sam.)* Musta been hard on your wife, having t'be blind all her life. Me, I don't even like the dark. I'm afraid of it.

SAM: Well, she used t'tell me, of everything in the world, the two things she most wanted t'see was the face of a person and a tree. But she said she was happy just being here on this earth.

CASSIDY: How long ago was it she died?

SAM: Been almost five weeks now.

CASSIDY: You miss her?

SAM: Oh yeah. She loved watermelon. I used t'slice it up for her and pick out all the seed. *(Lacey twirls over to Turnip. Hooker stares at Sue Jack from across the room. She stares back.)*

LACEY: Hi Turnip.

TURNIP: Hi. You, ah, you wanna dance?

LACEY: Sure. You got a ticket?

TURNIP: I—no.

LACEY: Well, I gotta have a ticket.

TURNIP: Oh. Well, I guess I don't have the money t'buy one.

LACEY: *(A beat.)* Sorry, then. It's the rules.

SAM: *(To Cassidy.)* Is that your fellow?

CASSIDY: Who?

SAM: The young guy putting on the records. The one you've got your eye on.

CASSIDY: *(Indicating Turnip.)* Him? Oh no. He's just some nitwit. *(Indicating Hooker.)* I'm engaged t'the man on the staircase. *(A beat.)* He's in love with me.

(Sue Jack steps into the outdoor area. Carmichael is sitting on a bench smoking.)

CARMICHAEL: You wanna drink?

SUE JACK: I quit.

CARMICHAEL: You can't stand me, can you?

SUE JACK: Not really.

CARMICHAEL: It's funny but I like you.

SUE JACK: Well, you can afford to.

CARMICHAEL: There're two things I've always wanted to do to you. One of them was beat you in a game of cards.

SUE JACK: You're a slime, Whitt. A real slime.

CARMICHAEL: Come on. Play cards with me. Let's gamble. Come on. I wanna beat you.

SUE JACK: Shit. *(Sue Jack turns to go inside.)*

CARMICHAEL: Don't go inside.

SUE JACK: Screw you. Go buy some tickets if you wanna take up my time. My time is money. Big money.

(Sue Jack goes inside. Carmichael follows her. Hooker watches them both. Turnip is ringing the bell, indicating that the dance is over. Lacey rushes up to Sam and Cassidy and throws herself between them.)

LACEY: *(To Sam.)* Oh, dance with me. Next time let me be your partner. Let me be your one.

SAM: I'm getting kinda tuckered. Maybe I'll sit this one out.

LACEY: Fine, sit with me. I'm a sympathetic listener. *(She pulls him over to a table and starts plucking off tickets from his roll.)* I know how t'show ya a good time.

(Carmichael comes up to Hooker who has been staring at Sue Jack.)

CARMICHAEL: I'd like some more tickets. *(Carmichael takes out a large bill.)*

HOOKER: What're you still doing here?

CARMICHAEL: Waiting for you t'crack.

HOOKER: Forget about it. I'm not gonna crack. This place could be something great. Look at that lonely guy over there. He's having a damn ball. See that?

(Hooker, Carmichael, and Turnip all turn and watch Lacey chewing on Sam's red tie.)

CARMICHAEL: Ah yes, yes. How very picturesque.

(Music F—"Honeysuckle Rose"—starts to play. Carmichael turns and heads over to Sue Jack. Carmichael offers her a reel of tickets. She takes them. Hooker can't take his eyes off of them. Turnip continues to watch Lacey and Sam. Cassidy looks from Hooker to Turnip and back again.)

SUE JACK: *(Dancing and laughing.)* Oh that music sends me someplace, some-place—I wish I could tell you where. Take me away! Please, take me away!

HOOKER: Oh sweet Jesus. Holy Jesus.

TURNIP: What?

HOOKER: Look at Sue dancing. I'll never get over her. There's nobody else like her. Nobody else.

TURNIP: What're you saying?

HOOKER: I love her. I want her. Can't help it. Never could.

TURNIP: I don't get you.

(Cassidy walks over to Hooker and Turnip.)

CASSIDY: *(To Hooker.)* Hi. You wanna dance?

HOOKER: No. I'm going outside. *(Hooker exits out the side door.)*

TURNIP: *(To Cassidy.)* I'll dance with ya.

CASSIDY: Why don't ya go ask Lacey t'dance? She's the one you're so fond of.

(Cassidy turns and walks away.)

LACEY: *(To Sam.)* You like my hair?

SAM: It's the color of spun gold.

LACEY: It's all natural. You can feel it if ya want to. Go ahead. Run your fin-gers right through it.

SAM: *(To Lacey as he fondles her hair.)* I like women's hair. Why, I washed and rolled and fixed my wife's hair all up when she died.

LACEY: Well, don't look at me. I'm not dead yet. Where're your tickets?

SAM: They're all gone.

LACEY: Well, excuse me but I believe I have t'go and powder my nose. *(Lacey gets up and walks over to Turnip, counting her tickets. To Turnip.)* Ring the bell, sugar. I've already bled that fish dry. I gotta go reel in another one. *(Turnip looks at her coldly and then starts ringing the bell. He takes the record off. Music F stops. Cassidy goes over and sits next to Sam. He offers a stick of gum. Lacey runs over to Carmichael and Sue Jack.)*

LACEY: *(To Carmichael.)* Dance? Dance? Wanna dance? Wanna be mine?

CARMICHAEL: No thanks. *(He hands more tickets to Sue Jack.)*

(Music G—"Cryin' for the Carolines"—starts up.)

LACEY: I waltz, I foxtrot, I tango, I polka—

SUE JACK: Go ahead. I'm on break.

(Sue Jack hands a ticket to Lacey. Lacey grabs the ticket and pulls Carmichael tightly into her arms.)

LACEY: Come on now. Who's your sugar?

(Sue Jack goes over to pour herself some coffee. Turnip comes up to her.)

TURNIP: Boy oh boy.

SUE JACK: What?

TURNIP: Well, Hooker, he—he's gone and gotten himself back in love with you. Says he just can't help it. Says he never could.

SUE JACK: Look, I don't want him loving me.

(Turnip echoes.)

SUE JACK: We're finished.

TURNIP: You're finished. I don't get it.

SUE JACK: Where'd he go?

TURNIP: He's out back.

(Turnip motions to the side door. Sue Jack heads outside. As she goes she passes Lacey who is trying to French-kiss Carmichael.)

LACEY: *(To Carmichael.)* Come on, sugar, it's not like I've got trench mouth. Although once I did transmit the pinkeye to a man. But that was way back in Alabama.

TURNIP: I swear, I pray I never fall in love. It seems like such a terrible thing. *(Sue Jack comes outside. Hooker is there looking at the sky. He turns and looks at her then turns back to stare at the sky.)*

HOOKER: It's pitch-black out. Not a star in the sky. Isn't that an incredible sight. *(A beat.)* Come here to me.

SUE JACK: We're bad luck for each other.

HOOKER: I don't care.

SUE JACK: I'm not right for you.

HOOKER: You are.

SUE JACK: Well, I'm not the one who's gonna have your kid, am I?

HOOKER: No, you're not.

SUE JACK: She is.

HOOKER: That's right. That's how that went down.

SUE JACK: Do the right thing for once in your lousy life.

HOOKER: You're the right thing.

SUE JACK: I'm the wrong thing.

HOOKER: You're the only goddamned thing.

SUE JACK: Listen, Reed, I—I got sick in prison. I can't have another kid. Not ever.

HOOKER: Doesn't matter. It's okay. We'll do okay.

SUE JACK: No, look at me. I've lost it. The bloom of youth. It's gone. It's over. I jazzed it all away. But her, she's good for you, this Cassidy, I want you to have her and the kid and this place—

HOOKER: *(Overlapping.)* This is bullshit, woman. Just bullshit 'cause I don't want a goddamn thing in this world but for you to come here to me. Not a goddamn thing—

SUE JACK: I can't, Reed. I can't ever be with you—

HOOKER: What do you mean?

SUE JACK: It's over, Christ, just let it be. Let it be!

HOOKER: I'm not gonna let it be!

SUE JACK: Alright, you wanna know?! Ya gotta know.

HOOKER: *(Overlapping.)* Yeah, I wanna know! Yeah, I gotta know!

SUE JACK: You wanna know about Andy. You wanna know about our son? Well, it was my fault.

HOOKER: It was a miserable accident. Couldn't be helped. He pulled away to chase a hummingbird—

SUE JACK: Jesus Christ, don't you get it? There was no goddamn hummingbird. I went into a speak t'get a drink. I left him standing there on the porch. He ran off, a car hit him and I was sitting there in the bar, slinging back a shot of whiskey.

HOOKER: You said you held tight. You said he pulled away from you.

SUE JACK: I lied.

HOOKER: God Almighty.

(Sue Jack turns and goes back inside. Inside Turnip starts clanging the bell as Music G ends.)

SUE JACK: Hey! Yo! Friends! Let's play some cards!

TURNIP: Cards! Well, hot damn! Hot damn!

LACEY: What fun! What fun!

SUE JACK: Whitt, you game?

CARMICHAEL: Why yes, ma'am, I'm plenty game.

SUE JACK: Good. Fortuitously, I seem t'have a deck of playing cards right here in my silver evening bag.

CARMICHAEL: Well, now, as chance would have it I've a round tucked right inside my breast pocket.

SUE JACK: My, my, but good fortune certainly does abound. *(Sue Jack slings off her lace gloves.)*

TURNIP: Well, alright! Alright! Yes, sir! Yes, sir!

(They both sit down at a table and begin to expertly shuffle their decks. The others crowd around them, murmuring with excitement and amazement. Hooker enters.)

SUE JACK: So what do you say we make this a real quick gamble. Three games of cut. Best two outta three. Working with a his and her deck.

HOOKER: What's going on here?

SUE JACK: A friendly game of cards.

CARMICHAEL: A very friendly game. What're the stakes?

SUE JACK: If I win I want your three hundred and fifty-five dollar stake on the Lucky Spot. If you win, well, then we can finish off what we started over on Esplanade Avenue.

CARMICHAEL: Deal me in. I feel lucky.

HOOKER: What's this now, Miss Sue, you gonna sacrifice yourself t'save my waning, dying ass?

SUE JACK: I'm just paying off some debts. That's all, Hooker. Just paying off some debts.

HOOKER: There's no way. You don't have a prayer.

SUE JACK: Look, I lost most of our stinking money playing the horses and dogs and roosters. As I remember, I was always pretty good with cards.

HOOKER: Yeah, well, just look at your goddamn hands. They're all torn up, for Christ's sake.

SUE JACK: *(Angrily.)* Oh leave me alone. Just leave me the fuck alone! Here, cut. *(Sue Jack shoves the cards over to Carmichael.)*

CARMICHAEL: No, no, no. Ladies first.

SUE JACK: Ah, a gentleman's game. *(She cuts the cards.)* Queen of hearts. *(She shoves the cards to Carmichael.)* Cut.

(Carmichael cuts the cards.)

CARMICHAEL: Jack of spades.

(Cheers from the people watching the game.)

TURNIP: *(To Carmichael.)* Better luck next time, ol' buddy.

LACEY: She's still got the touch.

CARMICHAEL: And I still feel lucky. Cut.

(Sue Jack cuts the deck.)

SUE JACK: King of hearts.

(Turnip echoes.)

CARMICHAEL: And I thought this was a game of chance.

SUE JACK: Cut.

(Carmichael cuts the deck.)

CARMICHAEL: Hmm. King of spades.

SUE JACK: My, my my, a lot of court cards in this deck.

CARMICHAEL: Cut.

HOOKER: I'm not watching this. I have no part in this. You're on your own.

(Hooker goes and pours himself a drink.)

SUE JACK: Yeah, that's where I belong. *(To Turnip.)* Here, spit on my hands for luck.

(Turnip spits on her hands. She rubs them together then cuts the cards.)

SUE JACK: Five of clubs.

CASSIDY: Oh no.

TURNIP: Damn.

LACEY: Sweet Jesus.

(Carmichael cuts the deck.)

CARMICHAEL: Ah me. What have we here? Ace of diamonds.

CASSIDY: She lost.

SUE JACK: Let's have another go. What d'ya say t'a round of Mexican Sweat?

CARMICHAEL: But, I've won the pot, haven't I? Don't wanna risk losing that.

SUE JACK: Well, then I guess tonight's just not my night.

CARMICHAEL: Please, my good fortune embarrasses me. Now why don't you get your coat?

(Sue Jack goes and gets her coat and evening bag.)

CASSIDY: Where ya going?

SUE JACK: Oh, out jazzing around. Keep the party going till I get back.

(Carmichael escorts Sue Jack toward the front door. Hooker comes toward them.)

HOOKER: Let her go, Carmichael. She stays here.

CARMICHAEL: You may own that one, but this one here's a free woman.

SUE JACK: Come on now, Reed. A bet's a bet.

HOOKER: I said get the hell away from her.

(Hooker jerks Sue Jack away and starts going toward Carmichael. Carmichael draws a pearl-handled pistol and aims it at Hooker. Everyone freezes.)

CARMICHAEL: I don't think so. Unless maybe you want your face shot off.

SUE JACK: Alright now. Everything's fine. Let's just get outta here.

(Sue Jack and Carmichael head for the door. Carmichael keeps the gun aimed at everybody. They are almost out the door when Hooker grabs a chair to clobber Carmichael.)

HOOKER: No, goddamnit!

(Carmichael quickly fires two shots. Both of them barely miss Hooker.)

SUE JACK: Hooker! Jesus Christ!

HOOKER: Oh I'm fine. Just put my nerves a little on edge.

CARMICHAEL: Next time I shoot between the eyes.

HOOKER: Listen, Carmichael, I'll pay ya the three fifty-five she owes ya—we'll call it even.

CARMICHAEL: I don't believe you have it.

HOOKER: I do if I sell this place to you. You want it so damn bad. Here, I'll sign it over.

SUE JACK: Jesus, Hooker, don't be a goddamn idiot! Come on, Whitt. Let's go. *(Sue Jack tries to drag Carmichael out the door.)*

HOOKER: *(To Sue Jack.)* You're not going.

SUE JACK: Damn it t'hell! Just 'cause I go and make a fool outta myself doesn't mean you have to follow suit!

HOOKER: Screw it. I just won the place through freak luck. It ain't nothing t'me. This place is a joke. I'm sick of fooling with it. Here, Carmichael. Take the damn thing!

(Hooker signs the paper. Sue Jack rushes in and slams the paper down on the table.)

SUE JACK: Look, this is nothing to me. He's just one guy, one night. Christ, Reed, don't you realize how many men, how many times—

HOOKER: *(Overlapping.)* Stop it! Don't!

SUE JACK: *(Running on.)* ...How many nights there were just t'survive in that prison.

HOOKER: *(Overlapping.)* Shut up. You. Be still.

SUE JACK: There were days...

HOOKER: *(Overlapping.)* Stop! No more! Please! Please! Please! *(Hooker grabs her face in his hands and shakes her with a desperate passion.)* I can't have it. No more. Please.

(Hooker holds Sue Jack tightly. She stares at him dumbstruck; tears stream down her face. Cassidy watches Sue Jack and Hooker, feeling the electric passion between the couple. She turns and runs up the stairs.)

TURNIP: *(Reaching for her.)* Hey! Hey—

CASSIDY: *(Ripping off the rope ring.)* Let me be! Let me be—

(Hooker grabs Sue Jack to him. She pulls away. Hooker then gets the contract and hands it to Carmichael.)

HOOKER: There's the papers. Take them.

CARMICHAEL: Thank you.

SUE JACK: Damn, damn, damn! *(Sue Jack exits out the front door.)*

HOOKER: Goddamnit! Come back here. I'm not running after you.

SUE JACK: *(Offstage.)* I can't, Reed. It's no good. Let it go. Please, let it go.

HOOKER: *(Overlapping.)* I'm not running after you! You hear me? Sue Jack! *(A beat. He runs out the front door after her. Offstage.)* Sue Jack! *(Hooker re-enters.)* Hell. *(He slams out the kitchen door.)*

CARMICHAEL: Arrange to be out of here by January one. That's when the drilling crew—oh well, those high finance matters don't really concern you, poor people, now do they? Well, good night, everyone.

LACEY: Look, Mr. Carmichael—

CARMICHAEL: What?

LACEY: Don't go away lonesome. I'll keep ya company for the night.

CARMICHAEL: Well, it's funny. I've always liked blondes but I'm going to make an exception in your case. Good night now. *(Carmichael exits out the front door.)*

LACEY: Well, he certainly is a spoilsport, isn't he? A man like that doesn't do anybody any good. He's too prissy. Thinks just 'cause he's rich nobody but him matters in the whole wide world. *(She falls and trips.)* Oh, my poor ankle. *(To Turnip.)* Help me up, will you, sugar?

TURNIP: Are you sure your ankles are really weak?

LACEY: What?

TURNIP: Maybe you just pretend they're weak. Maybe you just like t'fall down.

LACEY: Don't be stupid. Nobody likes t'fall down.

TURNIP: No, you're wrong. A lot of people like t'fall down. And why not? It's easy. Ya just go right with the pull of things. Right with the flow. Ya don't ever gotta worry about standing on your own two feet. The only tough part is dragging yourself back up again. Getting back up. *(A beat.)* Yeah, that can be a lot of work.

LACEY: Then help me up. Please.

TURNIP: Help your own self up.

(Lacey drags herself to her feet.)

LACEY: Oooh!

(Hooker walks in from the kitchen carrying a jug of moonshine. He takes a slug. Lacey turns and looks at him.)

LACEY: Oooh! I just don't understand, people always despise me, no matter where I go! *(Lacey exits out the side door and disappears through the yard.)*

HOOKER: Women. Christ, they're all the same.

TURNIP: Sweet Jesus. Nobody's got any sense in this world; nobody. We just let it all slip right on past us. No wonder why we keep coming up empty-handed. No damn wonder.

(Turnip exits out the kitchen door. Hooker pauses a beat then turns to Sam.)

HOOKER: Well, looks like I spoiled everybody's Christmas Eve. So, you having a good time?

SAM: Oh yeah.

HOOKER: Good. I'll put on some more music.

(Hooker puts on Music H—"Sweet Lorraine." The music plays.)

HOOKER: Want some punch? We got cookies.

SAM: I'm, well, I'm outta tickets.

HOOKER: Forget about it. It's all on the house. Everything's all on the house.

(Hooker tosses Sam a cookie. The two men sway to the music a moment.)

HOOKER: Pretty tune.

(The music swells and the lights fade to blackout.)

SCENE III

The setting is the same. Cassidy sits at a table humming as she makes paper hats out of newspaper. She wears a simple dress and has a bow in her hair. The coffeepot is out on the counter. It is sunrise. Lacey sits on a stump in the outside area. She wears her tattered robe. Sue Jack comes in the front door. She wears the same dress she had on the night before. She carries a branch of holly.

CASSIDY: Good morning.

SUE JACK: 'Morning.

CASSIDY: It's a pretty morning.

SUE JACK: *(Undecided.)* Yeah.

CASSIDY: You alright?

SUE JACK: I—no.

CASSIDY: Well, I reckon I outta tell ya I broken off my marriage t' Hooker. Tore off the engagement ring. It's gone.

SUE JACK: Well, look, ya better forget about all that and make it up with him. It'll be alright. You'll just make it up.

CASSIDY: Ain't nothing t'make up. The thing is I can't never awaken no love in him for me—'cause, well, he's got you in his blood; you're his partner.

SUE JACK: I sure as hell don't know about that.

CASSIDY: I do. See I ain't stupid. I know people getting married's supposed to be in love with the people they's getting married to. Ya don't want somebody just marrying ya on the rebound. And it's funny but it makes me feel lighthearted, 'cause now I see, well, maybe love ain't a made-up lie like Santa Claus or something. Maybe it can be true. And if it's true, maybe I can find someone I'd shoot off guns for and find someone who'll hold my face and tell me, please, please, please. Or maybe he'll just, I don't know, give me a slice of watermelon and pick out all the seeds. Why, having this child don't even scare me no more. 'Cause if ya have this love inside ya it don't matter if your father was a lord in a castle or a bum on the road or a murderer in a cage. It don't matter. Well, here's a hat for ya. Merry Christmas.

(Cassidy puts a paper hat on Sue Jack's head. Turnip enters from right. He carries a branch of mistletoe. He spots Lacey.)

LACEY: Hi.

TURNIP: Hi. *(Turnip passes her and heads for the side door.)*

LACEY: I guess you think I'm just a gold digger. Well, maybe I am. But if I am it's 'cause I went broke trying t'crash the movies and all my stuff's in pawn and I don't even have a decent rag on my back. Gosh, the main thing I wanted outta life was fame, wealth, and adoration. Instead I'm poor and broke and nobody likes me.

TURNIP: I like talking t'ya. Ya seemed interested in what I had t'say.

LACEY: Really?

TURNIP: Yeah.

LACEY: Oh my, my, my! *(Lacey staggers around in a dither. Suddenly she realizes she is about to fall and quickly sits back down on the stump.)* How nice. Thank you very much, Turnip.

TURNIP: Tell me…

LACEY: Yes?!

TURNIP: Do you think I should change my name from Turnip t'something else? I mean, so people—so girls would like me better.

LACEY: Hmm. Well, ya know what they say, "A turnip by any other name would smell as sweet."

TURNIP: Never thought of it like that. Wanna go inside?

LACEY: Sure.

(Lacey stands up and they move from the outside area to the ballroom through the side door.)

LACEY: Merry Christmas, everyone!

SUE JACK AND CASSIDY: Merry Christmas.

LACEY: Look, I've brought over my spray bottle of genuine French perfume. As a gift I'm allowing everyone four sprays apiece. *(To Sue Jack.)* Here, sugar, you go first.

SUE JACK: Well, thanks, Lacey.

TURNIP: *(To Cassidy.)* Here, I brought ya some mistletoe.

SUE JACK: Mmm. Smells good.

TURNIP: If ya put it over two people's heads, they gotta kiss underneath it. *(He holds the mistletoe over their heads.)* See, like this. *(He kisses her.)* It's part of Christmas. *(He hands out the mistletoe to her.)*

CASSIDY: *(Taking it from him.)* Thanks. *(Cassidy goes solemnly up to Sue Jack.)* Oh look, you're under mistletoe. Kiss me quick.

(They kiss. Cassidy walks over to Lacey.)

CASSIDY: Now you're under mistletoe. Kiss me. It's part of Christmas.

(They kiss. Cassidy turns and says to Turnip.)

CASSIDY: What a fun gift.

(She holds the mistletoe over his head and they kiss again. Hooker and Sam enter the outdoor area. Hooker carries a sack of oranges. Sam carries some peppermint candy canes. Hooker still wears his evening clothes.)

HOOKER: How many sugar candies ya got?

SAM: 'Bout a dozen.

HOOKER: Well, that oughta be plenty. I'll eat one now. *(Hooker takes a candy cane, sits down on the bench and starts eating it.)*

SAM: Ain't we going in?

HOOKER: You go on in. I don't figure I'm gonna get such a heartwarming reception.

SAM: Well, alright. And thanks for having me over for Christmas. I didn't have no other place t'go.

HOOKER: No, me neither.

(Sam knocks on the side door and says "Hello." Everyone welcomes him.)

LACEY: Well, look who's here!

CASSIDY: Sam, come on in.

TURNIP: Hey, Merry Christmas.

SAM: Thanks. I hope ya don't mind me coming unexpected.

CASSIDY: Oh, no.

SAM: Hooker, he's the one asked me.

SUE JACK: Where is he anyway?

SAM: Just sitting out back. I brought y'all some sugar candies.

(Sam hands out the candy. Sue Jack heads for the side door.)

LACEY: Oh look! Sweets! Sugar sweets!

CASSIDY: Why, thanks, Sam.

TURNIP: Thanks.

(Sue Jack stands at the side door watching Hooker eat his candy cane on the bench.)

SUE JACK: Hi.

HOOKER: Hi. You're back.

SUE JACK: Yeah. Just now. I was out walking. And thinking. Did a lot of thinking.

HOOKER: What'd ya think?

SUE JACK: That I miss you. A lot. A real lot.

HOOKER: Yeah, well, sorry t'say—I miss you too.

SUE JACK: Ya do? Well, thanks. I appreciate it. God I—thanks.

HOOKER: Oh don't be so damn grateful. It makes me feel like an idiot.

SUE JACK: Sorry.

HOOKER: Forget it.

SUE JACK: Sure. I guess I don't really know how to be. I mean there's so much water under the bridge. So much muddy, muddy goddamn water.

HOOKER: Yeah, yeah. I know, I know. So do us both a favor and let's not wallow in it.

SUE JACK: We don't wanna wallow in it.

HOOKER: That reminds me. Our hog's gone. The Christmas pig. Somebody stole it. I don't know what t'do. You got any ideas?

SUE JACK: Well...let's see now. I passed by a pumpkin patch this morning. I could go borrow three or four and make us up some pumpkin pudding.

HOOKER: That'd be a treat. We haven't had that in, well, years.

SUE JACK: Yeah. It's been years. Hope I remember how t'make it.

HOOKER: Well, don't ya put a nickel in it?

SUE JACK: Right. Whoever finds the nickel in their portion will have a stroke of dumb luck.

HOOKER: Well, we sure could use some dumb luck.

SUE JACK: We sure could.

HOOKER: God Almighty. T'dumb luck. *(He reaches into the air, and a nickel appears in his fingers. He hands the nickel to Sue Jack.)*

SUE JACK: T'dumb luck.

(They both start to laugh.)

HOOKER: Now, Christ, will ya come here, please!

(They go into each other's arms.)

SUE JACK: *(After a beat.)* Merry Christmas, Reed.

HOOKER: Merry Christmas to you, sweet Sue.

(They kiss passionately. Inside Cassidy sits on top of a table. She wears a paper hat and waves a candy cane.)

CASSIDY: Once I had my fortune told and the fortune teller tol' me I had a future right here in the palm of my hand. Why, this could be the beginning of my future. This could be it!

(Music I—"Sunny Side of the Street"—starts to play on the record player. Sue Jack and Hooker enter from the side door.)

HOOKER: Merry Christmas, everyone! Merry Christmas!

ALL: *(To Hooker.)* Merry Christmas!

HOOKER: Here're some oranges for ya. *(Hooker starts throwing oranges to every-one from his sack.)*

TURNIP: Oranges, look! Oranges!

LACEY: I love citrus!

CASSIDY: They're beautiful!

HOOKER: Yeah, they are. Hey, I wanna dance! I wanna dance with every one of ya! It's Christmas morning and I wanna dance with everyone.

(Everyone starts dancing. They all keep changing partners. Men dance with women, men dance with men, women dance with women. People dance alone. Everyone dances with everyone else as the lights slowly fade to black-out and the music continues to play.)

END OF PLAY

THE DEBUTANTE BALL

WITH LOVE, TO GILBERT PARKER
FOR YOUR ETERNAL SUPPORT

Mary C. Vreeland, Kellie Overbey, and Carol Kane
in Manhattan Theatre Club's 1988 production of
The Debutante Ball.

photo by Gerry Goodstein

ORIGINAL PRODUCTION

The Debutante Ball was produced by Manhattan Theatre Club (Lynne Meadow, Artistic Director; Barry Grove, Managing Director) in New York City, on April 26, 1988. It was directed by Norman René; the set design was by Loy Arcenas; the costume design was by Walker Hicklin; the lighting design was by Debra Kletter; the sound design was by Joshua Starbuck; and the production stage manager was Mary Fran Loftus. The cast was as follows:

Jen Dugan Parker Turner	Ann Wedgeworth
Teddy Parker	Kellie Overbey
Violet Moone	Adina Porter
Hank Turner	Trey Wilson
Bliss White	Carol Kane
Brighton Parker	Bruce Norris
Frances Walker	Mary C. Vreeland

The Debutante Ball was produced by New York Stage and Film Company (Mark Linn-Baker, Max Mayer, Leslie Urdang, Producing Directors) at The Powerhouse Theater at Vassar College, in Poughkeepsie, New York, on July 28, 1988. It was directed by Evan Yionoulis; the set design was by Charles McCarry; the costume design was by Jess Goldstein; the lighting design was by Donald Holder; the production stage manager was William H. Lang; and the stage manager was Kathleen Farrar. The cast was as follows:

Jen Dugan Parker Turner	Tammy Grimes
Teddy Parker	Yeardley Smith
Violet Moone	Leah Maddrie
Hank Turner	Eddie Jones
Bliss White	Wendy Makkena
Brighton Parker	Joe Urla
Frances Walker	Margaret Arnold

The Debutante Ball had it's world premiere at South Coast Repertory (David Emmes, Producing Artistic Director; Martin Benson, Artistic Director), Costa Mesa, California, on April 9, 1985.

THE CHARACTERS

JEN DUGAN PARKER TURNER: 50s, the debutante's mother

TEDDY PARKER: 20, the debutante

VIOLET MOONE: 20, the maid

HANK TURNER: 50, Teddy's stepfather, Jen's second husband, a wealthy attorney

BLISS WHITE: 20s, Teddy's half-sister, Jen's older daughter

BRIGHTON PARKER: 20s, Teddy's cousin, Jen's nephew

FRANCES WALKER: 30s, Hank's deaf niece

THE SETTING

The setting of the entire play is the upstairs parlor and connecting bathroom in the Turner mansion located in Hattiesburg, Mississippi, a small Southern town. Both rooms should be designed with stunning opulent elegance. The occupants have only recently moved into the mansion; therefore, there is still a sense of perfection and polish, nothing has begun to tarnish.

There are six entrances and exits leading to the parlor. On stage left, there is an entrance that leads to the outer hallway and the main staircase; and there is a staircase leading up to the third story. Upstage there is an entrance that leads to the back stairway and on down into the kitchen, and there is also a balcony with a stone railing. Stage right there is a door leading to Jen's bedroom and a door leading to the bathroom. There is also a connecting door between Jen's bedroom and the bath; thus there are two entrances and exits to the bathroom.

The bathroom should be magnificent with a crystal chandelier, marble floors, gold faucets, and a dressing table. There is a toilet located far stage right in an alcove.

THE TIME

Autumn

ACT I
SCENE I

In the bathroom, Violet Moone, a black woman in a maid's uniform, is scrubbing the bathroom mirror. She pauses a moment, then begins making noises like a bird.

VIOLET: Caw, caw, ahya. Caw, caw.
   (In the parlor, Jen Parker Turner, a lovely, lithe woman with black flickering eyes, begins giving instructions to her daughter, Teddy Parker, who stands in the wings of the balcony dressed in her white debutante's gown. Teddy is a thin and strange-looking girl with large, frightened eyes and tight, colorless lips.)
JEN: And now, announcing Miss Theadora Jenniquade Parker.
   (Teddy slowly and stiffly moves to the center of the balcony. Throughout the following Teddy attempts to follow Jen's instructions.)
JEN: Now turn majestically toward the audience, filling the room with your stunningly youthful presence. Remember your eye contact. Keep the chin up. Now let's see an elegant shimmer of a smile. Yes! Oh Yes! Now for your grand bow. *(Jen demonstrates for Teddy.)* Remember your grand bow must be full, radiant, magnificent! You are one hundred times more beautiful and alive than any of the jackasses sitting out in that banquet hall. You're a goddess and they're all swine. Do you have that?
TEDDY: Yes, ma'am.
JEN: Fine. Now bow to the swine. Oh, wonderful, Teddy. Flawlessly done. Now for the ascension. Keeping the neck long, chin up. Eyes rising over the swine. Shimmering smile. Glorious. Now turn around, slowly, I want to see the whole gown. Oh, now isn't that magnificent. The cut of the back is simply divine. Don't you feel divine?
TEDDY: Divine. I feel divine.
JEN: Oh yes, and once you have on your jeweled cape and the diamond tiara—Oh, and of course, your corrective makeup.
TEDDY: Right, the corrective makeup. That'll help, won't it?
JEN: Goodness, yes. Lord knows we'd all be hideous without it. I know, I'll run down and get your cape. You go into my bathroom and fix your face with the new round-the-clock makeup kit. That way we'll be able to get a better sense of the ensemble as a whole.
TEDDY: Alright, Sweet Mama, I'll go fix it.
JEN: Good. *(Jen exits down the back stairs.)*

TEDDY: I'll go fix my face. My face. Face.

(In the bathroom Violet is scrubbing the floor. Once again she makes sounds like a bird.)

VIOLET: Caw, caw, ahya, ahya. Caw, caw, caw.

(Teddy bursts into the bathroom.)

VIOLET: Oh, you scared me.

TEDDY: Who are you?

VIOLET: Violet Moone. I'm working here…for today.

TEDDY: Why were you making those strange sounds?

VIOLET: I don't know. I's just thinking 'bout the time when I heard them birds.

TEDDY: What birds?

VIOLET: Well, first I thought it was some wild child crying. So I went outside in the pouring rain t'hunt for it and then flapping up outta the trees I saw all them colors flying. The most beautiful colors alive—just coming up outta them trees in the drowning rain. All them lost birds shrieking this wild, mournful cry like there ain't nothing left but dying. My mama come and tol' me that them was tropical parrot birds and they liked t'mimic the talk they hear. It always stuck with me wondering, 'bout where they would of heard such mournful crying t'recollect.

TEDDY: A lot of people cry. They could of heard it…anywhere.

VIOLET: Well, I come t'figure it musta been somewhere on the long journey that took them birds away from the warm, sunny climate they was so lonesomely homesick for. Ya see 'cause a bird's a sign.

TEDDY: What sorta sign?

VIOLET: A sign a' change. And that's why I'm going off to—sunny, tropical L.A., California. They got real sand there, and fruit trees and a big, big ocean a'water.

TEDDY: Umm. Well, maybe that's where I'll send my baby off to.

VIOLET: You got a baby?

TEDDY: (Pointing to her stomach.) Yeah. In here.

VIOLET: Oh.

TEDDY: Violet, would you please hand me the Band-Aid box from up there?

VIOLET: (Handing her the box.) Here.

TEDDY: Thank you. (Teddy opens the Band-Aid box, takes out a cigarette, and matchbook.) Wanna smoke?

(Violet shakes her head. Teddy lights up.)

TEDDY: Me, I love to smoke.

(Bliss White and Hank Turner enter from the main stairs carrying an enormous

amount of baggage: a tattered suitcase; a beat-up trunk; a box with a bad-
minton racket, board game, small, artificial Christmas tree tied to it with
rope, a birdcage, etc. Bliss has white skin and mauve lips. She carries a huge
stuffed animal. She is slender; her silky clothes seem to stick to her skin. Hank
is a big lumbering man. He looks uncomfortable in his expensive business
suit.)

HANK: I'm not sure where Jen got off to.

BLISS: Oh, oh, oh. Gracious God! Another stunning room!

HANK: Well, the third story still needs a lot of work, but Jen wanted us all
moved in here for Teddy's debutante deal.
(In the bathroom, Teddy smokes her cigarette as she mercilessly plucks her eye-
brows with a pair of tweezers.)

TEDDY: I don't like hair. I abhor it.

BLISS: And where is our prominent Hattiesburg Debutante? Why, she must
be on pins and needles.

HANK: She was, ah, down modeling her gown for us earlier this morning—
(Jen enters from the back stairway. She carries Teddy's satin cape.)

HANK: Jen, honey, hello—

BLISS: Oh, Mama, Mama! Sweet, Sweet Mama!

JEN: Bliss, you've arrived! My darling child.

BLISS: Oh, Mama, it's been so long. I've missed you so much!

JEN: Well, it's wonderful of you to come up from New Orleans for your sister's debut. I just hope you can—stay the weekend.

BLISS: Of course. I—of course. Delightful.

JEN: I've told Hank all about you. Isn't it true, we don't look a thing alike?

HANK: Well, you're both mighty good-looking to me.

BLISS: Oh, isn't he the charmer. Why, he'll just turn me giddy as a goose.

HANK: *(After a beat.)* So, Jen, how's Frances? Did she get in alright?

JEN: I don't know.

HANK: Didn't you pick her up?

JEN: Was I supposed to?

HANK: Good Lord, we discussed it thirty minutes last night!

JEN: Oh, now I remember. She was going to have pansies pinned to her lapel.

HANK: *(Looking at his watch.)* God, the poor girl was due in at the Trailway
Station over an hour and a half ago. Christ on a crutch! What's she
gonna do?! She can't call anyone! She can't talk!

JEN: I feel dreadful about this.

HANK: Well, I've got to get right over there and try to locate the girl. I just hope to hell I find her! Holy God and dog shit, don't let her be lost! *(Hank exits down the front stairway.)*

JEN: Poor Hank. He flares up like that since he stopped smoking. *(Jen takes a compact case out of her pocket, opens it, and takes out a cigarette.)*

BLISS: Yes, I can tell he's really a dear. Just a dear. Oh, Mama, you're smoking again.

JEN: Yes, damnit. Don't tell Teddy.

BLISS: Oh, I won't. I wouldn't. I won't.

(Violet enters from the bathroom. She carries a pail.)

JEN: Oh, Violet, go down front and start waxing the entrance hall. When you finish that, wash all the front windows, then start ironing the linen and stuffing the shrimp.

(Violet exits down the front stairs, making noises like a bird.)

JEN: Oh, the shrimp! I'm boiling butterfly shrimp! They've probably completely disintegrated. Bliss, you run this cape in to Teddy. She's down there in that bathroom.

BLISS: So, Mama, where shall I stay?

JEN: Oh, anywhere up on the third floor. I believe there's a bed up there somewhere.

(Jen exits down the back stairway. Bliss looks at the cape with envy. In the bathroom Teddy takes the tweezers and violently scratches her face.)

TEDDY: My Lord. My Lord. My face. My face.

(Bliss heads toward the bathroom.)

BLISS: Teddy! Teddy! Teddy Bear!

TEDDY: Bliss? Is that you?

(Bliss enters Jen's bathroom.)

BLISS: Oh, Teddy, there you are, honey! Give me a hug! I want a hug.

TEDDY: Oh, Bliss! Bliss!

BLISS: Lord in heaven, what a luxurious bathroom.

TEDDY: How are you?

BLISS: *(Pulling back and looking at Teddy.)* Good Christ, what's that on your face?

TEDDY: A scratch. A cat scratched me. It was beige colored.

BLISS: My God. Well, don't worry, we'll find something in here to fix it up with. *(Looking through her bag.)* Hmm. But first let me put on just a dash of mascara. I see people so much better when I'm wearing mascara. Oh God!

TEDDY: What?

BLISS: You're smoking again?

TEDDY: Don't tell Mama. Swear you won't tell Mama.

BLISS: Oh, I won't. I wouldn't. I won't.

(Teddy is dubious.)

BLISS: So how is Mama anyway? Do you think she still hates me for being born?

(Teddy shrugs. Bliss begins putting makeup on herself)

BLISS: It's so unfair. And now I'm forced to plead with her to take me in.

TEDDY: You mean to live here?

BLISS: I have no choice. I'm destitute, penniless, deserted, and alone. No one wants me. No one can stand me.

TEDDY: What happened to your dog trainer boyfriend?

BLISS: Oh, he said I couldn't dance. It's not true. I can dance. I dance. You've seen me dance!

TEDDY: Uh-huh.

BLISS: In an unprovoked rage, he threw all of my belongings out of the window. I had to scrape this blush up off the sidewalk and put it in a plastic bag. The few fine things from my marriage to the fat man were lost or destroyed. *(She sighs and begins putting makeup on Teddy.)* So anyway, how is my former husband doing? Is Tommy still repulsively overweight?

TEDDY: He's awfully large.

BLISS: And how's my baby, Butterball?

TEDDY: She's getting bigger and bigger.

BLISS: God, I'm sick with guilt I never send Butterball anything at all. And I do love her so. She's my one child. It's just I hate to think about her. *(About Teddy's makeup.)* There, that looks much better.

TEDDY: Tell me, Bliss, boys and men, they know, don't they? I mean they know a girl's eyelids aren't really colored bright green and her lips aren't really so dark and red and shiny. They know that, don't they?

BLISS: Of course they're aware it's something of an illusion.

TEDDY: Then why do they like it? Why do they want it? It's all a big trick.

BLISS: Well, uh, my, Teddy...

(The doorbell rings.)

BLISS: Ah, chimes! Chimes! I love the chimes! I wonder who's coming? I wonder who's there? Oh, who could it be?

(Teddy takes off her debutante gown.)

TEDDY: Brighton's coming over. He's taking me to the hair salon.

BLISS: Brighton is coming *here*? He's actually speaking to Mama?

(Teddy puts on a black raincoat. She pulls the hood up over her head.)

TEDDY: They all speak to her now that I'm having my debut.

BLISS: You mean Mama is back in Theadora Parker's good graces?

TEDDY: Yes, she is. Everyone has high hopes about my entrance into society. It's gonna turn everything around for us. I look divine in my gown.

BLISS: Divine. I'm sure. Divine.

(Brighton Parker enters from the front stairway with Violet leading him. Brighton is a very well dressed, proper young man. He wears horn-rimmed glasses and carries a cane.)

VIOLET: She's up here someplace.

BRIGHTON: *(About the room.)* Utterly atrocious. Ghastly. Hideous. Unspeakable. *(To Violet.)* I know you. Your mother, Candy Moone, used to work for my grandmother, Theadora.

VIOLET: Yeah, I remember that lady. She rode in a wheelchair and fixed my mama leftover luncheon meat sandwiches to go.

BRIGHTON: Yes, Grandmother's very generous. She's always thinking of others.

(Teddy puts a pair of wool socks on her hands.)

BLISS: Teddy, why are you wearing socks on your hands?

TEDDY: I wear them now instead of mittens.

BLISS: Oh, thank God for my pharmaceutical regimen.

(Bliss takes a pill. Teddy enters the parlor from the bathroom.)

BRIGHTON: Teddy, must you always wear that black raincoat?

TEDDY: You never know about the weather.

(Bliss enters from the bathroom.)

BLISS: Brighton! Brighton! It's me! I'm home. I've returned!

BRIGHTON: Yes, I see. So you have.

BLISS: Gracious Lord, merciful heavens, that's Daddy's doghead cane you're carrying. What in the world possesses you to fraternize with that grotesque piece of memorabilia?

BRIGHTON: Grandmother gave it to me after Uncle Theodore died. I carry it with me as a reminder.

BLISS: A reminder of gruesomeness.

BRIGHTON: Teddy, we don't have much time.

TEDDY: I'm all ready. I'm all fine.

BLISS: But first, won't y'all and the maid please help me carry up my luggage?

BRIGHTON: All of this is yours?

BLISS: I couldn't decide what to wear. So, Brighton, can you believe it? Mama's happily rich all over again.

(Teddy, Violet, Brighton, and Bliss start hauling luggage up the stairs.)

BRIGHTON: It is amazing. I never thought she'd marry that professional boor, even for the sake of money.

BLISS: Why, I hear Hank Turner's very brilliant. They say he can talk spun gold in a courtroom.

BRIGHTON: Yes, well, he did manage to save Aunt Jen's neck. And that was certainly quite a feat.

TEDDY: No talking, no talking, no talking about any trials. That's all over. That's all behind us.

BRIGHTON: *(To Teddy.)* Where're you going?

TEDDY: I'd like to wait down in the car. That big black car. *(Teddy exits down the main stairway.)*

BRIGHTON: She's upset. She's got problems.

VIOLET: I know 'bout one of 'em.

(They exit up the stairs. Jen comes up the back stairs carrying a beautiful bouquet of debutante roses.)

JEN: Teddy! Where are you, my darling child? My wondrous salvation? Your debutante bouquet has arrived.*(Jen enters the bathroom.)* Teddy? *(Jen sees Teddy is not there. She twirls around smelling the bouquet.)* They're so beautiful. Like all the untold secrets of the angels. *(Jen looks at herself in the mirror, smiling sweetly. Her smile disappears.)* Ah. Hmm, why'd you have to get to be such an old bag of bones?

(Violet and Brighton come walking down the stairs.)

BRIGHTON: It's amazing. The higher you go, the worse it gets. I'd rather live on a bed of nails than spend one night in this teratogeny.

VIOLET: It's kinda scary.

JEN: *(Exits from bathroom.)* Brighton! To see your face again.

BRIGHTON: Aunt Jen, hello.

JEN: Well, come here and kiss me, my cherished child.

BRIGHTON: I, no. No thank you.

JEN: Please. What's wrong? You always said I was your favorite aunt.

BRIGHTON: Yes, and Uncle Theodore was Grandmother's only son.

JEN: How pompous you've become clutching that silly cane. Oh well, we'll turn it all around. Here, just look at Teddy's debutante bouquet. Don't the roses remind you of the untold secrets of angels.

BRIGHTON: Yes, but angels don't keep secrets.

JEN: No, then where's Teddy? I want her to see it.

BRIGHTON: I believe she's down in Grandmother's limousine.

(Jen runs out on the balcony and waves below to Teddy.)

JEN: Teddy! Oh, Teddy!

BRIGHTON: God, who'd ever think it? Her with those frail white hands and flowered charm. Who'd ever believe?

VIOLET: What?

JEN: *(Disappears on the balcony.)* Look up here, child!

BRIGHTON: That she murdered her own husband in that violent fashion.

JEN: *(Offstage.)* Your bouquet, my angel!

VIOLET: Oh, Lordy! Is she the one from in the newspapers?

BRIGHTON: That's she.

VIOLET: And the girl in the white dress, was it her daddy was murdered?

BRIGHTON: *(Nods yes.)* Yes. My Uncle Theodore. Three years ago.

VIOLET: Got bludgeoned to death with a cast iron skillet.

JEN: *(Offstage.)* Tonight's going to be all you ever dreamed! I promise you! I promise!

(Lights fade to blackout.)

SCENE II

Bliss is standing with one leg in Jen's bathroom sink. She shaves her leg in a tattered peach teddy as she sings an upbeat Spanish song. Jen sits at her dressing table in a beautiful rose-colored slip. She is putting ointment onto sores on her skin.

JEN: *(Laughing with delight.)* Oh, how sweet it is! How divine!

BLISS: Marvelous, Mommie! Marvelous!

JEN: Just think, Bliss, tonight I'm going to get them all back—

BLISS: Resplendent revenge!

JEN: *(Running on.)* Everyone in this town who ever shunned or ostracized us.

BLISS: Let them eat words! Oh, let them eat words.

(Jen puts on a robe.)

JEN: Imagine. We'll all drive out to the ball—together again! Theadora Parker's going to enter my new house and shake my dirty hand which will be dripping with jewels and gold.

BLISS: Dear old Grandmama.

JEN: Ha! After my trial, the heartless bitch was happy to see all we had auctioned off to the highest bidder.

BLISS: Yes, she was very bitter about it all. Very bitter.

JEN: She's hoping tonight will give some new air of respectability to the memory of her infamous son. To the memory of her son. Why, this has got nothing to do with that wretched man.

BLISS: You never loved Daddy, did you, Mama? Even on your wedding day?

JEN: Of course not, Bliss. I told you that.

BLISS: I'm glad you're with Hank now.

JEN: Yes, well, I never get tired of marrying for money.

BLISS: No, why should you?

JEN: Exactly. Teddy needs every advantage. She's been put on probation up at Ole Miss. The Tri-Delts have threatened to expel her—for idiosyncratic behavior.

BLISS: Well, frankly, her social skills do need a good deal of refining. She went out today wearing socks on her hands instead of mittens. She's just trying to get attention. It's repulsive. She's smoking again, too.

JEN: No! Oh, Goddamnit! The little liar! What am I going to do?

BLISS: (*Shaving under her arm.*) You've done all you can. You've married Hank. You have this splendid mansion for her to live in. Why, tonight she's going to be presented at the Hattiesburg Debutante Ball in a Paris gown strewn with antique pearls. It really oughta be enough for anyone. (*Cutting herself with the razor.*) Aaah! Damnation! I cut myself. Look at this gash.

JEN: (*Really sick.*) No, I can't. I swear. Really, I used to look at bloody things, now they get me so sick.

BLISS: It's alright. I'll soak it up. It's not so bad.

(*Bliss soaks up the blood. Jen leaves the bathroom and goes into the main room. Hank comes up the main stairway. He is dripping with sweat.*)

HANK: She's nowhere to be found! I've had to notify the police. They're all out searching for her. An Officer Shackelford is waiting downstairs to keep us posted.

(*Bliss enters the living room in her teddy.*)

BLISS: (*Showing her underarm.*) Look, Mama, the bleeding has spontaneously subsided.

(*Hank paces over by the phone.*)

HANK: God, I just don't know what to do. I can't call up my dying sister and tell her I've lost her only child. Oh, what have I done?! What have I done?! (*Hank goes to pour himself a straight bourbon.*)

JEN: Oh, Hank, please, don't start drinking now. Remember tonight's Teddy's Debutante Ball.

HANK: Screw the ball, woman! I've lost my deaf niece!

(*Violet comes up the back stairs with a huge tray of unpolished silver, silver polish, and rags. Violet is uneasy in Jen's presence.*)

JEN: Oh, Violet, thank goodness. You've brought up the silver.

BLISS: My rings! I haven't got on my rings! I'm flushed all over with embarrassment. I'm simply dishabille without them.

JEN: *(To Violet.)* The flowers! The flowers! Have they arrived?

VIOLET: Big bunches of 'em.

(Bliss flees into Jen's bathroom to retrieve her rings.)

JEN: *(To Violet.)* Bring the red ones up here. The white ones stay below.

VIOLET: That's where I'll keep 'em.

(Violet exits down the back stairs. Hank pours himself another drink.)

HANK: God Almighty. God Almighty.

JEN: Hank, please, I know you're upset—

HANK: Yes, Jen, I am upset. Very upset.

(Bliss enters the main room, spraying herself with perfume.)

BLISS: I'm drenching myself in lilac perfume. That's all there is to do.

HANK: My sister, Sue, is literally eaten up with cancer—

BLISS: *(Still spraying.)* Ugh.

HANK: She could drop dead any minute—

BLISS: *(Still spraying.)* Poor thing.

HANK: She sends her only daughter down here to go to this goddamn ball in a last-ditch effort to find a husband—

BLISS: *(Still spraying.)* How pathetic!

HANK: And what do we do? We lose the girl! She's gone. She's lost. She wasn't picked up.

JEN: Please, she's not lost. She's misplaced. Frances will be retrieved. It's inevitable.

HANK: It'd suit you just fine if she never showed up. You didn't want my family included. Admit it, Jen. You never did.

JEN: We're all delighted to have Frances.

HANK: You're not delighted, Jen. You never even found her a date. You didn't mail out her invitation. You're convinced she won't fit in. Come on! Face it! Look at the evidence!

JEN: She will fit in. We'll fit her in! Now please, Hank, stop raving like a lunatic—go out on the balcony and have a cigarette.

HANK: I don't smoke anymore!

JEN: Yes, you do. You do. *(Jen takes a cigarette and lighter out of her robe pocket, lights the cigarette, and hands it to Hank.)* There you are. There's your smoke.

HANK: Alright, Jen. Alright. *(Hank goes out on the balcony to smoke his cigarette.)*

BLISS: Men. They're all wild. They're all crazy.

JEN: I know how to handle him. I can run him. It's just sometimes I don't have the patience. There's only so much I can bear to swallow.

BLISS: Absolutely. I don't know why his niece had to be invited. She's spent her whole life on some dirt poor farm. She's probably never been to an occasion of any sort. I'm sure she can't dance; she can't hear; she can't make chitchat.

(Violet enters up the back stairway with an armload of red flowers.)

VIOLET: Here're the red ones. The white ones are staying below.

BLISS: *(Swooning.)* Oh, how lovely! How divine! Mama, I must have a corsage for tonight. I need money for an enormous arrangement. I want to erupt with foliage.

(Jen starts arranging the flowers.)

JEN: Yes, you expect to be given everything your heart desires. You'll just lap it right up off a silver platter. Why, my father never even once gave me a gift or a remembrance of any kind.

BLISS: Yes, you told me.

JEN: At Christmas time I'd invent pets he'd given me, like a pony or a puppy or a parakeet.

BLISS: I remember you named your pony Dodie.

JEN: Later I'd tell all my friends and acquaintances the pet had died. That way I was able to save face. That's how I did it.

BLISS: Yes, I know all that, Mama.

JEN: Well, then, polish the silver! Do something useful! Life isn't just some parade passing by!

(Bliss starts polishing the silver.)

JEN: Violet, bring up the party favors. I want to arrange them in this urn. That way they'll be a surprise. No one will know what they're picking. No one will see what's coming.

VIOLET: Caw, caw, ahya! *(Violet exits down the back stairway.)*

JEN: Christ, I'd love to fire her. Unfortunately, I can't. I fired all the help yesterday. Do you know she's the only person in the whole town Hank could find who'd come in and work for me today. What am I, a leper?

(Teddy and Brighton come up the main stairway. Teddy wears a black raincoat with the hood pulled up over her head and socks on her hands.)

TEDDY: *(Breathlessly.)* Listen, everyone, there's a policeman downstairs. He's smoking a cigar in the front hallway. What's he want? Mama, who's he come for?

BLISS: Oh, he's only here about that deformed, I mean, deaf girl, Hank's niece. She's still lost.

TEDDY: Oh, well, I hope they find her.

JEN: Don't worry. We're going to find Frances. Everything will work out perfectly. It always does. Now, Teddy, what time is your friend David Brickman arriving from Atlanta?

TEDDY: Oh. Oh, him. Him. This is very upsetting.

JEN: What?

TEDDY: He's not coming.

JEN: What do you mean he's not coming? This has been arranged for months. His name's in the program. He's your official escort.

TEDDY: I know, I know. It's dreadful. But his mother called up and said he fell down out on his lawn and broke his limb in two.

JEN: He what?

TEDDY: His left limb just broke in two.

JEN: But this can't be.

(Teddy sniffs, then quickly pulls off her hood to show her hair which has been put up on her head in a bouffant style. Violet comes up the back stairway with a basket of party favors.)

TEDDY: How do you like my hair? They did a nice job. Don't you see how the hairpiece adds a lot of fullness to the head.

BRIGHTON: *(It's very attractive.)*

BLISS: *(Overlapping from "like my hair.")* Well, they certainly poofed it out.

VIOLET: *(Overlapping from "nice job.")* Real fancy.

JEN: Give me his number, Teddy. I'm calling his parents. This is an outrage. You tell me this boy is from one of the finest families in Atlanta and he does this!

TEDDY: Please, Mama, he didn't mean to take the spill.

JEN: I'll spill him! He can't back out on us at the last minute. Get me his number, Teddy. Goddamnit, the little bastard's not gonna ditch us like dirt. Now run get me his number!

TEDDY: Yes, Mama. I'll go get the number. I'll go get it. *(Teddy runs down the hall to her bedroom.)*

JEN: I won't be stepped on anymore. No one is ruining this night! No one!

BLISS: Please, it's alright, Mama. Don't get upset. Whatever you do—just don't—do it.

JEN: *(To Bliss.)* Did you clean up all of that hair in my bathroom sink?

BLISS: I think so.

JEN: Well, make sure! You know how I hate hair! I abhor it! I can't stand to look at it. It makes my skin crawl. Now, go and check on that hair.

BLISS: It's always the same whenever I come home. It's always the same. *(Bliss runs into the bathroom and lights up a cigarette.)*

JEN: Violet, go brew some tea. We need tea!

(Violet exits down the back stairway.)

JEN: *(To Brighton.)* Why are you looking at me like that?

BRIGHTON: It's so bewildering to me how I ever could have believed in your foolish charm.

JEN: You were a lonely, fanciful child. We made each other laugh. I used to let you bake buttermilk biscuits. You'd always eat a ball of the dough.

BRIGHTON: Yes, I enjoyed eating that ball of dough. I found it tasty. I believe I actually preferred it to the biscuits.

(Teddy enters.)

TEDDY: Here, Sweet Mama. Here's the number.

JEN: Thank you. *(Jen goes to the phone.)*

BRIGHTON: *(To Teddy.)* Why can't anything ever work out with you people?

TEDDY: We're snake-bit.

JEN: Teddy, the telephone number you've given me is missing a digit.

TEDDY: Let me see. I thought it was correct. It's the one he gave me. Oh no, I must have deleted a digit.

JEN: Goddamnit, I'm all set to bless them straight to hell. Call information! We need directory assistance!!!

(Teddy goes to call on the phone.)

BRIGHTON: Really, Aunt Jen, if the boy's leg is broken, I can't understand what good it's going to do to make a scene.

JEN: That young man is going to honor his commitment to Teddy. He's obligated to us. He'll have to send a replacement.

TEDDY: They're unlisted. They're so rich and powerful they're not even listed.

JEN: Please, Teddy, don't worry. We'll fix it. I'm sure Brighton knows some marvelous young men.

BRIGHTON: Me? You can't expect me! Good Lord, this is the very day of the ball. All of my affiliates have made arrangements months in advance.

TEDDY: They're all booked up.

JEN: Oh, come on, Brighton, anyone will do. A young boy. A grandfather type. We're not being particular at the moment. Think! Think!

BRIGHTON: Let me think. Let me think! Let me think!! No, I can't think! I can't think! There's no one.

TEDDY: No one.

BRIGHTON: No one at all.

JEN: Well, then you'll just have to take her yourself.

BRIGHTON: That's impossible. As the official representative from the Parker family, I'm presenting her at the ball. The escort has got to be different from the presenter.

JEN: Oh, you're right. God. Good God.

TEDDY: Please, Sweet Mama. Don't despair. I have a good solution.

JEN: What?

TEDDY: I'll send regrets. I'll say I have an acid stomach.

BRIGHTON: I suppose if things can't be done properly. I mean, the whole purpose of tonight was to enhance the Parker family image, not to disgrace it further.

JEN: (Overlapping.) Shut up! You're not talking anymore. Shut up! Shut up! Let me think. Let me think. Hank! You'll go with Hank. That's all. It's a radical move, but he's all we've got. Hank!

TEDDY: Mama, wait—

JEN: (Calling out on the balcony.) Hank, dear, are you about!

BRIGHTON: You'll make us all laughingstocks.

(Hank enters from the balcony.)

HANK: Yes, Jen, what is it?

JEN: Hank, dear, we've run into a little snag. Teddy requires an escort for this evening's ball. And she's hoping you'll comply.

HANK: You want me to be her date?

JEN: (To Teddy.) See, dear, he'd be delighted.

BRIGHTON: This is ridiculous. The escort is supposed to be a young, eligible man, not some ancient old goat who's married to the debutante's mother.

TEDDY: (In a whisper.) Unfortunately, I don't think he can waltz. I observed him at your wedding and he couldn't waltz.

JEN: Nonsense. Hank has a natural grace. Here, take her in your arms. Spin her around the ballroom floor.

(Teddy and Hank awkwardly begin to waltz.)

JEN: See there. There's nothing to it. Try to breathe. Breathe. Keep breathing.

(Hank steps on Teddy's foot.)

TEDDY: Ah, my toes! He stepped on my toes! I think they're all broken for good!	HANK: I'm so sorry. I'm such an ox. I'm known for my clumsiness.
JEN: Teddy, please, Hank	BRIGHTON: She doesn't want to go with him. It's

would never break your
toes. We'll rehearse his
waltzing. It won't be a problem.

apparent. I think we all know
why.

TEDDY: Oh, please, Sweet Mama, I just don't think I can go. My toes are broken.

JEN: Listen to me, Teddy. I wish we could find you the perfect escort. I've tried so hard to make this night just what you wanted. Why do you think I've spent this last year planning and preparing and coordinating everything especially for you? Why, I had the florist make up nine different rose bouquets before I approved the one that was exactly exquisitely right for your ensemble. I know I can never change the past. But please, please don't deny me this ferocious dream I have of giving you a future.

TEDDY: Yes. I'll go with him. He'll be my date.

JEN: Fine, glorious.

HANK: I don't like twisting her arm.

BRIGHTON: She despises the man.

TEDDY: I'll need a lot of makeup, though. A lot of it. All over my face.

JEN: We'll dance all night.
It will be a spectacular occasion.
We'll always remember it.

(Violet enters from the main stairway with a tea tray.)

VIOLET: The deaf girl. She's come. She's down there. She's gotten all dusty!

(Everyone heads out the front hall doorway.)

HANK: Frances. Thank God! She's alive! Thank God. My dear, Frances.

JEN: *(Overlapping.)* See there! I knew it would all work out perfectly!

BRIGHTON: *(Overlapping.)* It's unbelievable! Now the deaf girl comes! Tonight will be so mortifying.

TEDDY: *(Relishing the idea.)* I wonder what it's like for her when she can't even hear anything at all. Nothing at all.

(They all exit. Bliss sits alone in Jen's bathroom. She powders herself with an enormous powder puff. Frances Walker enters the parlor from the back stairway. She is tall and strong and wears a dust-covered suit. She moves awkwardly around the room carrying her dust-laden suitcase and shoes. Bliss moves from the bathroom into the main room to get a drink to wash down some pills she is taking. Bliss spots Frances.)

BLISS: Oh, hello.

(Frances has had three summers of training at a deaf school, so she knows some sign language and can read lips somewhat. However, since almost no

one around her knows sign language, she has invented her own way of com-
municating—a very unique pantomime along with attempts at speaking
words. This will have to be developed by the actress.)

BLISS: Well, how do you do? I'm Bliss White.

FRANCES: "HELLO, I'M FRANCES WALKER."

BLISS: Pardon? What's that? Oh! Oh, my God! You're the cousin. *(Bliss takes*
a pill, yelling and enunciating.) Yes, so won-der-ful to meet you. I'm *Bliss*
White. *Comprende vous, ma chere?*

(Frances nods yes and no.)

BLISS: Yes, Bliss. *Je m'appelle,* Bliss.

FRANCES: "BLISS."

BLISS: Yes! Very good! *Très bien! Asseyez vous gentilmente.* While I go get some
help.

(Frances shakes her head in utter despair. She can hardly refrain from crying.)

FRANCES: "THIS HOUSE IS TOO BIG. TOO BEAUTIFUL."

BLISS: *(Overlapping.)* What's wrong? Why, you did very well.

FRANCES: "WHY DID I EVER COME? WHAT A FOOL!"

BLISS: Oh, I shouldn't have been speaking French.

FRANCES: "MY MAMA'S SICK!"

BLISS: *(Running on.)* Why was I speaking *Français!* Good gracious! Silly me.

FRANCES: "I MUST GO. HOME. I GO. I GO."

BLISS: Oh no, don't go. Stay here. Stay. Stay! Sit! Sit!

FRANCES: "SIT. I'M NO DOG. I HATE DOGS."

BLISS: Perhaps you'd like some tea.

FRANCES: "WHEN I WALK, THIS DOG GROWLS AT ME AND BITES."

BLISS: *(Overlapping.)* Oh my! This is ghastly! Mama. Somebody. Help. Help me!

FRANCES: "OH, I DON'T BELONG HERE. I'M ALL DIRTY."

BLISS: Oh Lord. Oh Lordy.

FRANCES: "LOOK AT THIS. I'M COVERED WITH FILTH."

BLISS: *(Overlapping.)* What? What? Oh dear, dear, dear.

FRANCES: *(Overlapping.)* "UGH, MY FEET. SMELL MY FEET."

BLISS: Your feet?

FRANCES: "OH, THEY STINK."

BLISS: Stink? Your feet stink. Your feet stink!

FRANCES: *(Overlapping.)* "YEAH. YEAH. THEY DO!"

BLISS: Oh, well, here, we'll just spray them with perfume. We'll drench them
in perfume. *(Bliss starts spraying Frances' feet with perfume.)* There. That's
good. I'll make it right. You'll have fun. It will be a beautiful night for
you. Your feet are lovely now. Just lovely.

(Frances looks up at Bliss and smiles.)
FRANCES: "YOU ARE SO BEAUTIFUL."
BLISS: Yes. Well, anyway. Yes. *(Bliss sprays herself with perfume.)*
(Lights fade to blackout.)

SCENE III

*It is evening. Violet is wearing a formal maid's uniform. She is helping Hank
finish dressing for the ball. Hank fidgets as Violet hooks him into his black
cummerbund. Hank has a shred of toilet tissue stuck to his face over a cut he
got shaving. Champagne has been laid out. The tea service has been cleared.*

HANK: This waist thing's too tight. I feel like a stuck hog.

VIOLET: That's as loose as it'll go.

HANK: Damn! T'hell with all this debutante crap. It's turned Jen into a crazy
woman. Why, it was no surprise to me when the maids and cook quit
yesterday.

VIOLET: *(Picking up his cuff links.)* Here, I'll get on your studs.

HANK: I just can't tell you, Violet, how much I appreciate your coming t'help
us out here on such short notice. I wish you'd consider staying with us
on a permanent basis.

VIOLET: Well, thing is come Monday morning, me and my kids are headed
out for L.A., California.

HANK: I tell you, Violet, breaking into the entertainment world is not going
to be nearly as simple as you may imagine. How would your mama have
felt about you hauling all your kids off to a strange place like California?

VIOLET: Well, I know, Mr. Turner, that at my age I've already been a jailbird
and nobody expects much outta me. But I'll prove 'em wrong.

HANK: I hope so, Violet, but I have some grave doubts about the practicality
of your plans.

VIOLET: Thing is ever since I was alive I've had this longing t'be a circus
clown. Originally, I thought you had to be born a clown, and I cried all
the time thinking how badly I felt 'cause I could never be turned from
a black colored person into a funny clown person. Then one day watching TV, I discovered that clowns were man-made and if I just learned out
at the circus school in California—I could change myself and become
one, too. From then on, a whole wide life appeared up before me.

(Suddenly Jen appears at the top of the stairs in a glamorous satin emerald

gown. She carries a dazzling gold jewelry case under her arm. Hank "oohs" at the sight of her.)

JEN: Good evening, everyone! Oh, let's illuminate the sky! What a night! What a time! Oh, I'm so filled with excitement!

(Violet rushes out onto the balcony and starts lighting small lanterns.)

HANK: God, your face.

JEN: What?

HANK: It sparkles.

JEN: Oh, Hank. Hank! Hank!

HANK: *(Overlapping.)* Like a Christmas tree when you smile. Like a lit up Christmas tree.

JEN: *(Laughing.)* Yes, I feel aglow. I feel aglow.

HANK: God, to hear you laugh. You know that first year we were married the only thing that ever made you smile even faintly was sitting and watching a rainstorm come in.

JEN: Yes, you'd sit there with me and we'd watch the rain flood down.

HANK: Later on you got to where you'd laugh just a little. Lord, it made me cry to hear you laugh so thin and strange. All I wanna do is be with you and hear your laughter soar.

JEN: No, don't ever leave me.

(Teddy enters from her room. She wears her debutante's gown, a white satin cape, silver slippers, and carries a glittering evening bag. She looks as though she is ready for battle.)

TEDDY: Here I am, Mama! I'm ready for the ball!

JEN: What a vision! Isn't she a vision!

HANK: Oh my goodness, she's pretty.

JEN: A belle! A real Southern belle.

TEDDY: Clang, clang, clang.

JEN: Here now, you must wear this diamond necklace. It's the perfect adornment to your gown. *(Jen takes a glittering necklace out of the jewel box.)*

TEDDY: Diamonds galore.

JEN: Isn't it beautiful. Like a treasure from a cherub's tomb. Hank gave it to me for our anniversary.

HANK: I love to give your mama things.

(Jen goes to put the necklace on Teddy.)

HANK: Remember the first gift I ever gave you?

JEN: The Pontiac?

HANK: No, honey, you were still in jail and I brought you in that homegrown tomato.

JEN: It's magnificent. How it sets off your eyes.

HANK: You said it was the best tomato you'd ever had.

JEN: Run look at your sweet self in the mirror. You're the purest angel. The dearest one.

(Teddy goes into Jen's bathroom and stares at herself in the mirror.)

HANK: You said each bite was like an endless summer. Don't you remember the tomato?

JEN: Yes, of course, I'm very fond of vegetables. *(Holding up her jewels.)* Let me see, what should I wear? I want to appear enormously enriched! I want them all to be speechless with envy.

HANK: God, you look so beautiful to me, I can't hardly stand it.

JEN: Oh, butter me up some more. Please, butter me up some more.

(Violet enters from the balcony. All the outdoor lanterns have been lit.)

HANK: *(To Violet.)* Violet, come in here and look at her! Why, I'd like to eat her right up with a silver spoon. Mmm, mmm. Gobble, gobble.

JEN: *(Uncomfortable.)* Hank, please, butter me up, but don't fry me in fat.

HANK: Sorry, I just can't help it. *(Hank knocks over a vase of flowers.)*

JEN: Oh, Hank, watch out! Those fresh flowers were sent in special for tonight!

HANK: I'll get something t'sweep it up with.

(The doorbell rings.)

JEN: God, that's Teddy's grandmother. They're here. *(To Hank.)* What's that toilet paper doing stuck on your face?

HANK: *(Pulling it off)* Oh.

JEN: Oh, Hank, would you run upstairs and lock my jewels back in the safe?

HANK: Alright.

JEN: Oh, and Hank, please don't come down without your jacket. Violet, would you get him his jacket? *(To Hank.)* Now, Hank, I know how much fun it is for you to let everyone think you're just a loud, crazy, red-neck who happens to have a brilliant mind; and if you want to hide behind that facade, well, that's up to you, because Teddy and I will be proud of you no matter what. And that's just the way we feel.

(Jen exits down the main stairway. Hank turns to Violet, who is sweeping up the flowers.)

HANK: Great. She's using reverse psychology on me. How brilliant. God, she's really changed since the day I met her in that little ol' county jail cell. I tell you one thing, Violet, a woman in distress is enormously attractive to a man. And if he thinks he's gonna be able to offer a bit of solace to her despair, well, he's a greased and cooked goose.

(Hank exits up the staircase with the jewel box. Violet exits down the back stairway. In the bathroom, Teddy puts roll-on deodorant behind her knees. Frances slowly opens the bathroom door. She wears a homemade dress and holds a white fur stole lovingly in her arms.)

FRANCES: *(Tentatively holding out the fur.)* "HI...COULD I...COULD I WEAR..."

TEDDY: Have it. Have it. It's yours.

(Frances' face lights up. She throws the fur around her shoulders and spins around the room.)

FRANCES: "OH, THANK YOU, TEDDY, THANK YOU! MANY WARM THANKS."

(Bliss bursts into the bathroom wearing a green gown.)

BLISS: See there. I told you she'd let you wear it!

FRANCES: "IT'S THE SOFTEST THING I'VE EVER FELT IN MY LIFE."

BLISS: Yes, and it does make all the difference in the world! Oh, Teddy, Teddy. My God, if I were only in your slippers, this would be the most thrilling night of my life. Why, I could burst into hysterical tears thinking about how I was never ever allowed to be a debutante. Oh God, never to be allowed. Not allowed. The agony.

(Teddy moans from her bowels.)

BLISS: Oh, good God, don't be such a silly. Things aren't that serious. Here, let's go out and have some pink champagne.

(They all move out into the parlor.)

BLISS: Come on now, we must be gay and frivolous tonight and spin ourselves into a high, high fever.

(Frances awkwardly imitates the way Bliss is spinning and gliding across the floor. As she pours champagne.)

BLISS: That's it, Frances! Oh, what a stunning carriage! Doesn't she have the most stunning carriage!

TEDDY: Oh, she does! Boy, she does. Clang! Clang! Clang!

(Bliss hands out glasses of champagne.)

BLISS: Here now, we must all drink up. It's a scientific fact that people who don't drink severely limit their spiritual development!

(They all clink glasses and dance about. Hank appears at the top of the stairs. He slides down the banister. They all look up at him and gasp.)

HANK: Good evening, ladies!

FRANCES: "UNCLE HANK!"

BLISS: What an athletic performance! What an amazing feat!

HANK: My, and don't the three of you look so pretty! Like three angels on a cake!

FRANCES: *(Giving him a glass of champagne.)* "PUNCH!"

HANK: Well, thank you, Frances. Cheers, everyone. Cheers.

BLISS: I'm putting on some music! We must dance!

HANK: *(To Teddy.)* Well, I have been practicing, if you'd like to give it a whirl, Miss Teddy.

(The waltzing music begins.)

TEDDY: Dancing's not for me.

HANK: I'll look out for your toes.

TEDDY: I'm saving myself for the ball.

(Bliss waves a rose at Hank with a smile.)

BLISS: I'll dance with you. *(Bliss slings the rose over her shoulder.)*

HANK: Perhaps she's right. I am awful clumsy.

BLISS: Oh, come on now. No fool, no fun.

(Bliss and Hank start dancing awkwardly. Frances watches with awe.)

BLISS: Ah, I love dancing. I've always dreamed of spending my life as a ballerina doll spinning madly on top of a jeweled music box. *(Picking up a quarter that she spots.)* Oh, look, a quarter! *(Pressing the coin into his palm.)* Here, you must keep it for me. *(Turning to Teddy and Frances.)* Look, everyone, isn't he marvelous! Why, he's just a natural!

(Teddy watches with interest as Frances applauds the couple. Jen and Brighton enter from the main stairway.)

JEN: Oh, very good! Why, Hank, your waltzing is looking so much better! Just don't let Bliss trip you up with her sense of rhythm. She's always been such an awkward dancer.

(Bliss stops dancing and goes to the record player.)

HANK: Jen, please don't treat the girl like that.

JEN: Treat her like what? Teddy, Brighton's brought up your grandmother's tiara. Go put it on and then hurry downstairs.

(Brighton hands Teddy the tiara. Bliss scratches the needle across the record. There is a horrible screech. Bliss kicks the wall with her foot and bangs on it with her fist. Everyone looks at her.)

JEN: Really, Bliss, please. I don't want to get into another tiff. I was just teasing you, silly.

BLISS: Teasing me? That's teasing?

JEN: Yes, because, you see, dancing is something that has always come so easily to me—

BLISS: *(Swallowing pills with champagne.)* Well, we all pale by comparison to you.

JEN: Good then. You just keep on taking those pills, but they're going to kill you just like they killed Judy Garland. Only you won't have any fame, or money to show for it!

HANK: Jen—

JEN: *(To Hank.)* And if you want to stay here and defend this pill-popper, please do! Everyone else, we're leaving right now!

(Jen exits out the hall door. Bliss stops taking pills.)

HANK: Sorry, honey. Sometimes I guess you'd just as soon she hit you with a stick.

BRIGHTON: A stick perhaps, but not an iron skillet.

HANK: Hey! You think that's funny?

BRIGHTON: No, you're right. It's never funny when somebody gets away with murder.

(Hank grabs Brighton's tuxedo lapel.)

HANK: You smug little bastard. You don't know shit.

BRIGHTON: Maybe not. But ask Teddy. She knows the truth.

TEDDY: *(To Brighton.)* I don't know anything. You're a liar. There's nothing that I know. Shut up. Just shut up! Oh, I need some more makeup. On my face. My face. *(Teddy goes to the bathroom where she proceeds to put on massive amounts of makeup.)*

HANK: *(To Brighton.)* After tonight I don't want you around here. I hope I'm making myself clear. *(Hank exits down the main stairway.)*

BRIGHTON: You people! You people! You're all festering with secrets and lies. And that man! That man! Did you see how he walks? Just like a pig. *(Brighton laughs with a snort.)*

BLISS: Did you know, Brighton, that you snort when you laugh?

BRIGHTON: No, I wasn't aware of it.

(He laughs and snorts once more. Bliss slings her champagne in his face.)

BLISS: Then perhaps you'd better suppress your mirth.

(Brighton glares at her, too furious to move. Frances watches, amazed.)

BRIGHTON: *(To Bliss.)* Strange. Somehow, I always knew you were never really part of my family. Your mannerisms are different. They're affected and coarse. The older you get, the more apparent it becomes.

(Brighton turns and exits down the back stairway. Teddy comes out of the bathroom covered with makeup, wearing the tiara on her head. She holds and pushes up the skin on her face with her hands.)

TEDDY: Oh, my face, the skin up on my face. They say it never stops growing.

It just starts slowly sagging and slipping down. And soon, it'll kinda be hanging there like globs of meat on a bone. *(Teddy stops at the bar and takes a slug of bourbon from the bottle.)*

BLISS: You are so sophomoric, Teddy. Sometimes you are so goddamn sophomoric!

TEDDY: *(Squirting breath spray.)* I gotta go see my grandmother, Theadora. She's waiting down there for me. We're going off to the ball. But first I'd better remind her to hold that excess falling skin up on her face.

BLISS: Go on down to your precious grandmother! I don't want any part of her or the rest of them! I'm glad my father was a fruit picker!!!
(Teddy exits down the main stairway. Bliss turns to Frances. She mimes some of the following for Frances.)

BLISS: Theodore wasn't my real father. Mama pretended he was, even though she was four months gone by the time they got married.

FRANCES: "A BABY?"

BLISS: Yes. Me. I was the baby. My fruit-picker father shot himself in the heart when he found out about her wedding.

FRANCES: "HURT HEART."

BLISS: Exactly. All of this came out at Mama's trial. My debut was canceled. I married Tommy to escape; things went sour; I fled. Still there was a relief in knowing Theodore Parker bore me no relation. He was an abusive drug addict as well as an embezzler and thief. Even so, it's awful Mama—killed him. Ah, well, as you can see, it's all been very Byzantine. *(Bliss moves around the room. She feels sticky all over.)* God, these underpants are sticking to my skin. Here, let me get rid of them.
(Bliss reaches up under her skirt and shimmies off her green silk underpants. Frances watches amazed.)

BLISS: Sometimes I simply can't bear underwear. They're so nasty.
(Frances suddenly reaches up under her dress and takes off her cotton panties and holds them up triumphantly. Bliss shakes her panties at Frances. Frances shakes hers at Bliss. Laughing, Bliss runs with her panties to the balcony window and throws them over the edge.)

BLISS: *Au revoir.*
(Frances holds her panties between her teeth and then slings them over the balcony railing. She looks back at Bliss and shrugs. Bliss bursts into hysterical laughter. Frances starts laughing, too. They collapse together on the floor in heaps of laughter.)

BLISS: Oh, God! Oh, God! I must go to the pot. Quick! Oh, God!

(Bliss gets up and rushes into the bathroom. Frances rushes after her. Bliss hikes up her skirt as she dashes to the toilet in the alcove.)

BLISS: Ah, what a relief! I have a teeny-tiny bladder. Everyone in our family does. That was the thing about being married to the fat man, all of his family had huge bladders. They could go solid months without peeing. *(Bliss gets up, flushes the toilet, and goes to put on more mascara. Frances is brushing on powder blush with a large makeup brush. Brighton and Violet come up the back stairway. Violet carries a tray of enormous corsages. Brighton is cleaning his jacket with a damp rag.)*

BRIGHTON: Look, there, I'm stained for the night. I'm just livid. Actually, Ms. Moone, since my Uncle Theodore's death I've tried to assume a refined appearance and a serious manner to show respect for my grandmother's relentless grief. I feel it is my mission in life. I've found that people need a mission. Otherwise there's confusion and if there is one thing we all must avoid, Ms. Moone, that is confusion.

VIOLET: There's a whole mess of that going on.

BRIGHTON: Yes, indeed, and it's not to be trifled with.

(Bliss and Frances come out of the bathroom into the parlor.)

BRIGHTON: Oh, horrors!

BLISS: *(To Frances.)* Just ignore him.

BRIGHTON: I'm stuffing the cleaning bill for this down your throat.

(Brighton turns away. Bliss sees the corsages.)

BLISS: Why, look! The corsages have arrived! The bouquets for our breasts.

VIOLET: *(To Bliss.)* Here's yours right here. It's the biggest one of all. I guess someone must adore you a whole lot.

BLISS: Well, yes, I sent it to myself. What I love most about corsages is the fact that they're so very, very beautiful for only one night. How special that makes the one night.

(Frances is excitedly smelling all of the flowers. She picks up Teddy's bouquet, then puts it back.)

VIOLET: Here, Frances, this one's for you.

(Frances takes the corsage with delight, then starts to pin it on Violet.)

VIOLET: Oh no, it's not for me.

(Frances picks up the bouquet and offers it.)

BLISS: No, Frances. Violet doesn't get a corsage. She's not going. She's the maid.

(Teddy comes rushing in from the main stairway. She is white with fear and is pulling at her hairpiece.)

TEDDY: Oh, Lord—Oh, Lord. No, no. I can't go. I can't go to the fancy ball.

BRIGHTON: Teddy, what's wrong? Are you alright?

TEDDY: Grandmother says I look just like my daddy. She says I'm his spitting image. *(Looking into her veins.)* She says she can see the Parker blood inside me. She can see it!

BLISS: Oh, that old bitch is blind as a bat.

TEDDY: I think I'd better not go. I think there are rats inside my hairpiece.

BRIGHTON: We're in trouble. Big trouble.

TEDDY: *(Running on.)* Rats! Rats! I knew it all along. I'd better not go. *(Teddy exits into the bathroom and slams the door shut.)*

BLISS: Darling Teddy, always looking at the world through rose-colored glasses.

(Jen bursts into the room. She carries Teddy's cape and evening bag. In the bathroom, Teddy starts pulling apart her hairpiece.)

JEN: Where's Teddy. Where'd she go? Bliss?!

(Bliss indicates the bathroom.)

BLISS: *La toilette.*

JEN: Please, everyone, get yourselves together. We've got to leave here this minute. I mean it, everyone! This minute! Violet, run over to my room and bring me my sable fur, it's lying out on the bed.

(Bliss and Frances go up the stairs. Violet exits to Jen's room. Jen goes into the bathroom with Teddy. Brighton exits down the main stairway.)

JEN: Teddy, what are you doing?

TEDDY: *(Pulling at her hair.)* Do you see any rats in here? I thought I saw some rats.

JEN: Jesus, child, are you having a breakdown?

TEDDY: Am I? I could be. I don't know. I wish Daddy were here. See, otherwise, they'll all look at me and it'll just remind them of how he died and how he can't be here tonight.

JEN: Look, Teddy, even if your daddy had survived he wouldn't be here tonight. He would have been convicted of embezzlement and fraud. He'd be stuck in jail for life.

TEDDY: Alive though. He'd be alive.

JEN: Let it go, Teddy. Please. There's nothing left I can do. Let it go.

TEDDY: It just sticks in my mind how Daddy brought me that Peter Rabbit coloring book after my thumb got smashed.

JEN: Well, does it also stick in your mind how he smashed your thumb and how he poured scalding chili over my head and what he did to the gold-fish?

TEDDY: He wasn't a well man. I know that. Oh, Mama, it just won't ever heal up. It's raw scabs over raw scabs and now it's all ripping away.

JEN: Teddy, don't do this. Not now.

TEDDY: They're all gonna see through me. Inside me.

(Hank enters the parlor from the main stairway.)

HANK: *(Yelling.)* Hey, people! Let's get this show on the road! Jen?! Hey, Jen!

JEN: *(From bathroom.)* Yes, darling! We're coming!

HANK: Well, Theadora's being wheeled out to her car right now. She wants Teddy to ride in there with her!

JEN: *(Rapidly trying to do something with Teddy's torn-down hair.)* We'll be right there!

HANK: *(Pouring a drink.)* Okay, but you'd better hurry. The roads to hell are paved with the skulls of unpresented debutantes!

TEDDY: Why did you have to marry him?

JEN: I needed help. We had no money. I couldn't let you take that job in the school cafeteria. You'd never have gotten into a proper sorority.

TEDDY: I didn't care. I would have done the work. I would have done anything not to lose you again, or hurt you. Hurt you to help me. Oh, my face. My face.

(Teddy pulls away from Jen, and rushes to the toilet to vomit. Jen wets a towel and goes to wash Teddy's face.)

JEN: God, Teddy. How much have you been drinking? Are you going to be alright?

TEDDY: Uh-huh. It's just…Mama, I'm pregnant.

(Jen stares at her wide-eyed.)

HANK: *(Looking at his watch.)* Hey, as a personal favor to me, could we all head out of here before the goddamned sunrise!?

JEN: Whose is it? Is it that boy's from Atlanta? Is it that David Brickman's?

TEDDY: There isn't any David Brickman from Atlanta. I just made him up.

JEN: What?

TEDDY: I was gonna be dead by now, it wasn't gonna matter. But now I gotta wait for this thing to be born. Even though I know it's going to be born horrible.

HANK: Let's move out! Roll 'em, roll 'em, roll 'em!

(Jen starts singing "We Wish You a Merry Christmas" in a frantic whisper, as she works with Teddy's hair.)

HANK: Hey, everyone! Let's get organized. Roll 'em, people! Roll 'em!

(Brighton enters from the main stairway.)

BRIGHTON: Grandmother's waiting on all of y'all down in her car.

HANK: Relax. Settle down!

BRIGHTON: This is extremely rude.

HANK: Relax. The night is young.

(Hank heads for the bar. He knocks into the silver vase of party favors causing the vase to tumble to the floor: Sparkling colored prizes spill out across the rug. Jen stops singing.)

HANK: Ah, Hell's fire! All the goddamn party favors. If I'm not the clumsiest man ever put on God's earth.

(Hank kneels down on the floor and starts sweeping the prizes back into the silver vase. Bliss and Frances come down the stairs carrying their wraps and evening bags.)

BLISS: Oh, look at the treasures! The treasures. *(Bliss picks up a paper crown covered with glitter that is among the party favors.)* A princess' crown!

(Hank turns away from them, then turns back toward them wearing a red nose that fell from the silver vase.)

HANK: Honk. Honk.

(Jen and Teddy enter the parlor from the bathroom. Teddy wears her cape and her tiara; her hair is a mess. Frances picks up a gold fan.)

JEN: Oh, no, Hank, those party favors were to be given out after the ball.

HANK: No problem. We'll put 'em all back.

JEN: We're going, everyone, now! *(To Hank.)* Oh, Hank, come here. *(She takes the red nose off of Hank and drops it into the silver vase.)*

BRIGHTON: *(Overlapping, to Teddy.)* Teddy, you and I are riding with Grandmother. We must hurry. They're out there waiting.

BLISS: *(Overlapping.)* Teddy, dear, what's happened to your hair? You've destroyed your hair.

JEN: She's going to fix it in the car.

BRIGHTON: *(To Teddy, handing her the debutante bouquet and a corsage.)* Teddy, these are for you. You'll have to pin them on in the car. *(To everyone.)* Hurry up! Hurry up! Everyone's waiting.

HANK: *(Overlapping, to Bliss and Frances. They both keep their party favors.)* My, what a lucky man I am tonight, escorting all these beautiful dolls to the Hattiesburg Debutante Ball.

(Brighton, Teddy, Hank, Bliss, and Frances all exit out the hall door as Jen talks rapidly to Violet while pinning on her corsage.)

JEN: *(Overlapping.)* We'll be returning about two A.M. so be sure the canapés are prepared and the bar is set up. You can heat up the hot hors d'oeuvres after we've arrived.

VIOLET: Alright. *(Helping Jen into her fur coat.)* My, this is a fine silky fur.

JEN: Don't worry, Violet, when you're my age, You'll have a fur that's just as fine and just as silky and you will have earned every Goddamned hair on it. Just like I have. 'Bye-'bye now.

VIOLET: 'Bye.

(Jen exits out the hall door. Blackout.)

END OF ACT I

ACT II
SCENE I

Finger sandwiches, various canapés, and exotic cheeses have been put out on silver platters. Teddy appears walking barefoot along the balcony railing, swinging her cape. Her dress is torn and dirty. She no longer wears the hairpiece.

TEDDY: Clang! Clang! Clang! I'm not a bell. Not a bell! No bell. *(Teddy jumps off the balcony railing and comes into the room. She is crazed with jubilation.)* Look, one cheese knife. *(Her eye catches the cheese knife. She picks it up and starts slashing at her face.)* Okay. Fine. Face. The face. Face. Whole face.
(Violet enters from the back stairs with a tray. She slings the tray aside and knocks the knife out of Teddy's hand.)
VIOLET: What you wanna do? Look here, there's blood.
TEDDY: *(With a fierce crazed triumph.)* Violet, I'm no belle. Mama, she wanted me to go to that ball and be a belle. But me, I'm no belle.
VIOLET: *(Handing Teddy a napkin.)* There now. Hold that to the cut.
TEDDY: A while ago, see, I was staying by myself at an old hotel up in Oxford, Mississippi. After supper one night I got on the elevator to ride up to my room. And just as the doors were about to close, a man stepped inside to ride up with me. I glanced over and saw his left arm was cut off right above the elbow. He wore a short-sleeved shirt and you could see the scarred nub. Then I caught sight of his face where the whole side of it was just...missing. I felt sick and sticky, and wanted to get off the ride. My legs buckled out from under me; he reached his good arm out to help me up. But I said to him, "You get away from me, you ugly man." Then the elevator stopped. The doors opened. But he didn't move. He just stayed hovering over in a corner with this weepy cry coming from inside his throat.
VIOLET: Uh-huh. Well, I'm sure it wasn't the first time people turned scared on him and caused his feelings to be injured. I reckon he'd better get used to it.
TEDDY: Violet, do you remember that baby I spoke to you about?
VIOLET: Yeah.
TEDDY: It's his baby.
VIOLET: The bad-looking one on the elevator?

TEDDY: Uh-huh. I kinda just did it to be polite. I was at a point, you see, where I couldn't take on any more, ah, bad feelings, guilt. Just no more. *(Teddy offers a cigarette from a Band-Aid box.)* Wanna smoke?

VIOLET: No thanks.

(Teddy sniffs.)

TEDDY: After we did it he said to me, "Mm-mm good." Can you believe it? "Mm-mm good."

VIOLET: Kinda like you was M&M's or somptin'.

TEDDY: Yeah. I still smell him on my skin sometimes. *(She sniffs.)* God. I gotta stop that.

VIOLET: What?

TEDDY: Sniffing. I sniff when I'm afraid.

VIOLET: What are you afraid of?

TEDDY: *(A chill runs through her.)* Hidden things. *(She sniffs.)* Did you ever have hidden things?

VIOLET: I used to write secrets in jars and bury the jars outside in the dirt.

TEDDY: What kinda secrets did you bury?

VIOLET: Different things I had to get offa my chest.

TEDDY: I know how that feels. On your chest. I've got things on my chest.

VIOLET: What things?

TEDDY: Certain acts. Irredeemable acts.

(Honking horns and screeching cars are heard.)

TEDDY: Wait! Wait! Oh, it's them. Look, there they are. Brighton's jumping out of the limousine heading for the front door swinging his cane.

VIOLET: Oh, yeah. And there's the rest of 'em pulling up behind. Why, who's that leaning outta the window? Looks like they's getting sick to their stomach.

TEDDY: That's Frances. I recognize the cape. Oh, there's Mama. Look at her shaking her fists up at the sky.

BRIGHTON: *(Offstage.)* Teddy! Teddy, are you here?

TEDDY: She's not gonna want me now. She's through with me. Finished.

(Brighton comes into the room from the main stairway.)

BRIGHTON: There you are! Thank God I found you before your mother caught up with you.

TEDDY: I bet she wants me dead.

BRIGHTON: What happened to your face?

TEDDY: There was a dreadful accident.

BRIGHTON: Christ. Listen to me, Teddy, I spoke to Grandmother Theadora tonight. She's aware of the damage Aunt Jen inflicted on you by forcing you to lie for her at the trial; saying she acted in self-defense. Everyone saw there wasn't a mark on her.

JEN: *(Offstage.)* Teddy! Teddy! Theadora Jenniquade!

(Violet exits down the back stairway.)

BRIGHTON: Grandmother wants you to come live with her. She wants to give you a chance to get away from your mother and regain your, well, your sanity.

JEN: *(Offstage.)* Teddy! Are you here in this house? Are you here?

BRIGHTON: In my opinion it's your only hope.

JEN: *(Offstage.)* Teddy!

TEDDY: Yes, I'll go. You tell her though. You break the news.

(Teddy disappears out onto the balcony. Jen and Bliss burst into the room from the main stairway. Jen searches through the second floor calling for Teddy. Bliss helps halfheartedly.)

JEN: Teddy! Teddy!

BLISS: Teddy! Teddy Bear.

JEN: Teddy! Teddy! She's not here. God, to think I've always feared an early death. Christ, if only I'd had one!

BLISS: You can't make silk purses out of sows' ears.

JEN: *(Lighting up a cigarette from a package she keeps stuck under her garter.)* But why act like a banshee? Why destroy all I've done for her?

BRIGHTON: Perhaps, if you hadn't brought along that professional boor you call a husband, we could have managed to escape with some small semblance of dignity.

BLISS: Not after Teddy made her first bow with her gown pulled up over her head and two feet of toilet paper stuck to her slipper.

JEN: Oh, and then later I found her crawling under the banquet table smearing cream cheese onto people's shoes.

BRIGHTON: Was that before or after Hank broke Mrs. Carver's toe when he waltzed?

JEN: After. It was right before he instigated that horrific brawl. I started searching all over for Teddy as soon as I discovered her hairpiece floating in the punch bowl.

BLISS: Disgusting.

BRIGHTON: Yes, but the most pathetic display was how Mrs. Rover kept pumping that idiot Frances for information about the reconciliation of our families.

BLISS: Poor Frances. Everyone knew she'd fallen right off the turnip truck. No one even asked her to dance.

JEN: When I find that girl, I'm going to shake her till her teeth fall out of her face. How could she do this to me?! It's inexcusable! Everything was rehearsed!

(Hank and Violet burst in from the main stairway. Hank's shirt is torn, his face is bruised. He no longer wears his bow tie or jacket. They are lugging in Frances who is sprawled all over the place. She drags Teddy's white stole along after her. It is covered with champagne, dirt, and vomit.)

HANK: That's right, get her in here. Watch out for her head.

JEN: Oh, God.   BRIGHTON: Oh, my.

(Jen runs to the bathroom to get a towel. Brighton grabs a wastepaper can.)

HANK: Lay her over here. Sit her up. She might choke herself like that. Frances, Baby? It's your Uncle Hank, here. Hey, are you gonna be okay?

(Jen enters from the bathroom.)

FRANCES: "YES, I—I—. WHAT WILL MAMA SAY?"

HANK: Huh?

FRANCES: "NO ONE MARRIED ME! NO ONE ASKED ME TO DANCE."

HANK: I'm sorry, I don't understand what you're saying.

FRANCES: "WHEN MAMA—WHEN SHE DIES, SHE'LL KNOW I'M AN OLD MAID. NO ONE ASKED ME TO DANCE!"

HANK: Please, Baby.

FRANCES: "OH, LOOK! I RUINED TEDDY'S CAPE! LOOK! MAYBE I CAN WASH IT OUT. YES. LET IT WASH OUT."

(Frances runs into the bathroom and starts trying to clean Teddy's soiled cape. Violet follows after her.)

HANK: God, I hate it when I can't understand what she's trying to say. I just hate it.

BLISS: She was saying no one asked her to dance and she ruined Teddy's cape.

HANK: Oh, yeah, well, I got that part t'do with Teddy's cape. So, ah, how about Teddy? Has anyone heard from her?

BLISS: No, she just ran off into the night. She does that very well, running off into the night.

JEN: It's a family trait.

HANK: Hmm. So, some party, eh? But look, folks, if we were always gonna do everything perfect, why bother being born, right?

(Bliss and Brighton voice general groans of despair.)

JEN: Yeah, right.

HANK: Hey, do I detect a pall of doom? *(To Jen.)* Please, what can I do to make you happy? Hey now! Could I do a jig?!

(Hank does a silly jig. Hank flips the top of his toupee up and down several times. Jen screams in disgust and rises to her feet.)

HANK: Please, Jen, any fall from your grace is unbearable to me. Look, I'm sorry about that scuffle.

JEN: Scuffle?! You broke a man's nose, tore up half the ballroom, and destroyed a whole event!

HANK: I didn't like how some of those people were treating us.

JEN: Do you think I did? Christ, I picked up a butter knife at the buffet table and everyone fled in horror. God knows it wasn't easy being the only murderess at the ball. But I stood there and stood it and smiled. I did it for Teddy. God, how could she betray me like that?

BRIGHTON: Listen, Aunt Jen, about Teddy, well, Grandmother Theadora was very upset about how things went tonight.

(Violet and Frances enter the main room from the bathroom.)

JEN: Oh, really, Brighton. How surprising. Violet, please pass around the hors d'oeuvres.

BRIGHTON: She, well, Grandmother, honestly feels Teddy's future is in grave jeopardy if she stays, well, with you. I, ah, spoke to Teddy and she agreed to go live with Grandmother for a time.

JEN: Brighton, why are you telling me such useless lies? Don't you think I know my own daughter?

BRIGHTON: No, not particularly. *(He calls out the balcony door.)* Teddy! Teddy, will you come in here, please! I need your corroboration. *(Brighton goes out onto the balcony.)*

JEN: Is she out there? Is she here?

(Brighton enters with Teddy. Teddy keeps her head down.)

JEN: Teddy, Teddy, look at me. Look at me. What happened to your face?

TEDDY: It broke out. I ate a lot of chocolate and it's all broken out.

BRIGHTON: Just look at her, Aunt Jen. You've done this to her. You've made her crazy. Go on, tell her, Teddy. Tell your mother you're going to stay with Grandmother from now on.

JEN: Yes, tell me, Teddy. Tell me that.

TEDDY: I thought it might be an idea.

JEN: I see.

(Jen goes out onto the balcony. There is a long moment of silence. Bliss moves up to Teddy.)

BLISS: *(To Teddy.)* She's mad at you. You're nothing but a disappointment. She hates the sight of you.

(Bliss moves away from Teddy. After a moment Jen enters from the balcony.)

JEN: Teddy, will you just tell me one thing? Where has my enchanted child gone?

TEDDY: I don't know, Mama.

JEN: Why do you want to leave me? Haven't we always been the closest of friends?

TEDDY: I thought you'd want me gone.

JEN: No. Oh, no. You're all I've got that's good. If I lose you, I have nothing. You're all the hope I have left.

BLISS: What about me, Mama? Don't you care anything for me? For *moi?* I'm not just some sack of garbage. I'm your oldest child. I inherited your elegance. I resemble you in every way. She—She looks like some drowned rat.

JEN: Bliss, don't start in on this. Not tonight.

BLISS: You're obviously jealous of my angelic beauty. That's why you shun and neglect me.

JEN: Neglect you? I neglect you? Well, please, let us not forget about little Butterball when we speak of neglected children. When was the last time you saw your child? What did you send her for her birthday? I never once have forgotten *your* birthday. Although I wish to God I could!

BLISS: Christ, why didn't they keep you in jail? I wish they'd stuck you in a hole forever! I hate you!

JEN: You! You think I could be jealous of you! You dream you're some beautiful lady, but you're nothing but a Southern strumpet whore!

BLISS: Oh really, Mama, well, fuck you!

JEN: You! You bring all your filthy baggage in here to intrude on my life, but I'm throwing you out! Out! Do you hear me! Out! Out! Out!

BLISS: *(Overlapping.)* Fuck you, Mother. Just fuck you! Fuck you! Fuck you dead!

JEN: You're an unproductive being! A worthless mis-creation! You're cheap! Cheap! Cheap!

(Bliss can no longer endure the abuse. She flees up the stairs.)

BLISS: *Aahh! Aahh!* No more!

(Bliss trips on the stairs and falls. Frances rushes up to her.)

FRANCES: "OH BLISS! DEAR BLISS!"

BLISS: *Ugh!* Look at you! There's green food between your teeth! You ugly, ugly thing! Get away from me! Keep away!

(Frances flees into the bathroom to brush her teeth. Bliss exits up the stairway.)

JEN: Maybe I'm not a very good mother. Maybe I never should have had any children after all.

BRIGHTON: Your wife's insane.

HANK: I know. I'm aware of it all.

JEN: Teddy, go put on some shoes. Pack some things. We're leaving here tonight.

TEDDY: Leaving tonight?

JEN: I'm getting you out of this town for good. I don't like these people influencing you. Move! Do you hear me?! Move! Move!

BRIGHTON: *(Overlapping.)* What are you so afraid of, Aunt Jen? Christ, no one's trying to get Teddy to reverse her testimony. Besides, they can't try you twice for the same murder.

JEN: *(To Teddy; running on.)* And put on some makeup. Your face is a mess. Fix it right!

(Teddy exits to her bedroom.)

BRIGHTON: *(Overlapping.)* Teddy! Teddy! Aunt Jen, you can't do this. I'm calling Grandmother.

JEN: Not from my house. Get out of my house. I'll rip you to shreds. I know how it's done.

BRIGHTON: You can be sure there are measures we can take.

JEN: Violet, show my nephew to the door. Don't let him lose his way.

BRIGHTON: I'll be back. I'll be back tonight.

(Violet and Brighton exit down the main stairway.)

JEN: Hank. Oh, Hank, we've got to leave here right away. I hate this town! I hate these people! I'd like to chop up every dreadful one of them and burn them all to ash ruins!

HANK: Sure, I understand. Things didn't go—the way you'd hoped. Look, I'll make us a reservation at the Hotel Royal. We can stay there a week. Let things settle down.

JEN: You don't understand. I don't want to go to New Orleans for a week's vacation. I want to move away from here for good. God, I just wish I knew—I just wish I knew where we'd—fit in. Let's see. Have you ever been to Pennsylvania? How about Delaware? Or, or Maine? Yes, Maine's way, way up there, isn't it? We could do well in Maine.

HANK: Jen, we can't just pick up and move lock, stock and barrel. All my work's here. And this house. Christ, I just spent three fortunes building you this huge, enormous house. You said you loved this house.

JEN: I don't love it. I don't. I want to go away. We'll never be able to live in this town. It was foolish to try. I'll go get my jewels. We'll hire movers to handle the rest. *(Jen starts up the stairs to get her jewels.)*

HANK: Jen, please. You're overwrought. Your rational mind has gone askew.

JEN: You don't understand. Teddy's in trouble. She's pregnant.

HANK: Ah, Lord.

JEN: We'll have to get rid of it. I won't let her life be ruined like mine was, but we can't do it here. We'll take care of all that up in Maine.

HANK: Have you talked to Teddy about this? What does she want to do?

JEN: She wants what I want.

HANK: Have you asked her?

JEN: Teddy's surrounded by people that are breaking her down, turning her against me. I've got to get her safe. And if you won't help me, I'll go without you.

HANK: We're married. We stay together. You can't go without me.

JEN: Yes, I can. Don't think you can hold me here. I own all of the jewelry upstairs in that safe. It's registered in my name. I saw to it this time that I wouldn't be left holding nothing.

HANK: Is that what you think? That I'd leave you holding nothing? When have I ever been cheap with you? Why, I've given you everything your blood-cold bitch heart's desired. You've used me up real good.

JEN: I never asked you for all of your help and salvation. I didn't want to end up owing you a whole lot of blood I could never pay back.

HANK: Don't worry, Jen, you don't owe me a goddamn thing. Not blood or nothing. You're free and clear. Go on. Go! Oh, wait. All the jewelry's yours, right? Well, here's my watch. Take it. *(He slings it at her.)* And my ring. And these; they're all yours. *(He slings his cuff links at her.)* Live it up! Here, take some silver with you! It's a bonus prize! *(Hank slings a silver tray and goblets across the room.)*

JEN: Look at you! Just look! You're nothing but a redneck bull. God, am I sick of trying to keep you penned in.

HANK: Nothing worked, did it? The new clothes, the toupee, the fancy manicure. Christ, you even changed my toothpaste brand and deodorant bar. Tell me, wasn't there anything about me you could stand besides my money?

JEN: No, there was nothing. Nothing at all.

HANK: Which car do you want to take with you?

JEN: We'll take the Lincoln.

HANK: Alright. I'll go get it out of the garage and pull it around front for you.

(Hank exits down the main stairway. Jen goes into the bathroom where Frances is sitting at the dressing table scrubbing her teeth with a wash rag.)

JEN: You! This is my bathroom. Get out! I've got to pack. I'm through with all of you. Leave me alone.

(Frances flees into the parlor. Jen slings various random toilet articles into a quilted bag, then exits into her bedroom. Violet comes up the back stairway with a large tray. Frances sees her and starts to head up the stairs. Violet begins picking up various hors d'oeuvre plates. Frances haughtily motions to Violet to pour her a glass of champagne. Violet pours the champagne. Frances demands her to fill the glass. Violet fills the glass. Frances slings the wine into Violet's face. Violet exits down the back stairway. Frances walks around the room with a sense of gloating victory. After a few moments her sense of triumph turns to regretful despair. She sinks to the floor in anguish. Bliss comes down the stairway. She is taking a pill and humming a sad French song. Without noticing Frances, she goes to the phone and dials.)

BLISS: *(Into phone.)* Yes, hello? Is this Tommy?…Well, hi, this is Blissy. I'm, oh, just visiting here in town for a while…Yes, right, for Teddy's Debutante Ball. How's my little girl? How's Butterball—did she know I was going to the ball?…Oh, well, anyway tell her I'm going to give her the jeweled princess' crown I received as a party favor. I want her to have it…Listen, Tommy, could I, ah, could I come see you sometime?…Well, it's just, I—I miss you and Butterball an awful lot, and I'd really like to maybe—try and come back home…Right. Well, of course, I know it's very difficult to live with me day in and day out…It's just I can't seem to make it on my own. My last employer accused me of lying about graduating from high school. He said I couldn't make change properly. I've got to tell you, I just don't know what's going to become of me…Yes. Certainly, I understand how you feel…Uh-huh. I see…No, really it was just a—fleeting fancy I had. You see, it occurred to me that I'd be able to teach Butterball how to tell time and tie her shoe. I didn't learn how to do those two things until very late and I remember feeling so badly about it…You will? Well, good then. That's very good. So, Tommy, good-bye. *(Bliss puts the phone down. With a laugh.)* Oh, well, maybe it was a mistake sleeping with every one of his friends before leaving the state.

(Bliss goes to the tape player and punches a button. A Chopin waltz plays. Bliss turns off the light, dances alone then spots Frances who is sitting on the floor staring at her.)

BLISS: Look, I'm sorry I said that about the green in your teeth.

FRANCES: "LOOK HERE. IT'S GONE."

BLISS: Yes. I'm sorry. I don't mean to be cruel. I just have this sort of hole inside me. This desperate longing to love and be loved. Somehow it cripples me. It makes me be cruel.

FRANCES: "YES. LOVE. HOLE."

BLISS: Yes. You understand me. I can talk to you.

(Bliss touches Frances softly. The moment is very potent. Bliss gets up and runs to the balcony. Frances follows her.)

BLISS: Oh, smell that night grass. I love t' smell nice things.

(They smell the grass. Then gently, slowly, they begin dancing together.)

BLISS: *(Still dancing.)* Look at the moon. A rose pink moon.

FRANCES: *(Touching Bliss' lips.)* "IT'S RED...IT'S RED JUST LIKE YOUR LIPS."

(Bliss reaches for Frances' hand. She kisses the palm of it softly. Then she holds Frances' hand in hers as she kisses Frances full on the lips. Bliss continues kissing Frances passionately on the neck and shoulders, as she feels the fullness of her breasts.)

BLISS: Yes, just two lost souls dancing on the rooftop together.

(Bliss pulls Frances to the floor as she unzips her dress. Jen enters the parlor from her room. She has changed out of her gown into traveling clothes. She wears her mink coat and carries a suitcase. She turns on the light and sees Bliss and Frances.)

JEN: Oh, and I thought they considered that something of a taboo down in this part of the state.

(Frances leaps up and rushes off down the back stairway. Bliss gets up and looks after Frances. Jen starts up the stairs.)

JEN: Cheap. You're cheap, cheap, cheap.

BLISS: That's not true. I don't believe you anymore. It's not true.

(Jen exits up the stairs. Bliss exits out onto the balcony. Teddy enters from the hallway. She wears her debutante gown with black loafers and carries a round makeup bag. Violet enters from the back stairway. She has changed into a worn-out fraternity T-shirt, polyester pants, and a worn-down pair of shoes.)

VIOLET: I'm ready to go home.

TEDDY: Alright. We'll take you. We're going, too. *(Teddy gets a cheese knife, pulls up her skirt, and cuts her leg.)*

VIOLET: I can't get involved with you people no more.

TEDDY: I'm just slicing away at it. That's all I can do for now. After I have the child of the elevator man, then I can stop it for good. Violet, have you ever wanted to stop it for good?

VIOLET: I did one time. It was after my mama died eating them leftover lunch meat sandwiches this white lady'd given over to her. I felt such hatred inside my heart I went out wild on the streets and stole whatever I wanted and didn't have. They caught me and I paid my time. Now I'm starting new.

TEDDY: Me; I can't start new. I got too many things on my chest. I keep trying to push them down, but they keep gripping back up at me.

VIOLET: Just like an old snapping turtle.

TEDDY: Huh?

VIOLET: A snapping turtle. They don't never let loose till it thunders.

TEDDY: But it never does thunder. I got all this lightning inside me. But it won't ever thunder.

VIOLET: Then you make it thunder. You make it. Ya don't wanna end up like my brother. He just laid himself down on a railroad track and died.

TEDDY: Why'd he do that?

VIOLET: I guess he just couldn't see no other way.

(After a moment Jen comes hurrying down the staircase with her jewels.)

JEN: Teddy, are you packed? Teddy?

TEDDY: *(Turning to her.)* Mama—

JEN: What?

TEDDY: I can't go.

JEN: Why not?

TEDDY: I'm afraid.

JEN: Afraid of what?

TEDDY: Afraid of you.

JEN: Christ. Jesus Christ. How can that be? I've given up everything for you. Everything.

TEDDY: Don't give up any more. I don't want it.

JEN: Yes you do. You're in trouble. You need help. I'll get you a doctor. We'll fix it. It won't be a problem.

TEDDY: But it is a problem. It is.

BRIGHTON: *(Offstage.)* Teddy! Teddy!

HANK: *(Offstage.)* Get out! I'll tear your head off!

BRIGHTON: *(Offstage.)* Stay away from me! Get away! Teddy!

(Hank and Brighton come racing up the front stairway.)

JEN: *(Overlapping.)* Don't let him in here! Keep him out!

BRIGHTON: Take your hands off—

HANK: I'm sick of dealing with you people. *(Hank slings Brighton across the room.)* All of you. I mean all of you.

BRIGHTON: Teddy, Grandmother's outside in her car.

JEN: Hank. Get him out. Hank—

(Hank starts up the stairs.)

BRIGHTON: She wants to talk to you.

JEN: She's not talking to anyone.

TEDDY: Yes I am. There's something I have to say.

JEN: You are not saying anything. You're coming with me.

TEDDY: No way, no way. I'm having this baby. I'm not gonna kill it too. I'm not killing anybody anymore.

BRIGHTON: Teddy, what do you mean?

JEN: Don't listen to her. She's utterly deluded. She's having a breakdown. Leave her alone.

TEDDY: *(Overlapping.)* I'm not afraid of telling anymore. I'm sorry, Mama. I'm past afraid.

JEN: Shut up! You'll ruin all I've done for you. You'll destroy your whole life! Don't do this to me!

TEDDY: *(Overlapping.)* Give up, Mama. You can't stop me. You never could.

BRIGHTON: *(Overlapping.)* Teddy, what is it? What are you saying?

TEDDY: I'm saying how I did it. I smashed Daddy with that black pan and he fell over into his turnip greens cold dead. It was me that killed him. It was me that smashed him dead!

BRIGHTON: *(Overlapping.)* Christ. Oh Christ.

JEN: *(Overlapping as she violently shakes Teddy.)* She's a liar! She's smoking again too! She says she doesn't smoke but she does! I know it! I've smelt it on her. *(She begins slapping Teddy repeatedly. She slings her across a chaise lounge.)* You liar! Traitor! Shut up! Shut up your mouth! I'll knock it off! I'll shut it up for good!

(Hank comes down the stairs and pulls Jen away.)

HANK: God, stop, Jen. Christ, stop!

(Teddy groans in agony as blood falls into the lap of her white gown.)

TEDDY: Oh no! Oh no! I knew it would be born horrible!

JEN: *(Overlapping.)* My God. My God.

BRIGHTON: Holy God. Please, please.

(Hank rushes to Teddy and holds her in his arms.)

HANK: It's alright, Teddy. *(To Brighton.)* Call the hospital. *(To Teddy.)* It'll be alright.

(Brighton goes to the phone.)

TEDDY: *(Reaching her arms out to Jen.)* Mama!! I want my Mama! Please, Mama!

JEN: *(Overlapping.)* Yes. Alright. Okay.

(Jen goes to the floor and takes Teddy in her arms. Hank moves away from them.)

JEN: I'm here, baby. I'm right here.

(Blackout.)

SCENE II

It is early the following morning. Frances is sitting on the sofa in her dusty traveling clothes staring out into space. Her suitcase sits by the stairway. Violet enters from the back stairway with a breakfast tray. She looks exhausted. She sets the tray down on the coffee table. Francis looks up at Violet and then hides her face. Violet looks at her and turns away. Hank enters from Jen's bedroom carrying a large suitcase.

HANK: Violet, hello. Thanks for getting the breakfast. Listen, soon as Teddy comes back from the hospital we'll be heading up to Pontotoc. My sister Sue's taken a turn for the worse. I'll drop you home on the way.

VIOLET: Good.

HANK: *(Handing her an enormous wad of money.)* Look, ah, here's your money. I'm adding in a little extra for all the inconveniences we've caused you. I apologize for everything. I'm deeply embarrassed 'bout all those events happening. But people in this world'll love each other and hate each other—you never know which; there's a wonderment to it all.

VIOLET: Yeah, well, I'll go down and get my things so I can go home.

HANK: Okay.

(Violet exits down the back stairway. Hank sits down with Frances.)

HANK: Hey, how ya doing? *(He takes the silver cover off of the breakfast plate.)* Mmm. Look here what we've got for breakfast this morning. Lotsa good fresh eggs and sausage. Here, try some.

(Frances shakes her head.)

HANK: Well, how 'bout some hot grits? I know you like your grits. Here, we'll fix it up for you with a load of butter; and then give it some good ole salt and pepper. Yeah. Now stir it all around. There you go.

(Hank offers her the bowl of grits. Frances shakes her head.)

FRANCES: "YOU'RE VERY NICE, UNCLE HANK, BUT I JUST DO NOT FEEL HUNGRY."

HANK: What? Not enough butter? Here, we'll add more butter. I like mine buttery too. Now, come on now. Ya gotta eat something. It's a long drive home. A really long drive all the way t'Pontotoc.

FRANCES: "PLEASE, I DON'T WANT IT. PLEASE!"

HANK: Well, look, then you don't have to eat it. Here, I can go on and eat it myself. Hell, it's fixed just like I like it.
(Hank takes a big bite of grits. Bliss enters the parlor from the main stairway. She still wears her evening gown.)

BLISS: Hi, we're back. Teddy's downstairs. I think she feels a little weak. Maybe you should help carry her up to her room.

HANK: Alright. Good. Be glad to. *(Hank exits down the main stairway.)*

BLISS: I heard they called about your mother.

FRANCES: "YES."

BLISS: She's…doing poorly.

FRANCES: "YES. VERY."

BLISS: I'm so sorry. *(A beat.)* Frances.

FRANCES: "HUH? "

BLISS: I hope I didn't—I mean last night—I guess, I just…like you very much.

FRANCES: "YOU DO?"

BLISS: Uh-huh. I do. Yes.

FRANCES: "OH."

BLISS: Yes.

FRANCES: "BLISS?"

BLISS: Yes?

FRANCES: "WHEN I GO HOME—"

BLISS: Home.

FRANCES: "YES, I'D LIKE—I MEAN IF YOU—IT'S JUST—"

BLISS: What? What?

FRANCES: "BLISS, WOULD YOU WANT TO GO HOME WITH ME?"

BLISS: Enchanté. Delightful. Yes.

FRANCES: "GOOD."

BLISS: Good. Yes. Well, then I've got to run and go change. And pack. I'll—just be a minute.

FRANCES: "I'LL HELP YOU."

BLISS: Help, yes, alright. Thank you. Alright.

(Bliss and Frances exit up the stairs. Hank carries Teddy into the parlor from the main stairway. Teddy wears a brand-new quilted robe.)

TEDDY: But you really don't need to carry me. I can walk fine. You could pull out your back.

HANK: You're light as a feather.

TEDDY: *(Seeing breakfast tray.)* Oh, look, is that food? I'm starving.

HANK: *(Putting her down.)* Sure. Here, sit down and eat. There's a whole plate that's wasting. *(Handing her a plate.)* There you go.

TEDDY: Great.

HANK: Here, you want some butter on your grits? It's a lot better with butter.

TEDDY: Oh, yes. I love butter. And salt and pepper too.

HANK: *(Stirring.)* Okay. There you go. *(Watching her take a bite.)* Good?

TEDDY: Yeah. That's good.

HANK: Well…good.

TEDDY: *(As she eats.)* Hank.

HANK: Yeah?

TEDDY: Did you always know I was guilty of Daddy dying?

HANK: Well, now, guilt can only be determined by a jury of your peers in a court of law. But ask me if I knew you did it. Yeah, I knew.

TEDDY: Did she tell you?

HANK: Lord, no. God, Jen lied every which way. It's just I had my suppositions. Though 'course I never knew about the exact circumstances surrounding the deal. I just figured you didn't intend to actually, ah…

TEDDY: Kill him.

HANK: Yeah.

TEDDY: *(Putting jam on her toast.)* I don't think I did. Maybe. He broke into the house really crazy that evening. He kept yelling about how he was gonna break Mama all up; cut her to stringy pieces. Seems he'd just found out about her filing for divorce. I served him some coffee and turnip greens, trying t' calm him down. But then he slings the sugar bowl at my chest and starts screaming about how there's not enough sugar, it's not full enough and he's sick of scraping the bottom of the bowl—and he's gonna scrape the bottom of her bowl with this switchblade knife he pulls out. Well, I go to get a broom t' clean up the sugar, but then I hear Mama's car. He hears it too and stops yelling and just sits silently eating turnip greens off the blade of his knife. The car door slams and I hear Mama coming up the walk, that's when I just grab the black skillet and walk back over and smash his skull. To stop him. Just t' stop him till she can run away. That's all I wanted—to let her run away.

HANK: Sure. That's all you wanted.

TEDDY: I cry sometimes thinking how little I miss him.

HANK: Hell, there's no way to blame you for doing what you did.

(Teddy looks at him, then looks away.)

HANK: Nah. I'm just curious about why you went on and hit him the seven more times.

TEDDY: I didn't. She did.

HANK: What?

TEDDY: Yeah. Mama came in and saw what I'd done, but she told me Daddy wasn't really dead. Then she took the pan and kept on hitting him, telling me she was the one that was doing it, that I never did!

HANK: *(Wryly amazed.)* Jesus, Jen.

TEDDY: But we both knew the truth. It was a bad lie to keep between us.

(Bliss and Frances come down the stairway. They are carrying Bliss' luggage. Bliss is dressed for traveling.)

BLISS: *(To Frances.)* No, really, I think I'd be quite marvelous at hoeing the corn and skinning potatoes.

HANK: Oh, good, Frances.

BLISS: *(Running on.)* Why, people in our family are known for their muscular shoulder blades.

HANK: *(To Frances.)* We need t' head out right away.

BLISS: *(To Hank.)* I'm going too. Frances asked me to come.

HANK: Well fine. *(Hank exits down the main stairway carrying a load of luggage.)*

FRANCES: "'BYE, TEDDY. I HAD A LOVELY TIME."

TEDDY: *(To Frances.)* Oh, well, thank you for coming.

BLISS: *(To Teddy, as she hands her the princess' crown.)* See that Butterball gets this princess' crown. Tell her it's from her mama. Take care, Teddy Bear. *(Brighton enters from the main stairway. He wears a suit but is quite disheveled. He no longer carries the cane.)*

BRIGHTON: Teddy! Teddy!

TEDDY: Good-bye, Bliss.

BLISS: Farewell, farewell.

(Bliss and Frances exit down the main stairs.)

BRIGHTON: Good-bye. Good-bye. *(Brighton turns to Teddy.)* Teddy, why did you tell Grandmother? Why did you tell her about what you did? Why in the world?

TEDDY: I got tired.

BRIGHTON: Tired? You got tired? Fine. Well, it was a dreadful mistake. I don't know what she's going to do. She's certainly not going to take you in.

TEDDY: Yes, I know, she told me.

BRIGHTON: Well, what are you going to do? You can't stay here, with all these—these unhealthy dynamics.

TEDDY: Yes. I'd like some time to get on my feet. Could I stay out at your lake cottage till I do that?

BRIGHTON: No. Oh no. But Grandmother would never approve. She'd consider me a traitor. Good Lord. Good heavens! I don't understand anything. Life! It's a horrible, hopeless mystery chock-full of confusion. Oh, well, go pack your things. I'll drive you out to the lake. Let me pull the car around. Confusion. What can you do about it? There it is.

(Brighton exits down the main stairway and Teddy exits to her bedroom. Jen enters up the back stairway. She wears the fur coat. Jen looks around the room and shivers. Hank enters from the main stairway.)

HANK: Hello, I—

JEN: Hank—

HANK: I have to get these bags. We're on our way to Pontotoc.

JEN: Yes—well—so…

HANK: So…

JEN: … Do you want me to be gone when you get back?

HANK: Whatever.

JEN: Well, anyway, my lost angel, you're better off without me.

HANK: Yeah, 'cause it's been a constant struggle to prove my worth to you.

JEN: I guess there's just some blackness buried so deep inside my chest you never could have pulled it out with a pair of pliers.

HANK: God. Then there's only one problem.

JEN: What's that?

HANK: I won't be able t' see your face sparkle no more.

JEN: Oh please…Butter me up. Butter me up some more.

(Hank picks up the bags and exits down the main stairway. Jen turns and goes into her bathroom. She is devastated. She turns on the bath water.)

JEN: Oh God. Oh God. *(Jen throws her blue bath crystals into the tub. She stirs the water with her trembling hand and chants.)* Please, please, please. Stop please, please.

(Jen leaves the bathroom and goes into her bedroom. Teddy enters the parlor from her room, dressed in jeans and a shirt, carrying a suitcase. She hears the water running in Jen's bathroom. Teddy sets down her suitcase. She goes out

onto the balcony. Violet enters up the back stairway. She carries a large tote bag that has "Le Bag" written on it.)

VIOLET: Is Mr. Turner ready to leave?

TEDDY: Yes. He went downstairs.

VIOLET: Alright.

TEDDY: *(Glancing out on the balcony.)* Oh, look! Out there!

VIOLET: What?

TEDDY: A bird.

VIOLET: Where?

TEDDY: Right there, Violet. By the white branch!

VIOLET: Yeah! I see. There it goes! It was green.

TEDDY: Uh-huh, green.

(Teddy and Violet look at each other. Violet turns and exits down the main stairway. Jen enters the bathroom nude with a large towel wrapped around her shoulders. She is trembling like a newborn bird. She walks over to the tub and puts her hand in the water to feel the temperature. She turns off the running water, drops the towel, and gets into the tub. Teddy, who hears the water stop, walks over to the door and goes inside the room.)

TEDDY: Hello.

JEN: Teddy.

TEDDY: Your psoriasis has broken out again.

JEN: I know. It's spreading. *(Looking at her skin.)* God, look how the ravages of time have conquered me. All these cracks and sores and ugliness. I hate it so much. Being trapped inside this—body.

TEDDY: You need to visit the doctor up in Memphis again. Where's your tube of medicine?

JEN: On the counter.

(Teddy gets the tube and Jen's compact case that holds the cigarettes.)

TEDDY: You wanna smoke?

JEN: Sure. Let's have a smoke.

(Teddy lights up a cigarette and hands it to Jen. She lights another one for herself. Then she gently begins rubbing the ointment over her mother's sores. Brighton enters from the main stairway. He glances around the room looking for Teddy. He picks up the small suitcase.)

BRIGHTON: *(Calling toward Teddy's room.)* Teddy, I had this idea! I could pick up some biscuit dough on the way to the cottage. *(He laughs with a snort.)* Teddy?! I've got your bag. I'll be down in the car. *(Brighton exits down the main stairway.)*

JEN: Are you leaving?

TEDDY: Yes.

JEN: Alright.

TEDDY: Mama?

JEN: What?

TEDDY: I don't have a feeling anymore like it's never gonna get better.

JEN: You don't?

TEDDY: No.

JEN: Why's that?

TEDDY: It's like I can smell the rain coming and I can feel it's gonna start to thunder.

JEN: It is? It's gonna thunder?

TEDDY: Yeah, and that ole snapping turtle's gonna let loose and I'll just be standing there in the rain and in the thunder and these arms will want to hold onto somebody and have their arms holding onto me.

JEN: Hmm. Well. I hope so. I, well, I…Yes. Good. Yes.

(Teddy continues putting on the ointment, as they both smoke cigarettes and the lights fade to blackout.)

END OF PLAY

BETH HENLEY was awarded the Pulitzer Prize in Drama and the New York Drama Critics Circle Award for Best American Play for her first full-length play, *Crimes of the Heart,* which was the co-winner in 1979 of the Great American Play Contest sponsored by the Actors Theatre of Louisville prior to its move to New York. *Crimes of the Heart* has since been produced in many of our leading resident theatres, on a major national tour, and in many countries throughout the world. Ms. Henley's second play, *The Miss Firecracker Contest,* has been produced in several regional theatres in the United States and in London at the Bush Theatre, and opened in the spring of 1984 at the Manhattan Theatre Club. It subsequently transferred for an extended run off-Broadway and was published in the Ten Best Plays of 1983–84. Ms. Henley's third play, *The Wake of Jamey Foster,* had its premiere at the Hartford Stage Company prior to its presentation on Broadway, directed by Ulu Grosbard. Ms. Henley's one-act play *Am I Blue* was produced at the Circle Repertory Company in New York. It is included in the Best Short Plays of 1983. Her play *The Debutante Ball* was presented in the spring of 1985 at the South Coast Repertory in Costa Mesa, California, and was presented in a substantially revised version at the Manhattan Theatre Club and the New York Stage and Film Company in the spring and summer of 1988, respectively. Subsequently, it was presented in London at the Hampstead Theatre Club in the spring of 1989. Her play, *The Lucky Spot,* was presented at the Williamstown Theatre Festival in the summer of 1986 and had its New York premiere at the Manhattan Theatre Club in 1987. It had its London premiere in the spring of 1991. *Abundance* had its premiere at the South Coast Repertory and opened at the Manhattan Theatre Club in the fall of 1990 and was produced at The Riverside Theatre in London in the fall of 1995. Her play *Signature* was given a workshop at the New York Stage and Film Company in the summer of 1990 and had a full production at the Charlotte Repertory Theatre in the spring of 1995. *Control Freaks* premiered at Chicago's Center Theatre in 1992 and opened at the Met Theatre in Los Angeles in July, 1993, under the direction of Ms. Henley. Her play *Revelers* had a production in the summer of 1994 under the auspices of New York Stage and Film at Poughkeepsie, N.Y. *L-Play* was the premiere production at the Unicorn Theatre in Stockbridge, Massachusetts, 1995. Ms. Henley's play, *Impossible Marriage,* was produced at the Roundabout Theatre, 1998–99. Her newest play, *Family Week*, has been optioned for a New York production.

Ms. Henley wrote the screenplay for the acclaimed film version of *Crimes of the Heart* for which she was nominated for an Academy Award. The film was directed by Bruce Beresford and starred Diane Keaton, Jessica Lange, Sissy Spacek, and Sam Shepard. She also wrote the screenplay for *Miss Firecracker* starring Holly Hunter, Mary Steenburgen, and Tim Robbins. She wrote the screenplay for *Nobody's Fool* which starred Rosanna Arquette and Eric Roberts and a teleplay for the PBS series, *Trying Times.*

She was born and raised in Mississippi, graduated from Southern Methodist University, and lives in Los Angeles with her son Patrick.